THE POTATO
AND RICE BIBLE

THE POTATO
AND RICE BIBLE

OVER 350 DELICIOUS, EASY-TO-MAKE RECIPES FOR TWO
ALL-TIME STAPLE FOODS, FROM SOUPS TO BAKES,
SHOWN STEP BY STEP IN 1500 GLORIOUS PHOTOGRAPHS

ALEX BARKER, SALLY MANSFIELD AND CHRISTINE INGRAM

HERMES
HOUSE

This edition is published by Hermes House, an imprint of Anness Publishing Ltd,
Blaby Road, Wigston, Leicestershire LE18 4SE; info@anness.com

www.hermeshouse.com; www.annesspublishing.com

If you like the images in this book and would like to investigate using them for publishing,
promotions or advertising, please visit our website www.practicalpictures.com
for more information.

Publisher: Joanna Lorenz
Senior Cookery Editor: Linda Fraser
Project Editors: Sarah Ainley and Toria Leitch
Assistant Editor: Martin Goldring
Copy Editor: Jenni Fleetwood and Leslie Mandel-Viney
Designers: Jane Coney, Penny Dawes and Margaret Sadler
Photography: Dave Jordan (RICE introduction), Dave King (RICE recipes),
Steve Moss (POTATO introduction) and Sam Stowell (POTATO recipes)
Food for Photography: Alex Barker (POTATO techniques),
Sara Lewis (RICE techniques), Eliza Baird (POTATO recipes)
and Jennie Shapter (RICE recipes)
Additional Recipes: Roz Denny, Jacqueline Clarke, Joanna Farrow,
Shirley Gill, Sarah Gates, Steven Wheeler, Hilaire Walden,
Christine France, Rosamund Grant, Sheila Kimberley, Liz Trigg,
Carla Capalbo, Carole Clements, Judy Jackson, Ruby Le Bois,
Chris Ingram, Matthew Drennan, Elizabeth Wolfe-Cohen,
Shehzad Hussain, Rafi Fernandez, Manisha Kanini, Laura Washburn,
Andi Clevely, Katherine Richmond and Jennie Shapter
Indexer: Vikki Robinson

ETHICAL TRADING POLICY

Because of our ongoing ecological investment programme, you, as our customer, can
have the pleasure and reassurance of knowing that a tree is being cultivated on your
behalf to naturally replace the materials used to make the book you are holding.
For further information about this scheme, go to www.annesspublishing.com/trees

A CIP catalogue record for this book is available from the British Library

Previously published as *Potato & Rice*

NOTES

For all recipes, quantities are given in both metric and imperial measures and, where
appropriate, in standard cups and spoons. Follow one set of measures, but not
a mixture, because they are not interchangeable.

Standard spoon and cup measures are level. 1 tsp = 5ml, 1 tbsp = 15ml,
1 cup = 250ml/8fl oz.
Australian standard tablespoons are 20ml. Australian readers should use 3 tsp in
place of 1 tbsp for measuring small quantities.

American pints are 16fl oz/2 cups. American readers should use 20fl oz/2.5 cups in
place of 1 pint when measuring liquids.

Electric oven temperatures in this book are for conventional ovens. When using a fan
oven, the temperature will probably need to be reduced by about 10–20°C/20–40°F.
Since ovens vary, you should check with your manufacturer's instruction book for guidance.

Medium (US large) eggs are used unless otherwise stated.

PUBLISHER'S NOTE

Although the advice and information in this book are believed to be accurate and true at
the time of going to press, neither the authors nor the publisher can accept any legal
responsibility or liability for any errors or omissions that may have been made nor for
any inaccuracies nor for any loss, harm or injury that comes about from following
instructions or advice in this book.

CONTENTS

INTRODUCTION

Potato and rice are tremendously
important foodstuffs, and this is
easy to see throughout the long and
surprisingly colourful histories of their
cultivation. In some countries these foods are associated
with gods and spirits because they have stood the test of
time as reliable crops. In Peru, a potato goddess was
thought to protect the harvest, and even today in
South-east Asia, rice barns are regarded as
sacred temples and the home of the rice
spirit in the months between
harvesting and planting.

The potato is the staple food
for two-thirds of the world's
population, while rice is an
essential ingredient in every one of

the world's major cuisines. From China and the Far East through India, the Middle East, Africa, Europe and the Americas, rice is central to the daily diet.

Potato and rice are popular for a number of reasons. Significantly, they are resilient crops and are relatively easy to produce and, consequently, cheap to buy. Even better, they can provide a nutritious and filling meal: both are excellent sources of complex carbohydrates and are low in fat and salt; the potato is also the most important source of vitamin C for much of the world.

Perhaps what makes these foods unique, however, is the fact that they taste so very good. There are an astonishing number of varied and delicious recipes for potatoes and rice, and the very best of them are featured in this book. Enjoy!

POTATO

INTRODUCTION

*The potato feeds two-thirds of
the world's population and is
an all-time favourite vegetable.
This book opens with a fascinating
look at the history of the potato,
and traces the extraordinary
journey from the Indians in the
pre-Inca Andes to the dinner tables
of today. The extensive introduction
section covers essential preparation
and cooking techniques, and a
comprehensive reference directory
provides an illustrated guide to the
world's best potato varieties.
Finally, there is a feast of over
150 recipes — old favourites and
adventurous new creations — to
celebrate the enormous versatility of
this humble vegetable.*

THE HISTORY OF THE POTATO

THERE ARE FEW more important foods in the world than the potato. Its history goes back to the early days of man – a past spanning feast and famine. It has long played a vital role as the best all-round source of nutrition for mankind, and will continue to do so in the future.

The potato was discovered by pre-Inca Indians in the foothills of the Andes Mountains in South America. Archaeological remains have been found dating from 400 BC on the shores of Lake Titicaca, in ruins near Bolivia, and on the coast of Peru. Cultivated by the Incas, it influenced their whole lives. The Peruvian potato goddess was depicted holding a potato plant in each hand. The South American Indians measured time by the length of time it took to cook potatoes to various consistencies. Potato designs were found in Nazca and Chimu pottery. Raw slices of potato placed on broken bones were thought to prevent rheumatism.

The original potatoes, ranging from the size of a nut to a small apple, and ranging in colour from red and gold to blue and black, flourished in these temperate mountain plateaux. The first recorded information about the potato

was written in 1553 by the Spanish conquistador Pedro Cieza de Leon and soon potatoes joined the treasures carried away by these Spanish invaders. They became standard food on Spanish ships, and people began to notice that the sailors who ate them did not suffer from scurvy.

The first known purchase of the potato was by a hospital in Seville in 1573. Its cultivation spread quickly throughout Europe via explorers such as

Above: A ceramic plate made by the Incas, which typically would have been used for serving potatoes

Sir Francis Drake, who is reputed to have brought potatoes back to Britain. These are thought to have been cultivated on Sir Walter Raleigh's estate in Ireland, 40,000 acres of land given to him by Queen Elizabeth I expressly to grow potatoes and tobacco. Botanists and scientists were fascinated by this novel plant – it was mentioned in John Gerard's herbal list in 1597 – and potatoes may first have been grown mainly for botanical research. During Charles II's reign, the Royal Society recognized the potato as being nutritional and inexpensive and, with the ever-present fear of famine and war, governments in Europe tried to persuade their farmers to start growing this valuable crop in quantity.

However the potato also carried with it a reputation. As part of the nightshade family, it was thought to be poisonous or to cause leprosy and syphilis and to be a dangerous aphrodisiac. In France, a young chemist, Antoine Augustin Parmentier, set about converting the French and their King Louis XVI with his potato delicacies (hence his name is now used often in connection with potato dishes), and Marie Antoinette was persuaded to wear potato blossoms in her hair. But in some cases it took more than just

Above: The Golden Hind *in which Sir Francis Drake brought potatoes back to Britain*

Above: The potato flower

in the 1840s. Over a million people died and it is hardly surprising that the potato became known as the white or Irish potato, to distinguish it from the sweet potato.

The Irish took their love of the potato with them when they moved in large numbers to the north of England, as well as to Europe and America to escape the famine. The British government had by now accepted the potato as a nutritious, cheap and easily grown food and were encouraging the use of allotments for potato growing; "potato patches" as they became known in the Victorian era. The fear of another potato crop disaster through disease, along with the new-found appreciation of its table value caused intense interest in improving potato varieties throughout Europe. At the International Potato Show at London's Alexandra Palace in

1879 there were reputed to have been several hundred varieties on show. By the turn of the century the potato was the accepted main vegetable crop and was exported throughout Europe.

POTATOES IN THE WORLD TODAY

Now the potato is the staple food for two-thirds of the world's population and our third most important food crop. It is the best all-round source of nutrition known to man, second only to eggs for protein and better even than soya beans, the protein food of the second half of the 20th century. Growing potatoes is also the world's most efficient means of converting land, water and labour into an edible product – a field of potatoes produces more energy per acre per day than a field of any other crop.

persuasion. King Frederick of Prussia ordered his people to plant potatoes to prevent famine but had to enforce these orders by threatening to cut off the noses and ears of those who refused. European immigrants introduced potatoes to North America but it was not until Irish immigrants took the potato to Londonderry, New Hampshire in 1719, that it began to be grown in any quantity. Early in the 19th century, Lord Selkirk also emigrated with a group from the Isle of Skye in Scotland to settle in an area known as Orwell Point on Prince Edward Island, Canada. With him he took potatoes and the community survived on potatoes and cod for many years.

By the end of the 18th century, the potato was becoming a major crop, particularly in Germany and Britain. The Irish peasants were eating a daily average of ten potatoes per person, 80 per cent of their diet. In addition, potatoes were fodder for their animals who provided their milk, meat and eggs. This total dependence proved to be disastrous for the Irish when the blight of *Phytophthora infestans* struck the potato harvest in three successive years

Above: The great exhibition hall at London's Alexandra Palace

*Above: The sweet potato or yam flower (*Ipomoea batatas*)*

surrato, *pompiterre, bombiderre, castanhola* (chestnut from Spain) are some of the European ones. Chinese names include *shanyao* (mountain medicine), *didan* (ground egg), *fanzaishu* (potato with many children) and *aierlanshu* (Irish potato), to mention but a few.

THE POTATO PLANT CYCLE

The potato is related to both the tomato and the tobacco plant. Its botanical name is *Solanum tuberosum*, from the *Solanaceae* family, and the only edible part is the tuber. The plant is bushy and sprawling with clusters of dark green leaves. It produces flowers which range in colour from white to purple or striped and occasionally grows yellow-green fruits which contain anything from 100 to 300 kidney-shaped seeds. When grown from seed (or seed potato) it sprouts upwards producing a shoot, and downwards producing a root. The shoot first forms leaves, then flowers and as they die back the excess energy is stored as starch below ground in tubers at the ends of the roots. These tubers, the potatoes, grow larger as more and more starch is produced.

Potato tubers have several small indentations or external buds (as consumers we call them eyes and cut them out before eating them) which, when allowed to grow, form new stems or sprouts. Some of these will successfully grow into new plants using the stored food in the tuber. This original tuber is known as a seed potato which home growers and most commercial growers buy every year. In fact, you only need a piece of potato with one bud in, not even the whole potato, to produce one potato plant.

Producing the plant from seed is a much more complex process. The flower grown from this seed needs pollinating and it is only when this occurs in a controlled environment that you can be sure what the resultant plant will be like. In all the major potato growing countries there are seed potato producers and breeding centres where researchers are constantly developing

Statistics for potato production around the world show up many interesting factors. Russia is still the world's largest potato producer with Poland, China and the USA not far behind them.

Consumption trends, however, are now changing the demands which are put upon potato growers. This is due mainly to the trend towards Mediterranean eating which is heavily based on alternative starch foods, such as pasta and rice. Although potatoes are still a major seller the bulk of those sold

are pre-packed, many in the form of chips. Part of this consumption of chips is in a frozen form, and is worldwide, with America and the Far East setting the trend. Freezing potatoes is certainly not new, however. The early Incas, 2,000 years ago, turned potatoes into a form of convenience food called chuno, by a process of natural freezing and drying which meant they could be kept for much longer.

Throughout the world the potato goes under many other names: *pomme de terre, kartoffel, patata, batateirs, batala*

Above: A selection of rare potatoes, clockwise from top, Mr Bressee, International Kidney, Blue Catriona, Champion, Edgecote Purple, Arran Victory

FROM FIELD TO TABLE

The potato grows in over 180 countries, from an altitude of sea level to 14,000 feet, under a wider range of climatic conditions than any other staple food. It matures faster too, taking from 90 to 140 days. Yet much still depends on the grower knowing his or her potato, finding the right potato for the market and then making the most of the environment – a technology on its own.

Large scale potato production is highly mechanized, from planting to harvesting. Rows of furrows are made in the field by machines, ready for mechanical planters to drop in the seed potatoes. Machines aided by computer determine the depth of the troughs, the spacing of seed potatoes and soil fertilization, monitoring for pests and diseases and crop spraying as well. In good time for harvesting, the plant is left to finally mature and be ready for picking, which is done by machine, several rows at a time. The potatoes, separated from soil and stones by machines and briefly air dried, are stored in insulated boxes in controlled ventilation warehouses. Those going to local market are graded by size or riddled before being bagged or put into sacks.

new breeds. The Netherlands, the USA, Peru and the UK are key centres and, as with rare breeds of animals, the researchers log those that go out of favour or fashion, endeavouring to keep these breeds going for future reference and genetic research. Their main aim, however, is to develop new breeds which will enable more efficient potato production for the various climates throughout the world. These include breeds that can resist viruses and diseases or ones that will store better for longer, and breeds which provide the culinary qualities that certain markets demand, such as being good for chipping and processing. It is rare, of course, that all the desired qualities are found in one plant – in fact on average only one in 100,000 seedlings ever becomes registered as a cultivar (a possible new breed).

Only then does a seed go into field trials and it could be at least another 3–4 years before it is seen on the commercial market. There are several thousand varieties in existence throughout the world therefore, although only a fraction of those are in regular production. Countries with seed potato research centres provide key information annually for their seed producers. In Britain there are about 700 varieties held at the Department of Agriculture and Fisheries for Scotland listed in the Douglas M MacDonald collection. The Potato Association of America classifies up to 4,000 varieties but the International Potato Centre in Peru (CIP) has the largest gene bank, holding 3,694 cultivars.

Although varieties such as Blue Don, Elephant, King Kidney, Perthshire Red, The Howard and Victoria – some dating as far back as the 16th century – have become extinct, other more famous names are in various collections for posterity. These include Congo, a bright blue potato from pre-1900, Edgecote Purple and Champion. Other aged varieties are being revived, through the success of research and supermarket innovation. Names such as Mr Bressee, Blue Catriona and Arran Victory are returning to our shops. Home growers, buying from seed catalogues, now have an even more exciting wealth of new varieties to experiment with.

Above: Grading potatoes by size using a riddling machine

After harvesting, potatoes are stored or cured at a temperature of 15–18°C/ 59–65°F before being put into long-term storage at a temperature just above freezing. This helps to prevent sprouting but potatoes going into storage for up to ten months may also be sprayed. At these temperatures the potato starch can be affected and turn to sugar, so before processing the potatoes go back into short-term storage at the curing temperature to convert the sugars back to starch. On smaller farms and in areas where farm workers are readily available, many of these jobs are still done partially by hand. In more rural regions potatoes can still sometimes be found stored in clamps where the potatoes are stacked up under piles of soil and straw to keep them dry and frost-free.

Above: The Yanaimilla and the Compis (see below) are descendants of the original South American potatoes

Potatoes are classified by the length of time they take to mature although this can be affected by the weather and the climate. First earlies, also called new potatoes, are planted in early spring for harvesting, after some 100–110 days, in early summer. Second earlies, as the name implies, are planted in late spring and harvested, after 110–120 days, from mid to late summer as late new potatoes. Maincrop potatoes are planted in the spring but not harvested for at least 125–140 days in late summer. These are the potatoes which go into long-term storage for sale in the next season, whilst earlies go straight into the shops.

When a young potato is dug up it has fragile, flaky skin. As it matures the skin sets and after a certain length of time will no longer flake and the flesh becomes much more starchy. Maincrop potatoes have to be kept in the ground maturing as long as possible to produce skins which are thick enough to survive in long-term storage. You will now find that you can buy a young, new Maris Piper for instance, which is small and flaky, at the same time as you can buy the large, firm maincrop Maris Piper, since each may be grown in different areas by different producers.

NUTRITION

The potato is the single most important source of vitamin C for much of the world, in particular the poorer countries where there is little fruit and certainly no other dietary supplements. We all need vitamin C to help fight off infections and to keep muscle, skin and bones healthy. Unlike many vegetables, the entire potato is edible and nutritious, providing important amounts of protein, vitamins and minerals, and it can be cooked in ways to suit most climates, ethnic traditions and cooking abilities. More than that, for the Western societies which are suffering from the excesses of good food, potatoes can provide a useful amount of one of the key elements needed in our modern healthy diet – fibre.

Above: The Compis, like the Yanaimilla, are only grown by local Andean Farmers

The bulk of the potato, about 75 per cent or more according to how you cook it, is made up of water. The largest

Above: Baked potatoes are a valuable source of protein, fibre and vitamin C

amount of the rest – 17 per cent – is starch, known also as complex carbohydrate. Current recommendations for the Western diet suggest that we should get at least 40 per cent of our food energy – our total calorie consumption per day – from starchy foods such as potatoes. One large baked potato, approximately 300g/11oz, will provide about 250 calories. Potatoes also contain 2.1 per cent protein, 1.3 per cent fibre, good quantities of vitamin C, almost no fat and other important trace elements such as foliate (for red blood cells), potassium (which helps calm the nerves) and iron (which helps oxygen travel easily around the body). New potatoes have a particularly high vitamin C content and a 100g/3¾oz serving can provide 23 per cent of our daily requirement.

The way potatoes are stored and cooked also affects their nutritional content. Vitamin C can be lost during long storage in too much light and it can also be lost whilst they are soaking in water before and during the cooking process. Chips, surprisingly, are not such a bad way of cooking potatoes as they are often portrayed. They manage to retain more of the vitamin C because the method of cooking involves less soaking in water and, if oven-baked, 100g/3¾oz chips will actually have fewer calories than 100g/3¾oz of fruit and nut mix.

GROWING YOUR OWN POTATOES

Potatoes usually grow well in most soils, and whether you have a small corner or a large plot, whether you have years of experience or are a novice gardener, they will produce a worthwhile result for relatively little effort. Just 900g/2lb of seed potatoes can give around 23kg/50lb potatoes, so unless you have plenty of storage space or have a large family you may only need to plant a small amount or stagger the harvesting. Early potatoes produce a smaller crop than maincrop potatoes so they also require less space.

PREPARATION

Prepare the ground in the autumn before it gets too hard, clearing the weeds and digging in a good compost or manure, about one bucketful to 1sq m/1.2sq yds. A couple of weeks before planting, dig over the ground adding fertilizers as recommended. Potatoes need a lot of space; a 900g/2lb seed bag will require 0.9–1.2sq m/3–4sq ft of soil for instance. Seed potatoes can be put in trays at the end of January in a cool room or warmed greenhouse, to encourage the sprouts to grow earlier and give a better crop.

PLANTING

In most climates first earlies can be planted from mid-spring; in colder regions wait until late spring.

1 Make drills or shallow trenches about 10cm/4in deep and 45cm/18in apart with a hoe, or up to 60cm/2ft apart for maincrop potatoes, Place the seed potatoes, sprouts uppermost, into them.

2 Fill in the drills with soil, increasing the height of soil over the potato seed for protection.

3 For easier, weed-free growth and frost protection, plant the seeds under black plastic. Secure the edges of the plastic under soil.

4 Make several cross-shaped slits where the potatoes will be planted, making sure they are covered with at least 5cm/2in of soil.

PROTECTING

As the shoots start to appear, draw up more soil over the seed potato into a ridge, giving protection against frost, and continue this earthing-up process every two weeks until the foliage meets between the rows or you have soil mounds about 15cm/6in high. Water occasionally in a very dry spring or more frequently for earlies.

HARVESTING

Early potatoes should be ready for harvesting from early summer in milder climates – as a rough guide after about 12–14 weeks. You could start by carefully pushing away earth from the higher part of the ridges to remove any that are ready. Replace the soil if they are still too small.

Maincrop potatoes, on the other hand, have to be held in the ground until the foliage dies down, so the tubers can keep growing and the skin sets firmly for longer storage. To be sure, lift one or two potatoes, as above, and try rubbing the skin. If it rubs off easily the potatoes are not ready.

1 Dig up the potatoes with a large fork and sort them into groups by size. Leave them on the ground for an hour or two to dry off.

2 Store them in large sacks made of hessian if you can find them, or in string bags. Slatted boxes are suitable too, but use straw to both protect the potatoes from bruising and keep them frost-free and dry. Keep in a dark, cool but not damp place such as a garage, as long as it does not get too cold.

PREPARATION TECHNIQUES

The method you use to prepare your potatoes affects the mineral and vitamin content, and the cooking technique.

CLEANING POTATOES

Most potatoes you buy today are very clean, especially those from supermarkets and pre-packed potatoes, so giving them a light wash will probably be sufficient before boiling them. Locally grown potatoes, farm shop or home-grown potatoes may still have some earth attached to them, so give them a light scrub before cooking. If you are not going to cook them immediately avoid scrubbing the potatoes with water as they can start to go mouldy in warm or damp weather.

1 If the potatoes are very dirty, use a small scrubbing brush or a gentle scourer to clean and remove the peel of the new potatoes.

2 Remove any green or discoloured patches or black eyes carefully, using a pointed knife or potato peeler, unless you are going to peel them after cooking, at which stage they will come out of their skins easily.

PEELING POTATOES

It is well known that much of the goodness and flavour of a potato is in the skin and just below it. You can boil the potatoes and then peel them afterwards when they are cool enough to handle. The taste is much fresher and earthier if they are prepared this way and perfect for eating plain or simply garnished. Leave the skins on occasionally, which gives more taste and added texture, plus a vital source of roughage and fibre to the diet. Save any peelings you have left over for a very healthy version of crisps.

To peel potatoes use a very sharp potato peeler (there are many different varieties to choose from) to remove the thinnest layer possible in long even strips. Place the potatoes in a saucepan of water so they are just covered until ready to cook, but preferably cook them immediately to avoid any loss of vitamin C.

If you cook potatoes in their skins and want to peel them whilst hot ready for eating immediately, hold the hot potato with a fork and then gently peel off the skin – the skin tends to peel more easily while the potatoes are still hot.

SCRAPING POTATOES

Really new potatoes peel very easily, often just by rubbing them in your hands. You can tell a good new potato, when buying them, by how easily the skin rubs or flakes off.

With a small sharp knife scrape away the flaky skin and place in just enough water to cover.

RUMBLING

This wonderfully old-fashioned word refers to a catering machine with a large revolving bowl and rough, grater-like sides. The potatoes rumble around until the skins are eventually scratched or scraped off. There is one product available for the domestic market which peels the potatoes in the same way.

Wash the potatoes, place in the peeler drum with water as directed, then turn on to speed 2–3 and leave for several minutes. Remove any that are peeled and then continue until the rest are ready. Transfer to a pan of cold water ready for cooking. Don't put in more potatoes than recommended or they may come out misshapen.

GRATING BY HAND

Potatoes can be grated before or after cooking, depending on how you will be using them. They are easier to grate after cooking, when they have had time to cool, and can be grated on a large blade straight into the cooking dish or frying pan. Be sure you don't overcook the potatoes, especially if they are floury, as they will just fall to pieces. Floury potatoes are ideal for mashing, while waxy potatoes are a good choice for making rösti or hash.

Raw potatoes exude a surprising amount of starchy liquid that is vital to helping some dishes stick together. Check before you start whether you need to keep this liquid. The recipe should also tell you whether to rinse off the starchy liquid or just dry the potatoes on kitchen paper. Don't grate the potatoes too soon as the flesh quickly begins to turn brown.

Using a standard grater, grate raw potatoes on a board.

Or if you need the liquid, grate into a medium bowl using either the medium or large blade. Squeeze the liquid from the potatoes by hand.

CHOPPING

Potatoes are often required to be chopped for recipes such as salads and dishes using leftovers. If you are cooking them first the best potatoes to choose are the waxy ones which stay nice and firm. They chop most easily when they are cold and peeled.

To chop, cut the potato in half, then half again and again until it is cut up evenly, as small as is required.

DICING

If the recipe calls for dice this means you have to be much more precise and cut the potato into even shaped cubes. This is usually so that all the sides brown neatly or the pieces cook through evenly.

1 To dice, trim the potato into a neat rectangle first (keep the outside pieces for mash, or to add to a soup), then cut the rectangles into thick, even slices.

2 Turn the stack of slices over and cut into thick batons and finally into even cubes of the size needed for the recipe you are using.

SLICING BY HAND

It may not always matter how neatly and evenly you slice your potatoes, but for some dishes it will affect both the appearance of the finished dish and the cooking time. Try to cut all slices the same thickness so that they cook evenly. Use a large knife for the best results, and make sure that it is sharp otherwise it may slip and cause a nasty cut. To make rounder slices cut across the width of the potato, for longer slices cut along the length of the potato. If you need to slice cooked potatoes for a recipe, be sure to slightly undercook them so they don't fall to pieces either in the dish or when slicing, and let them get really cold before handling them. For most casseroles and toppings cut them about 3mm/⅛in thick.

Put the tip of the knife on the work surface or board first, then press the heel of the knife down firmly to create nice even slices.

SLICING WITH A MANDOLINE

A relative of the musical instrument of the same name, the mandoline has several different cutting blades which vary both the size and shape of the cut potato. The blades are fitted into a metal, plastic or wooden framework for ease of use. It can produce slices from very thin to very thick, as well as fluted slices for crinkle-cut style crisps. It's quite a dangerous gadget, and needs handling with respect because of its very sharp blades. You can cut different thicknesses as required, such as, medium thick (about 2–3mm/$\frac{1}{16}$–$\frac{1}{8}$in) for sautéed potato slices and very thin for crisps.

Plain Slices

Fix the blade to the required thickness, then holding the potato carefully slide it firmly up and down or across the blade. Use the handle or gadget that is provided with some versions to hold on to whenever possible.

Crinkle-cut

For crinkle-cut slices cut the potato horizontally down the fluted blade. Take particular care when the potato gets smaller as it is easy to cut one's fingers on the blade.

Waffled Crisps

For the fancy waffled crisps (*pomme gaufrettes*), cut horizontally down the blade, rotating each time you slice to get a lattice effect.

MAKING CRISPS BY HAND

Home-made crisps are the best, but they can be very fiddly if you do not have the right tools for making them. For a large batch slice the potatoes in a food processor, but for a small batch the slicing blade on a standard grater should give thin enough potato slices if you use it carefully. You can also use a sharp knife to make crisps, but you need to be very careful.

Grating Crisps

To make thin crisps, hold a standard grater firmly on a chopping board, placing a damp cloth on the board to anchor the grater to it and prevent it from sliding. Slide the potato down over the slicing blade carefully. Be sure the grater or mandoline has a very sharp blade. Adjust it to the right thickness or, if it's not adjustable, you will find that the harder you press, the thicker the crisps will be.

Slicing Crisps

This method is best if you want to make small quantites of thick crisps. Hold one end of the potato firmly in your hand and cut thin slices – 3mm/$\frac{1}{8}$in thick – with a sharp knife, on a chopping board. Slicing crisps with a knife means that it is easier to adjust the thickness. Remember that the thicker the slice, the less oil will be absorbed by the potato during cooking.

MAKING RIBBONS BY HAND

Thin ribbons, which also deep fry into delicious crisps, can be simply cut with a potato peeler. (Any leftover odd shapes can go into the stockpot.)

To make ribbons, peel the potato like an apple to give very long strips. Work quickly, or put the ribbons in a bowl of cold water as you go, to prevent them turning brown.

CHIPS

The French give their chips various names, depending on how thin or thick they are cut. The larger you cut them the healthier they will be, since they will absorb less fat during the cooking. You can also make chips with their skins on, giving additional fibre.

Traditional English Chips

Use the largest chipping potatoes and cut the potatoes into 1.5cm/⅝in thick slices, or thicker if you wish.

Turn the slices on their side and cut into 1.5cm/⅝in batons, or slightly thicker or thinner if you prefer.

Chip Wedges

For a healthier alternative cut your chips, extra thick, into wedge shapes. First cut the potatoes in half lengthwise, then into long thin wedges.

Pommes Frites

Cut as for chips but slice again into neat, even batons about 6mm/¼in thick, either by hand or machine.

Pommes Allumettes

Cut the potato into a neat rectangle by removing the rounded sides, then into thin slices and julienne strips about half the thickness of *pommes frites*.

Pommes Pailles (Straw Chips)

Cut the potatoes as for *pommes allumettes* into even finer julienne strips. They are usually pan fried.

Chip-cutter Chips

Chips can be cut with a special chip cutter (see equipment section) and some mandolines. Cut the potatoes to a suitable size to fit.

Left: Four different sizes of chips, from bottom left clockwise – English chips, pommes pailles, pommes frites, pommes allumettes

HASSELBACK AND FAN POTATOES

Children often refer to these as hedgehogs as they look quite spiky when roasted to a crispy, golden brown. Peel and dry the potatoes then slice as shown, brush with oil and then put them to roast as soon as possible before they begin to discolour.

To make hasselback potatoes, cut large potatoes in half and place cut side down on a board. With a sharp knife, cut very thin slices across the potato from end to end, slicing deep but not quite through the potato.

To make potato fans, use medium potatoes of long or oval shape and cut them at a slight angle, slicing almost but not quite through the potato, keeping the back section still attached. Press the potato gently on the top until it flattens and fans out at the same time. If you have not cut far enough through it will not fan very much, but if you have cut too far it will split into sections. The best way to cook both these potatoes is to cook them with melted butter and oil and roast them in the oven, preheated to 190°C/375°F/Gas 5, for 40–50 minutes.

SHAPED POTATOES

Occasionally it is fun to spend the time making potatoes into an artistic creation. You might try these out with children when you are encouraging them to get more involved with preparing and cooking family meals. Use the offcuts for making mash or to thicken soups.

To make potato balls use large firm potatoes for the best results. Peel them and then using a large round or shaped melon baller push it firmly into the potato, twist, and ease out the potato shape. Keep in water until ready to cook, pat dry on kitchen paper and roast or sauté as usual.

To make turned potatoes, first peel small to medium firm potatoes (or quartered large potatoes), trim the ends flat and then cut or trim with a small knife into rugby ball shapes 2.5–5cm/1–2in long.

To make potato wedges, cut potatoes in half lengthways, then into quarters and then into eighths. Brush with oil and oven roast or deep fry. The larger the pieces of potato the less fat they will absorb.

PREPARING POTATOES BY MACHINE

Some machines will do many of the jobs already mentioned, such as peeling, grating, slicing, chipping and puréeing, with great speed but not with the precision of your own hands. To get the best results, always cut the potatoes to the same size, use the slowest speed or pulse so you can control the results, and cook the cut potatoes immediately or rinse and dry on kitchen paper to prevent browning.

Home-cooked chips are always the best kind, and cutting them by hand can be time consuming. So use a machine to prepare them for cooking. Fit the correct blade attachment and pack sufficient potatoes in the tube of the food processor so they can be pushed down. Turn on to the slowest speed and press the potato down with the plunger. The harder you press the plunger the thicker the chips will be.

They may turn out slightly bent but that won't affect the taste. For nice evenly sliced potatoes change the attachment on the machine and pack the potatoes so that they will remain facing the same direction and continue as above.

COOKING TECHNIQUES

There are endless different ways of cooking potatoes. However, the best technique depends on both the potato variety and the dish you are cooking.

BLANCHING

Potatoes are blanched (part-cooked) to soften the skin for easy peeling, to remove excess starch for certain recipes and to par-cook before roasting. Use a draining spoon or basket to remove large pieces of potato but when cooking smaller potatoes, place the potatoes in a chip basket for easy removal.

Place the prepared potatoes in a pan of cold water. Bring slowly to the boil and boil gently for 2–5 minutes depending on their size, then drain and use or leave in the cooling water until required.

BOILING

This is the simplest way of cooking potatoes. Place potatoes of a similar size, either whole or cut into chunks, with or without skins (sweet potatoes are best cooked in their skins to retain their bright colour) in a pan with sufficient water just to cover them. Sprinkle on 5–10ml/1–2 tsp salt or to taste, and bring slowly to the boil. Floury potatoes need very gentle boiling or you may find the outside is cooked before the inside is ready and they will become mushy or fall apart in the pan. New potatoes, which have a higher vitamin C content, should be put straight into boiling water and cooked for about 15 minutes and not left soaking. Very firm salad potatoes can be put into boiling water, simmered for

5–10 minutes and then left to stand in the hot water for another 10 minutes until required.

1 Place the potatoes in a large pan and just cover with salted water and a tight-fitting lid. Bring to the boil and leave to gently boil for 15–20 minutes depending on the size and type of potato. Boiling too fast tends to cook the potato on the outside first so it becomes mushy and falls apart before the middle is cooked.

2 When they are finished cooking, drain the potatoes through a colander and then return them to the pan to dry off, as wet or soggy potatoes are not very appetizing.

3 For really dry, peeled potatoes (for mashing for instance), leave them over a very low heat so any moisture can escape. In the north of England they sprinkle the potatoes with salt and shake occasionally until the potatoes stick to the sides of the pan.

4 In Ireland the potatoes are wrapped in a clean tea towel until ready to serve dry and fluffy.

STEAMING

All potatoes steam well but this gentle way of cooking is particularly good for very floury potatoes and those which fall apart easily. Small potatoes, such as new potatoes, steamed in their skins taste really delicious. Make sure potatoes are cut quite small, in even-size chunks or thick slices. Leaving cooked potatoes over a steaming pan of water is also a good way to keep them warm for several minutes.

1 Place prepared potatoes in a sieve, colander or steamer over a deep pan of boiling salted water. Cover as tightly as possible and steam for 5–7 minutes if sliced or cut small, increasing the time to 20 minutes or more if the potatoes are quite large.

2 Towards the end of the cooking time, test a few of the potatoes with a sharp knife, and when cooked, turn off the heat and leave until you are ready to serve them.

3 As an alternative, place a handful of fresh mint leaves in the bottom of the steamer before cooking. The flavour of the mint will penetrate during cooking.

FRYING

The key to successful frying is good fat. A mixture of butter and oil gives good flavour yet allows a higher cooking temperature than just butter.

Shallow Frying

Use a heavy-based large frying pan to allow an even distribution of heat and sufficient room to turn the food.

1 Heat about 25g/1oz/2 tbsp butter and 30ml/2 tbsp oil until bubbling. Put an even layer of cooked or par-cooked potatoes in the hot fat taking care not to splash yourself. Leave for 4–5 minutes until the undersides turn golden.

2 Turn the potatoes over gently with a large fish slice once or twice during cooking until golden brown all over.

Deep Frying

When deep frying, whether you use oil or solid fat, be sure it is fresh and clean. The chips must be well dried as water can cause the fat to bubble up dangerously. Always fry in small batches so the temperature does not drop too much when you add the food and it can cook and brown evenly. Remove any burnt pieces after each batch as this can taint the fat.

To deep fry chips, fill either a chip pan, a deep heavy saucepan with tight-fitting lid, or a deep-fat fryer, about half full with clean fat. Heat to the required temperature by setting the thermostat or test if the oil is hot enough by dropping in a piece of bread; it should turn golden in one minute.

When making chips they are best "blanched" first in hot fat to cook through and seal them without browning. These can then be removed, drained and frozen when cool. Give them a final cooking when you are almost ready to eat, to crisp them up and turn them golden brown.

1 Before frying, dry the chips very thoroughly in a cloth or kitchen paper. Any water or moisture will make the fat splash and spit.

2 Heat the basket in the fat first, then add the chips to the basket (don't overfill or they will not cook evenly), and lower slowly into the pan. If the fat appears to bubble up too much remove the basket and cool the fat slightly.

3 Shake the pan of chips occasionally to allow even cooking, and cook until they are crisp and golden. Remove with a draining spoon or chip basket and drain well against the side of the pan first.

4 Tip the chips on to kitchen paper to get rid of the excess fat before serving, sprinkled with salt.

Deep frying temperatures

- To blanch and seal chips 160°C/325°F
- To quickly fry fine straw chips and crisps and to second cook chips 190°C/375°F

Potato Baskets

1 Cut potatoes into thin, even slices and dry on kitchen paper without rinsing. You will need two wire potato baskets or ladles. Line the larger one evenly with overlapping slices, covering the base well, then clamp the smaller basket inside this one.

2 Slowly immerse in very hot fat for 3–4 minutes until starting to turn golden brown.

3 Remove from the heat, separate the ladles and ease out the basket. Drop back into the fat for another 1–2 minutes until golden.

4 Serve filled with vegetables, stir-fried meat, or sweet and sour prawns.

Safe deep frying

- Never overfill the pan, with either fat or food.
- Always use a tight-fitting lid.
- Have ready a large, very thick cloth to throw over the pan in case of fire.
- NEVER throw water on to a chip pan full of hot or burning fat as it will explode.

BAKING

One of the most comforting and economical meals is a salt-crusted potato baked in its jacket with a fluffy centre that is golden with melted butter and cheese.

Sweet potatoes can be cooked in exactly the same way, sprinkled with a little demerara sugar and topped with soured cream and crispy bacon.

Allow a 275–350g/10–12oz potato for a good size portion and choose the ones recommended for baking, such as Marfona, Maris Piper, Cara or King Edward. Cook in the middle of a hot oven at 220°C/425°F/Gas 7 for 1–1½ hours for very large potatoes or 40–60 minutes for medium potatoes. To test that they are cooked, squeeze the sides gently to make sure that they are sufficiently soft.

1 Wash and dry baking potatoes thoroughly then rub with good oil and add a generous sprinkling of salt. Cook on a baking tray as above.

2 To speed up cooking time and to ensure even cooking throughout, cook the baking potatoes on a skewer, or on special potato baking racks.

3 When really tender cut a cross in the top of each potato and set aside to cool slightly.

4 Hold the hot potato in a clean cloth and squeeze gently from underneath to open up.

5 Place the open potatoes on individual serving plates and pop a lump of butter in each one.

6 For a quick and simple topping, add a little grated tangy Cheddar or similar hard cheese, or a dollop of soured cream and some chopped fresh herbs, such as chives, parsley or coriander. Season with plenty of salt and ground black pepper.

Baked Potato Skins

Bake the potatoes at 220°C/425°F/Gas 7 for 1–1½ hours for large potatoes and 40–60 minutes for medium. Cut in half and scoop out the soft centres. (Mash for a supper or a pie topping.)

Brush the skins with melted butter, margarine or a mixture of butter and oil and return to the top of the oven, at the same temperature, for 20 minutes or until really crisp and golden.

Potato Parcels

Baking a potato in a foil or greaseproof paper parcel, or in a roasting bag, makes for a very tasty potato with no mess and no dirty dishes, if you're careful. If you leave the potatoes in their skins you could prepare them well in advance and put them in to cook in an automatic oven before you get home.

Wash or scrub and dry small potatoes, then wrap them up in a parcel with several knobs of butter, a sprinkle of seasoning and a sprig or two of mint, tarragon or chives. Bake at 190°C/375°F/Gas 5 for about 40–50 minutes for 450g/1lb potatoes.

COOKING IN A CLAY POT

This is most like cooking in a bonfire or under a pile of earth – but here the potatoes take on a deep woody aroma and intense flavour without all the charring and smoke. The terracotta potato pot takes a generous 450g/1lb of potatoes easily. As with all clay pot utensils it should be soaked for 10–20 minutes before using. Use small, even-size potatoes, preferably in their skins. Always place the pot in a cold oven and let the temperature gradually increase to 200°C/400°F/Gas 6. Cook for 40–50 minutes and then test with a pointed knife to see if they are ready.

1 Put the prepared potatoes in the clay pot, toss in 30–45ml/2–3 tbsp of good, preferably extra virgin olive oil or melted butter and sprinkle with roughly ground salt from a mill and pepper. Add your favourite flavourings, such as one large unpeeled clove of garlic, a thick piece of streaky smoked bacon, chopped, or fresh herbs.

2 Put the covered pot in the cold oven and allow to heat to 200°C/400°F/Gas 6. After 40–50 minutes test with a knife. Serve straight from the pot.

MICROWAVED POTATOES

Baking potatoes in the microwave is an enormous time saver, as long as you don't expect the crunchy crust of oven-cooked potatoes. New potatoes and potato pieces can be cooked very quickly and easily. In both cases prick the potato skins first, to prevent bursting. To bake, allow 4–6 minutes per potato, with the setting on a high temperature, increasing by 2–4 minutes for every additional potato. As a guide for smaller boiled potatoes, allow 10–12 minutes per 450g/1lb of cut potatoes on high, or follow the manufacturer's instructions.

Place large potatoes in a circle on kitchen paper on the microwave tray, make cuts around the middle so the skins don't burst and turn once during the cooking process.

Place small potatoes in a microwave bowl with 30–45ml/2–3 tbsp boiling water. Cover tightly with microwave film and pierce two or three times to allow steam to escape during cooking. Leave for 3–5 minutes before draining, adding a knob or two of butter, seasoning and a sprig of mint.

Alternatively, cover the potatoes with a close-fitting microwave lid and cook them using the same method as for the microwave film covered bowl.

Standing time

Allow sufficient standing time afterwards so the potatoes are evenly cooked. Large, baked potatoes should be left to stand for 10 minutes wrapped in serviettes. This will keep them warm before serving and ensure even cooking.

PRESSURE-COOKING

If you want baked potatoes or large potatoes to be cooked in a hurry, or if you want to make a quick and easy mash, this is an ideal cooking method, but it's important to make sure you do not to overcook them, otherwise the potatoes will become dry and floury. Follow the instructions in your manual and allow up to 12 minutes cooking time for large whole potatoes; less for smaller ones. You can cook the potatoes in their skins, which speeds up the process further. Once the potatoes are ready, carefully reduce steam pressure so that they do not overcook.

ROASTING

Melt-in-the-mouth crisp roasties are what Sundays were meant for, so here are some pointers to make sure you get them right every time.

For soft, fluffy-centred roast potatoes, you need to use large baking potatoes – Wilja, Maris Piper, Record, Désirée and Kerr's Pink all give excellent results. Peel (you can roast potatoes in their skins but you won't get the crunchy result most people love), and cut into even-size pieces. Blanch for 5 minutes, then leave in the cooling water for a further 5 minutes to par-cook evenly. Drain well and return to the pan to dry off completely. Well-drained potatoes with roughed up surfaces produce the crispiest results.

A successful roast potato also depends on the fat you cook them in and the temperature. Beef dripping gives the best flavour, although goose fat, if you are lucky enough to find some, is delicious and gives a very light, crisp result. With other roasts you can use lard or, where possible, drain off enough dripping from the joint. A vegetarian alternative is a light olive oil, or olive and sunflower oils mixed.

The fat in the tin must be hot enough to seal the potato surfaces immediately. Use a large enough roasting pan so that you have room to turn the potatoes at least once. Don't leave the almost cooked potatoes in too much fat as they will become soggy. Serve as soon as they are ready for maximum crispness.

1 Blanch the peeled chunks of potato and drain, then shake in the pan or fork over the surfaces to rough them up.

2 Pour a shallow layer of your chosen fat into a good heavy roasting tin and place it in the oven, heating it to a temperature of 220ºC/425ºF/Gas 7. Add the dry, forked potatoes and toss immediately in the hot oil. Return to the top shelf of the oven and roast for up to one hour.

3 Once or twice during cooking remove the roasting tin from the oven and, using a spatula, turn the potatoes over to evenly coat them in fat. Then drain off any excess fat so they can crisp up and brown more easily.

Flavourings

Flavourings you could try are:
- Curry powder mixes.
- Ground hazelnuts or other nuts.
- Dry seasoning mixes such as Italian Garlic Seasoning or Cajun Seasoning.
- Sesame seeds.
- Garlic and herb breadcrumbs.
- Grated Parmesan cheese.

Healthy Wedges

As a healthier alternative to deep-fried chips and roasties, serve wedges of dry-roasted potatoes sprinkled with various seasonings. Bake at 190ºC/375ºF/Gas 5, turning often until golden and crisp.

1 Cut large baking potatoes into long thin wedges. Toss in a small amount of very hot sunflower oil in a roasting tin.

2 Sprinkle on seasonings, turn the wedges over several times and bake for 30–40 minutes, turning and testing once or twice.

MASHING AND PURÉEING

The ubiquitous mashed potato has seen a revival in recent years, from a favourite comfort food into a fashion food purely by the addition of olive oil or Parmesan cheese. Every chef and every trendy restaurant today produces their own version. It shows what can be done with a simple ingredient, but you've got to start with good mash. When choosing your potatoes remember that floury potatoes produce a light fluffy mash, while waxy potatoes will result in a dense, rather gluey purée which needs lots of loosening up. Boil even-size potatoes until very well cooked but not falling apart and dry them well, as watery potatoes will give a soggy, heavy mixture. Cold potatoes mash best of all. Sweet potatoes also mash well, to serve as a savoury or sweet dish.

You can mash potatoes in several ways: using a hand masher, which gives a very smooth result; pressing the potatoes through a ricer, sieve or mouli grater, which gives a very light and fluffy result; using a fork, which can result in a slightly lumpy, uneven mixture; or using a pestle-type basher. An electric hand-held mixer can be used but don't be tempted to blend or purée them in the food processor as the end product will be a very solid, gluey mixture, ideal for turning into soup.

Making Mash

There are a number of different hand mashers available for sale but the best ones are those that have a strong but open cutting grid. Simply push down on the cooked potatoes, making sure you cover every area in the pan and you will get a smooth, yet textured result.

Press potatoes through a ricer for an easy way to prepare light and fluffy mash. For a low-calorie side dish, press the potatoes straight into a heated bowl.

Alternatively beat in a generous knob of butter, some creamy milk and seasoning to taste, then continue mashing until you have a creamy, fluffy mixture.

Quick Mash Toppings

There are many simple ways to make mashed potatoes look more exciting and even tempt youngsters to try something new and unusual.

Rough up the topping on a shepherd's pie by running a fork through it.

An alternative decorative effect can be created using the back of a spoon to gently swirl the potato into soft hollows and peaks.

For a more chunky topping, use two matching spoons to make scoops or quenelle shapes, carefully moulding the potato around the sides of the spoons.

A quick and easy pattern to achieve is a lattice design. Run with a fork up and down the pie topping, before brushing with egg and then placing under a pre-heated grill to brown.

Piping Mashed Potatoes

Smooth and creamy mashed potatoes will pipe beautifully, and your results can look professional with very little practice. But it does have to be really smooth mash, since any lumps will ruin your efforts and may clog up the piping bag and nozzle. Place a large, star nozzle in a large clean piping bag and using a spoon fill the bag two-thirds with mash. Use your left hand to hold and guide the nozzle and your right hand to squeeze the potato down the bag. Practise a few times on a board, doing it slowly at first.

Duchesse Potatoes and Rosettes

These are the fancy portions which are often served in hotels. Rosettes are piped on to baking trays, brushed with beaten egg and baked until just golden to serve as a vegetable accompaniment to a main meal. They are very easy to make at home, however, if you want to impress your friends at a dinner party. You will need to use a firmer mashed potato than normal. To do this simply add egg yolks instead of milk to the potatoes in the pan and combine well. Brush with an egg glaze: 1 small egg, beaten with 15–30ml/1–2 tbsp water will give a thin mixture. Bake at 190°C/375°F/Gas 5 until golden brown.

1 Place a large, clean piping bag, fitted with a star nozzle, in a jug to hold it steady. Spoon in the thickened mashed potato until the bag is two-thirds full.

2 Start by squeezing out a small circle of potato, moving the nozzle slowly in one direction.

3 Then, still squeezing gently, fill in the centre and lift the bag up to make a cone shape.

Piped Topping

1 The same shape as above, made with a smaller nozzle, can be used to give a pie a very professional topping.

2 Bake the topping in the oven, preheated to 190°C/375°F/Gas 5 for 10-15 minutes, or grill for 5 minutes.

Potato Nests

These make a great meal for young children or an attractive dish for dinner. Fill with asparagus spears, fresh peas, sweetcorn, baked beans, soft cheese, chicken, fish or mushrooms in a creamy sauce and heat through.

1 Using the same nozzle as for duchesse potatoes pipe a large circle, or oval, on to a baking sheet or on to greaseproof paper.

2 Then fill in the base and pipe over the outer circle again to give height to the sides. Glaze and bake as for duchesse potatoes.

Piped Edgings

Many dishes can have piped potato edges. Most well known is the individual starter Coquilles St Jacques, where the potato holds the fish and creamy sauce safely in the scallop shell.

Pipe a circle, just like the potato nests, but around the edge of a cleaned scallop shell or a china version of this. Brush with egg, fill with fish mixture and then grill until golden.

Mash Flavours

To make a Mediterranean version beat in salt, pepper and good quality olive oil to give a smooth soft mixture. Serve sprinkled with plenty of finely grated Parmesan cheese.

To make a wickedly rich mash, add thick cream or crème fraîche and grated fresh nutmeg. Mix thoroughly and serve with more grated nutmeg.

To make a lovely creamy mixture, beat in good, preferably extra virgin olive oil, and enough hot milk to make a smooth, thick purée. Then flavour to taste with salt and ground black pepper and stir in a few fresh basil leaves or parsley sprigs, chopped.

Chopped, cooked cabbage, spring onions and leeks are all regional favourites which add lots of flavour to a family supper dish.

Try a spicy mixture of chilli powder, or very finely chopped chilli and chives to sprinkle over a creamy mash.

To make a crunchy texture, place a few bacon rashers under a hot grill and once they are nice and crispy, chop them up and sprinkle over the potato.

To make a nutty mash, try toasted, flaked almonds or roughly chopped nuts of your choice.

USING COOKED POTATOES

Potatoes are one of the most versatile leftovers to have in the fridge, so it is well worth cooking extra when you make them, especially if a member of the family cannot tolerate wheat or cereals. You can use mashed potatoes in fish cakes, to thicken soups or stews, to make breads and scones and for a very light pastry to use in traditional savoury dishes or quiches. Grated, cooked potato can be used for rösti, hashes, omelettes, tortillas, and even to beef up a salad.

Potato Pastry

1 Rub 100g/4oz/8 tbsp dripping, lard or butter into 450g/1lb/4 cups sifted plain flour and add 450g/1lb mashed potatoes, 10ml/2 tsp salt, 1 beaten egg and sufficient milk so that when you draw the mixture together it is smooth but firm. Chill the pastry in the fridge for 10 minutes before use.

2 Roll the pastry out on a floured surface to an even thickness and use to line a suitable dish or tin. Chill the pastry in the dish again for 1 hour before pricking the bottom and filling as wished.

Potato Croquettes

1 Enrich a firm mash with egg, as for duchesse potatoes, season or add flavourings to taste, then shape into small cylinders, rolling out with a little flour or cornflour to prevent sticking.

2 Brush lightly with beaten egg, then coat or dip into any favourite mixture, like nibbed or flaked almonds or grated cheese mixed with breadcrumbs.

3 Shallow fry in butter and oil, turning occasionally until golden brown and warmed through. Croquettes can also be deep fried, or baked until golden brown. (Try putting a nugget of cheese in the middle before cooking for a delicious starter or supper dish.)

Rösti

1 Grate cold, par-cooked, waxy potatoes, on the largest side of a grater into a bowl and season to taste.

2 Heat a mixture of butter and oil in a heavy-based non-stick pan and, when bubbling, put in spoonfuls of the grated potato and flatten down neatly. Cook over low to medium heat until the rösti are golden and crisp underneath, which takes about 7–10 minutes.

3 Turn each of the rösti over with a fish slice, taking care that they do not fall apart and continue cooking for another 5 minutes or until really crisp.

4 To prepare one large rösti, spoon the potato mixture into the bubbling fat, flatten out evenly and leave to cook over a medium heat for about 10 minutes or until turning golden underneath. To turn the rösti over easily invert it on to a large plate – use a plate that fits right into the pan over the potato.

5 Turn the pan and plate over carefully so that the rösti slips on to the plate without breaking up.

6 Gently slide it back into the pan, with an extra knob of butter if necessary. Continue cooking for another 10 minutes or until crisp underneath. Serve cut into generous slices.

BUYING AND STORING

Now that there is such a variety of potatoes to choose from, suited for every kind of cooking, it is important to think about how you plan to use your potatoes before you shop for them. Being tempted by some lovely little creamy International Kidneys or pale Pink Fir Apple potatoes, when what you want to make is a velvety thick soup or the topping for a shepherd's pie, won't give you complete success. Look at the Potato Index so that next time you go shopping you can choose the right varieties of potatoes to suit your menu ideas. If you always like to eat the skins and are concerned about what may be sprayed on them, then you would be well-advised to buy organic potatoes. Or grow your own – a very easy and rewarding task if you have the space.

When buying new potatoes check that they are really young and fresh by scraping the skin, which should peel off easily. New potatoes have a high vitamin C content so buy and eat them as fresh as possible for maximum goodness.

Maincrop potatoes should be firm. Avoid any which are soft, flabby, sprouting or have a white dusty mould.

Check for any green patches. These are a sign that the potatoes have been stored in the light and, although the rest of the potato is fine to eat, you do need to cut out these poisonous patches.

STORING

Potatoes have come from the dark and like to stay in the dark, and they do not keep too well unless carefully stored. In the warmth of a centrally heated kitchen they can start sprouting; the dampness of a cold fridge will make them sweaty and mouldy, and in too much light they begin to lose their nutritional value and start turning green. New potatoes in particular should be eaten within two or three days, to prevent mould forming on the surface. Unless they can be kept in the dark, it is better to buy in small quantities, a few pounds at a time, so that they are used quickly.

If you prefer to buy your potatoes in bulk, by the sack or in a large paper bag, then you need to find a dark, dry larder or garage, where they won't freeze in cold weather but the temperature is low enough not to encourage the growth of any sprouts.

If you are storing your potatoes in the house, put them into an open storage rack or basket or a well aerated bin in a dry, dark room.

When you buy potatoes in plastic bags remove them from the bags immediately you get them. Then store them in a suitable place.

Read the storage and keeping times of pre-packed potatoes, since these come in many varieties. Some are ready to cook, and others are already peeled or cleaned. You can even buy potatoes with seasonings or flavoured butter nowadays, but these are best consumed soon after purchasing, again read the packet for correct storage times.

PLANNING AHEAD

If you like to be organised and peel potatoes in advance – don't. Storing peeled potatoes in water will remove almost every trace of vitamin C. Even storing them tightly covered but without water in the fridge will result in nasty black potatoes.

A much better option is to almost fully cook the potatoes in their skins, leaving them very firm. They can be refrigerated like this, covered, for 2–3 days. Then when you come to use them, peel and chop the potatoes and reheat in the microwave or cook for a further 3–5 minutes with mint, or use as you would normally in a recipe. You should also find that they have far more flavour.

You can store already mashed potato covered with cling-film ready to make into rissoles or toppings.

FREEZING POTATOES

Raw potato does not freeze at all well as it goes mushy, but cooked potato freezes quite well, although it has a tendency to go watery, so make sure it is very well dried before freezing.

Pipe duchesse potatoes or rosettes on to a baking tray, freeze until hard and store in a container. Cook from frozen.

Croquettes, rissoles, potato cakes and rösti should be individually wrapped or separated by greaseproof paper and then packed in fours or eights. Partly defrost them if they contain any meat or fish, then cook as for the original recipe.

Chips can be cooked but not browned, ready for a last minute really hot fry to crisp them. Freeze them on trays and then transfer to bags. Partly defrost on kitchen paper to remove any particles of ice before deep frying in small batches.

POTATO PRODUCTS

There are many forms of prepared potato available in the shops today. Instant mashed potato, in powder or flake form, is very easy to use and now comes with popular flavour additions; potato flour makes a healthy alternative to wheat, and canned new potatoes mean a salad is made in seconds. Foil pouches contain ready-to-fry potato suppers with a very long shelf life, and an array of seasonings could give your baked potatoes, slices or wedges a welcome spark of flavour.

EQUIPMENT

The right piece of equipment for the job always makes life easier and you may find that there are now gadgets available that you haven't come across. Some tools, like potato peelers, become old friends too. If you are used to using one particular style you will be loath to change. Just glancing at the selection of equipment now available, it's difficult to know where to start. If you could try out a gadget before buying it, like trying on a dress, you would have an easier time choosing the right one. This list is designed to help.

The horizontal-angled blades are fast and easy to use on large potatoes.

Peeler with brush For dirty work you could try a swivel-blade peeler with brush attached.

Thick-grip peeler Many peelers now have good, thick grips which make light work of any peeling job and are much easier on the muscles for those with arthritic problems.

Left: Peeler with brush

Twin-bladed peeler Takes a little time getting used to, but if you are preparing large quantities of big potatoes you could be grateful for this efficiency.

Coloured peeler Modern kitchen colours are now echoed in the design of kitchen equipment such as peelers, but following the trend doesn't always produce quality products. Enjoy them for what they are, a touch of fun in the kitchen, and hope that they also work well.

Above: Lancashire peelers

Peelers

Lancashire peeler This is the most traditional peeler, with a solid handle, often made from wood and string, and a rigid blade. They are firm and last well and also double up as a corer.

Stainless steel peeler Lightweight and inexpensive. The sharpest ones will give the thinnest peel. Beware the very cheap ones with stainless steel blades that bend, snap or blunt very quickly.

Above: Stainless steel peeler

Swivel-blade peeler These are for left- or right-handed people, but they are not very strong for heavy-duty work.

Above: Thick-grip peelers

Above: Twin-bladed peeler

Above: Coloured peelers

Above: A selection of graters, including single-sided, box and standard shapes

Graters

The sturdier the better is the only approach if you want a grater for heavy-duty work, like grating large, raw potatoes. Standard or box graters are ideal and can have four or more sides with several different size blades, often including a slicer which acts like a mandoline. Some have simple removable base trays or come in their own box container, making it unnecessary to dirty a board or plate and leaving no messy trail. Single-sided graters can be difficult to hold unless you steady them with a damp cloth, but they are ideal to place over a bowl so that you can grate straight in. If you plan to put your grater in the dishwasher, look for a stainless steel one without too much plastic.

Paring Knives

These are one of the most important items in the kitchen, especially for small fiddly jobs. Choose a knife with a short enough blade to allow you to use your thumb as well, but not too short or you won't be able to use it for small chopping jobs. The knife should be curved but not serrated and it should have a sharp point. Don't be tempted by those with removable peeler blades, as these are easily lost and remove too much skin.

Above: Paring knives

Mandolines

The original mandoline was a simple wooden implement with adjustable flat or fluted blades. It was designed for chefs to cut wafer-thin slices of potato, or other hard foods like carrots, for making crisps and game chips and for shredding and chipping. Take care, as they can give your hands a nasty cut.

Modern mandolines These now often come in their own supporting plastic frame or box, sometimes with a shredder or chipper blade as well. They can have two or three blades which are adjustable to give variable thicknesses, and these are flat or fluted. Some of the plastic ones are machine washable and come with a gadget for holding the last part of the vegetable to protect you from slicing your fingertips.

For large quantities of chips and crisps where the thickness needs to be exact, a more professional mandoline is available, but it is very expensive.

Wire Baskets

Using a wire basket is the easiest way to remove a batch of chips quickly from hot fat or quantities of potato from boiling water. When putting potatoes into hot fat do be sure the basket is heated in the fat first or the potatoes will stick to it.

Left: Mandoline

Long-handled wire baskets For blanching or frying chips in, these come in various sizes. Be sure to choose one that fits your pan almost exactly.

Small baskets Used for removing small quantities or pieces of potato when blanching or frying. There is a special attached pair for making potato nests.

Steamers

Steaming gives a very light potato and has nutritional benefits since it allows far less of the vitamins to be lost during cooking. Electric steamers are excellent for large quantities of potatoes. Chinese steamer baskets, which have their own lids,

are also good, especially as you can stack them up and steam several different foods at once. Clean steamers well to remove the potato starch – this is easiest done whilst they are warm.

Stainless steel steamer Can be bought with its matching pan, or separately to stand over a similar sized pan. It should

Above: Stainless steel steamer

also have a lid which makes it very useful for keeping cooked potatoes warm until needed.

Collapsible steamer These will fit into most sizes of pan. Alternatively, use a colander or sieve with your pan lid.

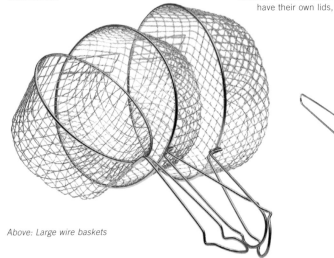

Above: Large wire baskets

Above: Attached baskets

Below: Metal ricer

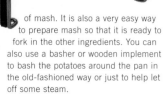

Below: Mouli grater

Ricers and Mashers

A ricer is a small rigid sieve with a pusher that makes the cooked potato come through looking like grains of rice.

Potato was often served like this, riced directly into a warmed serving dish without any butter or milk added – a much healthier version

of mash. It is also a very easy way to prepare mash so that it is ready to fork in the other ingredients. You can also use a basher or wooden implement to bash the potatoes around the pan in the old-fashioned way or just to help let off some steam.

Original metal ricer This has a triangular shaped bowl and is very sturdy. The round ricer doesn't take quite so much potato in the bowl.

Plastic ricer These are machine washable. They can have two sizes of blades, for smooth or textured results.

Mashers These come in various shapes and with different size holes, so you can choose accordingly if you prefer a smooth or rough mash. Some, but not all mashers, are machine washable.

Wooden basher A strong tool, which can give a chunky or fine result.

Large mouli grater This gives a very smooth result, and is suitable for puréeing or preparing a baby's dinner.

Left: Mashers

Electrical Equipment

Food processor If you frequently slice, shred or chip potatoes then a processor with these attachments could be a great time-saver. Different models have different attachments so research well before you buy. Most will have one slicer and one shredder blade, some will have additional sizes of blades and shredders and some also have chipper attachments.

Potato peeler It only takes a few minutes to peel the potatoes, whilst you are doing other things. It does leave a slightly rough surface on the potatoes which is good for roasting, but don't put too many in the machine at one time.

Deep-fat Fryers

Chip frying is one of the greatest causes of house fires so if you are a chip-loving family, it is essential that you buy an efficient deep-fat fryer (electric or not). Check the size before you buy as some can be quite small. Cooking chips in smaller quantities gives better results, and you should never be tempted to put in too many chips as the fat may bubble over. Don't buy a cheap fryer thinking it is saving you money because it won't last as long and will probably not be as safe. For the most efficient results be sure to keep the fryer well cleaned, change the oil frequently and preferably after each use. A good non-electric deep-fat fryer should be quite heavy, with a strong heatproof handle or handles and good-fitting basket and lid.

Electric deep-fat fryers These have a thermostatically controlled temperature gauge so you fry at the right temperature, giving the crispest results. They often include specified temperature guides or controls for certain frying tasks. The fat and chips are in a sealed container which avoids smells and spitting fat and removes much of the danger. Most can be taken to pieces for easy cleaning or have removable electric cords and some have Perspex lids so that you can see the chips cooking.

Above: Deep-fat fryer

Potato Bake Stands

To speed up baking you can push your potatoes on to skewers, or stand them upright on a special potato bake stand, which can save up to one-third of the cooking time.

Above: Food processor

Above: Potato bake stand

Chip Cutters

Manual chip cutters can certainly take the time out of chip making but you will always have to cut the potato to fit the model before you start cutting chips. It really would be good if you could try these out first though, as they rely entirely on brute force. Blades should be removable for easy washing and the rest of the machine should also be easily washable.

Flat chip cutter This gives very neat, if small, chips, but is hard work.

Upright chip cutter Slightly easier to push down, this cutter has two sizes of blade but is very limited on the size of potato it can take.

Above: Scrubbing brushes

Above: Upright chip cutter

Scrubbing brushes

For easily cleaning mud off potatoes, a small brush is ideal. The bristles should be firm without being too hard on the skins as you do not want to remove then while you are scrubbing.

Potato Pots

The two terracotta and clay pots illustrated are designed specifically for potatoes, giving an earthy taste and an easy method of cooking. Remember to soak the pots in water before using, as it is this moisture which is important in the cooking.

Potato Ballers

To make potato garnishes or shapes, the large side of a potato baller is ideal if you have a firm wrist.

Right: Potato pots

Potatoes of the World

WITH THE REVIVAL OF OLD POTATO BREEDS and the creation of many new and unusual breeds, potatoes are fast becoming a hot fashion food. We can now choose from small, flaky new potatoes with their buttery sweet flavour; traditional maincrops with soft earthy tasting floury centres; waxy golden maincrop potatoes with velvety firm texture; small misshapen speciality potatoes which give delicious crunch to salads, omelettes and casseroles; and a growing collection of vivid red or pink, purple and blue potatoes trendy enough to grace many a London or New York restaurant menu.

This resumé includes a description of each potato along with details of origin, availability, suitability for cooking and, where relevant, for home growing. The potatoes are listed alphabetically in their most familiar name. Their seasonal details, classified according to how early in the season they are ready for digging up, are listed as: First Early, Second Early, Maincrop (early and late).This simply means that, anywhere in the world, the first earlies are the first new potatoes on the market ready for eating fresh and young, the second earlies are still theoretically a new potato although the skin will have begun to set so they will not be scrapers, whilst the maincrop potatoes which are on the market throughout most of the year are the ones that can be picked and stored for many months. However, the consumer may be even more confused by the fact that some potatoes are now being picked young for the early market as well as at full size for the maincrop market and others, which are transported from around the world, arrive labelled as new during the maincrop season! The label (if any) and the retailer may be able to help you but this index should be your best guide.

Ajax
Second Early
Origin: Netherlands
Availability: Netherlands,
Pakistan, Vietnam
Suitability for cooking: Boiling,
Chipping, Roasting
Description: Oval, with
smooth yellow skin, pale
yellow firm flesh,
slightly bland in
flavour

Alcmaria
First Early
Origin: Netherlands, 1970
Availability: Italy, United Kingdom
Suitability for cooking: Baking, Boiling
and most other methods
Description: Long, oval, with yellow skin
and firm flesh, and shallow eyes

Above: Ailsa
Above left: Alcmaria
Below: Alex

Accent
First Early
Origin: Netherlands, 1994
Availability: Netherlands, United Kingdom
(not widely available yet)
Suitability for cooking: Boiling, Salad
Description: Uniform oval or round shape,
light yellow smooth skin, waxy flesh
which holds its shape, and bland taste.
Scrapes easily and good for sautéeing
Home growing: Available

Agria
Maincrop
Origin: West Germany, 1985
Availability: Canada, New Zealand,
Switzerland, United Kingdom
Suitability for cooking: Baking, Boiling,
Chipping, Processing, Roasting
Description: Good size oval shape, deep
yellow flesh and good flavour

Ailsa
Maincrop
Origin: Scotland, 1984
Availability: United Kingdom
Suitability for cooking: Boiling, Chipping,
Processing
Description: Round or oval medium
potato, white skinned with light, creamy-
coloured flesh and pleasant flavour, with
a floury texture
Home growing: Available

Alex
Second Early
Origin: Denmark, 1995
Availability: Europe,
United Kingdom
Suitability for cooking: Salad
and most other methods
Description: Splash of blue on
the skin, creamy waxy texture
and good mild flavour
Home growing:
Good

Anna
Maincrop
Origin: Irish Republic, 1996
Availability: Irish Republic,
United Kingdom
Suitability for cooking: Baking and boiling
Description: Uniform shape with smooth
white skin and creamy while floury flesh;
often sold pre-packed

Anya
Second Early
Origin: Scotland, 1997
Availability: United Kingdom
Suitability for cooking: Boiling, Salad and
speciality uses
Description: Small finger potato, knobbly
long oval shape with pale
pink beige skin, white
flesh, a waxy
texture and
pleasant
nutty
flavour

Ambo   *Above: Ambo*
Maincrop
Origin: Irish Republic, 1993
Availability: Irish Republic, New Zealand,
Switzerland, United Kingdom
Suitability for cooking: Baking, Boiling
and quite good all-round variety
Description: Creamy skin with
large pink eye patches
and very white, bland
floury flesh

Aminca
First Early
Origin: Netherlands,
1977
Availability: Denmark,
Italy, United Kingdom
Suitability for cooking:
Baking, Boiling, Chipping
Description: Oval, medium
to large potato, with light
yellow skin and cream or
light yellow flesh, medium
deep eyes, and dry
texture. Often used for
crisp production

Above: Anya
Top right: Aminca

Arran Banner
Maincrop – early
Origin: Scotland, 1927
Availability: Cyprus, New Zealand,
Portugal, United Kingdom
Suitability for cooking: Boiling
Description: Round potato with quite
deep eyes and white skin and a firm,
creamy flesh

Arran Comet
First early
Origin: Scotland, 1957
Availability: United Kingdom
Suitability for cooking: Boiling, Chipping
Description: Round to oval with white
skin and creamy flesh. Excellent early
season new potato, not quite so easily
found now

Arran Consul
Maincrop – early
Origin: Scotland, 1925
Availability: United Kingdom

Suitability for cooking: Boiling, Baking,
Mashing, Roasting and generally good
all-round variety
Description: Round with white skin and
creamy flesh. Reputed to be "the potato
that helped win the war", as it provided
good food for little money

Arran Victory *Irish Blues*
Maincrop – late
Origin: Scotland, 1918
Availability: United Kingdom (now rare in
England and limited in Scotland and
Northern Ireland)
Suitability for cooking: Baking, Boiling,
Roasting and other methods
Description: Oval shape with deep purple
skin and bright white flesh. This is the
oldest Arran variety still available, it is a
very tasty potato with a floury texture and
though not easy to find it is having a
revival of interest so it is well worth
looking out for
Home growing: Available

Above: Arran Victory
Below from left to right: Arran Banner,
Arran Comet, Arran Consul (top right)

Atlantic

Maincrop – early/mid-season
Origin: USA, 1978
Availability: Australia, Canada, New
Zealand, USA (North Carolina)
Suitability for cooking: Baking, Boiling,
Chipping, Mashing, Processing, Roasting
Description: Oval to round shape with
light, scaly, buff skin and white flesh.
Used largely for chips and crisps
Home growing: Available

Ausonia

Second Early
Origin: Netherlands, 1981
Availability: Greece, Netherlands,
United Kingdom
Suitability for cooking: Baking, Boiling
and most other methods
Description: Oval shape with white skin
and light yellow mealy flesh. It is
susceptible to discolouring after cooking.
Predominantly sold in various
pre-packed forms
Home growing: Available

Avalanche

Maincrop – early
Origin: Northern Ireland, 1989
Availability: United Kingdom (still rare)
Suitability for cooking: Boiling, Mashing

Description: Round or oval, medium
potatoes, with white skin, firm, creamy
flesh and good, slightly sweet flavour
Home growing: Available

Avondale

Maincrop
Origin: Irish Republic, 1982
Availability: Canary Isles, Egypt, Hungary,
Israel, Morocco, Pakistan, Portugal,
Spain, Sri Lanka, United Kingdom
(but still rare)
Suitability for cooking: Quite good
all-round variety
Description: Round or oval with pale,
beige skin and creamy flesh. It has a
moist waxy texture and mellow flavour

Barna

Maincrop – late
Origin: Irish Republic, 1993
Availability: Irish Republic,
United Kingdom
Suitability for cooking: Boiling, Roasting
Description: Uniform, oval red-skinned
potato with white slightly waxy flesh and
warm, nutty taste
Home growing: Available

Above: Atlantic
Left: From top to bottom, Avalanche,
Avondale, Barna

Belle de Fontenay *Boulangère Henaut*
Maincrop – early
Origin: France, 1885
Availability: Australia, France,
United Kingdom (occasionally)
Suitability for cooking: Boiling,
Mashing, Salad
Description: Long, slightly bent shape
with pale yellow skin, yellow flesh, firm
and waxy with an excellent buttery
flavour. One of the old classic potatoes of
French cuisine but popular with modern
chefs. Improves with storage. Good
eaten with skins on and tossed in
salad dressings
Home growing: Good

BelRus
Maincrop – late
Origin: USA, 1978
Availability: Canada, USA (north-eastern
states and North Florida)
Suitability for cooking: Baking,
Chipping, Mashing
Description: Uniform, long smooth
potatoes with dark thick russeted skin

and creamy coloured flesh. Exceptional
cooking qualities, excellent in gratins and
when steamed; the heavy russeting gives
a thick and crunchy skin when baked

BF15
Second Early
Origin: France, 1947
Availability: France (seldom found
outside France)
Suitability for cooking: Boiling,
Salad
Description: Long, slightly bent,
with smooth yellow skin and
yellow flesh, firm and waxy
with very good flavour.
Derivative of Belle de Fontenay
but slightly earlier
Home growing: Available

Bintje
Maincrop – early
Origin: Netherlands, 1910
Availability: Australia, Brazil, Canada,
Denmark, Finland, Italy, Netherlands,
New Zealand, Sweden, Thailand,

United Kingdom
Suitability for cooking: Baking, Boiling,
Chipping, Processing, Roasting, Salad
Description: Long, oval, with pale yellow
skin and starchy flesh and a really
distinctive flavour. Used largely for chips
and processing
Home growing: Available

Above: BelRus
Main picture: Clockwise from right,
BF15, Bishop, Bintje

Bishop (the)
Maincrop – late
Origin: United Kingdom, 1912
Availability: United Kingdom
Suitability for cooking: Boiling, Roasting, Salad
Description: Long, oval potatoes, with white skins and yellow nutty-flavoured flesh. Recently popular variety
Home growing: Available

British Queen(s)
Second Early
Origin: Scotland, 1894
Availability: United Kingdom
Suitability for cooking: Baking, Boiling, Roasting, Processing, Salad
Description: Kidney-shaped, with smooth white skin and very white flesh which is dry, floury and has a very good taste. Best cooked with skins on to retain excellent flavour. Very popular at the turn of the century and having a revival

CalWhite
Maincrop
Origin: USA, 1997
Availability: Canada, USA (California, Idaho)
Suitability for cooking: Baking, Chipping, Processing
Description: Oblong shape with buff-white smooth skin and white flesh

Cara White and Red
Maincrop – late
Origin: Irish Republic, 1976
Availability: Cyprus, Egypt, Irish Republic, Israel, United Kingdom
Suitability for cooking: Baking, Boiling, Chipping and all other methods, especially wedges.
Description: Round or oval, white skin with pink eyes, cream flesh, mild flavour and moist, waxy texture. There is a pink-skinned variety which has creamy flesh
Home growing: Good, but not in very wet soil

Carlingford
First Early
Origin: Northern Ireland, 1982
Availability: Australia, United Kingdom
Suitability for cooking: Baking, Boiling, Chipping
Description: Round or oval with white skin and flesh, eyes shallow to medium, firm and waxy cooked texture and distinctive flavour. An excellent new or baby potato. Best not overcooked, very good steamed, microwaved and baked in wedges. Relatively new potato but growing in popularity
Home growing: Available

Above left: British Queen
Above right: Carlingford
Below: Cara White

Centennial Russet
Maincrop
Origin: USA, 1977
Availability: USA (California, Colorado, Idaho, Oregon, Texas, Washington)
Suitability for cooking: Baking, Boiling, Mashing
Description: Oblong to oval with thick, dark, netted skin, shallow eyes and white floury flesh

Champion
Maincrop – late
Origin: United Kingdom, 1876
Availability: No longer commercially grown, only found in collections
Suitability for cooking: Excellent all-round variety
Description: Round potato with white skin and yellow flesh on the inside. It has an excellent flavour. It was hugely successful for very many years until much of the stock was affected by blight, but remained Ireland's favourite until the 1930s

Charlotte *Noirmoutier*
Maincrop
Origin: France, 1981
Availability: France, Germany, Italy, Switzerland, United Kingdom
Suitability for cooking: Baking, Boiling, Salad
Description: Pear or long oval shape with pale yellow skin, yellow flesh, firm waxy texture and a hint of chestnut flavour. Excellent steamed and in salads. Especially popular in France
Home growing: Good

Catriona and Blue Catriona
Second Early
Origin: Scotland, 1920; Blue Catriona, United Kingdom, 1979
Availability: United Kingdom (mainly for gardeners, in few shops)
Suitability for cooking: Baking, Boiling and all other methods
Description: Large kidney-shaped potato with skin that has beautiful purple splashes around the eyes, pale yellow flesh and a very good flavour.
Home growing: Available

Above: Centennial Russet
Left: Catriona

Chieftain
Maincrop
Origin: USA, 1966
Availability: Canada, USA
Suitability for cooking: Baking, Boiling
Description: Oblong to round with a fairly smooth, bright red skin and white flesh. Good for most methods of cooking except chipping

Chipeta
Maincrop – late
Origin: USA, 1993
Availability: Canada, USA (Colorado, Idaho)
Suitability for cooking: Baking, Boiling, Chipping, Processing
Description: Round with white skin and patches of russeting, creamy white flesh. Mainly developed for chipping

Claret
Maincrop – early
Origin: Scotland, 1996
Availability: Scotland
Suitability for cooking: Good all-round
Description: Smooth rosy red skin, with a round to oval shape and cream, firm flesh
Home growing: Good

Top: Claret, Chieftain
Above: Cleopatra, Colmo

Cleopatra
First Early
Origin: Netherlands, 1980
Availability: Algeria, Hungary
Suitability for cooking: Boiling
Description: Oval with pink/red blemished skin and light yellow, dense flesh

Colmo
First Early
Origin: Netherlands, 1973
Availability: Netherlands, United Kingdom
Suitability for cooking: Boiling and good for all other methods
Description: Medium-round, or oval-shaped potato, with white skin and light yellow firm flesh on the inside. Good for making mashed potatoes

Congo

Maincrop – late
Origin: Congo
Availability: Australia, United Kingdom
(for curiosity and fun for gardeners, not
in shops)
Suitability for cooking: Boiling,
Mashing, Salad
Description: Striking small, thin and
knobbly shape, with very dark, purple-
black shiny skin and beetroot black
flesh. The flavour is surprisingly bland
and the texture stodgy. It is dry when
cooked but still retains its colour, making
it impressive in salads and as a garnish.
Peel after cooking and either boil briefly,
steam or microwave. Makes good
mashed potatoes or gnocchi
Home growing: Available mainly as a
curiosity. Since they are small and dark,
you might need to harvest them on a
bright day

Above right: Désirée
Below: Congo

Delcora

Maincrop – early
Origin: Netherlands, 1988
Availability:
Netherlands, New
Zealand
Suitability for cooking:
Boiling, Chipping,
Mashing
Description: Long oval
potato with pink/red
skin and light
yellow flesh
which is not
floury and
has good
flavour

Désirée

Maincrop
Origin: Netherlands, 1962
Availability: Algeria, America, Argentina,
Australia, Cameroon, Chile, Iran, Irish
Republic, Malawi, Morocco, Netherlands,
New Zealand, Portugal, Sri Lanka,
Pakistan, Tunisia, Turkey, United Kingdom
Suitability for cooking: Baking, Boiling,
Chipping, Mashing, Roasting, Salad and
all other methods
Description: Oval shape with shallow
eyes and smooth red skin, pale creamy
yellow flesh, firm texture and good taste.
Said to be the world's most popular red-
skinned potato. It is often sold direct
from the farm and markets in large
quantities as well as loose or pre-packed.
Good roasted or cooked as wedges or
slices; holds its shape
Home growing: Good

Diamant

Maincrop – early
Origin: Netherlands, 1982
Availability: Cameroon, Canada, Egypt,
New Zealand, Pakistan
Suitability for cooking: Baking, Boiling
Description: Long oval shape, rough
white skin with light yellow, firm, waxy
flesh and nutty, sharp aftertaste. Popular
in the 1930s

Below: Duke of York
Bottom: Clockwise from top left,
Diamant, Ditta, Dr McIntosh

Ditta
Second Early
Origin: Austria, 1950
Availability: Austria, Netherlands,
United Kingdom
Suitability for cooking: Boiling, Roasting
Description: Long, oval potato with
rough, brownish skin, pale yellow flesh
and firm waxy texture. When cooked
it has a very buttery taste, and an almost
melt-in-the-mouth flavour

Dr McIntosh
Maincrop – early
Origin: United Kingdom, 1944
Availability: New Zealand, United
Kingdom (rarely found today)
Suitability for cooking: Baking, Boiling,
quite good all-round
Description: Oval potato with quite a long
shape to it with white skin and light,
creamy flesh

Draga
Second Early
Origin: Netherlands, 1970
Availability: Iran, New Zealand
Suitability for cooking: Boiling, Mashing,
Salad, Good all-round variety
Description: Round, white/yellow skin,
creamy flesh, full-flavoured with waxy
texture. Keeps well

Duke of York *Eersteling*
First Early
Origin: Scotland, 1891
Availability: Netherlands, France,
United Kingdom
Suitability for cooking: Boiling and most
other methods
Description: Long, oval, with pale
whitish-yellow skin, light yellow flesh, firm
cooked texture and rich, sweet flavour.
Best eaten young
Home growing: Very popular

Duke of York Red *Rode Eersteling*
First Early
Origin: Netherlands, 1842
Availability: Netherlands, United
Kingdom (but quite rare)
Suitability for cooking: Boiling, Salad
Description: Long, oval, very red potato
with light yellow tasty flesh. Loses its
colour when cooked
Home growing: Available

Dunbar Standard
Maincrop – late
Origin: Scotland, 1936
Availability: United Kingdom, Ireland

Suitability for cooking: Good all-round
Description: Long, oval white-skinned
potato with white flesh. Its full flavour
and firmness suit most forms of cooking.
Home growing: Available. Does well in
heavy soil

Dundrod
First Early
Origin: Northern Ireland, 1987
Availability: Canada, Netherlands,
Northern Ireland, Sweden,
United Kingdom
Suitability for cooking: Boiling,
Chipping, Mashing
Description: Oval to round
shaped potatoes with light
yellow skin and creamy
white flesh on the
inside. Moderately
waxy, so rarely falls
apart. A very popular
choice of potato for
making chips in fish
and chip shops

Edgcote Purple
Maincrop – early
Origin: United Kingdom, 1916
Availability: Collections only
Description: Long, oval potatoes with
blue skin and light yellow flesh.
Although it was an excellent cooker it
never became popular and is no longer
commercially available

Edzell Blue
Second Early
Origin: Scotland, pre-1915
Availability: Scotland (very little
now grown)
Suitability for cooking: Boiling, Mashing
Description: Round, blue-skinned with
bright white flesh, floury and tasty. Boil
with care as it falls apart easily. Very good
steamed and in microwave recipes
Home growing: Available

Eigenheimer
Maincrop – second early
Origin: Netherlands, 1893
Availability: Netherlands, Zaire (rarely
seen elsewhere)
Suitability for cooking: Chipping
Description: Oval, white skin and yellow
flesh, great for frying and chips, a
favourite of Dutch gardeners

Top left: Duke of York Red
Top right: Edzell Blue
Left: Dunbar Standard

Estima
Second Early
Origin: Netherlands, 1973
Availability: Algeria, Northern Europe
Suitability for cooking: Baking, Boiling,
Chipping, Roasting, and most
other methods
Description: Uniform oval shape with
shallow eyes, light yellow skin and flesh,
firm moist texture and mild flavour.
Most widely grown second early and has
an exceptionally long season. Makes a
particularly good baking potato early in
the year – very popular at the moment.
One of the first to destroy the myth that
yellow potatoes could not be popular
Home growing: Good

Elvira
Origin: Unknown
Availability: Italy
Suitability for cooking: Boiling, Chipping
Description: Medium oval potato with
shallow eyes, yellow skin and creamy
yellow flesh

Epicure
First Early
Origin: United Kingdom, 1897
Availability: Canada, United Kingdom
Suitability for cooking: Baking, Boiling
Description: Round, white skin and
creamy white flesh, firm texture, but with
deep eyes and a distinctive flavour.
The traditional Ayrshire potato and still
grown extensively in Scottish gardens
Home growing: A popular and easy to
grow variety

Top left: Estima
Above right: Elvira
Right: Epicure

Fianna
Maincrop – early
Origin: Netherlands, 1987
Availability: Netherlands, New Zealand,
United Kingdom

Suitability for cooking: Baking, Chipping,
Mashing, Processing, Roasting
Description: Smooth white skin and firm
flesh, with pleasant, floury texture
Home growing: Available

Forty Fold
Maincrop – early
Origin: United Kingdom, 1893;
Russet, United Kingdom, 1919
Availability: United Kingdom (very limited)
Suitability for cooking: Quite good all-
round variety
Description: Irregular tubers with deep
eyes, white or vivid purple skin splashed
with white or russet, creamy flesh, and
good flavour. The potato was a popular
Victorian speciality which is currently
being revived
Home growing: Available

Above: Forty fold, white and russet
Left: Fianna

Francine
Maincrop
Origin: France, 1993
Availability: France, Germany,
United Kingdom
Suitability for cooking: Boiling, Salad
Description: Red skin, white/cream flesh,
soft yet waxy texture and an
earthy taste. Great for gratins and
for steaming

Frisia
Maincrop – early
Origin: Netherlands
Availability: Bulgaria, Canada, Europe,
New Zealand
Suitability for cooking: Baking, Boiling,
Roasting, Salad
Description: Oval, creamy yellow-skinned
potato with white flesh and a moist,
slightly waxy texture

Gemchip

Maincrop – late
Origin: USA, 1989
Availability: Canada, USA (Colorado, Idaho, Oregon, Washington)
Suitability for cooking: Baking, Boiling, Chipping, Processing
Description: Short and round with smooth, light tan skin and white flesh with the occasional scaly patch

Golden Wonder

Maincrop – late
Origin: United Kingdom, 1906
Availability: United Kingdom
Suitability for cooking: Boiling, Processing, Roasting
Description: Large oval potato with light yellow flesh and russet/brown skin, very floury when cooked and tasty. Creates some of the best crisps and the flavour improves with long storage.
Home growing: Good for home growing, popular in Scotland

Goldrush

Maincrop
Origin: North Dakota, 1992
Availability: Canada, USA
Suitability for cooking: Baking, Boiling, Roasting, quite good all-round
Description: A new russet type, oblong potato with light brown netted skin and very white flesh and good flavour.

Granola

Second Early – early main
Origin: West Germany, 1975
Availability: Australia, Germany, India, Indonesia, Nepal, Netherlands, Pakistan, Switzerland, Turkey, Vietnam
Suitability for cooking: Baking, Boiling, Chipping
Description: Oval with brilliant yellow skin and creamy yellow flesh

Home Guard

First Early
Origin: Scotland, 1942
Availability: United Kingdom (mainly in Cornwall and Pembrokeshire)
Suitability for cooking: Boiling, Chipping, Roasting and most other methods
Description: Round to oval, white skin and creamy white flesh, quite floury dry texture and good, almost bitter flavour. A World War II favourite, one of the first new potatoes to arrive on the market and at its best eaten early
Home growing: Good

Ilam Hardie

All year
Origin: Unknown
Availability: South Africa, New Zealand
Suitability for cooking: Baking, Boiling, Chipping, Mashing, Roasting, Salad, and most other methods
Description: Yellow skinned with white flesh, floury and well flavoured

International Kidney *Jersey Royal*

Maincrop – early
Origin: United Kingdom, 1879
Availability: Australia, Europe, United Kingdom
Suitability for cooking: Boiling, Salad
Description: Long ovals with very flaky, white/yellow skin and creamy white flesh, waxy with delicious buttery flavour. The International Kidney, developed in England in the 1870s and is slightly smaller than the original Jersey Royal. many countries have tried to grow the Jersey Royal, but only in Jersey's rich soil does this prized potato grow so well and it is now exported to many corners of the world.
Home growing: Available

Left: Francine
Above: Gemchip

Karlena
Origin: E. Germany, 1993
Availability: Egypt, France, Germany, Hungary, Israel, Scandinavia, United Kingdom (still very limited)
Suitability for cooking: Baking, Chipping, Mashing, Roasting
Description: A medium size round yellow skinned potato with golden yellow flesh and warm distinctive flavour but very floury. It is excellent as a very early season boiling potato; main season it is good steamed in skins, roasts and chips very well, but boil with care to avoid disintegration

Katahdin
Maincrop – late
Origin: USA, 1932
Availability: Canada, New Zealand, USA
Suitability for cooking: Baking, Boiling, Salad, and most other methods
Description: Round to oblong shape, with buff, smooth, thin skin and white, waxy, moist flesh. Most popular in Maine until recently

Irish Cobbler *America*
First Early
Origin: USA, 1876
Availability: Canada, South Korea, USA
Suitability for cooking: Boiling, Chipping, Mashing and most other methods.
Description: Round white, medium to large potato, smooth creamy white skin and flesh. Was widely grown in the United Kingdom at the turn of the century probably because it matures earlier than others but has not been grown much since World War I – except in the USA. It is difficult to grow and bruises easily
Home growing: Available

Itasca
Maincrop
Origin: Minnesota, 1994
Availability: Canada, USA
Suitability for cooking: Baking, Boiling, Chipping, Mashing, Roasting
Description: Oblong to round shaped potato with smooth, pale skin and creamy white flesh

Jaerla
First Early
Origin: Netherlands, 1969
Availability: Algeria, Argentina, Greece, Netherlands, Turkey, Yugoslavia
Suitability for cooking: Baking, Boiling

and most other methods
Description: Long, oval light skinned with light yellow flesh and firm texture

Kanona
Maincrop
Origin: USA, 1989
Availability: Canada, USA
Suitability for cooking: Baking, Boiling, Chipping, Processing
Description: Large round potatoes with a white slightly netted skin and white flesh

Above: Irish Cobbler
Below: Katahdin

Kennebec
Maincrop
Origin: USA, 1948
Availability: Argentina, Australia, Canada, Italy, New Zealand, Portugal, South Korea, Taiwan, Uruguay, USA
Suitability for cooking: Baking, Boiling, Chipping, Mashing, Roasting, Processing and most other methods
Description: Largish oval to round shaped potato, with smooth, buff, white skin and white flesh. Widely grown in many parts of the world now as it is adaptable and consistent. Was mainly used for chip processing but less so now although still a good all-round potato. A favourite variety for gardeners in North America

Kepplestone Kidney
Second Early – early main
Origin: United Kingdom, 1919
Availability: Not commercially available
Suitability for cooking: Boiling
Description: Blue skinned, classically shaped potatoes with yellow flesh and rich buttery taste
Home growing: Good

Kerr's Pink
Maincrop – late
Origin: Scotland, 1917
Availability: Irish Republic, Netherlands, United Kingdom
Suitability for cooking: Baking, Boiling, Chipping, Mashing, Roasting
Description: Round, pink skin, creamy white flesh, quite deep eyes, mealy, floury cooked texture
Home growing: Available

Above: From left to right, Kennebec, Kepplestone Kidney, Karlena
Below: Kerr's Pink

King Edward and Red

Maincrop
Origin: United Kingdom, 1902
(red 1916)
Availability: Australia, Canary Isles, New
Zealand, Portugal, Spain,
United Kingdom
Suitability for cooking: Baking,
Chipping, Mashing, Roasting and
most other methods
Description: Oval to kidney shape. White
skin with pink colouration, cream to pale
yellow flesh, floury texture. For much of
the twentieth century it was the most
popular potato in Britain and has seen a
fall and rise in popularity since
Home growing: Available

Kipfler

Maincrop
Origin: Austria, 1955
Availability: Australia (rarely available)
Suitability for cooking: Baking, Boiling,
Chipping, Roasting, Salad and most
other methods
Description: Yellow flesh and skin, small
to medium size, elongated, often called
finger potato. They have a waxy texture
when cooked and a buttery, nutty taste.
Not ideal for chipping but microwaves
well and excellent in salads

Krantz

Maincrop
Origin: USA, 1985
Availability: Canada, USA
Suitability for cooking: Baking, Boiling,
Chipping, Processing
Description: Oblong with brown russet
skin and white flesh

Linzer Delikatess

Second Early
Origin: Austria, 1976
Availability: Austria, United Kingdom
(very rare)
Suitability for cooking: Boiling, Salad
Description: Small, oval- to pear-shaped
potato with a pale yellow skin and yellow
flesh. Firm and waxy texture. The flavour
is similar to Ratte, but not so distinctive.
Good cold and in most cooked dishes
where you need firmness
Home growing: Available

Lumper

Maincrop – early
Origin: Ireland, 1806
Availability: Collections only
Description: Round, oval potato with
white skin and flesh and very deep eyes
giving it a lumpy shape. Lacking in
flavour.Dating back to the Irish famine
when it was a mainstay of the potato crop
but was nearly wiped out. Its poor
cooking qualities eventually led to the
Lumper being consigned to the history
books and seed collections only

Above: King Edward
Left: Lumper

Maori Chief *Peru*
Early
Origin: New Zealand
Availability: New Zealand
Suitability for cooking:
Boiling, Roasting, Salad
Description: Purple/black
skin, dark purple/black
flesh, with a sweet new
potato flavour. The very
tender skin doesn't need
peeling, tastes good
eaten within ten days of
harvesting. There is also a
variety found in New
Zealand, with a buttery yellow
flesh, which has caused much debate
as to which is the true original Maori
Chief potato

Marfona
Second Early
Origin: Netherlands, 1975
Availability: Cyprus, Greece, Israel,
Netherlands, Portugal, Turkey,
United Kingdom
Suitability for cooking: Baking, Boiling,
Chipping, Mashing
Description: Round oval with light beige
to yellow skin and flesh, smooth waxy
texture with slightly sharp taste
Home growing: Available

Maris Bard
First Early
Origin: United Kingdom, 1972
Availability: United Kingdom
Suitability for cooking: Boiling and most
other methods
Description: White skin, white to cream
flesh, soft yet waxy with an earthy taste.
One of the most widely grown first
earlies. Can disintegrate on cooking late
in the season and lose its taste
Home growing: Available

Magnum Bonum
Maincrop – late
Origin: United Kingdom, 1876
Availability: Nepal, United
Kingdom (collections only)
Suitability for cooking: Baking,
Boiling, Mashing, Roasting
Description: Long, oval-shaped
potato with white skin and dry, mealy
white flesh. Has an excellent flavour.
One of the early very successful potatoes
which proved to be both a good grower,
an excellent eater and withstood blight.
The Victorians were delighted to find
such a continually good cropper which
eventually was used in producing other
renowned potatoes, such as
today's King Edward

Majestic
Maincrop – early
Origin: Scotland, 1911
Availability: Italy, United Kingdom (now
only in Scotland for seed potato)
Suitability for cooking: Baking,
Boiling, Mashing
Description: Large oval with white skin
and soft white flesh, and a mild flavour.
Was the most widely grown variety in
Britain at one time but no longer suits the
marketplace and is mainly grown for
gardeners and prefers dry conditions
Home growing: Available

Top left: Marfona
Right: Maori Chief

Maris Peer
Second Early
Origin: United Kingdom, 1962
Availability: United Kingdom
Suitability for cooking: Boiling,
Chipping, Salad
Description: Round- to oval-shaped
potato with cream skin and flesh, eyes
shallow to medium, firm cooked texture.
Good when young to use as new potatoes
since they do not break up on cooking,
and the large later season ones bake well
either whole or in wedges
Home growing: Available

Maris Piper
Maincrop – early
Origin: United Kingdom, 1964
Availability: Portugal, United Kingdom
Suitability for cooking: Baking, Chipping,
Processing, Roasting
Description: Oval, cream skin and flesh
and pleasant floury texture and taste.
One of Britain's most popular potatoes,
especially in fish and chip shops but
breaks up easily if overcooked
Home growing: Good

Minerva
First Early
Origin: Netherlands, 1988
Availability: Netherlands
Suitability for cooking: Boiling, Chipping

Description: Oval-shaped potato with
white skin and creamy yellow flesh on
the inside. It is particularly good for
boiling since it retains a firm texture
when cooked

Mona Lisa
Second Early
Origin: Netherlands, 1982
Availability: France, Greece,
Netherlands, Portugal
Suitability for cooking: Baking, Boiling,
Chipping, Mashing, Roasting, Processing
Description: Long oval, sometimes
kidney-shaped with yellow skin and
flesh, waxy but becomes floury when
cooked. Has a good nutty flavour. Grows
quite large for a new potato but is
surprisingly versatile in cooking. Not
grown a great deal commercially yet
Home growing: Available

Mondial
Maincrop – early
Origin: Netherlands, 1987
Availability: Greece, Israel, Netherlands,
New Zealand
Suitability for cooking: Baking, Chipping,
Mashing, Roasting
Description: Long oval with yellow skin
and flesh and a slightly mealy texture
Home growing: Good in most conditions

Above: Maris Piper
Left: Clockwise from top, Mondial, Mona
Lisa, Morene

Monona

Maincrop – early
Origin: USA, 1964
Availability: Canada, USA (north central and north-eastern states)
Suitability for cooking: Baking, Boiling, Chipping
Description: Round or oval, with buff-white skin and white flesh. Mainly goes for chip processing

Morene

Maincrop – early
Origin: Netherlands, 1983
Availability: Netherlands, United Kingdom
Suitability for cooking: Baking, Boiling, Chipping, Processing
Description: Large, long oval potatoes with white skin and creamy coloured mealy flesh. During cooking the flesh has a tendency to break up so do not over-boil
Home growing: Available

Nadine

Second Early
Origin: Scotland, 1987
Availability: Australia, Canary Isles, New Zealand, Spain, United Kingdom
Suitability for cooking: Baking, Boiling, Mashing, Salad
Description: Creamy yellow skin and white flesh, firm, waxy texture but slightly disappointing taste. Sometimes available as small new potatoes with soft young skins which scrub easily. The larger ones are good baked and in wedges
Home growing: Available

Navan

Maincrop – late
Origin: Irish Republic, 1987
Availability: Irish Republic, United Kingdom

Suitability for cooking: Baking, Chipping, Roasting
Description: Oval, with white-buff skin, creamy flesh and pleasant flavour. Has a firm, waxy texture
Home growing: Available

Top: Nadine
Above: Monona

Below: Nicola

Nicola
Maincrop – all year
Origin: West Germany, 1973
Availability: Australia, Austria, Cyprus, Egypt, France, Germany, Israel, Morocco, New Zealand, Portugal, Switzerland, Tunisia, United Kingdom
Suitability for cooking: Baking, Boiling, Chipping, Mashing, Roasting, Salad, and most other cooking methods
Description: Oval to long oval, with smooth yellow skin and deep yellow flesh. The texture is waxy with an excellent buttery taste. Originally grown in Mediterranean countries but now the salad-style potato has become so popular that it is being grown much more widely. Ideal for all-round use as well as being particularly good in salads – also good

steamed, sautéed and sliced for dishes taking longer to cook
Home growing: Good

Nooksak
Maincrop – late
Origin: USA, 1973
Availability: Canada, New Zealand, USA
Suitability for cooking: Baking, Boiling, Processing
Description: Oblong, slightly flat potatoes with heavily russeted skin and very white flesh. Excellent keeping potato, good for baking

Norchip
Second Early
Origin: North Dakota, 1968
Availability: Canada, USA

(North Carolina, Dakota)
Suitability for cooking: Baking, Boiling, Chipping
Description: Round to oblong shape with smooth white skin and white flesh. Excellent chipping qualities

NorDonna
Maincrop
Origin: North Dakota, 1995
Availability: Canada, USA
Suitability for cooking: Baking, Boiling, Roasting, Salad
Description: Oval- to round-shaped potatoes with dark red skin, white flesh and a good flavour. Good for microwave cooking, in soups and served cold

Above: Norchip

Norland
Early
Origin: North Dakota, 1957
Availability: Canada, USA, United Kingdom
Suitability for cooking: Baking, Boiling, Mashing, Salad
Description: Oblong, slightly flat with medium-red skin and creamy flesh. Also popular and available in Europe is the Red Norland with a rich red skin and pale flesh
Home growing: Available

Norwis
Maincrop
Origin: USA, 1965
Availability: USA
Suitability for cooking: Baking, Boiling, Chipping, Processing
Description: Large ovals, slightly flat with smooth, light tan to white skin and pale, creamy, yellow flesh

Above: Norwis

Onaway
Early
Origin: USA, 1956
Availability: Canada, USA (north-eastern states and Michigan)
Suitability for cooking: Baking, Boiling
Description: Short and round with smooth, creamy white skin and flesh

Patrones
Maincrop – early
Origin: Netherlands, 1959
Availability: Australia, Indonesia, Malawi, Pakistan, Vietnam
Suitability for cooking: Baking, Boiling, Roasting, Salad
Description: Small, oval- to pear-shaped, with light golden-yellow skin and flesh and a firm waxy texture. These potatoes are great for steaming, gratins and for rösti

Penta
Second Early
Origin: Netherlands, 1983
Availability: Canada, Netherlands
Suitability for cooking: Baking, Boiling, Mashing, Roasting
Description: Round, with quite deep pink/red eyes, creamy white skin and rich, creamy flesh. A fairly new Maincrop potato which has a tendency to disintegrate on boiling. Good for steaming and microwave dishes

Top: Penta
Left: Onaway

Pentland Hawk

Maincrop – early
Origin: Scotland, 1966
Availability: United Kingdom
Suitability for cooking: Baking, Boiling,
Chipping, Processing, Roasting
Description: Oval, white skin and creamy
flesh, with a good flavour.
Very popular in Scotland as it cooks well.
It is an excellent keeper, but has a slight
tendency to discolour after cooking. At its
best late in the season
Home growing: Available

Pentland Javelin

First Early
Origin: Scotland, 1968
Availability: United Kingdom
Suitability for cooking: Boiling, Salad
Description: Medium-sized oval, white
skin, white flesh, soft waxy texture. It is
a good new potato but also bakes and
roasts well later in the season
Home growing: Good

Pentland Marble

First Early
Origin: Scotland, 1970
Availability: United Kingdom
Suitability for cooking: Boiling, Salad
Description: Round to oval, white-
skinned with light yellow waxy flesh.
Good small, early, waxy salad potato,
unlike most of the other Pentlands
and only recently reintroduced into
the market
Home growing: Available

Pentland Squire

Maincrop – early
Origin: Scotland, 1970
Availability: United Kingdom
Suitability for cooking: Baking, Mashing,
Processing, Roasting
Description: Oval, white skin and creamy
white flesh, very floury texture and
good flavour. Very good baker and
popular with fish and chip shops
Home growing: Good

Pentland Crown

Maincrop
Origin: Scotland, 1959
Availability: United Kingdom (Scotland,
but rarely seen in shops), Malawi
Suitability for cooking: Baking,
Boiling, Roasting
Description: Oval to round with white
skin and creamy white flesh. The first of
the Pentland varieties to become
popular in the Seventies, especially in
eastern England but out of favour now
as it doesn't have the cooking
qualities required
Home growing: Available

Pentland Dell

Maincrop – early
Origin: Scotland, 1961
Availability: New Zealand, South Africa,
United Kingdom
Suitability for cooking: Baking, Chipping,
Processing, Roasting
Description: Medium-sized, oval potato
with white skin, creamy white flesh,
and a firm fairly dry texture.
It has a tendency to disintegrate during
boiling but can bake well
Home growing: Available

*Above: Clockwise from top, the
Pentland collection, Hawk, Javelin, Dell,
Marble, Crown, Squire*

Picasso
Maincrop – early
Origin: Netherlands, 1992
Availability: Balearic Islands, CIS,
Cyprus, Egypt, Netherlands, Spain,
Portugal, United Kingdom
Suitability for cooking: Boiling, Salad
Description: Small, oval-round potato
with quite deep red eyes, pale skin, with
white waxy flesh
Home growing: Available

Pike
Maincrop
Origin: Pennsylvania, 1996
Availability: Canada/USA
Suitability for cooking: Baking, Boiling,
Chipping, Processing
Description: Medium, spherical potatoes
with quite deep eyes, buff-coloured,
slightly netted skin and creamy flesh.
Has a tendency to discolour after it has
been cooked

Pimpernel
Maincrop – early
Origin: Netherlands, 1953
Availability: Chile, Malawi, Norway, South
Africa, Zaire

Suitability for cooking:
Good all-round
Description: An
oval shaped potato
with pink to red skin
and yellowish-
coloured flesh on
the inside

Pink Eye *Southern Gold,*
Sweet Gold or Pink Gourmet
Early
Origin: United Kingdom, 1862
Availability: Australia
Suitability for cooking: Boiling, Mashing,
Salad and most other methods
Description: A small, smooth, creamy-
skinned potato, with purple/blue blush,
and creamy yellow flesh, floury texture
and a nutty taste. Although it originated
in Kent, it is now only grown in Australia
and is commonly available as a new
potato variety

Pink Fir Apple
Maincrop – late
Origin: France, 1850
Availability: Australia, France,
United Kingdom

Suitability for cooking:
Baking, Boiling, Roasting, Salad
Description: Long, knobbly, misshapen
potatoes with a pink blush on white skins
and creamy yellow flesh. Firm and waxy
with a delicious, nutty flavour. Best
cooked in skins. Having a revival now but
they have always been popular with
gardeners as they are good keepers. The
shape makes them impossible to peel
until cooked, but they are best cold in
salads and tossed in warm dressings, or
served as new potatoes
Home growing: Good for home growing,
although tubers form clusters of roots
under stem and can be prone to blight

Above: Picasso
Left: Pink Fir Apple

Pompadour
Maincrop – early
Origin: Netherlands, 1976
Availability: France
Suitability for cooking: Boiling, Salad
Description: Long, oval and regular in
shape with light yellow skin and flesh.
Also good steamed and served on their
own for a starter

Premiere
First Early
Origin: Netherlands, 1979
Availability: Bulgaria, Canada,
Netherlands, United Kingdom
Suitability for cooking: Baking, Boiling,
Chipping, Roasting
Description: Large, oval potatoes with
light yellow skin, firm yellow flesh and
good flavour. Not as waxy as many
early potatoes
Home growing: Available

Primura
First Early
Origin: Netherlands, 1963
Availability: Denmark, Italy, Netherlands
Suitability for cooking: Boiling, Chipping
Description: Oval to round, medium size,
yellow skin, light yellow flesh, shallow
eyes and firm texture

Ratte (La) *Cornichon or Asparges
or Princess*
Maincrop – early
Origin: France, 1872
Availability: Australia, Denmark, Germany,
France (has only recently begun to be
grown outside France), United Kingdom
Suitability for cooking: Boiling, Salad
Description: Long, tubular, almost
banana-shaped, not as knobbly as Pink
Fir. Has brown/yellow skin and creamy
flesh, which is firm and waxy with a
delicious nutty flavour. Very good for
eating cold, exceptionally popular in
France and growing in popularity in other
parts of the world
Home growing: Good

*Above: From top to bottom, Ratte,
Record*

Record
Maincrop – early
Origin: Netherlands, 1932
Availability: Greece, Holland, Yugoslavia,
United Kingdom (grown in Britain for
processing market)
Suitability for cooking: Baking, Chipping,
Mashing, Roasting, Processing
Description: White skin with pinkish
tinges, light yellow to yellow flesh, mealy
texture and great flavour. Versatile potato
often sold by the sack in farm shops
Home growing: Available

*Above: From left to right, Primura,
Premiere*

Red Pontiac *Dakota Chief*
Maincrop – early
Origin: USA, 1983
Availability: Algeria, Australia, Canada, Philippines, Uruguay, USA (south-eastern states), Venezuela
Suitability for cooking: Baking, Boiling, Mashing,
Roasting, Salads
Description: Round to oval potatoes with dark red, sometimes netted skin, quite deep eyes and white waxy flesh. A red-skinned variety with worldwide popularity. Good for use in microwave cooking
Home growing: Available

Red Rascal
Maincrop
Origin: Unknown
Availability: New Zealand
Suitability for cooking: Baking, Mashing, Roasting
Description: Red-skinned and yellow-fleshed, slightly floury with good flavour

Red Rooster
Maincrop – early
Origin: Irish Republic, 1993
Availability: Irish Republic
Suitability for cooking: Baking, Boiling, Chipping, Processing, Roasting, Salad
Description: Flattish, oval potato with bright red skin and firm buttery, yellow, mild-tasting flesh. Fairly new potato not yet widely available outside Ireland
Home growing: Available

Red LaSoda
Maincrop – late
Origin: USA, 1953
Availability: Algeria, Australia, Canada, Uruguay, USA (south-eastern states), Venezuela

Suitability for cooking: Baking, Boiling, Roasting
Description: Round to oval with smooth, deep-red skin, quite deep eyes and creamy white flesh. Ideal for most cooked and baked dishes

Right: Red LaSoda
Above: Red Rooster
Left: Red Pontiac

Above: From left, Romano, Rocket, Roseval

Red Ruby
Maincrop
Origin: USA, 1994
Availability: Canada, USA
Suitability for cooking: Baking, Boiling
Description: Oblong in shape with dark red skin which has patches of russeting and bright white flesh. An attractive winter potato

Remarka
Maincrop
Origin: Netherlands, 1992
Availability: Netherlands, Portugal, Spain, United Kingdom
Suitability for cooking: Baking, Boiling, Chipping, Roasting
Description: Large oval potato with creamy white skin, pale yellow flesh and good flavour. Makes a particularly good baking potato
Home growing: Available for home growing and ideal for organic gardening as it is a very disease-resistant variety

Rocket
First Early
Origin: United Kingdom, 1987
Availability: New Zealand, United Kingdom
Suitability for cooking: Baking, Boiling, Chipping, Mashing, Roasting, Salad
Description: Uniformly round, white-skinned, white flesh, firm, waxy and well flavoured. This is one of the earliest potatoes
Home growing: Available

Romano
Maincrop – early
Origin: Netherlands, 1978
Availability: Balearic Islands, Cameroon, CIS, Hungary, Netherlands, Portugal, Spain, United Kingdom
Suitability for cooking: Baking, Boiling, Mashing, Roasting and most other methods
Description: Round to oval, red skin with creamy flesh, soft dry texture, with a pleasant, mild nutty taste. Lovely colour which tends to pale during cooking to a soft rusty beige
Home growing: Available

Roseval
Second Early – early main
Origin: France, 1950
Availability: Australia, France, Israel, New Zealand, United Kingdom
Suitability for cooking: Boiling, Salad
Description: Oval shape with dark red, almost purple skin with golden yellow flesh. Waxy texture with a really good buttery flavour. A very distinctive-looking potato which has a great flavour and is very popular in microwave cookery
Home growing: Good

Above: Remarka

Russet Burbank *Idaho Russet*
or Netted Gem
Maincrop – late
Origin: USA, 1875
Availability: Australia, Canada, New
Zealand, United Kingdom (for
commercial use only), USA (north-west,
central and mid-eastern states)
Suitability for cooking: Baking, Chipping,
Mashing, Processing, Roasting
Description: Oval to long in shape,
russeted skin with pale yellow to white
flesh, floury and full of flavour, and
turning a bright colour when cooked.
The potato which made Idaho famous for
potatoes and therefore is often referred
to as an Idaho potato. Hugely popular in
America for some time and more recently
found in McDonald's fries. Most
widespread potato grown in Canada

Above left: Russet Burbank
Below: Royal Kidney

Rosine
Maincrop – early
Origin: Brittany, 1972
Availability: France
Suitability for cooking: Boiling, Salad
Description: Great in steamed dishes and
gratins, also in salads

Description: Round-shaped potato with
creamy white skin and white flesh on the
inside. It falls midway between being
waxy and floury in texture when cooked.
This potato has a really good flavour and
is good for use in many dishes

Rouge (La)
Maincrop – late
Origin: USA, 1962
Availability: Canada, USA (south-eastern
and eastern states)
Suitability for cooking: Boiling, Roasting
Description: Medium size, irregular
flattened round/oval with smooth bright
red skin, quite deep eyes and creamy
white flesh. Brilliant colour which fades
in storage, but an attractive winter
potato. Very popular in Florida

Royal Kidney
Second Early
Origin: United Kingdom, 1899
Availability: United Kingdom (but
now grown in Majorca for United
Kingdom market)
Suitability for cooking: Salad
Description: Kidney-shaped, smooth
white skin with pale yellow flesh and
waxy texture. Good eaten cold so works
particularly well in salads

Rua
Maincrop – early
Origin: New Zealand, 1960
Availability: New Zealand
Suitability for cooking: Baking, Boiling,
Chipping, Mashing, Roasting, Salad and
most other methods

Russet Norking
Maincrop
Origin: USA, 1977
Availability: Canada, USA
Suitability for cooking: Baking, Boiling, Chipping
Description: Oblong-shaped potato with medium-heavy russet skin and creamy white flesh

Russet Norkotah
Second Early
Origin: North Dakota, 1987
Availability: Canada, USA
Suitability for cooking: Baking, Chipping
Description: Oval long, darkly russeted potatoes with white flesh

Russet Nugget
Maincrop – late
Origin: Colorado, 1989
Availability: Canada, USA
Suitability for cooking: Baking, Boiling, Chipping, Processing, Roasting
Description: Oblong, slightly flat potatoes with evenly russeted skin and creamy white flesh

Russet Ranger
Maincrop – late
Origin: USA, 1991
Availability: Canada, USA (Colorado, Idaho, Oregon, Washington)
Suitability for cooking: Baking, Boiling, Chipping, Processing
Description: Long, russet or tannish-skinned potatoes, with bright white flesh

Samba
Maincrop – early
Origin: France, 1989
Availability: France, Portugal, Spain
Suitability for cooking: Baking, Boiling, Mashing and most other methods
Description: Regular, oval shape, white skin with yellow flesh and floury texture when cooked

Russet Century
Maincrop – late
Origin: USA, 1995
Availability: USA
Suitability for cooking: Baking, Boiling, Mashing, Roasting
Description: Long, cylindrical and slightly flat potatoes with pale, buff-coloured, slightly russeted skin and creamy flesh

Russet Frontier
Second Early
Origin: USA, 1990
Availability: Canada, USA
Suitability for cooking: Baking, Boiling, Chipping

Description: Long, oval potatoes with light, slightly russeted skins and creamy white flesh

Russet Lemhi
Maincrop – late
Origin: USA, 1981
Availability: USA
Suitability for cooking: Baking, Chipping and most other methods
Description: Large oblong with a tannish-brown netted skin and white eyes

Above: From top, Russet Frontier, Russet Burbank

Sangre
Maincrop
Origin: Colorado, 1982
Availability: Canada, USA
(western states)
Suitability for cooking: Baking, Boiling
Description: Oval shape with smooth
dark red skin, slightly netted, and
creamy flesh

Sante
Maincrop – early
Origin: Netherlands, 1983
Availability: Bulgaria, Canada,
Netherlands, United Kingdom
Suitability for cooking: Baking, Boiling,
Chipping, Roasting
Description: Oval or round with white
or light yellow skin and flesh and dry
firm texture. These have become the
most successful organic potato and are
often sold young as new potatoes too
Home growing: Available

Saxon
Second Early
Origin: United Kingdom, 1992
Availability: United Kingdom (still rare)
Suitability for cooking: Baking,
Boiling, Chipping
Description: This variety has white skin
and flesh, a firm moist texture and
excellent flavour. New general purpose
potato which is still finding its niche and
is very popular in the pre-packed
potato market
Home growing: Available

Sebago
Maincrop – late
Origin: USA, 1938
Availability: Australia, Canada, Malaysia,
New Zealand, South Africa, USA
(Northern states), Venezuela
Suitability for cooking: Baking, Boiling,
Chipping, Mashing, Roasting, Salad
Description: Round to oval shape, with
ivory white skin and white flesh.
Especially good for both boiling
and mashing. Most widely grown
potato in Australia

*Above: From left to right, Sante, Saxon
(bottom), Sebago*

Above: Sangre

Above: Sebago

Sharpe's Express
First – Second Early
Origin: United Kingdom, 1900
Availability: Not for commercial markets though occasionally available in Scotland
Suitability for cooking: Quite good all-round
Description: Oval to pear shaped, with white skin and creamy flesh. Needs careful cooking, especially when boiling
Home growing: Occasionally available for home growing

Shepody
Maincrop – early
Origin: New Brunswick, Canada, 1980
Availability: Canada, New Zealand, USA (Northern states)
Suitability for cooking: Baking, Boiling, Chipping, Mashing
Description: Long, oval shape, with white, slightly netted skin, light creamy yellow flesh and dry starchy texture. Developed for the chip processing market in America and seldom found in supermarkets

Shetland Black *Black Kidney*
Second Early
Origin: United Kingdom, 1923
Availability: United Kingdom (very limited)
Suitability for cooking: Boiling, Mashing
Description: Inky blue/black skin with yellow flesh and unique purple ring inside. Very fluffy and floury with an exceptionally sweet, buttery flavour. An attractive potato which, if handled carefully, can be great in salads or served simply with butter. Also good mashed, but the colour goes slightly grey/blue
Home growing: Available

Top: Shepody
Left: From top to bottom, Skerry Blue, Swedish Black, Shetland Black

Shula
Maincrop – early
Origin: United Kingdom, 1986
Availability: Scotland, but still rare
Suitability for cooking: Boiling, Mashing,
Roasting, quite good all round
Description: Oval shape, partly pink skin,
with light creamy flesh
Home growing: Occasionally available

Sieglinde
Second Early
Origin: West Germany, 1935
Availability: Cyprus, Germany
Suitability for cooking: Boiling, Roasting
Description: Long, oval

shape, with white skin and yellow flesh.
Beware of overcooking as they tend to
break up easily

Skerry Blue
Maincrop – late
Origin: United Kingdom, *c.*1846
Availability: United Kingdom (not
commercially available)
Suitability for cooking: Boiling
Description: Rich violet skin with deep
purple and white mottled or creamy
flesh. Has a superb flavour
Home growing:
Available

Snowden
Maincrop – all year
Origin: USA, 1990
Availability: Canada, USA
Suitability for cooking: Baking, Boiling,
Chipping, Processing
Description: Round, slightly flat potato
with mildly netted, light tan skin and
creamy flesh. Primarily used in
Canada for the chip processing market

Spunta
Second Early
Origin: Netherlands, 1968
Availability: Argentina, Australia, Cyprus,
Greece, Indonesia, Italy, Malaysia,
Mauritius, Netherlands, New Zealand,
Portugal, Thailand, Tunisia, United
Kingdom, Vietnam
Suitability for cooking: Baking, Boiling,
Chipping, Mashing, Roasting, Salad and
most other methods
Description: Medium-large, long potato,
often kidney- or pear-shaped, with light
yellow skin and golden flesh
Home growing: Occasionally available

Top: Spunta
Above: Snowden

Stroma
Second Early
Origin: Scotland, 1989
Availability: New Zealand, United
Kingdom (still rare)
Suitability for cooking: Baking, Boiling,
Mashing, Roasting
Description: Attractive long, oval
potato with pink/red skin, yellow/pink
flesh, floury texture and good flavour
Home growing: Available

Superior
Second Early
Origin: USA, 1962
Availability: Canada, South Korea,
USA (North Carolina)
Suitability for cooking: Chipping and
most other methods
Description: Round to oblong,
irregular shape with buff skin,
occasionally slightly russeted or netted,
and white flesh. Best early in the season

the West Indies, Africa and Asia and
has seen a rise in popularity in
Western cuisine

Above: Superior

Swedish Black
Origin: Unknown
Availability: Collections only
Suitability for cooking: Baking,
Boiling, Mashing
Description: Bluish-purple skinned
medium to large potato with very deep
eyes giving irregular shape. Blue flesh is
very mealy on cooking

Sweet Potato
Maincrop
Origin: South America
Availability: Widely grown in southern
United States and Pacific Islands,
Japan, Soviet Union
Suitability for cooking: Baking,
Boiling, Mashing, Processing,
Roasting and most other
methods
Description: Two
varieties, white skinned
and red-brown
skinned, both with
yellow flesh and quite
a waxy texture. The redder
are sweeter and firmer.
The sweet potato is
unrelated to the white potato
or to the yam. However it has all
the same characteristics: the
edible part is the tuber which can vary in
skin and flesh colour and can be treated
just like the potato. It is a staple food in

Toolangi Delight
Origin: Australia
Availability: Australia (still new, so rarely
available yet)
Suitability for cooking: Baking, Boiling,
Chipping, Mashing, Roasting, Salad and
good all-round variety
Description: A truly distinctive purple
skin and pure smooth white flesh which
is dry when cooked. It is one of the few
potatoes bred in Australia where it is
often used to make gnocchi

Above: Sweet Potato

Up to Date

Maincrop – late
Origin: Scotland, 1894
Availability: Burma, Cyprus, Malawi,
Mauritius, Nepal, South Africa,
United Kingdom
Suitability for cooking: Quite good all-round variety
Description: Flattish oval shape, white
skin and flesh with a good flavour.
First potato to be grown in Cyprus for
export and still mainly grown for small
international markets. It was the main
variety available at the turn of the century
in the United Kingdom

Valor

Maincrop – early
Origin: Scotland, 1993
Availability: Canary Isles, Israel,
United Kingdom
Suitability for cooking: Baking, Boiling
Description: Oval potato with white skin
and creamy white flesh. A new potato not
yet widely available in the shops
Home growing: Available

Tosca

Maincrop – late
Origin: United Kingdom, 1987
Availability: United Kingdom (still rare)
Suitability for cooking: Good
all-round variety
Description: Oval-shaped potato with
pink to red skin and light yellow pleasant
tasting flesh

Ulster Prince

First Early
Origin: United Kingdom, 1947
Availability: Irish Republic, United
Kingdom (very small quantities)
Suitability for cooking: Baking, Boiling,
Chipping, Roasting
Description: Large, kidney-shaped potato
with white skin and white flesh. This
potato is best eaten early in the season
when the flavour is delicious
Home growing: Available

Ulster Sceptre

First Early
Origin: Northern Ireland, 1963
Availability: Northern Ireland

Suitability for cooking: Boiling, Roasting,
Salad and most other methods
Description: Smaller ovals, with yellow-white skin and creamy waxy firm flesh.
Sometimes blackening can occur after
cooking which has seen it gradually
being edged out of the market place

Top left: Tosca
Left: Ulster Prince (top), Ulster Sceptre
Above: Up to Date

White Rose *American Giant, Wisconsin Pride, California Long White*
First Early
Origin: USA, 1893
Availability: Canada, USA (California, Oregon, Washington)
Suitability for cooking: Baking, Boiling, Mashing
Description: Large, very long and flat with smooth white skin and quite deep eyes, and bright white flesh. Not as popular as it used to be

Wilja
Second Early
Origin: Netherlands, 1967
Availability: Netherlands, Pakistan
Suitability for cooking: Boiling, Chipping, Mashing, Roasting
Description: Long, oval shape with pale yellow skin and flesh, quite firm, with a slightly dry texture. Second most widely grown of the second-early potatoes. Often available in maincrop season
Home growing: Available

Vanessa
First Early
Origin: Netherlands, 1973
Availability: Netherlands, United Kingdom
Suitability for cooking: Boiling, Roasting, Salad
Description: Long oval with pink to red skin and light yellow flesh
Home growing: Available

Viking
Maincrop
Origin: North Dakota, USA, 1963
Availability: Canada, USA
Suitability for cooking: Baking, Boiling, Mashing and most other methods
Description: Ranging from large oblong to round with smooth, pale red skin and very white flesh

Vitelotte *Truffe de Chine*
Origin: Unknown
Availability: France, United Kingdom (very rare)
Suitability for cooking: Boiling, Salad
Description: Long, thin and smallish purple/black finger potatoes with dark greyish blue flesh. Firm waxy texture with a mild nutty taste. The colour does not fade on cooking. The name Truffe de Chine is not often used in France since there is also a Chinese Truffle (Truffe de Chine) found which causes confusion

Top right: Wilja
Above: Vitelotte
Right: White Rose

Winston
First Early
Origin: Scotland, 1992
Availability: New Zealand,
United Kingdom
Suitability for cooking: Baking, Chipping,
Roasting, Salad
Description: A uniform, oval-shaped
potato with almost no eyes, creamy white
skin and very firm texture. These
potatoes make particularly good early
season bakers
Home growing: Available

Right: Winston
Below: Yukon Gold

Yukon Gold
Second Early – Maincrop
Origin: Ontario, Canada, 1980
Availability: Canada, USA
(California, Michigan)
Suitability for cooking: Baking,
Boiling, Chipping
Description: Large, oval to round potato
with buff-coloured skin, yellow flesh, pink
eyes and a slightly mealy texture. An
excellent baking potato with a delicious
flavour, which is very popular in the
international speciality market. This was
the first successful North American
yellow-fleshed potato
Home growing: Available

Potato Recipes

Soups

Nothing beats a steaming hot bowl of soup, whether it's thick and creamy or light with a delicate broth. When potatoes are used as a base or as a finishing touch they add a special touch to the dish as well as a delicious texture. The flavour combinations are simply endless, from an Italian Minestrone Genoa to a spicy Chorizo Soup or a classic Leek and Potato Soup.

CHILLED LEEK AND POTATO SOUP

THIS CREAMY-SMOOTH COLD VERSION OF THE CLASSIC VICHYSSOISE IS SERVED WITH THE REFRESHING TANG OF YOGURT AS A TOPPING.

SERVES FOUR

INGREDIENTS

25g/1oz/2 tbsp butter
15ml/1 tbsp vegetable oil
1 small onion, chopped
3 leeks, sliced
2 medium floury potatoes, diced
600ml/1 pint/2½ cups
    vegetable stock
300ml/½ pint/1¼ cups milk
45ml/3 tbsp single cream
a little extra milk (optional)
salt and ground black pepper
60ml/4 tbsp natural yogurt and
    fried chopped leeks, to serve

1 Heat the butter and oil in a large pan and add the onion, leeks and potatoes. Cover and cook for 15 minutes, stirring occasionally. Bring to the boil, reduce the heat and simmer for 10 minutes.

2 Stir in the stock and milk and cover again.

3 Ladle the vegetables and liquid into a blender or a food processor in batches and purée until smooth. Return to the pan, stir in the cream and season.

4 Leave the soup to cool, and then chill for 3–4 hours. You may need to add a little extra milk to thin down the soup, as it will thicken slightly as it cools.

5 Ladle the soup into soup bowls and serve topped with a spoonful of natural yogurt and a sprinkling of leeks.

LEEK, POTATO <u>AND</u> ROCKET SOUP

ROCKET ADDS ITS DISTINCTIVE, PEPPERY TASTE TO THIS WONDERFULLY SATISFYING SOUP.
SERVE IT HOT, GARNISHED WITH A GENEROUS SPRINKLING OF TASTY CIABATTA CROÛTONS.

SERVES FOUR TO SIX

INGREDIENTS
50g/2oz/4 tbsp butter
1 onion, chopped
3 leeks, chopped
2 medium floury potatoes, diced
900ml/1½ pints/3¾ cups light
    chicken stock or water
2 large handfuls rocket, roughly
    chopped
150ml/¼ pint/⅔ cup double cream
salt and ground black pepper
garlic-flavoured ciabatta croûtons,
    to serve

1 Melt the butter in a large heavy-based pan then add the onion, leeks and potatoes and stir until the vegetables are coated in butter. Heat the ingredients until sizzling then reduce the heat to low.

2 Cover and sweat the vegetables for 15 minutes. Pour in the stock or water and bring to the boil then reduce the heat, cover again and simmer for 20 minutes until the vegetables are tender.

3 Press the soup through a sieve or pass through a food mill and return to the rinsed-out pan. (When puréeing the soup, don't use a blender or food processor, as these will give the soup a gluey texture.) Add the chopped rocket to the pan and cook the soup gently, uncovered, for 5 minutes.

4 Stir in the cream, then season to taste and reheat gently. Ladle the soup into warmed soup bowls and serve with a scattering of garlic-flavoured ciabatta croûtons in each.

LEEK AND POTATO SOUP

THESE TWO VEGETABLES MAKE A REALLY TASTY AND SUBSTANTIAL, SIMPLE SOUP, AND ARE READILY AVAILABLE THROUGHOUT THE YEAR, MAKING THEM IDEAL FOR ANY SEASON.

SERVES FOUR

INGREDIENTS
50g/2oz/4 tbsp butter
2 leeks, chopped
1 small onion, finely chopped
350g/12oz floury potatoes, chopped
900ml/1½ pints/3¾ cups chicken or
   vegetable stock
salt and ground black pepper
crusty bread, to serve

1 Heat 25g/1oz/2 tbsp of the butter in a large heavy-based saucepan, add the chopped leeks and onion and cook gently, stirring occasionally so that they do not stick to the bottom of the pan, for about 7 minutes until softened but not browned.

2 Add the potatoes to the pan and cook, stirring occasionally, for 2–3 minutes. Add the stock and bring to the boil then reduce the heat, cover and simmer gently for 30–35 minutes until the vegetables are very tender.

3 Season to taste, remove the pan from the heat and stir in the remaining butter in small pieces. Serve hot with slices of thick crusty bread.

COOK'S TIP
If you prefer your soup to have a smoother consistency, simply press the mixture through a sieve or pass through a food mill once it is cooked. Don't use a food processor as it can give the potatoes a gluey texture.

CLAM, MUSHROOM AND POTATO CHOWDER

THE DELICATE, SWEET SHELLFISH TASTE OF CLAMS AND THE SOFT EARTHINESS OF WILD MUSHROOMS COMBINE WITH POTATOES TO MAKE THIS A GREAT MEAL ON ITS OWN — FIT FOR ANY OCCASION.

SERVES FOUR

INGREDIENTS
48 clams, scrubbed
50g/2oz/4 tbsp unsalted butter
1 large onion, chopped
1 celery stick, sliced
1 carrot, sliced
225g/8oz assorted wild mushrooms,
   such as chanterelles, saffron milk-
   caps, chicken of the woods or
   St George's mushrooms, sliced
225g/8oz floury potatoes,
   thickly sliced
1.2 litres/2 pints/5 cups light
   chicken or vegetable stock, boiling
1 thyme sprig
4 parsley stalks
salt and ground black pepper
thyme sprigs, to garnish

1 Place the clams in a large saucepan, discarding any that are open. Put 1cm/½in of water in the pan, cover, bring to the boil and steam over a medium heat for 6–8 minutes until the clams open (discard any clams that do not open).

2 Drain the clams over a bowl, remove the shells from each one and chop. Strain the cooking juices into the bowl, add the chopped clams and set aside.

3 Add the butter, onion, celery and carrot to the pan and cook gently until softened but not coloured. Add the mushrooms and cook for 3–4 minutes until their juices begin to appear. Add the potatoes, the clams and their juices, the stock, thyme and parsley stalks.

4 Bring to the boil then reduce the heat, cover and simmer for 25 minutes. Season to taste, ladle into soup bowls, and garnish with thyme.

SWEETCORN AND POTATO CHOWDER

THIS CREAMY YET CHUNKY SOUP IS RICH WITH THE SWEET TASTE OF CORN. IT'S EXCELLENT SERVED WITH THICK CRUSTY BREAD AND TOPPED WITH SOME MELTED CHEDDAR CHEESE.

SERVES FOUR

INGREDIENTS

1 onion, chopped
1 garlic clove, crushed
1 medium baking potato, chopped
2 celery sticks, sliced
1 small green pepper, seeded, halved
  and sliced
30ml/2 tbsp sunflower oil
25g/1oz/2 tbsp butter
600ml/1 pint/2½ cups stock or water
300ml/½ pint/1¼ cups milk
200g/7oz can flageolet beans
300g/11oz can sweetcorn kernels
good pinch dried sage
salt and ground black pepper
Cheddar cheese, grated, to serve

1 Put the onion, garlic, potato, celery and green pepper into a large heavy-based saucepan with the oil and butter.

2 Heat the ingredients in a large saucepan until sizzling then reduce the heat to low. Cover and cook gently for about 10 minutes, shaking the pan occasionally.

3 Pour in the stock or water, season with salt and pepper to taste and bring to the boil. Reduce the heat, cover again and simmer gently for about 15 minutes until the vegetables are tender.

4 Add the milk, beans and sweetcorn – including their liquids – and the sage. Simmer, uncovered, for 5 minutes. Check the seasoning and serve hot, sprinkled with grated cheese.

GALICIAN BROTH

IN THIS HEARTY MAIN MEAL SOUP THE POTATOES COOK IN THE GAMMON STOCK, ABSORBING ITS RICH FLAVOUR AND GIVING IT A SALTY TASTE, SO BE CAREFUL NOT TO OVER SEASON IT.

SERVES FOUR

INGREDIENTS
    450g/1lb gammon, in one piece
    2 bay leaves
    2 onions, sliced
    10ml/2 tsp paprika
    675g/1½lb baking potatoes, cut into
      large chunks
    225g/8oz spring greens
    425g/15oz can haricot or cannellini
      beans, drained
    salt and ground black pepper

COOK'S TIP
Peel the potatoes if you prefer, but the flavour is best with the skin left on.

1 Soak the gammon overnight in cold water in the fridge. Drain and put in a large saucepan with the bay leaves and onions. Pour over 1.5 litres/2½ pints/6¼ cups fresh cold water.

2 Bring to the boil then reduce the heat and simmer very gently for about 1½ hours until the meat is tender. Keep an eye on the pan to make sure it doesn't boil over.

3 Remove the meat from the cooking liquid and leave to cool slightly. Discard the skin and any excess fat and cut the meat into small chunks. Return to the pan with the paprika and potatoes. Return to the boil, then reduce the heat, cover and simmer for 20 minutes until the potatoes are tender.

4 Meanwhile cut away the cores from the greens. Roll up the leaves and cut into thin shreds. Add to the pan with the beans and simmer, uncovered, for about 10 minutes. Remove the bay leaves. Season with salt and pepper to taste and serve hot.

VARIATION
Bacon knuckles can be used instead of the gammon. The bones will give the stock a delicious flavour. Freeze any stock you don't use.

CREAMED SPINACH AND POTATO SOUP

THIS IS A DELICIOUS LOW-FAT CREAMY SOUP. THIS RECIPE USES SPINACH BUT OTHER VEGETABLES WOULD WORK JUST AS WELL, SUCH AS CABBAGE OR SWISS CHARD.

SERVES FOUR

INGREDIENTS
  1 large onion, finely chopped
  1 garlic clove, crushed
  900g/2lb floury potatoes, diced
  2 celery sticks, chopped
  1.2 litres/2 pints/5 cups
    vegetable stock
  250g/9oz fresh spinach leaves
  200g/7oz/scant 1 cup low-fat
    cream cheese
  300ml/½ pint/1¼ cups milk
  dash of dry sherry
  salt and ground black pepper
  chopped fresh parsley, to garnish
  crusty bread, to serve

1 Place the onion, garlic, potatoes, celery and stock in a large saucepan. Simmer for 20 minutes.

2 Season the soup and add the spinach, cook for a further 10 minutes. Remove from the heat and cool slightly.

3 Process the soup in batches in a food processor or food mill and return to the saucepan.

4 Stir in the cream cheese and milk, simmer and check for seasoning. Add a dash of sherry and serve crusty bread and chopped fresh parsley.

POTATO AND GARLIC BROTH

ALTHOUGH THERE IS PLENTY OF GARLIC IN THIS SOUP, THE END RESULT IS NOT OVERPOWERING. SERVE PIPING HOT WITH BREAD, AS THE PERFECT WINTER WARMER.

SERVES FOUR

INGREDIENTS
  2 small or 1 large whole head of
    garlic (about 20 cloves)
  4 medium potatoes, diced
  1.75 litres/3 pints/7½ cups
    vegetable stock
  salt and ground black pepper
  flat leaf parsley, to garnish

VARIATION
Make the soup more substantial by placing in each bowl a slice of French bread which has been toasted and topped with melted cheese. Pour the soup over so that the bread soaks it up.

1 Preheat the oven to 190°C/375°F/Gas 5. Place the unpeeled garlic bulbs or bulb in a small roasting tin and bake for 30 minutes until they are soft in the centre.

2 Meanwhile, par-boil the potatoes in a large saucepan of lightly salted boiling water for 10 minutes.

3 Simmer the stock for 5 minutes. Drain the potatoes and add to the stock.

4 Squeeze the garlic pulp into the soup, reserving a few cloves to garnish, stir and season to taste. Simmer for 15 minutes and serve garnished with whole cloves and parsley.

SMOKED HADDOCK AND POTATO SOUP

"CULLEN SKINK" IS A CLASSIC SCOTTISH DISH USING ONE OF THE COUNTRY'S TASTIEST FISH.
THE RESULT IS A THICK, CREAMY SOUP WITH A RICH, SMOKY FISH FLAVOUR.

SERVES SIX

INGREDIENTS
350g/12oz smoked haddock fillet
1 onion, chopped
bouquet garni
900ml/1½ pints/3¾ cups water
500g/1¼lb floury potatoes, quartered
600ml/1 pint/2½ cups milk
40g/1½oz/3 tbsp butter
salt and ground black pepper
snipped chives, to garnish
crusty bread, to serve

1 Put the haddock, onion, bouquet garni and water into a large heavy-based saucepan and bring to the boil. Skim the scum from the surface, then cover, reduce the heat and poach gently for 10–15 minutes until the haddock flakes easily.

2 Lift the haddock from the pan and cool slightly, then remove the skin and bones. Flake the flesh and put to one side. Return the skin and bones to the pan and simmer, for 30 minutes.

3 Strain the fish stock and return to the pan, then add the potatoes and simmer for about 25 minutes. Remove the potatoes from the pan. Add the milk to the pan and bring to the boil.

4 Mash the potatoes with the butter, then whisk into the soup. Add the flaked fish to the pan and heat through. Season. Ladle into soup bowls, sprinkle with chives and serve with crusty bread.

NORTH AFRICAN SPICED SOUP

*CLASSICALLY KNOWN AS HARIRA, THIS SOUP IS OFTEN SERVED IN THE EVENING DURING RAMADAN,
THE MUSLIM RELIGIOUS FESTIVAL WHEN FOLLOWERS FAST DURING THE DAYTIME FOR A MONTH.*

SERVES SIX

INGREDIENTS
 1 large onion, chopped
 1.2 litres/2 pints/5 cups
   vegetable stock
 5ml/1 tsp ground cinnamon
 5ml/1 tsp turmeric
 15ml/1 tbsp grated ginger
 pinch cayenne pepper
 2 carrots, diced
 2 celery sticks, diced
 400g/14oz can chopped tomatoes
 450g/1lb floury potatoes, diced
 5 strands saffron
 400g/14oz can chick-peas, drained
 30ml/2 tbsp chopped fresh coriander
 15ml/1 tbsp lemon juice
 salt and ground black pepper
 fried wedges of lemon, to serve

1 Place the onion in a large pot with 300ml/½ pint/1¼ cups of the vegetable stock. Simmer gently for about 10 minutes.

2 Meanwhile, mix together the cinnamon, turmeric, ginger, cayenne pepper and 30ml/2 tbsp of stock to form a paste. Stir into the onion mixture with the carrots, celery and remaining stock.

3 Bring the mixture to a boil, reduce the heat, then cover and gently simmer for 5 minutes.

4 Add the tomatoes and potatoes and simmer gently, covered, for 20 minutes. Add the saffron, chick-peas, coriander and lemon juice. Season to taste and when piping hot serve with fried wedges of lemon.

KALE, CHORIZO AND POTATO SOUP

THIS HEARTY WINTER SOUP HAS A SPICY KICK TO IT, WHICH COMES FROM THE CHORIZO SAUSAGE.
THE SOUP BECOMES MORE POTENT IF CHILLED OVERNIGHT AND IT IS WORTH BUYING THE BEST
POSSIBLE CHORIZO SAUSAGE TO IMPROVE THE FLAVOUR.

SERVES SIX TO EIGHT

INGREDIENTS
    225g/8oz kale, stems removed
    225g/8oz chorizo sausage
    675g/1½lb red potatoes
    1.75 litres/3 pints/7½ cups
      vegetable stock
    5ml/1 tsp ground black pepper
    pinch cayenne pepper (optional)
    12 slices French bread, grilled
    salt and ground black pepper

1 Place the kale in a food processor
and process for a few seconds to chop
it finely.

2 Prick the sausages and place in a
pan with enough water to cover.
Simmer for 15 minutes. Drain and
cut into thin slices.

3 Boil the potatoes for about
15 minutes or until tender. Drain, and
place in a bowl, then mash adding a
little of the cooking liquid to form a
thick paste.

4 Bring the vegetable stock to the boil
and add the kale. Add the chorizo and
simmer for 5 minutes. Add the paste
gradually, simmer for 20 minutes.
Season with black pepper and cayenne.

5 Place bread slices in each bowl, and
pour the soup over. Serve sprinkled
with pepper.

CREAM OF CAULIFLOWER SOUP

THIS SOUP IS LIGHT IN FLAVOUR YET SATISFYING ENOUGH FOR A LUNCHTIME SNACK.
YOU CAN TRY GREEN CAULIFLOWER FOR A COLOURFUL CHANGE.

SERVES SIX

INGREDIENTS

30ml/2 tbsp olive oil
2 large onions, finely diced
1 garlic clove, crushed
3 large floury potatoes, finely diced
3 celery sticks, finely diced
1.75 litres/3 pints/7½ cups
  vegetable stock
2 carrots, finely diced
1 medium cauliflower, chopped
15ml/1 tbsp chopped fresh dill
15ml/1 tbsp lemon juice
5ml/1 tsp mustard powder
1.5ml/¼ tsp caraway seeds
300ml/½ pint/1¼ cups single cream
salt and ground black pepper
shredded spring onions, to garnish

3 Add the cauliflower, fresh dill, lemon juice, mustard powder and caraway seeds and simmer for 20 minutes.

4 Process the soup in a blender or food processor until smooth, return to the saucepan and stir in the cream. Season to taste and serve garnished with shredded spring onions.

1 Heat the oil in a large saucepan, add the onions and garlic and fry them for a few minutes until they soften. Add the potatoes, celery and stock and simmer for 10 minutes.

2 Add the carrots and simmer for a further 10 minutes.

CORN AND SWEET POTATO SOUP

THE COMBINATION OF SWEETCORN AND SWEET POTATO GIVES THIS SOUP A REAL DEPTH OF FLAVOUR AS WELL AS MAKING IT LOOK VERY COLOURFUL.

SERVES SIX

INGREDIENTS
15ml/1 tbsp olive oil
1 onion, finely chopped
2 garlic cloves, crushed
1 small red chilli, seeded and
    finely chopped
1.75 litres/3 pints/7½ cups
    vegetable stock
10ml/2 tsp ground cumin
1 medium sweet potato, diced
½ red pepper, finely chopped
450g/1lb sweetcorn kernels
salt and ground black pepper
lime wedges, to serve

1 Heat the oil and fry the onion for 5 minutes until softened. Add the garlic and chilli and fry for a further 2 minutes.

2 In the same pan, add 300ml/½ pint/ 1¼ cups of the stock, and simmer for 10 minutes.

3 Mix the cumin with a little stock to form a paste and then stir into the soup. Add the diced sweet potato, stir and simmer for 10 minutes. Season and stir again.

4 Add the pepper, sweetcorn and remaining stock and simmer for 10 minutes. Process half of the soup until smooth and then stir into the chunky soup. Season and serve with lime wedges for squeezing over.

MINESTRONE GENOA

THE VARIATIONS ON THIS SOUP ARE ENDLESS. THIS PASTA-FREE VERSION IS PACKED WITH HEAPS OF VEGETABLES TO MAKE A SUBSTANTIAL, HEARTY LUNCH WITH CRUSTY BREAD.

SERVES SIX

INGREDIENTS
1.75 litres/3 pints/7½ cups
    vegetable stock
1 large onion, chopped
3 celery sticks, chopped
2 carrots, finely diced
2 large floury potatoes, finely diced
½ head of cabbage, very finely diced
225g/8oz runner beans, sliced
    diagonally
2 x 400g/14oz cans cannellini
    beans, drained
60ml/4 tbsp ready-made pesto sauce
salt and ground black pepper
crusty bread, to serve
freshly grated Parmesan cheese,
    to serve

1 Pour the stock into a large saucepan. Add the onion, celery and carrots. Simmer for 10 minutes.

2 Add the potatoes, cabbage, and beans and simmer for 10–12 minutes or until the potatoes are tender.

3 Stir in the cannellini beans and pesto, and bring the mixture to the boil. Season to taste and serve hot with crusty bread and plenty of freshly grated Parmesan cheese.

CATALAN POTATO BROAD BEAN SOUP

BROAD BEANS ARE ALSO KNOWN AS FAVA BEANS. WHILE THEY ARE IN SEASON FRESH BEANS ARE
PERFECT, BUT TINNED OR FROZEN WILL MAKE AN IDEAL SUBSTITUTE.

SERVES SIX

INGREDIENTS
    30ml/2 tbsp olive oil
    2 onions, chopped
    3 large floury potatoes, diced
    450g/1lb fresh broad beans
    1.75 litres/3 pints/7½ cups
        vegetable stock
    1 bunch coriander, finely chopped
    150ml/¼ pint/⅔ cup single cream
    salt and ground black pepper
    coriander leaves, to garnish

COOK'S TIP
Broad beans sometimes have a tough
outer skin, particularly if they are large.
To remove this, first cook the beans
briefly, peel off the skin, and add the
tender centre part to the soup.

1 Heat the oil in a large saucepan
and fry the onions, stirring occasionally,
for about 5 minutes until softened but
not brown.

2 Add the potatoes, beans (reserving a
few for garnishing) and stock to the
mixture in the saucepan and bring to
the boil, then simmer for 5 minutes.

3 Stir in the coriander and simmer for
a further 10 minutes.

4 Process in batches in a blender or
food processor, then return the soup to
the pan.

5 Stir in the cream (reserving a little for
garnishing), season, and bring to a
simmer. Serve garnished with more
coriander leaves, beans and cream.

SPANISH POTATO <u>AND</u> GARLIC SOUP

SERVED IN EARTHENWARE DISHES, THIS CLASSIC SPANISH SOUP SHOULD BE SAVOURED.

SERVES SIX

INGREDIENTS
    30ml/2 tbsp olive oil
    1 large onion, finely sliced
    4 garlic cloves, crushed
    1 large potato, halved and cut into
        thin slices
    5ml/1 tsp paprika
    400g/14oz can chopped
        tomatoes, drained
    5ml/1 tsp thyme leaves
    900ml/1½ pints/3¾ cups
        vegetable stock
    5ml/1 tsp cornflour
    salt and ground black pepper
    chopped thyme leaves, to garnish

1 Heat the oil in a large saucepan,
fry the onions, garlic, potato and
paprika for 5 minutes, until the onions
have softened, but not browned.

2 Add the tomatoes, thyme and stock
and simmer for 15–20 minutes until the
potatoes have cooked through.

3 Mix the cornflour with a little water to
form a paste and stir into the soup, then
simmer for 5 minutes until thickened.

4 Using a wooden spoon break the
potatoes up slightly. Season to taste.
Serve garnished with the chopped
thyme leaves.

Starters and Snacks

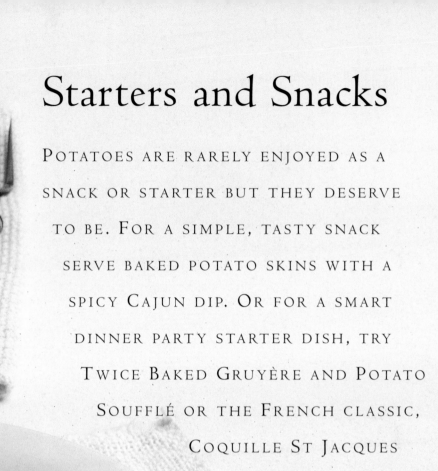

POTATOES ARE RARELY ENJOYED AS A
SNACK OR STARTER BUT THEY DESERVE
TO BE. FOR A SIMPLE, TASTY SNACK
SERVE BAKED POTATO SKINS WITH A
SPICY CAJUN DIP. OR FOR A SMART
DINNER PARTY STARTER DISH, TRY
TWICE BAKED GRUYÈRE AND POTATO
SOUFFLÉ OR THE FRENCH CLASSIC,
COQUILLE ST JACQUES
WITH ITS
DECORATIVE
POTATO-PIPED
BORDER.

COQUILLES ST JACQUES

A CLASSIC FRENCH STARTER, THAT CALLS FOR THE BEST QUALITY SCALLOPS POSSIBLE TO ENSURE A TRULY WONDERFUL RESULT. YOU WILL NEED FOUR SCALLOP SHELLS TO SERVE THESE.

SERVES FOUR

INGREDIENTS
  450g/1lb potatoes, chopped
  50g/2oz/4 tbsp butter
  4 large or 8 small scallops
  120ml/4fl oz/½ cup fish stock
For the sauce
  25g/1oz/2 tbsp butter
  25g/1oz/¼ cup plain flour
  300ml/½ pint/1¼ cups milk
  30ml/2 tbsp single cream
  115g/4oz/1 cup mature Cheddar
    cheese, grated
  salt and ground black pepper
  dill sprigs, to garnish
  grilled lemon wedges, to serve

1 Preheat oven to 200°C/400°F/Gas 6. Place the chopped potatoes in a large saucepan, cover with water and boil for 15 minutes or until tender. Drain and mash with the butter.

2 Spoon the mixture into a piping bag fitted with a star nozzle. Pipe the potatoes around the outside of a cleaned scallop shell. Repeat the process, making four in total.

3 Simmer the scallops in a little fish stock for 3 minutes or until just firm. Drain and slice the scallops finely. Set them aside.

4 To make the sauce, melt the butter in a small saucepan, add the flour and cook over a low heat for a couple of minutes, gradually add the milk and cream, stirring continuously and cook until thickened.

5 Stir in the cheese and cook until melted. Season to taste. Spoon a little sauce in the base of each shell. Divide the scallops between the shells and then pour the remaining sauce over the scallops.

6 Bake the scallops for 10 minutes or until golden. Garnish with dill. Serve with grilled lemon wedges.

TWICE BAKED GRUYÈRE
AND POTATO SOUFFLÉ

A GREAT STARTER DISH, THIS RECIPE CAN BE PREPARED IN ADVANCE IF YOU ARE ENTERTAINING AND GIVEN ITS SECOND BAKING JUST BEFORE YOU SERVE IT UP.

2 Stir in half of the Gruyère cheese and all of the flour. Season to taste with salt and pepper.

3 Finely chop the spinach and fold into the potato mixture.

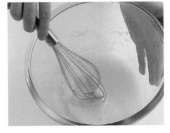

4 Whip the egg whites until they form soft peaks. Fold a little of the egg white into the mixture to loosen it slightly. Using a large spoon, fold the remaining egg white into the mixture.

5 Grease 4 large ramekin dishes. Pour the mixture in and place on a baking sheet and bake for 20 minutes. Remove from the oven and allow to cool.

6 Turn the soufflés out on to a baking sheet and scatter with the remaining cheese. Bake again for 5 minutes and serve with salad leaves.

SERVES FOUR

INGREDIENTS
  225g/8oz floury potatoes
  2 eggs, separated
  175g/6oz/1½ cups Gruyère, grated
  50g/2oz/½ cup self-raising flour
  50g/2oz spinach leaves
  butter for greasing
  salt and ground black pepper
  salad leaves, to serve

VARIATION
For a different flavouring try replacing the Gruyère with a crumbled blue cheese, such as Stilton or Shropshire Blue, which have a stronger taste to them.

1 Preheat the oven to 200°C/400°F/ Gas 6. Cook the potatoes in lightly salted boiling water for 20 minutes until very tender. Drain and mash with the 2 egg yolks.

New Potatoes with Mock Caviar and Cream Cheese

A perfect one-bite snack for a party that makes the most of tender new potatoes with their waxy texture. Danish mock caviar is another name for lumpfish roe.

MAKES THIRTY

INGREDIENTS
30 small new potatoes
200g/7oz/scant 1 cup full-fat
   cream cheese
15ml/1 tbsp chopped fresh parsley
1 jar Danish black mock caviar
   (lumpfish roe)
1 jar salmon roe
salt and ground black pepper
dill sprigs, to garnish

VARIATION
If you can't get hold of any mock caviar, then top the new potatoes with thin slices of smoked salmon.

1 Cook the potatoes in a large saucepan of boiling water for 20 minutes or until tender. Drain through a colander and then trim off both ends of each potato.

2 Sit the potatoes on the cut end. Beat the cream cheese and parsley together and season. Spoon the mixture on to the potatoes and top with a little mock caviar and salmon roe. Garnish with dill.

Potato Blinis

This crisp, light pancake originates from Russia, where it is served with the best caviar, or use the topping from the recipe above, if you prefer.

SERVES SIX

INGREDIENTS
115g/4oz maincrop potatoes, boiled
   and mashed
15ml/1 tbsp easy-blend dried yeast
175g/6oz/1½ cups plain flour
oil for greasing
90ml/6 tbsp soured cream
6 slices smoked salmon
salt and ground black pepper
lemon slices, to garnish

COOK'S TIP
These small pancakes can easily be prepared in advance and stored in the refrigerator until ready for use. Simply warm them up in a low oven.

1 In a large bowl, mix together the potatoes, yeast, flour and 300ml/½ pint/1¼ cups hand-hot water.

2 Leave to rise in a warm place for 30 minutes until the mixture has doubled in size.

3 Heat a non-stick frying pan and add a little oil. Drop spoonfuls of the mixture on to the preheated pan. Cook the blinis for 2 minutes until lightly golden on the underside, toss with a spatula and cook on the second side. Season to taste before serving.

4 Serve with a little soured cream and a small slice of smoked salmon folded on top. Garnish with black pepper and a small slice of lemon.

POTATO SKEWERS WITH MUSTARD DIP

POTATOES COOKED ON THE BARBECUE HAVE A GREAT FLAVOUR AND CRISP SKIN. TRY THESE DELICIOUS KEBABS SERVED WITH A THICK, GARLIC-RICH DIP.

SERVES FOUR

INGREDIENTS
For the dip
  4 garlic cloves, crushed
  2 egg yolks
  30ml/2 tbsp lemon juice
  300ml/½ pint/1¼ cups extra virgin
    olive oil
  10ml/2 tsp whole-grain mustard
  salt and ground black pepper
For the skewers
  1kg/2¼lb small new potatoes
  200g/7oz shallots, halved
  30ml/2 tbsp olive oil
  15ml/1 tbsp sea salt

1 Prepare the barbecue for cooking the skewers before you begin. To make the dip, place the garlic, egg yolks and lemon juice in a blender or a food processor fitted with the metal blade and process for a few seconds until the mixture is smooth.

2 Keep the blender motor running and add the oil very gradually, pouring it in a thin stream, until the mixture forms a thick, glossy cream. Add the mustard and stir the ingredients together, then season with salt and pepper. Chill until ready to use.

COOK'S TIP
Early or "new" potatoes, and salad potatoes have a firmness necessary to stay on the skewer. Don't be tempted to use other types of small potato, they will probably split or fall off the skewers during cooking.

3 Par-boil the potatoes in their skins in boiling water for 5 minutes. Drain well and then thread them on to metal skewers alternating with the shallots.

4 Brush the skewers with oil and sprinkle with salt. Cook over a barbeque for 10–12 minutes, turning occasionally, Serve with the dip.

POTATO SKINS WITH CAJUN DIP

DIVINELY CRISP AND NAUGHTY, THESE POTATO SKINS ARE GREAT ON THEIR OWN OR SERVED WITH THIS PIQUANT DIP AS A GARNISH OR TO THE SIDE.

SERVES TWO

INGREDIENTS
 2 large baking potatoes
 vegetable oil, for deep frying
For the dip
 120ml/4fl oz/½ cup natural yogurt
 1 garlic clove, crushed
 5ml/1 tsp tomato purée
 2.5ml/½ tsp green chilli purée or
  ½ small green chilli, chopped
 1.5ml/¼ tsp celery salt
 salt and ground black pepper

COOK'S TIP
If you prefer, you can microwave the potatoes to save time. This will take about 10 minutes.

1 Preheat the oven to 180°C/350°F/Gas 4. Bake the potatoes for 45–50 minutes until tender. Cut them in half and scoop out the flesh, leaving a thin layer on the skins. Keep the flesh for another meal.

2 To make the dip, mix together all the ingredients and chill.

3 Heat a 1cm/½in layer of oil in a large saucepan or deep-fat fryer. Cut each potato half in half again, then fry them until crisp and golden on both sides. Drain on kitchen paper, sprinkle with salt and black pepper and serve with a bowl of dip or a dollop of dip in each skin.

DEEP-FRIED NEW POTATOES
WITH SAFFRON AÏOLI

*SERVE THESE CRISPY LITTLE GOLDEN POTATOES DIPPED INTO A WICKEDLY GARLICKY MAYONNAISE —
THEN WATCH THEM DISAPPEAR IN A MATTER OF MINUTES!*

SERVES FOUR

INGREDIENTS
1 egg yolk
2.5ml/½ tsp Dijon mustard
300ml/½ pint/1¼ cups extra virgin
  olive oil
15–30ml/1–2 tbsp lemon juice
1 garlic clove, crushed
2.5ml/½ tsp saffron strands
20 baby, new or salad potatoes
vegetable oil, for deep frying
salt and ground black pepper

1 For the aïoli, put the egg yolk in a
bowl with the mustard and a pinch of
salt. Mix. Beat in the olive oil very
slowly, drop by drop, then in a thin
stream. Add the lemon juice.

2 Season the aïoli with salt and pepper
then add the crushed garlic and beat
the mixture thoroughly to combine.

3 Place the saffron in a small bowl and
add 10ml/2 tsp hot water. Press the
saffron with the back of a teaspoon, to
extract the colour and flavour, and leave
to infuse for 5 minutes. Beat the saffron
and the liquid into the aïoli.

4 Cook the potatoes in their skins in
boiling salted water for 5 minutes, then
turn off the heat. Cover the pan and
leave for 15 minutes. Drain the
potatoes, then dry them thoroughly
in a tea towel.

5 Heat a 1cm/½in layer of vegetable oil
in a deep pan. When the oil is very hot,
add the potatoes and fry quickly,
turning, until crisp and golden. Drain on
kitchen paper and serve hot with the
saffron aïoli.

MINI BAKED POTATOES WITH BLUE CHEESE

PERFECT AS FINGER FOOD FOR A PARTY, ESPECIALLY AS YOU CAN PREPARE THEM IN ADVANCE.

MAKES TWENTY

INGREDIENTS
  20 small new or salad potatoes
  60ml/4 tbsp vegetable oil
  coarse salt
  120ml/4fl oz/½ cup soured cream
  25g/1oz blue cheese, crumbled
  30ml/2 tbsp chopped fresh chives,
    for sprinkling

COOK'S TIP
This dish works just as well as a light
snack; if you don't want to be bothered
with lots of fiddly small potatoes, simply
bake an ordinary baking potato.

1 Preheat the oven to 180°C/350°F/
Gas 4. Wash and dry the potatoes. Pour
the oil into a bowl. Add the potatoes
and toss to coat well with oil.

2 Dip the potatoes in the coarse salt to
coat lightly. Spread out the potatoes on
a baking sheet. Bake for 45–50 minutes
until tender.

3 In a small bowl, combine the soured
cream and blue cheese.

4 Cut a cross in the top of each potato.
Press gently with your fingers to open
the potatoes.

5 Top each potato with a dollop of the
cheese mixture. It will melt down into
the potato nicely. Sprinkle with chives
on a serving dish and serve hot or at
room temperature.

SWEET POTATO CRISPS

*YOU CAN USE THESE PINK POTATOES TO MAKE SWEET OR SAVOURY CRISPS, AND THEY HAVE A LOVELY
COLOUR AND A UNIQUE, ALMOST FRUITY FLAVOUR.*

SERVES FOUR

INGREDIENTS
  2 medium sweet potatoes
  vegetable oil, for deep-frying
  salt

VARIATIONS
For a sweet version, sprinkle with
cinnamon and caster sugar, and toss
well, before cooling. You can prepare
yams in just the same way.

COOK'S TIP
These sweet potato crisps are delicious
served warm, but if you don't manage to
finish them they are equally good as a
cold snack. Serve with a dip, either
sweet or savoury.

1 Peel the sweet potatoes under cold
running water, cut into 3mm/⅛in thick
slices with a sharp knife or vegetable
slicer and place in a bowl of salted
cold water.

2 Heat a 1cm/½in layer of oil in a large
saucepan or deep-fat fryer. While the oil
is heating, remove the slices from the
water and pat dry on kitchen paper.

3 Fry a few slices at a time until crisp,
then drain on kitchen paper. Sprinkle
with salt and serve warm.

INDIAN POTATO PANCAKES

*ALTHOUGH CALLED A PANCAKE, THESE CRISPY SPICED CAKES ARE MORE LIKE A BHAJI. THEY MAKE AN
IDEAL STARTER FOR A MEAL WITH A CURRY AS THE MAIN DISH.*

MAKES TEN

INGREDIENTS
  300g/11oz potatoes, grated
  25ml/1½ tsp garam masala or curry
    powder
  4 spring onions, finely chopped
  1 large egg white, lightly beaten
  30ml/2 tbsp vegetable oil
  salt and ground black pepper
  chutney and relishes, to serve

COOK'S TIP
Don't grate the potatoes too soon before
use as the flesh will quickly turn brown.

1 Using your hands, squeeze the
excess liquid from the grated potatoes
and pat dry.

2 Place the dry, grated potatoes in a
separate bowl and add the spices,
spring onions, egg white and seasoning,
stir to combine.

3 Heat a non-stick frying pan over a
medium heat and add the oil.

4 Drop tablespoonfuls of the potato on
to the pan and flatten out with the back
of a spoon (you will need to cook the
pancakes in two batches).

5 Cook for a few minutes and then flip
the pancakes over. Cook for a further
3 minutes.

6 Drain on kitchen paper and serve
with chutney and relishes.

POTATO PIZZA

THIS "PIZZA" MADE OF MASHED POTATOES, WITH A ROBUSTLY FLAVOURED FILLING OF ANCHOVIES, CAPERS AND TOMATOES, IS A SPECIALITY OF PUGLIA IN NORTHERN ITALY.

SERVES FOUR

INGREDIENTS

    1kg/2¼lb floury potatoes
    120ml/4fl oz/½ cup extra virgin
        olive oil
    2 garlic cloves, finely chopped
    350g/12oz tomatoes, chopped
    3 anchovy fillets, chopped
    30ml/2 tbsp capers, rinsed
    salt and ground black pepper

1 Cook the potatoes in their skins in boiling water until tender. Drain well and leave to cool slightly. When they are cool enough to handle, peel and mash or pass through a food mill. Beat in 45ml/3 tbsp of the oil and season to taste. Set aside.

2 Heat another 45ml/3 tbsp of the oil in a medium saucepan. Add the garlic and the chopped tomatoes and cook over a medium heat for 12–15 minutes stirring a little to cook evenly, until the tomatoes soften and begin to dry out. Meanwhile preheat the oven to 200°C/400°F/Gas 6.

3 Oil a round shallow baking dish. Spread half the mashed potatoes into the dish in an even layer. Cover with the tomatoes, and dot with the chopped anchovies and the capers.

4 Spread over the rest of the potatoes in an even layer. Brush the top with the remaining oil and bake for 20–25 minutes until the top is golden brown. Sprinkle with black pepper and serve hot.

VARIATION
For a vegetarian version of this dish, simply omit the anchovies. A few pitted and chopped olives may be added to the filling instead. Add them in step 3, on top of the tomatoes.

SPICED SWEET POTATO TURNOVERS

THE SUBTLE SWEETNESS OF THESE WONDERFUL PINK "POTATOES" MAKES A GREAT TURNOVER FILLING WHEN FLAVOURED WITH A SELECTION OF LIGHT SPICES.

SERVES FOUR

INGREDIENTS

For the filling
    1 sweet potato, about 225g/8oz
    30ml/2 tbsp vegetable oil
    2 shallots, finely chopped
    10ml/2 tsp coriander seeds, crushed
    5ml/1 tsp ground cumin
    5ml/1 tsp garam masala
    115g/4oz/1 cup frozen petit pois,
      thawed
    15ml/1 tbsp chopped fresh mint
    salt and ground black pepper
    mint sprigs, to garnish
For the pastry
    15ml/1 tbsp olive oil
    1 small egg
    150ml/¼ pint/⅔ cup natural yogurt
    115g/4oz/8 tbsp butter, melted
    275g/10oz/2½ cups plain flour
    1.5ml/¼ tsp bicarbonate of soda
    10ml/2 tsp paprika
    5ml/1 tsp salt
    beaten egg, to glaze

1 Cook the sweet potato in boiling salted water for 15–20 minutes, until tender. Drain well and leave to cool. When cool enough to handle, peel the potato and cut into 1cm/½in cubes.

2 Heat the oil in a frying pan, add the shallots and cook until softened. Add the sweet potato and fry until it browns at the edges. Add the spices and fry, stirring, for a few seconds. Remove the pan from the heat and add the peas, mint and seasoning to taste. Leave to cool.

3 Preheat the oven to 200°C/400°F/Gas 6. Grease a baking sheet. To make the pastry, whisk together the oil and egg, stir in the yogurt, then add the melted butter. Sift the flour, bicarbonate of soda, paprika and salt into a bowl, then stir into the yogurt mixture to form a soft dough. Turn out the dough, and knead gently. Roll it out, then stamp it out into rounds.

4 Spoon about 10ml/2 tsp of the filling on to one side of each round, then fold over and seal the edges.

5 Re-roll the trimmings and stamp out more rounds until the filling is used up.

6 Arrange the turnovers on the prepared baking sheet and brush the tops with beaten egg. Bake in the oven for about 20 minutes until crisp and golden brown. Serve hot, garnished with mint sprigs.

MIDDLE EASTERN LAMB AND POTATO CAKES

*AN UNUSUAL VARIATION, THESE MINCED LAMB TRIANGLES ARE EASY TO SERVE HOT FOR A BUFFET,
OR THEY CAN BE EATEN COLD AS A SNACK OR FOR PICNICS.*

MAKES TWELVE TO FIFTEEN

INGREDIENTS
450g/1lb new or small, firm potatoes
3 eggs
1 onion, grated
30ml/2 tbsp chopped fresh parsley
450g/1lb finely minced lean lamb
115g/4oz/2 cups breadcrumbs
vegetable oil, for frying
salt and ground black pepper
mint leaves, to garnish
pitta bread and herby green salad,
  to serve

1 Cook the potatoes in a large pan of boiling salted water for 20 minutes until tender, then drain and leave to cool. Beat the eggs in a large bowl. Add the onion, parsley and seasoning and beat together.

2 When the potatoes are cold, grate them coarsely and stir into the egg mixture together with the minced lamb. Knead for 3–4 minutes until all the ingredients are thoroughly blended.

3 Take a handful of the lamb mixture and roll it into a ball. Repeat this process until all is used. Roll the balls in the breadcrumbs and then mould them into triangular shapes, about 13cm/5in long. Coat them in the breadcrumbs again on both sides.

4 Heat a 1cm/½in layer of oil in a frying pan over a medium heat. When the oil is hot, fry the potato cakes for 8–12 minutes until golden brown on both sides, turning occasionally. Drain on kitchen paper. Serve hot, garnished with mint and accompanied by pitta bread and salad.

IDAHO POTATO SLICES

*THIS DISH IS MADE FROM A LAYERED RING OF POTATOES, CHEESE AND HERBS. COOKING THE
INGREDIENTS TOGETHER GIVES THEM A VERY RICH FLAVOUR.*

3 Scatter some of the onion rings over the potatoes and top with a little of the cheese. Scatter over some thyme and then continue to layer the ingredients, finishing with cheese and seasoning.

4 Press the potato layers right down. (The mixture may seem quite high at this point but it will cook down.)

5 Pour the cream over and cook in the oven for 35–45 minutes. Remove from the oven and cool. Invert on to a plate and cut into wedges. Serve with a few salad leaves.

VARIATION
If you want to make this snack more substantial, top the wedges with slices of grilled bacon, or grilled red peppers.

SERVES FOUR

INGREDIENTS
   3 large potatoes
   butter, for greasing
   1 small onion, finely sliced into rings
   200g/7oz/1¾ cups red Leicester or
     mature Cheddar cheese, grated
   fresh thyme sprigs
   150ml/¼ pint/⅔ cup single cream
   salt and ground black pepper
   salad leaves, to serve

1 Preheat the oven to 200°C/400°F/
Gas 6. Peel the potatoes and cook in boiling water for 10 minutes until they are just starting to soften. Remove from the water and pat dry.

2 Finely slice the potatoes, using the straight edge of a grater or a mandoline. Grease the base and sides of an 18cm/7in cake tin with butter and lay some of the potatoes on the base to cover it completely. Season.

POLPETTES

YUMMY LITTLE FRIED MOUTHFULS OF POTATO AND TANGY-SHARP GREEK FETA CHEESE, FLAVOURED WITH DILL AND LEMON JUICE. SERVE AS A STARTER OR PARTY BITE.

SERVES FOUR

INGREDIENTS
  500g/1¼lb floury potatoes
  115g/4oz/1 cup feta cheese
  4 spring onions, chopped
  45ml/3 tbsp chopped fresh dill
  1 egg, beaten
  15ml/1 tbsp lemon juice
  salt and ground black pepper
  plain flour, for dredging
  45ml/3 tbsp olive oil
  dill sprigs, to garnish
  shredded spring onions, to garnish
  lemon wedges, to serve

1 Cook the potatoes in their skins in boiling lightly salted water until soft. Drain and leave to cool slightly, then chop them in half and peel while still warm.

2 Place in a bowl and mash. Crumble the feta cheese into the potatoes and add the spring onions, dill, egg and lemon juice and season with salt and pepper. (The cheese is salty, so taste before you add salt.) Stir well.

3 Cover and chill until firm. Divide the mixture into walnut-size balls, then flatten them slightly. Dredge with flour, shaking off the excess.

4 Heat the oil in a frying pan and fry the polpettes in batches until golden brown on both sides. Drain on kitchen paper and serve hot, garnished with spring onions, dill and lemon wedges.

SAVOURY POTATO CAKES

GOLDEN AND CRISP, BUT SOFT WHEN YOU BITE INTO THEM, THESE POTATO CAKES ARE WONDERFUL FOR BREAKFAST OR SUPPER, WITH OR WITHOUT ANYTHING ELSE.

SERVES FOUR

INGREDIENTS
450g/1lb waxy potatoes
1 small onion, grated
4 slices streaky bacon, finely chopped
30ml/2 tbsp self-raising flour
2 eggs, beaten
vegetable oil, for deep-frying
salt and ground black pepper
parsley, to garnish

VARIATION
For a vegetarian alternative, omit the bacon and replace it with red pepper.

1 Coarsely grate the potatoes, rinse, drain and pat dry on kitchen paper, then mix with the onion, half the bacon, flour, eggs and seasoning.

2 Heat a 1cm/½in layer of oil in a frying pan until really hot, then add about 15ml/1 tbsp of the potato mixture and quickly spread the mixture out with the back of the spoon taking care that it does not break up.

3 Add a few more spoonfuls of the mixture in the same way, leaving space between each one so they do not stick together, and fry them for 4–5 minutes until golden on the undersides.

4 Turn the cakes over and fry the other side. Drain on kitchen paper, transfer to an ovenproof dish and keep warm in a low oven while frying the remainder. Fry the remaining bacon and parsley and serve sprinkled over the hot cakes.

Salads

WARM OR CHILLED POTATOES ADD A NEW
DIMENSION TO SALADS. ADD FLAVOUR AND
COLOUR TO CHUNKY CUT POTATOES WITH
FRESHLY COOKED BEETROOT OR SLICED
RADISHES. OR TRY SWEET POTATO, BAKED
UNTIL SOFT IN THE CENTRE AND THEN
COMBINED WITH A CORIANDER AND LIME
DRESSING, A PERFECT COMBINATION OF
REFRESHING AND AROMATIC FLAVOURS.

Tangy Potato Salad

If you like a good kick of mustard, you'll love this combination. It's also well flavoured with tarragon, used in the dressing and as a garnish.

SERVES EIGHT

INGREDIENTS

1.55kg/3lb small new or salad
   potatoes
30ml/2 tbsp white wine vinegar
15ml/1 tbsp Dijon mustard
45ml/3 tbsp vegetable or olive oil
75g/3oz/6 tbsp chopped red onion
125ml/4fl oz/½ cup mayonnaise
30ml/2 tbsp chopped fresh tarragon,
   or 7.5ml/1½ tsp dried tarragon
1 celery stick, thinly sliced
salt and ground black pepper
celery leaves, to garnish
tarragon leaves, to garnish

VARIATIONS

When available, use small red or even
blue potatoes to give a nice colour to
the salad.

1 Cook the potatoes in their skins in boiling salted water for about 15–20 minutes until tender. Drain well.

2 Mix together the vinegar and mustard, then slowly whisk in the oil.

3 When the potatoes are cool enough to handle, slice them into a large bowl.

4 Add the onion to the potatoes and pour the dressing over them. Season, then toss gently to combine. Leave to stand for at least 30 minutes.

5 Mix together the mayonnaise and tarragon. Gently stir into the potatoes, along with the celery. Serve garnished with celery leaves and tarragon.

TOULOUSE POTATO SALAD

WELL-FLAVOURED SAUSAGES AND FIRM CHUNKY POTATOES MAKE A REALLY GREAT LUNCH,
SIMPLY DRESSED WITH A QUICK AND EASY VINAIGRETTE.

3 Peel the potatoes if you like or leave in their skins, and cut into 5mm/¼ in slices. Place them in a large bowl and sprinkle with the wine and shallots.

4 To make the vinaigrette, mix together the mustard and vinegar in a small bowl, then very slowly whisk in the oil. Season and pour over the potatoes.

SERVES FOUR

INGREDIENTS
   450g/1lb small waxy or
   salad potatoes
   30–45ml/2–3 tbsp dry white wine
   2 shallots, finely chopped
   15ml/1 tbsp chopped fresh parsley
   15ml/1 tbsp chopped fresh tarragon
   175g/6oz cooked garlic or
   Toulouse sausage
   chopped fresh parsley, to garnish
For the vinaigrette
   10ml/2 tsp Dijon mustard
   15ml/1 tbsp tarragon vinegar or
   white wine vinegar
   75ml/5 tbsp extra virgin olive oil
   salt and ground black pepper

1 Cook the potatoes in their skins in a large saucepan of boiling salted water for 10–12 minutes until tender.

2 Drain the potatoes, rinse under cold running water, then drain them again.

5 Add the chopped herbs to the potatoes and toss until well mixed.

6 Slice the sausage and toss with the potatoes. Season to taste and serve at room temperature with a parsley garnish.

THE SIMPLEST POTATO SALAD

THE SECRET OF THIS POTATO SALAD IS TO MIX THE POTATOES WITH THE DRESSING WHILE THEY ARE STILL HOT SO THAT THEY ABSORB IT. THIS IS PERFECT WITH GRILLED PORK, LAMB CHOPS OR ROAST CHICKEN OR FOR VEGETARIANS SERVE WITH A SELECTION OF ROASTED VEGETABLES.

SERVES FOUR TO SIX

INGREDIENTS
    675g/1½lb small new or
        salad potatoes
    4 spring onions
    45ml/3 tbsp olive oil
    15ml/1 tbsp white wine vinegar
    175ml/6fl oz/¾ cup good
        mayonnaise, preferably home-made
    45ml/3 tbsp snipped chives
    salt and ground black pepper

1 Cook the potatoes in their skins in a large saucepan of boiling salted water until tender.

2 Meanwhile, finely chop the white parts of the spring onions along with a little of the green parts; they look more attractive cut on the diagonal. Put to one side.

3 Whisk together the oil and vinegar. Drain the potatoes well and place them in a large bowl, then immediately toss lightly with the vinegar mixture and spring onions. Put the bowl to one side to cool.

4 Stir the mayonnaise and chives into the potatoes, season well and chill thoroughly until ready to serve. Adjust the seasoning before serving.

POTATO AND RADISH SALAD

RADISHES ADD A SPLASH OF CRUNCH AND PEPPERY FLAVOUR TO THIS HONEY-SCENTED SALAD. SO MANY POTATO SALADS ARE DRESSED IN A THICK SAUCE. THIS ONE HOWEVER, IS QUITE LIGHT AND COLOURFUL WITH A TASTY YET DELICATE DRESSING.

SERVES FOUR TO SIX

INGREDIENTS
    450g/1lb new or salad potatoes
    45ml/3 tbsp olive oil
    15ml/1 tbsp walnut or hazelnut oil
        (optional)
    30ml/2 tbsp wine vinegar
    10ml/2 tsp coarse-grain mustard
    5ml/1 tsp honey
    about 6–8 radishes, thinly sliced
    30ml/2 tbsp snipped chives
    salt and ground black pepper

VARIATIONS
Sliced celery, diced red onion and/or chopped walnuts would make good alternatives to the radishes if you can't get hold of any.

COOK'S TIP
For best effect, serve on a platter lined with frilly lettuce leaves.

1 Cook the potatoes in their skins in a large saucepan of boiling salted water until just tender. Drain the potatoes through a colander and leave to cool slightly. When cool enough to handle, cut the potatoes in half, but leave any small ones whole. Return the potatoes to a large bowl.

2 To make the dressing, place the oils, vinegar, mustard, honey and seasoning in a bowl. Mix them together until thoroughly combined.

3 Toss the dressing into the potatoes in the bowl while they are still cooling and leave to stand for an hour or so to allow the flavours to penetrate.

4 Finally mix in the sliced radishes and snipped chives and chill in the fridge until ready to serve.

5 When ready to serve, toss the salad mixture together again, as some of the dressing may have settled on the bottom and adjust the seasoning.

HOT HOT CAJUN POTATO SALAD

IN CAJUN COUNTRY WHERE TABASCO ORIGINATES, HOT MEANS REALLY HOT, SO YOU CAN GO TO TOWN WITH THIS SALAD IF YOU THINK YOU CAN TAKE IT!

SERVES SIX TO EIGHT

INGREDIENTS

8 waxy potatoes
1 green pepper, seeded and diced
1 large gherkin, chopped
4 spring onions, shredded
3 hard-boiled eggs, shelled
  and chopped
250ml/8fl oz/1 cup mayonnaise
15ml/1 tbsp Dijon mustard
salt and ground black pepper
Tabasco sauce, to taste
pinch or two of cayenne
sliced gherkin, to garnish
mayonnaise, to serve

1 Cook the potatoes in their skins in boiling salted water until tender. Drain and leave to cool. When they are cool enough to handle, peel them and cut into coarse chunks.

2 Place the potatoes in a large bowl and add the green pepper, gherkin, spring onions and hard-boiled eggs. Toss gently to combine.

3 In a separate bowl, mix the mayonnaise with the mustard and season with salt, black pepper and Tabasco sauce to taste.

4 Toss the dressing into the potato mixture and sprinkle with a pinch or two of cayenne. Serve with mayonnaise and a garnish of sliced gherkin.

CARIBBEAN POTATO SALAD

COLOURFUL VEGETABLES IN A CREAMY SMOOTH DRESSING MAKE THIS PIQUANT SALAD IDEAL TO SERVE ON ITS OWN OR WITH GRILLED OR COLD MEATS.

SERVES SIX

INGREDIENTS
  900g/2lb small waxy or
  salad potatoes
  2 red peppers, seeded and diced
  2 celery sticks, finely chopped
  1 shallot, finely chopped
  2 or 3 spring onions, finely chopped
  1 mild fresh green chilli, seeded and
  finely chopped
  1 garlic clove, crushed
  10ml/2 tsp finely snipped chives
  10ml/2 tsp finely chopped basil
  15ml/1 tbsp finely chopped parsley
  15ml/1 tbsp single cream
  30ml/2 tbsp salad cream
  15ml/1 tbsp mayonnaise
  5ml/1 tsp Dijon mustard
  7.5ml/½ tbsp sugar
  snipped chives, to garnish
  chopped red chilli, to garnish

1 Cook the potatoes in a large saucepan of boiling water until tender but still firm. Drain and leave to one side. When cool enough to handle, cut into 2.5cm/1in cubes and place in a large salad bowl.

2 Add all the vegetables to the potatoes in the salad bowl, together with the chilli, garlic and all the chopped herbs.

3 Mix together the cream, salad cream, mayonnaise, mustard and sugar in a small bowl. Stir well until the mixture is thoroughly combined and forms a smooth dressing.

4 Pour the dressing over the potato mixture and stir gently to coat evenly. Serve garnished with the snipped chives, and chopped red chilli.

WARM POTATO SALAD WITH HERB DRESSING

TOSS THE POTATOES IN THE DRESSING AS SOON AS POSSIBLE, SO THE FLAVOURS ARE FULLY ABSORBED.
USE THE BEST OLIVE OIL FOR AN AUTHENTIC MEDITERRANEAN TASTE.

SERVES SIX

INGREDIENTS
   1kg/2¼lb waxy or salad potatoes
   90ml/6 tbsp extra virgin olive oil
   juice of 1 lemon
   1 garlic clove, very finely chopped
   30ml/2 tbsp chopped fresh herbs
      such as parsley, basil or thyme
   salt and ground black pepper
   basil leaves, to garnish

1 Cook the potatoes in their skins in boiling salted water, or steam them until tender.

2 Meanwhile make the dressing. Mix together the olive oil, lemon juice, garlic, herbs and season the mixture thoroughly.

3 Drain the potatoes and leave to cool slightly. When they are cool enough to handle, peel them. Cut the potatoes into chunks and place in a large bowl.

4 Pour the dressing over the potatoes while they are still warm and mix well. Serve at once, garnished with basil leaves and black pepper.

WARM HAZELNUT AND PISTACHIO SALAD

TWO KINDS OF CRUNCHY NUTS TURN ORDINARY POTATO SALAD INTO A REALLY SPECIAL
ACCOMPANIMENT. IT WOULD BE LOVELY WITH COLD SLICED ROAST BEEF, TONGUE OR HAM, BUT YOU
CAN SERVE IT ON ITS OWN AS A HEALTHY SNACK.

SERVES FOUR

INGREDIENTS
   900g/2lb small new or salad potatoes
   30ml/2 tbsp hazelnut or walnut oil
   60ml/4 tbsp sunflower oil
   juice of 1 lemon
   25g/1oz/¼ cup hazelnuts
   15 pistachio nuts
   salt and ground black pepper
   flat leaf parsley sprig, to garnish

VARIATION
Use chopped walnuts in place of the hazelnuts. Buy the broken pieces of nut, which are less expensive than walnut halves, but chop them smaller before adding to the salad.

1 Cook the potatoes in their skins in boiling salted water for about 10–15 minutes until tender.

2 Drain the potatoes well and leave to cool slightly.

3 Meanwhile mix together the hazelnut or walnut oil with the sunflower oil and lemon juice. Season well.

4 Using a sharp knife, roughly chop the nuts.

5 Put the cooled potatoes into a large bowl and pour the dressing over. Toss to combine.

6 Sprinkle the salad with the chopped nuts. Serve immediately, garnished with flat leaf parsley.

CURRIED POTATO SALAD WITH MANGO DRESSING

THIS SWEET AND SPICY SALAD IS A WONDERFUL ACCOMPANIMENT TO ROASTED MEATS.

SERVES FOUR TO SIX

INGREDIENTS
15ml/1 tbsp olive oil
1 onion, sliced into rings
1 garlic clove, crushed
5ml/1 tsp ground cumin
5ml/1 tsp ground coriander
1 mango, peeled, stoned and diced
30ml/2 tbsp demerara sugar
30ml/2 tbsp lime juice
900g/2lb new potatoes, cut in half
  and boiled
15ml/1 tbsp sesame seeds
salt and ground black pepper
deep fried coriander leaves,
  to garnish

1 Heat the oil in a frying pan and fry the onion and garlic over a low heat for 10 minutes until they start to brown.

2 Stir in the cumin and coriander and fry for a few seconds. Stir in the mango and sugar and fry for 5 minutes, until soft. Remove the pan from the heat and squeeze in the lime juice. Season.

3 Place the potatoes in a large bowl and spoon the mango dressing over. Sprinkle with sesame seeds and serve whilst the dressing is still warm. Garnish with the coriander leaves.

POTATO SALAD WITH CAPERS AND BLACK OLIVES

A DISH FROM SOUTHERN ITALY, THE COMBINATION OF OLIVES, CAPERS AND ANCHOVIES IS PERFECT.

SERVES FOUR TO SIX

INGREDIENTS
900g/2lb large white potatoes
50ml/2fl oz/¼ cup white wine vinegar
75ml/5 tbsp olive oil
30ml/2 tbsp chopped flat leaf parsley
30ml/2 tbsp capers, finely chopped
50g/2oz/½ cup pitted black olives,
  chopped in half
3 garlic cloves, finely chopped
50g/2oz marinated anchovies
  (unsalted)
salt and ground black pepper

VARIATION
If you want to serve this dish to vegetarians, simply omit the anchovies, it tastes delicious even without them.

1 Boil the potatoes in their skins in a large pan for 20 minutes or until just tender. Remove from the pan using a slotted spoon and place them in a separate bowl.

2 When the potatoes are cool enough to handle, peel off the skins.

3 Cut the peeled potatoes into even chunks and place in a large, flat earthenware dish.

4 Mix together the vinegar and oil, season to taste and add the parsley, capers, olives and garlic. Toss carefully to combine and then pour over the potato chunks.

5 Lay the anchovies on top of the salad. Cover with a cloth and leave the salad to settle for 30 minutes or so before serving to allow the flavours to penetrate.

BAKED SWEET POTATO SALAD

THIS SALAD HAS A TRULY TROPICAL TASTE AND IS IDEAL SERVED WITH ASIAN OR CARIBBEAN DISHES.

SERVES FOUR TO SIX

INGREDIENTS
    1kg/2¼lb sweet potatoes
For the dressing
    45ml/3 tbsp chopped fresh coriander
    juice of 1 lime
    150ml/¼ pint/⅔ cup natural yogurt
For the salad
    1 red pepper, seeded and
        finely diced
    3 celery sticks, finely diced
    ¼ red skinned onion, finely chopped
    1 red chilli, finely chopped
    salt and ground black pepper
    coriander leaves, to garnish

1 Preheat the oven to 200°C/400°F/ Gas 6. Wash and pierce the potatoes all over and bake in the oven for 40 minutes or until tender.

2 Meanwhile, mix the dressing ingredients together in a bowl and season to taste. Chill while you prepare the remaining ingredients.

3 In a large bowl mix the red pepper, celery, onion and chilli together.

4 Remove the potatoes from the oven and when cool enough to handle, peel them. Cut the potatoes into cubes and add them to the bowl. Drizzle the dressing over and toss carefully. Season again to taste and serve, garnished with fresh coriander.

MARINATED BEEF AND POTATO SALAD

THIS DISH NEEDS TO MARINATE OVERNIGHT, BUT ONCE YOU HAVE DONE THAT IT IS VERY QUICK TO ASSEMBLE AND MAKES A SUBSTANTIAL MAIN MEAL.

SERVES SIX

INGREDIENTS
  900g/2lb sirloin steak
  3 large white potatoes
  ½ red pepper, seeded and diced
  ½ green pepper, seeded and diced
  1 small red skinned onion,
    finely chopped
  2 garlic cloves, crushed
  4 spring onions, diagonally sliced
  1 small cos lettuce, leaves torn
  salt and ground black pepper
  olive oil, to serve
  Parmesan cheese shavings, to serve
For the marinade
  120ml/4fl oz/½ cup olive oil
  120ml/4fl oz/½ cup red wine vinegar
  90ml/6 tbsp soy sauce

1 Place the beef in a large, non-metallic container. Mix together the marinade ingredients. Season with pepper and pour over the meat.

2 Cover and leave to marinate for several hours, or overnight.

3 To prepare the salad, drain the marinade from the meat and pat the joint dry. Preheat the frying pan, cut the meat carefully into thin slices and fry for a few minutes until just cooked on each side, but still slightly pink. Set aside to cool.

4 Using a melon baller, scoop out rounds from each potato. Boil in lightly salted water for 5 minutes or until just tender.

5 Drain and transfer to a bowl, and add the remaining ingredients. Transfer to a plate with the beef. Drizzle with a little extra olive oil and serve with Parmesan.

NEW POTATO AND QUAIL'S EGG SALAD

FRESHLY COOKED EGGS AND TENDER POTATOES MIX PERFECTLY WITH THE FLAVOUR OF CELERY SALT AND THE PEPPERY TASTING ROCKET LEAVES.

SERVES SIX

INGREDIENTS
900g/2lb new potatoes
50g/2oz/4 tbsp butter
15ml/1 tbsp snipped chives
a pinch of celery salt
a pinch of paprika
12 quail's eggs
a few rocket leaves
salt and ground black pepper
snipped chives, to garnish

COOK'S TIP
You can buy bags of rocket, on its own, or mixed with other leaves, in many supermarkets. It is also easy to grow from seed and makes a worthwhile addition to a herb patch.

1 Boil the potatoes in a large saucepan of salted water for 20 minutes or until tender. Meanwhile, beat the butter and chives together with the celery salt and the paprika.

2 Whilst the potatoes are cooking, boil the eggs for 3 minutes, drain and plunge into cold water. Peel the eggs under running water.

3 Arrange the rocket leaves on plates and divide the eggs between. Drain the potatoes and add the seasoned butter. Toss well to melt the butter and spoon the potatoes on to the plates. Garnish the salad with a few more chives.

BEETROOT AND POTATO SALAD

A BRIGHTLY COLOURED SALAD WITH A LOVELY TEXTURE. THE SWEETNESS OF THE BEETROOT CONTRASTS PERFECTLY WITH THE TANGY DRESSING.

SERVES FOUR

INGREDIENTS
4 medium beetroot
4 potatoes, peeled and diced
1 red-skinned onion, finely chopped
150ml/¼ pint/⅔ cup low-fat yogurt
10ml/2 tsp cider vinegar
2 small sweet and sour cucumbers, finely chopped
10ml/2 tsp creamed horseradish
salt and ground black pepper
parsley sprigs, to garnish

COOK'S TIP
To save yourself time and energy, buy ready cooked and peeled beetroot. They are readily available in most supermarkets.

1 Boil the beetroot in a large saucepan, in plenty of water for 40 minutes or until tender.

2 Meanwhile, boil the potatoes in a separate saucepan for 20 minutes until just tender.

3 When the beetroot are cooked, rinse and pull the skins off, chop into rough pieces and place in a bowl. Drain the potatoes and add to the bowl with the onions. Mix the yogurt, vinegar, cucumbers and horseradish. Reserve a little for a garnish and pour the remainder over the salad. Toss and serve with parsley sprigs and dressing.

ITALIAN SALAD

A COMBINATION OF ANTIPASTO INGREDIENTS AND POTATOES MAKES THIS A VERY SUBSTANTIAL DISH.

SERVES SIX

INGREDIENTS

    1 aubergine, sliced
    75ml/5 tbsp olive oil
    2 garlic cloves, cut into slivers
    4 sun-dried tomatoes in oil, halved
    2 red peppers, halved, seeded and
      cut into large chunks
    2 large baking potatoes, cut
      into wedges
    10ml/2 tsp mixed dried Italian herbs
    30–45ml/2–3 tbsp balsamic vinegar
    salt and ground black pepper

1 Preheat the oven to 200°C/400°F/
Gas 6. Place the aubergines in a
medium roasting tin with the olive oil,
garlic and sun-dried tomatoes. Lay the
pepper chunks over the aubergines.

2 Lay the potato wedges on top of the
other ingredients in the roasting tin.
Scatter the herbs over and season with
salt and black pepper. Cover the tin
with foil and bake in the oven for
45 minutes.

3 Remove from the oven and turn the
vegetables over. Then return to the oven
and cook uncovered for 30 minutes.
Remove the vegetables with a slotted
spoon. Add the vinegar and seasoning
to the pan, whisk and pour over the
vegetables. Garnish with salt and
black pepper.

PINK FIR APPLE POTATO SALAD

A RICH MUSTARD SAUCE GIVES THE POTATOES ADDED FLAVOUR AND COLOUR.

SERVES FOUR TO SIX

INGREDIENTS
5 eggs
30–45ml/2–3 tbsp Dijon mustard
200g/7oz jar mayonnaise
3 celery sticks, finely chopped
115g/4oz bacon lardons
900g/2lb Pink Fir Apple potatoes
30ml/2 tbsp chopped flat leaf parsley
salt and ground black pepper

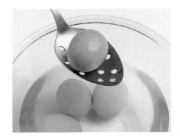

1 Place the eggs carefully into a saucepan of water and bring to the boil. Simmer for 5–8 minutes, drain and plunge the eggs straight into a bowl containing cold water.

2 Peel the eggs and mash three of them in a large bowl with a fork. Stir in the mustard, mayonnaise, celery and seasoning. Thin down with a little water if you wish. Set aside.

3 Dry fry the bacon until crisp and toss half of it into the mayonnaise mixture. Reserve the remainder.

4 Boil the potatoes for 20 minutes until tender. Drain and leave to cool. Toss into the mayonnaise mixture and spoon into a serving platter. Slice the remaining eggs and scatter over the salad with the reserved bacon pieces. Scatter the parsley over the top and serve.

Side Dishes

CLASSIC POTATO SIDE DISHES HAVE
LONG BEEN ESSENTIAL PARTNERS TO
NUMEROUS MAIN COURSES. FOR A
CHANGE, TRY SOMETHING A
LITTLE DIFFERENT TO SERVE
ALONGSIDE A SIMPLE ROAST, SUCH
AS BOULANGÈRE POTATOES OR
COLOURFUL CANDIED SWEET
POTATOES. AND ADD A GARLIC
TWIST TO A STEAMING PLATE
OF MASH — PERFECT ON ITS
OWN OR TO GO WITH A
MAIN COURSE.

MARQUIS POTATOES

A VARIATION ON THE DUCHESSE MIXTURE, FINISHED WITH A DELICIOUSLY TANGY TOMATO MIXTURE SET IN THE CENTRE OF THE POTATO NEST.

SERVES SIX

INGREDIENTS
   900g/2 lb floury potatoes
   450g/1lb ripe tomatoes
   15ml/1tbsp olive oil
   2 shallots, finely chopped
   25g/1oz/2 tbsp butter
   3 egg yolks
   60ml/4 tbsp milk
   chopped fresh parsley, to garnish
   sea salt and ground black pepper

1 Peel and cut the potatoes into small chunks, boil in lightly salted water for 20 minutes or until very tender. Meanwhile, blanch the tomatoes in boiling water and then plunge into a bowl of cold water. Peel the skins and then scoop the seeds out. Chop the tomato flesh.

2 Heat the olive oil in a large frying pan and fry the shallots for 2 minutes stirring continuously. Add the chopped tomatoes to the pan and fry for a further 10 minutes until the moisture has evaporated. Set aside.

3 Drain the potatoes through a colander and return to the pan and allow the steam to dry off. Cool slightly and mash well with the butter and 2 of the egg yolks and the milk. Season with salt and ground black pepper.

4 Grease a baking sheet. Spoon the potato into a piping bag fitted with a medium star nozzle. Pipe six oval nests onto the baking sheet. Beat the remaining egg with a little water and carefully brush over the potato. Grill for 5 minutes or until golden.

5 Spoon the tomato mixture inside the nests and top with a little parsley. Serve them immediately.

BERRICHONNE POTATOES

A POTATO DISH WITH A DIFFERENCE. THE TOP OF THE POTATOES WILL BE CRISPY WITH A SOFTLY COOKED BASE IN THE STOCK, ONIONS AND BACON.

SERVES FOUR

INGREDIENTS

900g/2 lb maincrop potatoes
25g/1oz/2 tbsp butter
1 onion, finely chopped
115g/4oz unsmoked streaky bacon,
   rinds removed
350ml/12fl oz /1½ cups
   vegetable stock
chopped parsley, to garnish
sea salt and ground black pepper

1 Preheat the oven to 200°C/400°F/Gas 6. Peel the potatoes and trim them into barrel shapes. Leave the potatoes to stand in a bowl of cold water.

2 Melt the butter in a frying pan. Add the onions, stir and cover with a lid. Cook for 2–3 minutes, until they are soft but not brown.

3 Chop the bacon and add to the onions, cover and cook for 2 minutes.

4 Spoon the onion mixture into the base of a 1.5 litres /2½ pints/6¼ cups rectangular shallow ovenproof dish. Lay the potatoes over the onion mixture and pour the stock over, making sure that it comes halfway up the sides of them. Season and cook for 1 hour. Garnish with chopped parsley.

BIARRITZ POTATOES

A COMBINATION OF CLASSIC MASHED POTATOES WITH FINELY DICED HAM AND PEPPERS MIXED IN. THIS DISH IS GREAT SERVED WITH ROASTED CHICKEN.

SERVES FOUR

INGREDIENTS
900g/2lb floury potatoes
50g/2oz/4 tbsp butter
90ml/6 tbsp milk
50g/2oz cooked ham, finely diced
1 red pepper, deseeded and
  finely diced
15ml/1tbsp chopped fresh parsley
sea salt and ground black pepper

1 Peel and cut the potatoes into chunks. Boil in lightly salted water for 20 minutes or until very tender.

2 Drain and return the potatoes to the pan and allow the steam to dry off over a low heat.

3 Either mash or pass the potatoes through a potato ricer. Add the butter and milk and stir in the cooked ham, peppers and parsley. Season and serve.

LYONNAISE POTATOES

TWO SIMPLE INGREDIENTS ARE PREPARED SEPARATELY AND THEN TOSSED TOGETHER TO CREATE THE PERFECT COMBINATION. THESE POTATOES GO VERY WELL WITH A SIMPLE MEAT DISH, SUCH AS STEAK OR PORK CHOPS. SERVE WITH A BOWL OF FRENCH BEANS, TOSSED IN BUTTER.

SERVES SIX

INGREDIENTS
900g/2lb floury potatoes
vegetable oil for shallow frying
25g/1oz/2 tbsp butter
15ml/1 tbsp olive oil
2 medium onions, sliced into rings
sea salt
15ml/1 tbsp chopped fresh parsley

VARIATION
For a more substantial version of this dish, ham or bacon can be added. Use about 50g/2oz chopped roast ham or bacon and fry with the onions until cooked through.

1 Scrub the potatoes clean and cook in a large saucepan with plenty of boiling water for 10 minutes.

2 Drain the potatoes through a colander and leave to cool slightly. When the potatoes are cool enough to handle, peel and finely slice them.

3 Heat the vegetable oil and shallow fry the potatoes in two batches for about 10 minutes until crisp, turning occasionally.

4 Meanwhile, melt the butter with the oil in a frying pan and fry the onions for 10 minutes until golden. Drain on kitchen paper.

5 Remove the potatoes with a slotted spoon and drain on kitchen paper. Toss with sea salt and carefully mix with the onions. Sprinkle with the parsley.

BYRON POTATOES

A MEAL IN ITSELF, THIS DISH IS BASED ON BAKED POTATOES WITH A RICH CREAMY CHEESE FILLING.

INGREDIENTS
   3 baking potatoes
   115g/4oz/1 cup mature Cheddar
   cheese, grated
   90ml/6 tbsp single cream
   sea salt and ground black pepper

COOK'S TIP
You can speed up this recipe by starting the potatoes off in the microwave. Prick the scrubbed potatoes well and place in a covered microwave dish. Cook on high until starting to soften – test after two minutes, then every minute. Place in the oven to crisp the skins and finish cooking for about 45 minutes.

1 Preheat the oven to 200°C/400°F/ Gas 6. Scrub the potatoes and pat dry. Prick each one with a fork and cook directly on the middle shelf for 1 hour 20 minutes.

2 Remove the potatoes from the oven and halve. Place the halves on a baking sheet and make shallow dips in the centre of each potato, raising the potato up at the edges.

3 Mix the cheese and cream together and divide between the potatoes.

4 Grill for 5 minutes until the cheese has melted and started to bubble. Serve hot, sprinkled with sea salt and black pepper.

BOULANGÈRE POTATOES

LAYERS OF POTATO AND ONIONS COOKED IN BUTTER AND STOCK. A DELICIOUS SAVOURY POTATO DISH THAT MAKES A GREAT ACCOMPANIMENT TO BOTH MEAT AND FISH.

INGREDIENTS
   butter for greasing
   450g/1lb maincrop potatoes, very
   finely sliced
   2 onions, finely sliced into rings
   2 garlic cloves, crushed
   50g/2oz/4 tbsp butter, diced
   300ml/½ pint/1¼ cups
   vegetable stock
   chopped parsley
   sea salt and ground black pepper

VARIATION
If you want to make this dish more substantial, add some grated cheese, sprinkled over the top just before you bake it.

1 Preheat the oven to 180°C/350°F/ Gas 4. Grease the base and sides of a 1.5 litre/2½ pint/6¼ cup ovenproof dish.

2 Line the dish with some of the sliced potatoes. Scatter some onions and garlic on top. Layer up the remaining potatoes and onions, seasoning between each layer.

3 Push the vegetables down into the dish and dot the top with the butter. Pour the stock over and bake in the oven for 1½ hours covering with foil after 1 hour if the top starts to over brown. Serve with parsley and plenty of salt and pepper sprinkled over the top.

POTATO LATKES

LATKES ARE TRADITIONAL JEWISH POTATO PANCAKES, FRIED UNTIL GOLDEN AND CRISP AND SERVED WITH HOT SALT BEEF OR APPLE SAUCE AND SOURED CREAM.

SERVES FOUR

INGREDIENTS
   2 medium floury potatoes
   1 onion
   1 large egg, beaten
   30ml/2 tbsp medium-ground
      matzo meal
   vegetable oil, for frying
   salt and ground black pepper

1 Coarsely grate the potatoes and the onion. Put them in a large colander but don't rinse them. Press them down, squeezing out as much of the thick starchy liquid as possible. Transfer the potato mixture to a bowl.

2 Immediately stir in the beaten egg. Add the matzo meal, stirring gently to mix. Season with salt and plenty of pepper.

VARIATION
Try using equal quantities of potatoes and Jerusalem artichokes for a really distinct flavour.

3 Heat a 1cm/½in layer of oil in a heavy-based frying pan for a few minutes (test it by throwing in a small piece of bread – it should sizzle). Take a spoonful of the potato mixture and lower it carefully into the oil. Continue adding spoonfuls, leaving space between each one.

4 Flatten the pancakes slightly with the back of a spoon. Fry for a few minutes until the latkes are golden brown on the underside, carefully turn them over and continue frying until golden brown.

5 Drain the latkes on kitchen paper, then transfer to an ovenproof serving dish and keep warm in a low oven while frying the remainder. Serve hot.

SWISS SOUFFLÉ POTATOES

A FABULOUS COMBINATION OF RICH AND SATISFYING INGREDIENTS — CHEESE, EGGS, CREAM, BUTTER AND POTATOES. THIS IS PERFECT FOR COLD-WEATHER EATING.

SERVES FOUR

INGREDIENTS

4 floury baking potatoes
115g/4oz/1 cup Gruyère
  cheese, grated
115g/4oz/8 tbsp herb-flavoured butter
60ml/4 tbsp double cream
2 eggs, separated
salt and ground black pepper

1 Preheat the oven to 220°C/425°F/ Gas 7. Prick the potatoes all over with a fork. Bake for 1–1½ hours until tender. Remove them from the oven and reduce the temperature to 180°C/350°F/Gas 4.

2 Cut each potato in half and scoop out the flesh into a bowl. Return the potato shells to the oven to crisp them up while making the filling.

3 Mash the potato flesh using a fork, then add the Gruyère, herb-flavoured butter, cream, egg yolks and seasoning. Beat well until smooth.

4 Whisk the egg whites in a separate bowl until they hold stiff but not dry peaks, then carefully fold into the potato mixture.

5 Pile the mixture back into the potato shells and place on a baking sheet. Bake in the oven for 20–25 minutes until risen and golden brown.

6 Serve the potatoes hot, sprinkled with fresh, snipped chives, if wished, and a bowl of mayonnaise to the side.

YORKSHIRE POTATO PUFFS

MINI YORKSHIRE PUDDINGS WITH A SOFT CENTRE OF HERBY POTATO MASH WILL BE DELICIOUS WITH THE SUNDAY ROAST, OR SERVE THEM FOR A WEEKDAY SUPPER WITH THE FAMILY'S FAVOURITE SAUSAGES.

MAKES SIX

INGREDIENTS
    275g/10oz floury potatoes
    creamy milk and butter for mashing
    5ml/1 tsp chopped fresh parsley
    5ml/1 tsp chopped fresh tarragon
    75g/3oz/⅔ cup plain flour
    1 egg
    120ml/4fl oz/½ cup milk
    vegetable oil or sunflower fat,
      for baking
    salt and ground black pepper

1 Cook the potatoes in a large saucepan of boiling water until tender, then mash with a little creamy milk and butter.

2 Stir in the chopped parsley and tarragon and season well to taste. Preheat the oven to 200°C/400°F/Gas 6.

3 Process the flour, egg, milk and a little salt in a food processor fitted with the metal blade or a blender to make a smooth batter.

4 Place about 2.5ml/½ tsp of oil or a small knob of sunflower fat in each of six ramekin dishes and place in the oven on a baking tray for 2–3 minutes until the oil or fat is very hot.

5 Working quickly, pour a small amount of batter (about 20ml/4 tsp) into each ramekin dish. Add a heaped tablespoon of the mashed potatoes and then pour an equal amount of the remaining batter in each dish. Bake for 15–20 minutes until the puddings are puffy and golden brown.

6 Using a palette knife, carefully ease the puddings out of the ramekin dishes and arrange on a large warm serving dish. Serve at once.

COOK'S TIP
Cook and mash the potatoes the day before to save time making a quick supper dish, or to prepare for a dinner party in advance.

GARLICKY ROASTIES

POTATOES ROASTED IN THEIR SKINS RETAIN A DEEP, EARTHY TASTE (AND, AS A BONUS, ABSORB LESS FAT TOO) WHILE THE GARLIC MELLOWS ON COOKING TO GIVE A PUNGENT BUT NOT OVERLY-STRONG TASTE TO SERVE ALONGSIDE OR SQUEEZED OVER AS A GARNISH.

SERVES FOUR

INGREDIENTS
    1kg/2¼lb small floury potatoes
    60–75ml/4–5 tbsp sunflower oil
    10ml/2 tsp walnut oil
    2 whole garlic bulbs, unpeeled
    salt

COOK'S TIP
If anyone really does not want to try the garlic paste, you can save the cloves to squeeze into your next pot of soup or mashed potato.

1 Preheat the oven to 240°C/475°F/ Gas 9. Place the potatoes in a pan of cold water and bring to the boil. Drain.

2 Combine the oils in a roasting tin and place in the oven to get really hot. Add the potatoes and garlic and coat in oil.

3 Sprinkle with salt and roast for 10 minutes. Reduce the heat to 200°C/400°F/Gas 6. Continue roasting, basting occasionally, for 30–40 minutes.

4 Serve each portion with several cloves of garlic.

POTATOES, PEPPERS AND SHALLOTS ROASTED WITH ROSEMARY

THESE POTATOES SOAK UP BOTH THE TASTE AND WONDERFUL AROMAS OF THE SHALLOTS AND ROSEMARY — JUST WAIT TILL YOU OPEN THE OVEN DOOR.

SERVES FOUR

INGREDIENTS
    500g/1¼lb waxy potatoes
    12 shallots
    2 sweet yellow peppers
    olive oil
    2 rosemary sprigs
    salt and ground black pepper
    crushed peppercorns, to garnish

1 Preheat the oven to 200°C/400°F/ Gas 6. Par-boil the potatoes in their skins in boiling salted water for 5 minutes. Drain and when they are cool, peel them and halve lengthways.

COOK'S TIP
Liven up a simple dish of roast or grilled lamb or chicken with these delicious and easy potatoes.

2 Peel the shallots, allowing them to fall into their natural segments. Cut each sweet pepper lengthways into eight strips, discarding seeds and pith.

3 Oil a shallow ovenproof dish thoroughly with olive oil. Arrange the potatoes and peppers in alternating rows and stud with the shallots.

4 Cut the rosemary sprigs into 5cm/2in lengths and tuck among the vegetables. Season the vegetables generously with salt and pepper, add the olive oil and roast, uncovered, for 30–40 minutes until all the vegetables are tender. Turn the vegetables occasionally to cook and brown evenly. Serve hot or at room temperature, with crushed peppercorns.

GLAZED SWEET POTATOES WITH BACON

SMOKY BACON IS THE PERFECT ADDITION TO THESE MELT-IN-THE-MOUTH SUGAR-TOPPED POTATOES.
THEY TASTE GREAT AS A CHANGE FROM ROAST POTATOES, WITH ROAST DUCK OR CHICKEN.

SERVES FOUR TO SIX

INGREDIENTS
  butter, for greasing
  900g/2lb sweet potatoes
  115g/4oz/½ cup soft light
    brown sugar
  30ml/2 tbsp lemon juice
  45ml/3 tbsp butter
  4 strips smoked lean bacon, cut
    into matchsticks
  salt and ground black pepper
  1 flat leaf parsley sprig, to garnish

1 Preheat the oven to 190°C/375°F/ Gas 5 and lightly butter a shallow ovenproof dish. Cut each unpeeled sweet potato crosswise into three and cook in boiling water, covered, for about 25 minutes until just tender.

2 Drain and leave to cool. When cool enough to handle, peel and slice thickly. Arrange in a single layer, overlapping the slices, in the prepared dish.

5 The potatoes are ready once they are tender, test them with a knife to make sure. Remove from the oven once they are cooked.

6 Preheat the grill to a high heat. Sprinkle the potatoes with parsley. Place the pan under the grill for 2–3 minutes until the potatoes are browned and the bacon is crispy. Serve hot.

3 Sprinkle over the sugar and lemon juice and dot with butter.

4 Top with the bacon and season well. Bake uncovered for 35–40 minutes, basting once or twice.

HERBY POTATO BAKE

WONDERFULLY CREAMY POTATOES WELL FLAVOURED WITH LOTS OF FRESH HERBS AND SPRINKLED WITH CHEESE TO MAKE A GOLDEN, CRUNCHY TOPPING.

SERVES FOUR

INGREDIENTS
butter, for greasing
675g/1½lb waxy potatoes
25g/1oz/2 tbsp butter
1 onion, finely chopped
1 garlic clove, crushed
2 eggs
300ml/½ pint/1¼ cups crème fraîche
   or double cream
115g/4oz/1 cup Gruyère, grated
60ml/4 tbsp chopped mixed fresh
   herbs, such as chervil, thyme,
   chives and parsley
freshly grated nutmeg
salt and ground black pepper

1 Place a baking sheet in the oven and preheat to 190°C/375°F/Gas 5. Butter an ovenproof dish.

2 Peel the potatoes and cut them into matchsticks. Set aside while you make up the sauce mixture. Start by melting the butter in a pan and fry the onion and garlic until softened. Remove from the heat to cool slightly. In a large bowl, whisk together the eggs, crème fraîche or cream and about half of the grated Gruyère cheese.

3 Stir in the onion mixture, herbs, potatoes, salt, pepper and nutmeg. Spoon the mixture into the prepared dish and sprinkle over the remaining cheese. Bake on the hot baking sheet for 50 minutes to 1 hour until the top is golden brown. Serve immediately, straight from the dish, as this will ensure that the potatoes stay really hot.

OVEN CHIP ROASTIES

THIS EASY ALTERNATIVE TO FRIED CHIPS TASTES JUST AS GOOD AND IS MUCH EASIER TO COOK.

SERVES FOUR TO SIX

INGREDIENTS
150ml/¼ pint/⅔ cup olive oil
4 medium to large baking potatoes
5ml/1 tsp mixed dried herbs
   (optional)
sea salt flakes
mayonnaise, to serve

VARIATION
Sweet potatoes also make fine oven chips. Prepare and roast in the same way as above, although you may find they do not take as long to cook.

COOK'S TIP
Oven chip roasties make great mid-week suppers served with fried eggs, mushrooms and tomatoes.

1 Preheat the oven to the highest temperature, generally 240°C/475°F/Gas 9. Lightly oil a large shallow roasting tin and place it in the oven to get really hot while you prepare the potatoes.

2 Cut the potatoes in half lengthwise, then into long thin wedges, or thicker ones if you prefer. Brush each side lightly with oil.

3 When the oven is really hot, remove the pan carefully and scatter the potato wedges over it, spreading them out in a single layer over the hot oil.

4 Sprinkle the potato wedges with the herbs and salt and roast for about 20 minutes, or longer if they are thicker, until they are golden brown, crisp and lightly puffy. Remove from the oven and serve with a dollop of mayonnaise.

GARLIC MASHED POTATOES

THESE CREAMY MASHED POTATOES ARE DELICIOUS WITH ALL KINDS OF ROAST OR SAUTÉED MEATS AS WELL AS VEGETARIAN MAIN DISHES AND ALTHOUGH IT SEEMS LIKE A LOT OF GARLIC, THE FLAVOUR TURNS SWEET AND SUBTLE WHEN COOKED IN THIS WAY.

SERVES SIX TO EIGHT

INGREDIENTS
    3 whole garlic bulbs, separated into
      cloves, unpeeled
    115g/4oz/8 tbsp unsalted butter
    1.5kg/3lb baking potatoes, quartered
    120–175ml/4–6fl oz/½–¾ cup milk
    salt and ground white pepper

COOK'S TIP
This recipe makes a very light, creamy purée. Use less milk to achieve a firmer purée, more for a softer purée. Be sure the milk is almost boiling or it will cool the potato mixture. Keep the purée warm in a bowl over simmering water.

1 Bring a small saucepan of water to the boil over a high heat. Add two thirds of the garlic cloves and boil for 2 minutes. Drain the pan and then peel the garlic cloves.

2 Place the remaining garlic cloves in a roasting tin and bake in a preheated oven at 200°C/400°F/Gas 6 for 30–40 minutes.

3 In a heavy-based frying pan, melt 50g/2oz/4 tbsp of the butter over a low heat. Add the blanched garlic cloves, then cover and cook gently for 20–25 minutes until very tender and just golden, shaking the pan and stirring occasionally. Do not allow the garlic to scorch or brown.

4 Remove the pan from the heat and cool. Spoon the garlic and melted butter into a blender or a food processor fitted with the metal blade and process until smooth. Tip into a bowl, press clear film on to the surface to prevent a skin forming and set aside.

5 Cook the potatoes in boiling salted water until tender, then drain and pass through a food mill or press through a sieve back into the saucepan. Return the pan to a medium heat and, using a wooden spoon, stir the potatoes for 1–2 minutes to dry out completely. Remove the pan from the heat.

6 Warm the milk over a medium-high heat until bubbles form around the edge. Gradually beat the milk, remaining butter and garlic purée into the potatoes. Season with salt, if needed, and white pepper, and serve hot, with the roasted garlic cloves.

CHAMP

SIMPLE BUT UNBELIEVABLY TASTY, THIS TRADITIONAL IRISH WAY WITH MASHED POTATOES MAKES AN EXCELLENT COMPANION FOR A HEARTY STEW OF LAMB OR BEEF.

SERVES FOUR

INGREDIENTS

900g/2lb floury potatoes
1 small bunch spring onions,
    finely chopped
150ml/¼ pint/⅔ cup milk
50g/2oz/4 tbsp butter
salt and ground black pepper

COOK'S TIP
If you make too much mashed potato, don't worry. It keeps well in the fridge and simply needs re-heating.

1 Cut the potatoes up into large chunks. Place in a large pan and cook in boiling water for 20 minutes until tender.

2 Meanwhile put the spring onions into a saucepan with the milk. Bring to the boil then reduce the heat and simmer until the spring onions are just tender.

3 Drain the potatoes well and leave to cool. When they are cool enough to handle, peel and return to the saucepan. Put the pan on the heat and, using a wooden spoon, stir for 1 minute until the moisture has evaporated. Remove the pan from the heat.

4 Mash the potatoes with the milk and spring onions and season. Serve hot with a pool of melted butter in each portion.

PERFECT CREAMED POTATOES

REAL CREAMED POTATOES ARE A SIMPLE LUXURY YOU WILL FIND IN ANY FASHIONABLE RESTAURANT TODAY BUT ARE SO EASY TO MAKE AT HOME AS WELL.

SERVES FOUR

INGREDIENTS
   900g/2lb firm but not waxy
      potatoes, diced
   45ml/3 tbsp extra virgin olive oil
   about 150ml/¼ pint/⅔ cup hot milk
   freshly grated nutmeg
   a few fresh basil leaves or parsley
      sprigs, chopped
   salt and ground black pepper
   basil leaves, to garnish
   fried bacon, to serve

COOK'S TIP
Choosing the right potato makes all the difference to creamed ones. A waxy variety won't be light and fluffy, and a potato which breaks down too quickly on boiling will become a slurry.

1 Cook the potatoes in boiling water until just tender but not too mushy. Drain very well. Press the potatoes through a special potato "ricer" (rather like a large garlic press) or mash them well with a potato masher. Do not use a food processor as it can give the potatoes a gluey consistency.

2 Beat in olive oil and enough hot milk to make a smooth, thick purée.

3 Flavour to taste with the nutmeg and seasoning, then stir in the chopped fresh herbs. Spoon into a warm serving dish and serve at once, garnished with basil leaves and fried bacon.

POTATOES with RED CHILLIES

IF YOU LIKE CHILLIES, YOU'LL LOVE THESE POTATOES! IF YOU'RE NOT A FAN OF FIERY FLAVOURS, THEN SIMPLY LEAVE OUT ALL THE CHILLI SEEDS AND USE THE FLESH BY ITSELF.

SERVES FOUR

INGREDIENTS
   12–14 small new or salad
      potatoes, halved
   30ml/2 tbsp vegetable oil
   2.5ml/½ tsp crushed dried
      red chillies
   2.5ml/½ tsp white cumin seeds
   2.5ml/½ tsp fennel seeds
   2.5ml/½ tsp crushed coriander seeds
   5ml/1 tsp salt
   1 onion, sliced
   1–4 fresh red chillies, chopped
   15ml/1 tbsp chopped fresh coriander
   chopped fresh coriander, to garnish

COOK'S TIP
To prepare fresh chillies, slit down one side and scrape out the seeds, unless you want a really hot dish. Finely slice or chop the flesh. Wear rubber gloves if you have very sensitive skin.

1 Cook the potatoes in boiling salted water until tender but still firm. Remove from the heat and drain off the water. Set aside until needed.

2 In a deep frying pan, heat the oil over a medium-high heat, then reduce the heat to medium. Add the crushed chillies, cumin, fennel and coriander seeds and salt and fry, stirring, for 30–40 seconds.

3 Add the sliced onion and fry until golden brown. Then add the potatoes, red chillies and coriander and stir well.

4 Reduce the heat to very low, then cover and cook for 5–7 minutes. Serve the potatoes hot, garnished with more fresh coriander.

STRAW POTATO CAKE

THIS DISH GETS ITS NAME FROM ITS INTERESTING STRAW–LIKE TEXTURE.

SERVES FOUR

INGREDIENTS
  450g/1lb firm baking potatoes
  25ml/1½ tbsp butter, melted
  15ml/1 tbsp vegetable oil
  salt and ground black pepper

1 Peel and grate the potatoes, then toss with melted butter and season.

2 Heat the oil in a large heavy-based frying pan. Add the potato and press down to form an even layer that covers the base of the pan. Cook over a medium heat for 7–10 minutes until the base is well browned.

3 Loosen the cake if it has stuck to the bottom by shaking the pan or running a knife under it.

4 To turn the cake, invert a large baking tray over the frying pan and, holding it tightly against the pan, turn them both over together. Lift off the frying pan, return it to the heat and add a little more oil if it looks dry. Slide the potato cake back into the frying pan, browned side uppermost, and continue cooking until the underside is crisp and golden.

5 Serve the cake hot, cut into individual wedges.

COOK'S TIP
Another nice way to serve this dish is to make several small cakes instead of a large one. They will not take quite so long to cook, so follow the method as for the large cake, but adjust the cooking time accordingly.

SAUTÉED POTATOES

THESE ROSEMARY-SCENTED, CRISP GOLDEN POTATOES ARE A FAVOURITE IN FRENCH HOUSEHOLDS.

SERVES SIX

INGREDIENTS
  1.5kg/3lb firm baking potatoes
  60–90ml/4–6 tbsp oil, bacon
    dripping or clarified butter
  2 rosemary sprigs, leaves chopped
  salt and ground black pepper

1 Peel and cut the potatoes into 2.5cm/1in slices.

2 Place the slices in a bowl of cold water and soak for 10 minutes. Drain, rinse and drain again, then pat dry.

3 In a large heavy-based frying pan, heat 60ml/4 tbsp of the oil, dripping or butter over a medium-high heat until very hot, but not smoking. Add the potatoes and cook for 2 minutes without stirring so that they seal completely and brown on one side.

4 Shake the pan and toss the potatoes to brown on another side and continue to stir and shake the pan until potatoes are evenly browned on all sides. Season with salt and pepper.

5 Add a little more oil, dripping or butter, reduce the heat to medium-low to low, and continue cooking the potatoes for 20–25 minutes until tender when pierced with a knife, stirring and shaking the pan frequently.

6 About 5 minutes before the end of cooking, sprinkle the potatoes with the chopped rosemary. Serve at once.

BUBBLE AND SQUEAK

WHETHER YOU HAVE LEFTOVERS, OR COOK THIS OLD-FASHIONED CLASSIC FROM FRESH, BE SURE TO GIVE IT A REALLY GOOD "SQUEAK" (FRY) IN THE PAN SO IT TURNS A RICH HONEY BROWN AS ALL THE FLAVOURS CARAMELIZE TOGETHER. IT IS KNOWN AS COLCANNON IN IRELAND, WHERE IT IS TURNED IN CHUNKS OR SECTIONS, PRODUCING A CREAMY BROWN AND WHITE CAKE.

SERVES FOUR

INGREDIENTS
   60ml/4 tbsp dripping, bacon fat or
   vegetable oil
   1 onion, finely chopped
   450g/1lb floury potatoes, cooked
   and mashed
   225g/8oz cooked cabbage or Brussels
   sprouts, finely chopped
   salt and ground black pepper

1 Heat 30ml/2 tbsp of the dripping, fat or oil in a heavy-based frying pan. Add the onion and cook, stirring frequently, until softened but not browned.

2 In a large bowl, mix together the potatoes and cooked cabbage or sprouts and season with salt and plenty of pepper to taste.

3 Add the vegetables to the pan with the cooked onions, stir well, then press the vegetable mixture into a large, even cake.

4 Cook over a medium heat for about 15 minutes until the cake is browned underneath.

5 Invert a large plate over the pan, and, holding it tightly against the pan, turn them both over together. Lift off the frying pan, return it to the heat and add the remaining dripping, fat or oil. When hot, slide the cake back into the pan, browned side uppermost.

6 Cook over a medium heat for 10 minutes or until the underside is golden brown. Serve hot, in wedges.

COOK'S TIP
If you don't have leftover cooked cabbage or Brussels sprouts, shred raw cabbage and cook both in boiling salted water until tender. Drain, then chop.

ORANGE CANDIED SWEET POTATOES

A TRUE TASTE OF AMERICA, NO THANKSGIVING OR CHRISTMAS TABLE IS COMPLETE UNLESS SWEET POTATOES ARE ON THE MENU. SERVE WITH EXTRA ORANGE SEGMENTS TO MAKE IT REALLY SPECIAL.

SERVES EIGHT

INGREDIENTS
900g/2 lb sweet potatoes
250ml/8 fl oz/1 cup orange juice
50ml/2fl oz/¼ cup maple syrup
5ml/1 tsp freshly grated ginger
7.5ml/1½ tsp ground cinnamon
6.5ml/1¼ tsp ground cardamom
7.5ml/1½ tsp salt
ground black pepper
ground cinnamon, to garnish
orange segments, to serve

1 Preheat the oven to 180°C/350°F/ Gas 4. Peel and dice the potatoes and then boil in water for 5 minutes.

2 Meanwhile, stir the remaining ingredients together. Spread out onto a non-stick shallow baking tin.

3 Drain the potatoes and scatter over the tray, cook for 1 hour, stirring the potatoes every 15 minutes until the potatoes are tender and they are well coated. Serve as a accompaniment to a main dish, with orange segments and ground cinnamon.

HASH BROWNS

*Crispy golden wedges of potatoes, "hashed" up with a little onion, are a favourite
American breakfast dish, but taste delicious anytime.*

SERVES 4

INGREDIENTS
    60ml/4 tbsp sunflower or olive oil
    450g/1lb cooked potatoes, diced
       or grated
    1 small onion, chopped
    salt and ground black pepper
    chives, to garnish
    tomato sauce, to serve

VARIATION
Turn this side dish into a main meal by
adding other ingredients to the potatoes
in the pan, such as cooked diced meat,
sliced sausages or even corned beef
for a northern English corned beef
hash supper.

1 Heat the oil in a large heavy-based
frying pan until very hot. Add the
potatoes in a single layer. Scatter the
onion on top and season well.

2 Cook on a medium heat, pressing
down on the potatoes with a spoon or
spatula to squash them together.

3 When the potatoes are nicely
browned underneath, turn them over in
sections with a spatula and fry until the
other side is golden brown and lightly
crispy, pressing them down again.

4 Serve hot with a garnish of chives
and tomato sauce alongside.

SPANISH CHILLI POTATOES

*The name of this Spanish tapas dish, "Patatas Bravas", means fiercely hot potatoes,
but luckily tapas are usually only eaten in small quantities!*

SERVES FOUR

INGREDIENTS
    900g/2lb small new or salad potatoes
    60ml/4 tbsp olive oil
    1 onion, finely chopped
    2 garlic cloves, crushed
    15ml/1 tbsp tomato paste
    200g/7oz can chopped tomatoes
    15ml/1 tbsp red wine vinegar
    2–3 small dried red chillies, seeded
       and finely chopped, or 5–10ml/
       1–2 tsp hot chilli powder
    5ml/1 tsp paprika
    salt and ground black pepper
    1 flat leaf parsley sprig, to garnish
    chopped fresh red chillies, to garnish

COOK'S TIP
If you don't like your potatoes to be too
fierce simply reduce the amount of
chilli to taste.

1 Cook the potatoes in their skins in
boiling water for 10–12 minutes until
just tender. Drain well and leave to cool,
then cut in half and reserve.

2 Heat the oil in a large pan and add
the onion and garlic. Fry them gently for
5–6 minutes until just softened. Stir in
the tomato paste, tomatoes, vinegar,
chillies or chilli powder and paprika and
simmer for about 5 minutes.

3 Stir the potatoes into the sauce
mixture until well coated. Cover and
simmer gently for 8–10 minutes until
the potatoes are tender.

4 Season the potatoes well and
transfer to a warmed serving dish.
Serve at once, garnished with a sprig
of flat leaf parsley. To make the dish
even hotter, add a garnish of chopped
fresh red chillies.

ALOO SAAG

TRADITIONAL INDIAN SPICES — MUSTARD SEED, GINGER AND CHILLI — GIVE A REALLY GOOD KICK TO POTATOES AND SPINACH IN THIS DELICIOUS AND AUTHENTIC CURRY.

SERVES FOUR

INGREDIENTS
  450g/1lb spinach
  30ml/2 tbsp vegetable oil
  5ml/1 tsp black mustard seeds
  1 onion, thinly sliced
  2 garlic cloves, crushed
  2.5cm/1in piece root ginger,
    finely chopped
  675g/1½lb firm potatoes, cut into
    2.5cm/1in chunks
  5ml/1 tsp chilli powder
  5ml/1 tsp salt
  120ml/4fl oz/½ cup water

COOK'S TIPS
To make certain that the spinach is dry, put it in a clean tea towel, roll up tightly and squeeze gently to remove any excess liquid. Choose a firm waxy variety of potato or a salad potato so the pieces do not break up during cooking.

1 Blanch the spinach in boiling water for 3–4 minutes.

2 Drain the spinach thoroughly and leave to cool. When it is cool enough to handle, use your hands to squeeze out any remaining liquid.

3 Heat the oil in a large saucepan and fry the mustard seeds for 2 minutes, stirring, until they begin to splutter.

4 Add the onion, garlic and ginger and fry for 5 minutes, stirring.

5 Stir in the potatoes, chilli powder, salt and water and cook for 8 minutes, stirring occasionally.

6 Finally, add the spinach to the pan. Cover and simmer for 10–15 minutes until the spinach is cooked and the potatoes are tender. Serve hot.

POTATOES IN A YOGURT SAUCE

TINY POTATOES WITH SKINS ON ARE DELICIOUS IN THIS FAIRLY SPICY YET TANGY YOGURT SAUCE.
SERVE WITH ANY MEAT OR FISH DISH OR JUST WITH HOT CHAPATIS.

SERVES FOUR

INGREDIENTS

12 small new or salad
  potatoes, halved
275g/10oz/1¼ cups natural
  low-fat yogurt
300ml/½ pint/1¼ cups water
1.5ml/¼ tsp turmeric
5ml/1 tsp chilli powder
5ml/1 tsp ground coriander
2.5ml/½ tsp ground cumin
5ml/1 tsp salt
5ml/1 tsp soft brown sugar
30ml/2 tbsp vegetable oil
5ml/1 tsp white cumin seeds
15ml/1 tbsp chopped fresh coriander
2 fresh green chillies, sliced
1 coriander sprig, to garnish
  (optional)

1 Cook the potatoes in their skins in boiling salted water until just tender, then drain and set aside.

2 Mix together the yogurt, water, turmeric, chilli powder, ground coriander, ground cumin, salt and sugar in a bowl. Set aside.

3 Heat the oil in a medium saucepan over a medium-high heat and stir in the white cumin seeds.

4 Reduce the heat to medium, and stir in the prepared yogurt mixture. Cook the sauce, stirring continuously, for about 3 minutes.

5 Add the fresh coriander, green chillies and potatoes to the sauce. Mix well and cook for 5–7 minutes, stirring occasionally.

6 Transfer to a serving dish, garnish with the coriander sprig, if wished and serve hot.

COOK'S TIP

If new or salad potatoes are unavailable, use 450g/1lb ordinary potatoes instead, but not the floury type. Peel them and cut into large chunks, then cook as described above.

MASALA MASHED POTATOES

THESE WELL-SPICED POTATOES ARE DELICIOUS SERVED ALONGSIDE RICH MEATS SUCH AS DUCK, LAMB OR PORK THAT HAS BEEN SIMPLY GRILLED OR ROASTED.

SERVES FOUR

INGREDIENTS

3 medium floury potatoes
15ml/1 tbsp mixed chopped fresh
  mint and coriander
5ml/1 tsp mango powder or chutney
5ml/1 tsp salt
5ml/1 tsp crushed black peppercorns
1 fresh red chilli, finely chopped
1 fresh green chilli, finely chopped
50g/2oz/4 tbsp butter or
  margarine, softened

1 Cook the potatoes in a large pan of lightly salted boiling water until tender. Drain very well. Mash them well with a potato masher.

2 Blend together the remaining ingredients in a small bowl.

3 Stir the mixture into the mashed potatoes reserving a little for a garnish and mix together with a fork.

4 Serve hot in a pile, with the remaining mixture on the top.

BOMBAY POTATOES

A CLASSIC GUJERATI (INDIAN VEGETARIAN) DISH OF POTATOES SLOWLY COOKED IN A RICHLY FLAVOURED CURRY SAUCE WITH FRESH CHILLIES FOR AN ADDED KICK.

SERVES FOUR TO SIX

INGREDIENTS

450g/1lb new or small salad potatoes
5ml/1 tsp turmeric
60ml/4 tbsp vegetable oil
2 dried red chillies
6–8 curry leaves
2 onions, finely chopped
2 fresh green chillies, finely chopped
50g/2oz coriander leaves,
  coarsely chopped
1.5ml/¼ tsp asafoetida
2.5ml/½ tsp each cumin, mustard,
  onion, fennel and nigella seeds
lemon juice
salt
fresh fried curry leaves, to garnish

1 Chop the potatoes into small chunks and cook in boiling lightly salted water with ½ tsp of the turmeric until tender. Drain, then coarsely mash. Set aside.

2 Heat the oil in a large heavy-based pan and fry the red chillies and curry leaves until the chillies are nearly burnt. Add the onions, green chillies, coriander, remaining turmeric, asafoetida and spice seeds and cook until the onions are tender.

3 Fold in the potatoes and add a few drops of water. Cook on a low heat for about 10 minutes, mixing well to ensure the even distribution of the spices. Remove the dried chillies and curry leaves.

4 Serve the potatoes hot, with lemon juice squeezed or poured over, and garnish with the fresh fried curry leaves, if you wish.

Meat and Poultry Dishes

THESE MEAT AND POULTRY DISHES MAKE THE MOST
OF THE POTATOES IN SEASON THROUGHOUT THE
YEAR. LAMB SHANKS SLOWLY COOKED IN SPICES
ARE FINISHED WITH HALVED NEW POTATOES.
CHICKEN IN A LIGHT SAUCE IS TOPPED WITH
HERBY DUMPLINGS MADE WITH MASHED POTATOES,
AND A RICH BEEF DISH IS FINISHED WITH A
CRISPY GRATED POTATO CRUST.

TEX-MEX BAKED POTATOES WITH CHILLI

CLASSIC CHILLI MINCE TOPS CRISP, FLOURY-CENTRED BAKED POTATOES. EASY TO PREPARE AND GREAT FOR A SIMPLE, YET SUBSTANTIAL FAMILY SUPPER.

SERVES FOUR

INGREDIENTS

2 large baking potatoes
15ml/1 tbsp vegetable oil, plus more
    for brushing
1 garlic clove, crushed
1 small onion, chopped
½ red pepper, seeded and chopped
225g/8oz lean beef mince
½ small fresh red chilli, seeded
    and chopped
5ml/1 tsp ground cumin
pinch of cayenne pepper
200g/7oz can chopped tomatoes
30ml/2 tbsp tomato paste
2.5ml/½ tsp fresh oregano
2.5ml/½ tsp fresh marjoram
200g/7oz can red kidney beans,
    drained
15ml/1 tbsp chopped fresh coriander
salt and ground black pepper
chopped fresh marjoram, to garnish
lettuce leaves, to serve
60ml/4 tbsp soured cream, to serve

1 Preheat the oven to 220°C/425°F/
Gas 7. Brush or rub the potatoes with a
little of the oil and then pierce them
with skewers.

2 Place the potatoes on the top shelf
of the oven and bake them for
30 minutes before beginning to
cook the chilli.

3 Heat the oil in a large heavy pan and
add the garlic, onion and pepper. Fry
gently for 4–5 minutes until softened.

4 Add the beef and fry until browned,
then stir in the chilli, cumin, cayenne
pepper, tomatoes, tomato paste,
60ml/4 tbsp water and the herbs. Bring
to a boil then reduce the heat, cover
and simmer for about 25 minutes,
stirring occasionally.

5 Stir in the kidney beans and cook,
uncovered, for 5 minutes. Remove from
the heat and stir in the chopped
coriander. Season well and set aside.

6 Cut the baked potatoes in half and
place them in serving bowls. Top with
the chilli mixture and a dollop of soured
cream. Garnish with chopped fresh
marjoram and serve hot accompanied
by a few lettuce leaves.

CORNED BEEF AND EGG HASH

This is real nursery, or comfort, food at its best! Whether you remember Gran's version, or prefer this American-style hash, it turns corned beef into a supper fit for any guest.

SERVES FOUR

INGREDIENTS
    30ml/2 tbsp vegetable oil
    25g/1oz/2 tbsp butter
    1 onion, finely chopped
    1 green pepper, seeded and diced
    2 large firm boiled potatoes, diced
    350g/12oz can corned beef, cubed
    1.5ml/¼ tsp grated nutmeg
    1.5ml/¼ tsp paprika
    4 eggs
    salt and ground black pepper
    deep fried parsley, to garnish
    sweet chilli sauce or tomato sauce,
      to serve

COOK'S TIP
Put the can of corned beef into the fridge to chill for about half an hour before using – it will firm up and cut into cubes more easily.

1 Heat the oil and butter together in a large frying pan. Add the onion and fry for 5–6 minutes until softened.

2 In a bowl, mix together the green pepper, potatoes, corned beef, nutmeg and paprika and season well. Add to the pan and toss gently to distribute the cooked onion. Press down lightly and fry without stirring on a medium heat for about 3–4 minutes until a golden brown crust has formed on the underside.

3 Stir the mixture through to distribute the crust, then repeat the frying twice, until the mixture is well browned.

4 Make four wells in the hash and carefully crack an egg into each. Cover and cook gently for about 4–5 minutes until the egg whites are set.

5 Sprinkle with deep fried parsley and cut into quarters. Serve hot with sweet chilli sauce or tomato sauce.

WILD MUSHROOM AND BACON RÖSTI

DRIED CEPS OR PORCINI MUSHROOMS HAVE A WONDERFUL WOODY, EARTHY AROMA AND TASTE.
WITH THE SALTY BACON LARDONS, THEY TURN POTATO RÖSTI INTO A MEMORABLE SUPPER.

SERVES FOUR

INGREDIENTS
675g/1½lb floury potatoes
10g/¼oz dried ceps or porcini
 mushrooms
225g/8oz very thick smoked bacon,
 cut into lardons or strips
2 thyme sprigs, chopped
30ml/2 tbsp chopped fresh parsley
30ml/2 tbsp vegetable oil
4 eggs, to serve
1 bunch watercress, to garnish
crushed peppercorns, to garnish

1 Cook the potatoes in a saucepan of boiling salted water for 5 minutes and not longer, as they need to remain firm enough to grate at the next stage.

2 Meanwhile cover the mushrooms with boiling water and leave to soften for 5–10 minutes. Drain and chop.

3 Fry the bacon gently in a non-stick pan until all the fat runs out. Remove the bacon using a slotted spoon and reserve the fat.

4 Drain the potatoes and leave to cool. When they are cool enough to handle, grate them coarsely, then thoroughly pat dry on kitchen paper to remove all moisture. Place them in a large bowl and add the mushrooms, thyme, parsley and bacon. Mix together well.

5 Heat the bacon fat with a little of the oil in the frying pan until really hot. Spoon in the rösti mixture in heaps and flatten. Fry in batches for about 6 minutes until crisp and golden on both sides, turning once. Drain on kitchen paper and keep warm in a low oven.

6 Heat the remaining oil in the hot pan and fry the eggs as you like them. Serve the rösti at once with the eggs, watercress and crushed peppercorns.

POTATO CHORIZO AND CHEESE TORTILLA

SLICED POTATOES AND CHILLI-HOT SAUSAGES MAKE A POTATO CAKE WITH A REAL KICK TO IT.

SERVES FOUR

INGREDIENTS
15ml/1 tbsp vegetable oil
½ onion, sliced
1 small green pepper, seeded and cut
 into rings
1 garlic clove, finely chopped
1 tomato, chopped
6 pitted black olives, chopped
275g/10oz cooked firm, waxy
 potatoes, sliced
225g/8oz sliced chorizo, in strips
1 fresh green chilli, seeded
 and chopped
50g/2oz/½ cup Cheddar
 cheese, grated
6 large eggs
45ml/3 tbsp milk
1.5ml/¼ tsp ground cumin
1.5ml/¼ tsp dried oregano
1.5ml/¼ tsp paprika
salt and ground black pepper
rocket leaves, to garnish

1 Preheat the oven to 190°C/375°F/ Gas 5. Line a 23cm/9in round cake tin with grease-proof paper.

2 Heat the oil in a large non-stick frying pan. Add the onion, green pepper and garlic and cook over a medium heat for 5–8 minutes until softened.

3 Spoon into the tin with the tomato, olives, potatoes, chorizo and chilli. Mix and sprinkle with cheese.

4 In a small bowl, whisk together the eggs and milk until frothy. Add the cumin, oregano, paprika and salt and pepper to taste. Whisk to blend.

5 Pour the egg mixture on to the vegetables, tilting the tin so that the egg mixture spreads evenly.

6 Bake for 30 minutes until set and lightly golden. Serve in wedges, hot or cold, with rocket leaves.

POTATO AND SAUSAGE CASSEROLE

YOU WILL FIND NUMEROUS VARIATIONS OF THIS TRADITIONAL SUPPER DISH THROUGHOUT IRELAND, BUT THE BASIC INGREDIENTS ARE THE SAME WHEREVER YOU GO — POTATOES, SAUSAGES AND BACON.

SERVES FOUR

INGREDIENTS
   15ml/1 tbsp vegetable oil
   4 bacon rashers, cut into
      2.5cm/1in pieces
   2 large onions, chopped
   2 garlic cloves, crushed
   8 large pork sausages
   4 large baking potatoes, thinly sliced
   1.5ml/¼ tsp fresh sage
   300ml/½ pint/1¼ cups
      vegetable stock
   salt and ground black pepper
   soda bread, to serve

1 Preheat the oven to 180°C/350°F/ Gas 4. Grease a large ovenproof dish and set aside.

2 Heat the oil in a frying pan. Add the bacon and fry for 2 minutes. Add the onions and fry for 5–6 minutes until golden. Add the garlic and fry for 1 minute, then remove the mixture from the pan and set aside.

3 Then fry the sausages in the pan for 5–6 minutes until golden brown.

4 Arrange the potatoes in the base of the prepared dish. Spoon the bacon and onion mixture on top. Season with the salt and pepper and sprinkle with the fresh sage.

5 Pour on the stock and top with the sausages. Cover and bake for 1 hour. Serve hot with fresh soda bread.

PORK ESCALOPES BAKED WITH APPLE AND POTATO RÖSTI

THE JUICES FROM THE PORK COOK INTO THE APPLES AND POTATOES GIVING THEM A WONDERFUL FLAVOUR AS WELL AS MAKING A DELICIOUS SAUCE.

SERVES FOUR

INGREDIENTS
 2 large potatoes, finely grated
 1 medium Bramley apple, grated
 2 garlic cloves, crushed
 1 egg, beaten
 butter, for greasing
 15ml/1 tbsp olive oil
 4 large slices Parma ham
 4 pork escalopes, about
  175g/6oz each
 4 sage leaves
 1 medium Bramley apple,
  cut into thin wedges
 25g/1oz/2 tbsp butter, diced
 salt and ground black pepper
 caramelized apple wedges, to serve

COOK'S TIP
Do not be tempted to overcook the pork
as it will start to dry out.

1 Preheat the oven to 200°C/400°F/
Gas 6. Squeeze out all the excess liquid
from the grated potatoes and apple. Mix
the grated ingredients together with the
garlic, egg and seasoning.

2 Divide the potatoes into 4 portions
and spoon each quarter on to a baking
sheet that has been lined with foil and
greased. Form a circle with the potatoes
and flatten out slightly with the back of
a spoon. Drizzle with a little olive oil.
Cook for 10 minutes.

3 Meanwhile, lay the Parma ham on a
clean surface and place a pork
escalope on top. Lay a sage leaf and
apple wedges over each escalope and
top each piece with the butter. Wrap the
Parma ham around each piece of meat,
making sure it is covered completely.

4 Remove the potatoes from the oven,
place each pork parcel on top and
return to the oven for 20 minutes.
Carefully lift the pork and potatoes off
the foil and serve with caramelized
wedges of apple and any cooking juices
on the side.

STEAK WITH STOUT AND POTATOES

THE IRISH WAY TO BRAISE BEEF IS IN STOUT OF COURSE AND TOPPED WITH THICKLY SLICED POTATOES. BAKE IT IN A MODERATE OVEN FOR LONG, SLOW TENDERISING IF YOU PREFER.

SERVES FOUR

INGREDIENTS

675g/1½lb stewing beef
15ml/1 tbsp vegetable oil
25g/1oz/2 tbsp butter
225g/8oz tiny white onions
175ml/6fl oz/¾ cup stout or dark beer
300ml/½ pint/1¼ cups beef stock
bouquet garni
675g/1½lb firm, waxy potatoes, cut into thick slices
225g/8oz/3 cups large mushrooms, sliced
15ml/1 tbsp plain flour
2.5ml/½ tsp mild mustard
salt and ground black pepper
chopped thyme sprigs, to garnish

3 Add the tiny white onions to the pan and cook for 3–4 minutes until lightly browned all over. Return the steak to the pan with the onions. Pour on the stout or beer and stock and season the whole mixture to taste.

5 Add the sliced mushrooms over the potatoes. Cover again and simmer for a further 30 minutes or so. Remove the steak and vegetables with a slotted spoon and arrange on a platter.

1 Trim any excess fat from the steak and cut into four pieces. Season both sides of the meat. Heat the oil and 10g/¼oz/1½ tsp of the butter in a large heavy-based pan.

2 Add the steak and brown on both sides, taking care not to burn the butter. Remove from the pan and set aside.

4 Next add the bouquet garni to the pan and top with the potato slices distributing them evenly over the surface to cover the steak. Bring the ingredients to a boil then reduce the heat, cover with a tight-fitting lid and simmer gently for 1 hour.

VARIATION

For a dish that is lighter, but just as tasty, substitute four lamb leg steaks for the beef, and use dry cider instead of the stout or beer, and lamb or chicken stock instead of beef.

COOK'S TIP

To make onion peeling easier, first put the onions in a bowl and cover with boiling water. Allow them to soak for about 5 minutes and drain. The skins should now peel away easily.

6 Mix the remaining butter with the flour to make a roux. Whisk a little at a time into the cooking liquid in the pan. Stir in the mustard. Cook over a medium heat for 2–3 minutes, stirring all the while, until thickened.

7 Season the sauce and pour over the steak. Garnish with plenty of thyme sprigs and serve the dish at once.

LAMB PIE WITH MUSTARD THATCH

SHEPHERD'S PIE WITH A TWIST, THE MUSTARD GIVING A REAL TANG TO THE POTATO TOPPING.

2 Fry the lamb in a non-stick pan, breaking it up with a fork, until lightly browned all over. Add the onion, celery and carrots to the pan and cook for 2–3 minutes, stirring, to stop the mixture sticking to the base.

3 Stir in the stock and cornflour mixture. Bring to the boil, stirring all the while, then remove from the heat. Stir in the Worcestershire sauce and rosemary and season with salt and pepper to taste.

4 Turn the lamb mixture into a 1.75 litre/3 pint/7 cup ovenproof dish and spread over the potato topping evenly, swirling with the edge of a palette knife. Bake for 30–35 minutes until golden on the top. Serve hot with a selection of fresh vegetables.

SERVES FOUR

INGREDIENTS
  800g/1¾lb floury potatoes, diced
  60ml/4 tbsp milk
  15ml/1 tbsp whole-grain or
    French mustard
  a little butter
  450g/1lb lean lamb, minced
  1 onion, chopped
  2 celery sticks, thinly sliced
  2 carrots, diced
  30ml/2 tbsp cornflour blended into
    150ml/¼ pint/⅔ cup lamb stock
  15ml/1 tbsp Worcestershire sauce
  30ml/2 tbsp chopped fresh rosemary,
    or 10ml/2 tsp dried
  salt and ground black pepper
  fresh vegetables, to serve

1 Cook the potatoes in a large saucepan of boiling lightly salted water until tender. Drain well and mash until smooth, then stir in the milk, mustard, butter and seasoning to taste. Meanwhile preheat the oven to 200°C/400°F/Gas 6.

VARIATION
Although the original shepherd's pie is made with lamb, most people make it with minced beef as well. To vary the potato topping slightly, try adding horseradish – either creamed or for an even stronger flavour, freshly grated.

LAMB AND NEW POTATO CURRY

THIS DISH MAKES THE MOST OF AN ECONOMICAL CUT OF MEAT BY COOKING IT SLOWLY UNTIL THE MEAT IS FALLING FROM THE BONE. CHILLIES AND COCONUT CREAM GIVE IT LOTS OF FLAVOUR.

SERVES FOUR

INGREDIENTS

- 25g/1oz/2 tbsp butter
- 4 garlic cloves, crushed
- 2 onions, sliced into rings
- 2.5ml/½ tsp each ground cumin, ground coriander, turmeric and cayenne pepper
- 2–3 red chillies, seeded and finely chopped
- 300ml/½ pint/1¼ cups hot chicken stock
- 200ml/7fl oz/scant 1 cup coconut cream
- 4 lamb shanks, all excess fat removed
- 450g/1lb new potatoes, halved
- 6 ripe tomatoes, quartered
- salt and ground black pepper
- coriander leaves, to garnish
- spicy rice, to serve

2 Stir in the hot stock and coconut cream. Place the lamb shanks in the liquid and cover the casserole with foil. Cook in the oven for 2 hours, turning the shanks twice, first after about an hour or so and again about half an hour later.

3 Par-boil the potatoes for 10 minutes, drain and add to the casserole with the tomatoes, then cook uncovered in the oven for a further 35 minutes. Season to taste and garnish with coriander leaves and serve with the spicy rice.

1 Preheat the oven to 160°C/325°F/Gas 3. Melt the butter in a large flameproof casserole, add the garlic and onions and cook over a low heat for 15 minutes, until golden. Stir in the spices and chillies, then cook for a further 2 minutes.

COOK'S TIP

Make this dish a day in advance if possible. Cool and chill overnight, then skim off the excess fat that has risen to the surface. Reheat thoroughly before you serve it.

POTATO, BEEF, BEETROOT AND MUSHROOM GRATIN

THIS VARIATION OF AN UNUSUAL POLISH MIX OF FLAVOURS PRODUCES A VERY HEARTY MAIN MEAL.
HORSERADISH AND MUSTARD ARE GREAT WITH BOTH THE BEEF AND THE BEETROOT, MOST OF WHICH
IS HIDDEN UNDERNEATH MAKING A COLOURFUL SURPRISE WHEN YOU SERVE IT.

SERVES FOUR

INGREDIENTS
30ml/2 tbsp vegetable oil
1 small onion, chopped
15ml/1 tbsp plain flour
150ml/¼ pint/⅔ cup vegetable stock
225g/8oz cooked beetroot, drained
    well and chopped
15ml/1 tbsp creamed horseradish
15ml/1 tbsp caraway seeds
3 shallots, or 1 medium
    onion, chopped
450g/1lb frying or grilling steak, cut
    into thin strips
225g/8oz assorted wild or cultivated
    mushrooms, sliced
10–15ml/2–3 tsp hot mustard
60ml/4 tbsp soured cream
45ml/3 tbsp chopped fresh parsley
For the potato border
900g/2lb floury potatoes
150ml/¼ pint/⅔ cup milk
25g/1oz/2 tbsp butter or margarine
15ml/1 tbsp chopped fresh dill
    (optional)
salt and ground black pepper

1 Preheat the oven to 190°C/375°F/
Gas 5. Lightly oil a baking or gratin
dish. Heat 15ml/1 tbsp of the oil in a
large saucepan, add the onion and fry
until softened but not coloured. Stir in
the flour, remove from the heat and
gradually add the stock, stirring until
well blended and smooth.

2 Return to the heat and simmer until
thickened, stirring all the while. Add the
beetroot (reserve a few pieces for the
topping, if you wish), horseradish and
caraway seeds. Mix gently, then put to
one side.

3 To make the potato border, first cook
the potatoes in a large saucepan with
plenty of boiling salted water for
20 minutes until tender. Drain well
through a colander and mash with the
milk and butter or margarine. Add the
chopped dill, if using, and season the
mixture with salt and pepper to taste.
Stir to combine the seasonings.

COOK'S TIP
If planning ahead, for instance for a
dinner party, this entire dish can be
made in advance and heated through
when needed. Allow 50 minutes baking
time from room temperature. Add the
beetroot pieces to the topping near the
end of the cooking time.

4 Spoon the potatoes into the prepared
dish and push well up the sides,
making a large hollow in the middle for
the filling. Spoon the beetroot mixture
into the well, evening it out with the
back of a spoon and set aside.

5 Heat the remaining oil in a large
frying pan, add the shallots or onion
and fry until softened but not coloured.
Add the steak and stir-fry quickly until
browned all over. Then add the
mushrooms and fry quickly until most
of their juices have cooked away.
Remove the pan from the heat and
gently stir in the mustard, soured
cream, seasoning to taste and half the
parsley until well blended.

6 Spoon the steak mixture over the
beetroot mixture in the baking dish,
sprinkling the reserved beetroot over the
top, cover and bake for
30 minutes. Serve hot, sprinkled with
the remaining parsley.

SLOW BAKED BEEF <u>WITH A</u> POTATO CRUST

*THIS RECIPE MAKES THE BEST OF BRAISING BEEF BY MARINATING IT IN RED WINE AND TOPPING IT
WITH A CHEESY GRATED POTATO CRUST THAT BAKES TO A GOLDEN, CRUNCHY CONSISTENCY. FOR A
CHANGE, INSTEAD OF GRATING THE POTATOES, SLICE THEM THINLY AND LAYER OVER THE TOP OF THE
BEEF WITH ONION RINGS AND CRUSHED GARLIC.*

SERVES FOUR

INGREDIENTS

    675g/1½lb stewing beef, diced
    300ml/½ pint/1¼ cups red wine
    3 juniper berries, crushed
    slice of orange peel
    30ml/2 tbsp olive oil
    2 onions, cut into chunks
    2 carrots, cut into chunks
    1 garlic clove, crushed
    225g/8oz/3 cups button
      mushrooms
    150ml/¼ pint/⅔ cup beef stock
    30ml/2 tbsp cornflour
    salt and ground black pepper
For the crust
    450g/1lb potatoes, grated
    15ml/1 tbsp olive oil
    30ml/2 tbsp creamed horseradish
    50g/2oz/½ cup mature Cheddar
      cheese, grated
    salt and ground black pepper

VARIATION
Any hard mature cheese is suitable for
cooking on the crust. Try Red Leicester
to add some colour, or Munster, for a
more pungent flavour.

1 Place the diced beef in a non-
metallic bowl. Add the wine, berries,
and orange peel and season with black
pepper. Mix the ingredients together
and then cover and leave to marinate
for at least 4 hours or overnight
if possible.

2 Preheat the oven to 160°C/325°F/
Gas 3. Drain the beef, reserving
the marinade.

3 Heat the oil in a large flameproof
casserole and fry the meat in batches
for 5 minutes to seal. Add the onions,
carrots and garlic and cook for 5
minutes. Stir in the mushrooms, red
wine marinade and beef stock. Simmer.

4 Mix the cornflour with water to make
a smooth paste. Stir into the pan.
Season, cover and cook for 1½ hours.

5 Make the crust 30 minutes before
the end of the cooking time for the
beef. Start by blanching the grated
potatoes in boiling water for 5 minutes.
Drain well and then squeeze out all the
extra liquid.

6 Stir in the remaining ingredients and
then scatter evenly over the surface of
the beef. Increase the oven temperature
to 200°C/400°F/Gas 6 and cook the dish
for a further 30 minutes so that the top
is crispy and slightly browned.

COOK'S TIP
Use a large grater on the food processor
for the potatoes. They will hold their
shape better whilst being blanched than
if you use a finer blade.

MOUSSAKA

THIS CLASSIC GREEK DISH WITH LAMB, POTATOES AND AUBERGINES IS LAYERED THROUGH WITH A RICH CHEESY TOPPING TO MAKE A SUBSTANTIAL MEAL.

SERVES SIX

INGREDIENTS
    30ml/2 tbsp olive oil
    30ml/2 tbsp chopped
       fresh oregano
    1 large onion, finely chopped
    675g/1½lb lean lamb, minced
    1 large aubergine, sliced
    2 x 400g/14oz cans
       chopped tomatoes
    45ml/3 tbsp tomato purée
    1 lamb stock cube, crumbled
    2 floury main crop
       potatoes, halved
    115g/4oz/1 cup Cheddar
       cheese, grated
    150ml/¼ pint/⅔ cup
       single cream
    salt and ground black pepper
    fresh bread, to serve

2 Stir in the lamb and cook for 10 minutes until browned. Meanwhile, grill the aubergine slices for 5 minutes until browned, turning once.

3 Stir the tomatoes and purée into the mince mixture, and crumble the stock cube over it, stir well, season with salt and pepper and simmer uncovered for a further 15 minutes.

4 Meanwhile, cook the potatoes in lightly salted boiling water for 5–10 minutes until just tender. Drain, and when cool enough to handle, cut into thin slices.

5 Layer the aubergines, mince and potatoes in a 1.75 litre/3 pint/7½ cup oval ovenproof dish, finishing with a layer of potatoes.

6 Mix the cheese and cream together in a bowl and pour over the top of the other ingredients in the dish. Cook for 45–50 minutes until bubbling and golden on the top. Serve straight from the dish, while hot, with plenty of fresh, crusty bread.

COOK'S TIP
The larger the surface area of the dish, the quicker the Moussaka will cook in the oven.

1 Preheat the oven to 180°C/350°F/ Gas 4. Heat the olive oil in a large deep-sided frying pan. Fry the oregano and onions over a low heat, stirring frequently, for about 5 minutes or until the onions have softened.

VARIATION
If you want to add more vegetables to the dish, use slices of courgette, grilled in the same way as the aubergines, instead of the sliced potato in the layers, then top the dish with a layer of well-seasoned mashed potatoes before pouring over the sauce. To make the dish even richer, add a sprinkling of freshly grated Parmesan cheese with each layer of aubergine.

IRISH STEW

SIMPLE AND DELICIOUS, THIS IS THE QUINTESSENTIAL IRISH MAIN COURSE. TRADITIONALLY MUTTON CHOPS ARE USED, BUT AS THEY ARE HARDER TO FIND THESE DAYS YOU CAN USE LAMB INSTEAD.

SERVES FOUR

INGREDIENTS
    1.5kg/2½lb boneless lamb chops
    15ml/1 tbsp vegetable oil
    3 large onions, quartered
    4 large carrots, thickly sliced
    900ml/1½ pints/3¾ cups water
    4 large firm potatoes, cut into chunks
    1 large thyme sprig
    15g/½oz/1 tbsp butter
    15ml/1 tbsp chopped fresh parsley
    salt and ground black pepper
    Savoy cabbage, to serve (optional)

COOK'S TIP
If you can't find boneless chops, use the same weight of middle neck of lamb. Ask the butcher to chop the meat into cutlets, which should then be trimmed of excess fat.

1 Trim any excess fat from the lamb. Heat the oil in a flameproof casserole, add the lamb and brown on both sides. Remove from the pan.

2 Add the onions and carrots to the casserole and cook for 5 minutes until the onions are browned. Return the lamb to the pan with the water. Season with salt and pepper. Bring to a boil then reduce the heat, cover and simmer for 1 hour.

3 Add the potatoes to the pan with the thyme, cover again, and simmer for a further hour.

4 Leave the stew to settle for a few minutes. Remove the fat from the liquid with a ladle, then pour off the liquid into a clean saucepan. Bring to a simmer and stir in the butter, then the parsley. Season well and pour back into the casserole. Serve with Savoy cabbage, boiled or steamed, if liked.

MIDDLE EASTERN ROAST LAMB AND POTATOES

WHEN THE EASTERN AROMA OF THE GARLIC AND SAFFRON COME WAFTING OUT OF THE OVEN, THIS DELICIOUSLY GARLICKY LAMB WON'T LAST VERY LONG!

SERVES SIX TO EIGHT

INGREDIENTS
    2.75kg/6lb leg of lamb
    4 garlic cloves, halved
    60ml/4 tbsp olive oil
    juice of 1 lemon
    2–3 saffron strands, soaked in
        15ml/1 tbsp boiling water
    5ml/1 tsp mixed dried herbs
    450g/1lb baking potatoes,
        thickly sliced
    2 large onions, thickly sliced
    salt and ground black pepper
    fresh thyme, to garnish

1 Make eight incisions in the lamb, press the garlic into the slits and place the lamb in a non-metallic dish.

2 Mix together the oil, lemon juice, saffron mixture and herbs. Rub over the lamb and marinate for 2 hours.

3 Preheat the oven to 180°C/350°F/ Gas 4. Layer the potatoes and onions in a large roasting tin. Lift the lamb out of the marinade and place the lamb on top of the potatoes and onions, fat side up and season.

4 Pour any remaining marinade over the lamb and roast for 2 hours, basting occasionally. Remove from the oven, cover with foil and rest for 10–15 minutes before carving. Garnish with thyme.

CHICKEN WITH POTATO DUMPLINGS

POACHED CHICKEN BREAST IN A CREAMY SAUCE TOPPED WITH LIGHT HERB AND POTATO DUMPLINGS MAKES A DELICATE YET HEARTY AND WARMING MEAL.

SERVES SIX

INGREDIENTS
    1 onion, chopped
    300ml/½ pint/1¼ cups
      vegetable stock
    120ml/4fl oz/½ cup white wine
    4 large chicken breasts
    300ml/½ pint/1¼ cups single cream
    15ml/1 tbsp chopped fresh tarragon
    salt and ground black pepper
For the dumplings
    225g/8oz main crop potatoes, boiled
      and mashed
    175g/6oz/1¼ cups suet
    115g/4oz/1 cup self-raising flour
    50ml/2fl oz/¼ cup water
    30ml/2 tbsp chopped mixed
      fresh herbs
    salt and ground black pepper

1 Place the onion, stock and wine in a deep-sided frying pan. Add the chicken and simmer for 20 minutes, covered.

2 Remove the chicken from the stock, cut into chunks and reserve. Strain the stock and discard the onion. Reduce the stock by one-third over a high heat. Stir in the cream and tarragon and simmer until just thickened. Stir in the chicken and season with salt and ground black pepper.

3 Spoon the mixture into a 900ml/1½ pint/3¾ cup ovenproof dish.

4 Preheat the oven to 190°C/375°F/Gas 5. Mix together the dumpling ingredients and stir in the water to make a soft dough. Divide into six and shape into balls with floured hands. Place on top of the chicken mixture and bake uncovered for 30 minutes.

COOK'S TIP
Make sure that you do not reduce the sauce too much before it is cooked in the oven as the dumplings absorb quite a lot of the liquid.

SPINACH AND POTATO STUFFED CHICKEN BREASTS

THIS DISH CONSISTS OF LARGE CHICKEN BREASTS, FILLED WITH A HERBY SPINACH MIXTURE, THEN TOPPED WITH BUTTER AND BAKED UNTIL MOUTH-WATERINGLY TENDER.

2 Stir the spinach into the potato with the egg and coriander. Season with salt and pepper to taste.

3 Cut almost all the way through the chicken breasts and open out to form a pocket in each. Spoon the filling into the centre and fold the chicken back over again. Secure with cocktail sticks and place in a roasting tin.

4 Dot with butter and cover with foil. Bake for 25 minutes. Remove the foil and cook for a further 10 minutes until the chicken is golden.

5 Meanwhile, to make the sauce heat the tomatoes, garlic and stock in a saucepan. Boil rapidly for 10 minutes. Season and stir in the coriander. Remove the chicken from the oven and serve with the sauce and fried mushrooms.

COOK'S TIP
Young spinach leaves have a sweeter flavour and are ideal for this dish.

SERVES SIX

INGREDIENTS
    115g/4oz floury main crop
        potatoes, diced
    115g/4oz spinach leaves,
        finely chopped
    1 egg, beaten
    30ml/2 tbsp chopped fresh coriander
    4 large chicken breasts
    50g/2oz/4 tbsp butter
For the sauce
    400g/14oz can chopped tomatoes
    1 garlic clove, crushed
    150ml/¼ pint/⅔ cup hot chicken stock
    30ml/2 tbsp chopped fresh coriander
    salt and ground black pepper
    fried mushrooms, to serve

1 Preheat the oven to 180°C/350°F/ Gas 4. Boil the potatoes in a large saucepan of boiling water for 15 minutes or until tender. Drain the potatoes, place them in a large bowl and roughly mash with a fork.

STOVED CHICKEN

"Stovies" were originally – not surprisingly – potatoes slowly cooked on the stove with onions and dripping or butter until falling to pieces. This version includes a delicious layer of bacon and chicken hidden in the middle of the vegetables.

SERVES FOUR

INGREDIENTS
butter, for greasing
1kg/2¼lb baking potatoes, cut into
    5mm/¼in slices
2 large onions, thinly sliced
15ml/1 tbsp chopped fresh thyme
25g/1oz/2 tbsp butter
15ml/1 tbsp vegetable oil
2 large bacon slices, chopped
4 large chicken joints, halved
600ml/1 pint/2½ cups chicken stock
1 bay leaf
salt and ground black pepper

COOK'S TIP
Instead of chicken joints, choose eight
chicken thighs or chicken drumsticks.

1 Preheat the oven to 150°C/300°F/
Gas 2. Arrange a thick layer of half the
potato slices in the bottom of a large
lightly greased heavy-based casserole,
then cover with half the onions. Sprinkle
with half of the thyme, and season with
salt and pepper to taste.

2 Heat the butter and oil in a large
heavy-based frying pan, add the bacon
and chicken, stirring frequently, and
brown on all sides. Using a slotted
spoon, transfer the chicken and bacon
to the casserole. Reserve the fat in
the pan.

3 Sprinkle the remaining thyme over
the chicken, season with salt and
pepper, then cover with the remaining
onion slices, followed by a neat layer of
overlapping potato slices. Season the
dish well.

4 Pour the stock into the casserole,
add the bay leaf and brush the potatoes
with the reserved fat. Cover tightly and
bake for about 2 hours until the chicken
is very tender.

5 Preheat the grill. Take the cover off
the casserole and place it under the
grill until the slices of potato are
beginning to turn golden brown and
crisp. Remove the bay leaf and
serve hot.

TURKEY CROQUETTES

A CRISP PATTY OF SMOKED TURKEY MIXED WITH MASHED POTATO AND SPRING ONIONS AND ROLLED IN BREADCRUMBS, SERVED WITH A TANGY TOMATO SAUCE.

3 Meanwhile, to make the sauce heat the oil in a frying pan and fry the onion for 5 minutes until softened. Add the tomatoes and purée, stir and simmer for 10 minutes. Stir in the parsley, season with salt and pepper and keep the sauce warm until needed.

SERVES FOUR

INGREDIENTS
  450g/1lb main crop potatoes, diced
  3 eggs
  30ml/2 tbsp milk
  175g/6oz smoked turkey rashers,
    finely chopped
  2 spring onions, finely sliced
  115g/4oz/2 cups fresh white
    breadcrumbs
  vegetable oil, for deep fat frying
For the sauce
  15ml/1 tbsp olive oil
  1 onion, finely chopped
  400g/14oz can tomatoes, drained
  30ml/2 tbsp tomato purée
  15ml/1 tbsp chopped fresh parsley
  salt and ground black pepper

1 Boil the potatoes for 20 minutes or until tender. Drain and return the pan to a low heat to make sure all the excess water evaporates.

2 Mash the potatoes with 2 eggs and the milk. Season well with salt and pepper. Stir in the turkey and spring onions. Chill for 1 hour.

4 Remove the potato mixture from the fridge and divide into 8 pieces. Shape each piece into a sausage shape and dip in the remaining beaten egg and then the breadcrumbs.

5 Heat the vegetable oil in a saucepan or deep-fat fryer to 175°C/330°F and deep fry the croquettes for 5 minutes, or until golden and crisp. Serve with the sauce.

COOK'S TIP
Test the oil is at the correct temperature by dropping a cube of bread on to the surface. If it sinks, rises and sizzles in 10 seconds the oil is ready to use.

LAYERED CHICKEN <u>AND</u> MUSHROOM POTATO BAKE

A DELICIOUS AND MOIST COMBINATION OF CHICKEN, VEGETABLES AND GRAVY IN A SIMPLE,
ONE-DISH MEAL TOPPED WITH CRUNCHY SLICES OF POTATO.

SERVES FOUR TO SIX

INGREDIENTS
15ml/1 tbsp olive oil
4 large chicken breasts, cut
   into chunks
1 leek, finely sliced into rings
50g/2oz/4 tbsp butter
25g/1oz/¼ cup plain flour
475ml/16fl oz/2 cups milk
5ml/1 tsp wholegrain mustard
1 carrot, very finely diced
225g/8oz/3 cups button mushrooms,
   finely sliced
900g/2lb main crop potatoes,
   finely sliced
salt and ground black pepper

1 Preheat the oven to 180°C/350°F/ Gas 4. Heat the oil in a large saucepan. Fry the chicken for 5 minutes until browned. Add the leek and fry for a further 5 minutes.

2 Add half the butter to the pan and allow it to melt. Then sprinkle the flour over and stir in the milk. Cook over a low heat until thickened, then stir in the mustard.

3 Add the carrots with the mushrooms. Season with salt and black pepper.

4 Lay enough potato slices to line the base of a 1.75 litre/3 pint/7½ cup ovenproof dish. Spoon one-third of the chicken mixture over. Cover with another layer of potatoes. Repeat layering, finishing with a layer of potatoes. Top with the remaining butter in knobs.

5 Bake for 1½ hours in the oven, covering with foil after 30 minutes' cooking time. Serve hot.

COOK'S TIP
The liquid from the mushrooms keeps the chicken moist and the potatoes help to mop up any excess juices.

ROASTED DUCKLING <u>ON A</u> BED <u>OF</u> HONEYED POTATOES

THE RICH FLAVOUR OF DUCK COMBINED WITH THESE SWEETENED POTATOES GLAZED WITH HONEY MAKES AN EXCELLENT TREAT FOR A DINNER PARTY OR SPECIAL OCCASION.

SERVES FOUR

INGREDIENTS
1 duckling, giblets removed
60ml/4 tbsp light soy sauce
150ml/¼ pint/⅔ cup fresh
  orange juice
3 large floury potatoes, cut
  into chunks
30ml/2 tbsp clear honey
15ml/1 tbsp sesame seeds
salt and ground black pepper

1 Preheat the oven to 200°C/400°F/
Gas 6. Place the duckling in a roasting
tin. Prick the skin well.

2 Mix the soy sauce and orange juice
together and pour over the duck. Cook
for 20 minutes.

3 Place the potato chunks in a bowl
and stir in the honey, toss to mix well.
Remove the duckling from the oven and
spoon the potatoes all around and
under the duckling.

4 Roast for 35 minutes and remove
from the oven. Toss the potatoes in
the juices so the underside will be
cooked and turn the duck over. Put
back in the oven and cook for a
further 30 minutes.

5 Remove the duckling from the oven
and carefully scoop off the excess fat,
leaving the juices behind.

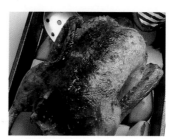

6 Sprinkle the sesame seeds over the
potatoes, season and turn the duckling
back over, breast side up, and cook for
a further 10 minutes. Remove the
duckling and potatoes from the oven
and keep warm, allowing the duck to
stand for a few minutes.

7 Pour off the excess fat and simmer
the juices on the hob for a few minutes.
Serve the juices with the carved
duckling and potatoes.

Fish Dishes

Fish takes only a short time to cook, so many of the recipes in this chapter use potatoes ready-cooked or very finely sliced. Try Jansson's Temptation, a classic Swedish dish made with matchstick potatoes and layered with anchovies and onions. Since fish lends itself well to being flaked it is ideal for mixing with mashed potato to make the tastiest of fish cakes.

SMOKED SALMON QUICHE WITH POTATO PASTRY

THE INGREDIENTS IN THIS LIGHT BUT RICHLY-FLAVOURED QUICHE PERFECTLY COMPLEMENT THE MELT-IN-THE-MOUTH PASTRY MADE WITH POTATOES.

SERVES SIX

INGREDIENTS
For the pastry
    115g/4oz floury maincrop
      potatoes, diced
    225g/8oz/2 cups plain flour, sifted
    115g/4oz/8 tbsp butter, diced
    ½ egg, beaten
    10ml/2 tsp chilled water
For the filling
    275g/10oz smoked salmon
    6 eggs, beaten
    150ml/¼ pint/⅔ cup full cream milk
    300ml/½ pint/1¼ cups double cream
    30–45ml/2–3 tbsp chopped fresh dill
    30ml/2 tbsp capers, chopped
    salt and ground black pepper
    salad leaves and chopped fresh dill,
      to serve

1 Boil the potatoes in a large saucepan of lightly salted water for 15 minutes or until tender. Drain well through a colander and return to the pan. Mash the potatoes until smooth and set aside to cool completely.

VARIATIONS
These quantities can also be used to make six individual quiches, which are an ideal size to serve as a starter or a light lunch. Prepare them as above, but reduce the cooking time by about 15 minutes. For extra piquancy, sprinkle some finely grated fresh Parmesan cheese over the top of each quiche before baking in the oven.

2 Place the flour in a bowl and rub in the butter to form fine crumbs. Beat in the potatoes and egg. Bring the mixture together, adding chilled water if needed.

3 Roll the pastry out on a floured surface and use to line a deep 23cm/9in round, loose-based, fluted flan tin. Chill for 1 hour.

4 Preheat the oven to 200°C/400°F/ Gas 6. Place a baking sheet in the oven to preheat it. Chop the salmon into bite-size pieces and set aside.

5 For the filling, beat the eggs, milk and cream together. Then stir in the dill and capers and season with pepper. Add in the salmon and stir to combine.

6 Remove the pastry case from the fridge, prick the base well and pour the mixture into it. Bake on a baking sheet for 35–45 minutes. Serve warm with mixed salad leaves and some more dill.

COOK'S TIPS
To ensure the base cooks through it is vital to preheat a baking sheet in the oven first. Make the most of smoked salmon offcuts for this quiche, as they are much cheaper.

COD, BASIL, TOMATO AND POTATO PIE

*NATURAL AND SMOKED FISH MAKE A GREAT COMBINATION, ESPECIALLY WITH THE HINT OF TOMATO
AND BASIL. SERVED WITH A GREEN SALAD, IT MAKES AN IDEAL DISH FOR LUNCH OR A FAMILY SUPPER.*

2 Melt 75g/3oz/6 tbsp of the butter in a large pan, add the onion and cook for about 5 minutes until softened and tender but not browned. Sprinkle over the flour and half the chopped basil. Gradually add the reserved fish cooking liquid, adding a little more milk if necessary to make a fairly thin sauce, stirring constantly to make a smooth consistency. Bring to the boil, season with salt and pepper, and add the remaining basil.

3 Remove the pan from the heat, then add the fish and tomatoes and stir gently to combine. Pour into an ovenproof dish.

SERVES EIGHT

INGREDIENTS
  1kg/2¼lb smoked cod
  1kg/2¼lb white cod
  900ml/1½ pint/3¾ cups milk
  1.2litres/2 pints/5 cups water
  2 basil sprigs
  1 lemon thyme sprig
  150g/5oz/10 tbsp butter
  1 onion, chopped
  75g/3oz/⅔ cup plain flour
  30ml/2 tbsp chopped fresh basil
  4 firm plum tomatoes, peeled
   and chopped
  12 medium main crop floury potatoes
  salt and ground black pepper
  crushed black pepper corns,
   to garnish
  lettuce leaves, to serve

1 Place both kinds of fish in a roasting tin with 600ml/1 pint/2½ cups of the milk, the water and the herb sprigs. Bring to a simmer and cook gently for about 3–4 minutes. Leave the fish to cool in the liquid for about 20 minutes. Drain the fish, reserving the cooking liquid for use in the sauce. Flake the fish, removing any skin and bone.

4 Preheat the oven to 180°C/350°F/Gas 4. Cook the potatoes in boiling water until tender. Drain then add the remaining butter and milk, and mash. Season to taste and spoon over the fish mixture, using a fork to create a pattern. You can freeze the pie at this stage. Bake for 30 minutes until the top is golden. Sprinkle with the crushed pepper corns and serve hot with lettuce.

CLASSIC FISH PIE

ORIGINALLY A FISH PIE WAS BASED ON THE "CATCH OF THE DAY". NOW WE CAN CHOOSE EITHER THE
FISH WE LIKE BEST, OR THE VARIETY THAT OFFERS BEST VALUE FOR MONEY.

SERVES FOUR

INGREDIENTS
   butter, for greasing
   450g/1lb mixed fish, such as
      cod or salmon fillets and
      peeled prawns
   finely grated rind of 1 lemon
   450g/1lb floury potatoes
   25g/1oz/2 tbsp butter
   salt and ground black pepper
   1 egg, beaten
For the sauce
   15g/½oz/1 tbsp butter
   15ml/1 tbsp plain flour
   150ml/¼ pint/⅔ cup milk
   45ml/3 tbsp chopped fresh parsley

3 Meanwhile make the sauce. Melt the butter in a saucepan, add the flour and cook, stirring, for a few minutes. Remove from the heat and gradually whisk in the milk. Return to the heat and bring to the boil then reduce the heat and simmer, whisking all the time, until the sauce has thickened and achieved a smooth consistency. Add the parsley and season to taste. Pour over the fish mixture.

4 Drain the potatoes well and then mash with the butter.

5 Pipe or spoon the potatoes on top of the fish mixture. Brush the beaten egg over the potatoes. Bake for 45 minutes until the top is golden brown. Serve hot.

COOK'S TIP
If using frozen fish defrost it very well first, as lots of water will ruin your pie.

1 Preheat the oven to 220°C/425°F/ Gas 7. Grease an ovenproof dish and set aside. Cut the fish into bite-sized pieces. Season the fish, sprinkle over the lemon rind and place in the base of the prepared dish. Allow to sit while you make the topping.

2 Cook the potatoes in boiling salted water until tender.

TUNA AND MASCARPONE BAKE

A ONE-DISH MEAL IDEAL FOR INFORMAL ENTERTAINING THAT MARRIES THE SMOKY FLAVOUR OF SEARED TUNA WITH A SWEET AND HERBY ITALIAN SAUCE.

SERVES FOUR

INGREDIENTS

4 x 175g/6oz tuna steaks
400g/14oz can chopped
   tomatoes, drained
2 garlic cloves, crushed
30ml/2 tbsp chopped fresh basil
250g/9oz/generous 1 cup
   mascarpone cheese
3 large potatoes
25g/1oz/2 tbsp butter, diced
salt and ground black pepper

VARIATION

This dish can easily be made into a side dish, simply leave out the tuna and prepare the other ingredients as before.

1 Preheat the oven to 200°C/400°F/Gas 6. Heat a griddle pan on the hob and sear the fish steaks for 2 minutes on each side, seasoning with a little black pepper. Set aside while you prepare the sauce.

2 Mix the tomatoes, garlic, basil and cheese together in a bowl and season to taste.

3 Grate half the potatoes and dice the other half. Blanch in separate pans of lightly salted water for 3 minutes. Drain.

4 Grease a 1.75 litre/3 pint/7½ cup ovenproof dish. Spoon a little sauce and some grated potato into it. Lay the tuna over with more sauce and the remaining grated potato. Scatter the diced butter and potatoes. Bake for 30 minutes.

POTATO AND SMOKED MUSSEL BAKE

THIS RECIPE USES SMOKED MUSSELS, WHICH HAVE A CREAMY TEXTURE AND RICH FLAVOUR, DELICIOUS WITH SOURED CREAM AND CHIVES. YOU CAN EASILY SUBSTITUTE SMOKED OYSTERS FOR THE MUSSELS.

SERVES FOUR

INGREDIENTS

2 large maincrop potatoes,
   cut in half
butter, for greasing
2 shallots, finely diced
2 x 85g/3¼oz tins smoked mussels
1 bunch chives, snipped
300ml/½ pint/1¼ cups soured cream
175g/6oz/1½ cups mature Cheddar
   cheese, grated
salt and ground black pepper
mixed vegetables, to serve

COOK'S TIP

To serve this dish for a dinner party, rather than serve it in a large dish, once it has cooked, stamp out rounds using a 5cm/2in cutter and serve on a bed of salad leaves.

1 Preheat the oven to 180°C/350°F/Gas 4. Cook the potatoes in a large saucepan of lightly salted boiling water for 15 minutes until they are just tender. Drain and leave to cool slightly. When cool enough to handle cut the potatoes into even 3mm/⅛in slices.

2 Grease the base and sides of a 1.2 litre/2 pint/5 cup casserole dish. Lay a few potato slices over the base of the dish. Scatter a few shallots over and season well.

3 Drain the oil from the mussels into a bowl. Slice the mussels and add them again to the reserved oil. Stir in the chives and soured cream with half of the cheese. Spoon a little of the sauce over the layer of potatoes.

4 Continue to layer the potatoes, shallots and the sauce. Finish with a layer of potatoes and sprinkle over the remainder of the cheese.

5 Bake for 30–45 minutes. Remove from the oven and serve while hot with a selection of mixed vegetables.

SMOKED HADDOCK AND NEW POTATO PIE

SMOKED HADDOCK HAS A SALTY FLAVOUR AND CAN BE BOUGHT EITHER DYED OR UNDYED. THE DYED FISH HAS A STRONG YELLOW COLOUR WHILE THE OTHER IS ALMOST CREAMY IN COLOUR.

SERVES FOUR

INGREDIENTS
450g/1lb smoked haddock fillet
475ml/16fl oz/2 cups
  semi-skimmed milk
2 bay leaves
1 onion, quartered
4 cloves
450g/1lb new potatoes
butter, for greasing
30ml/2 tbsp cornflour
60ml/4 tbsp double cream
30ml/2 tbsp chopped fresh chervil
salt and ground black pepper
mixed vegetables, to serve

VARIATIONS
Instead of using all smoked haddock for this pie, use half smoked and half fresh. Cook the two types together, as described in Step 1. A generous handful of peeled prawns is a good addition to this pie is you want to make it even more filling.

COOK'S TIP
The fish gives out liquid as it cooks, so it is best to start with a slightly thicker sauce than you might think is necessary.

1 Preheat the oven to 200°C/400°F/Gas 6. Place the haddock in a deep-sided frying pan. Pour the milk over and add the bay leaves.

2 Stud the onion with the cloves and place it in the pan with the fish and milk. Cover the top and leave to simmer for about 10 minutes or until the fish starts to flake.

3 Remove the fish with a slotted spoon and set aside to cool. Strain the liquid from the pan into a separate saucepan and set aside.

4 To prepare the potatoes, cut them into fine slices, leaving the skins on.

5 Blanch the potatoes in a large saucepan of lightly salted water for 5 minutes. Drain.

6 Grease the base and sides of a 1.2 litre/2 pint/5 cup ovenproof dish. Then using a knife and fork, carefully flake the fish.

7 Reheat the milk in the saucepan. Mix the cornflour with a little water to form a paste and stir in the cream and the chervil. Add to the milk in the pan and cook until thickened.

8 Arrange one-third of the potatoes over the base of the dish and season with pepper. Lay half of the fish over. Repeat layering, finishing with a layer of potatoes on top.

9 Pour the sauce over the top, making sure that it sinks down through the mixture. Cover with foil and cook for 30 minutes. Remove the foil and cook for a further 10 minutes to brown the surface. Serve with a selection of mixed vegetables.

BAKED MUSSELS AND POTATOES

THIS IMAGINATIVE BAKED CASSEROLE USES SOME OF THE BEST ITALIAN FLAVOURS – TOMATOES, GARLIC, BASIL AND, OF COURSE, PLUMP, JUICY MUSSELS.

SERVES TWO TO THREE

INGREDIENTS

750g/1¾lb large mussels, in
   their shells
225g/8oz small firm potatoes
75ml/5 tbsp olive oil
2 garlic cloves, finely chopped
8 fresh basil leaves, torn into pieces
2 medium tomatoes, peeled and
   thinly sliced
45ml/3 tbsp breadcrumbs
ground black pepper
basil leaves, to garnish

1 Cut off the "beards" from the mussels. Scrub and soak in several changes of cold water. Discard any with broken shells or ones that are open.

2 Place the mussels with a cupful of water in a large saucepan over a medium heat. As soon as they open, lift them out. Remove and discard the empty half shells, leaving the mussels in the other half. (Discard any mussels that do not open at this stage.) Strain any cooking liquid remaining through a layer of kitchen paper, and reserve to add at the final stage.

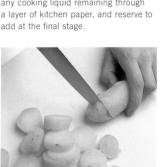

3 Cook the potatoes in a large saucepan of boiling water until they are almost tender. Drain and leave to cool. When they are cool enough to handle, peel and slice them.

4 Preheat the oven to 180°C/350°F/ Gas 4. Spread 30ml/2 tbsp of the olive oil in the bottom of a shallow ovenproof dish. Cover with the potato slices in one layer. Add the mussels in their half shells in one layer. Sprinkle with the garlic and basil. Cover with the tomato slices in one layer.

5 Sprinkle with breadcrumbs and black pepper, the reserved mussel cooking liquid and the remaining olive oil. Bake for about 20 minutes until the tomatoes are soft and the breadcrumbs are golden. Serve hot directly from the baking dish, and garnish with basil.

COD FILLET BAKED WITH SLICED POTATOES

COD FILLET BAKES PERFECTLY, ITS MILD FLAVOUR ENHANCED BY THE HERBS AND ITS JUICES GIVING FLAVOUR TO THE SLICED POTATOES UNDERNEATH.

SERVES FOUR

INGREDIENTS
2 large potatoes, sliced
600ml/1 pint/2½ cups water or
    fish stock
900g/2lb cod fillet, skinned and
    cut into 4 pieces
1 small bunch dill
1 small leek, shredded
50g/2oz/4 tbsp butter
olive oil, to drizzle
salt and ground black pepper
For the sauce
150ml/¼ pint/⅔ cup single cream
shredded leek, to garnish
snipped dill, to garnish

COOK'S TIP
The thicker the fillet of cod, the longer it will take to cook.

1 Preheat the oven to 200°C/400°F/ Gas 6. Cook the potatoes in the water or fish stock for 7–10 minutes or until tender. Drain and reserve the stock.

2 Season the cod pieces. Divide the potatoes into four portions. Arrange each one in an overlapping fan shape on a greased non-stick roasting tin.

3 Season the potatoes and snip some of the dill over each fan, reserving a little for the sauce. Scatter over the leeks, reserving some for the sauce and add a knob of the butter.

4 Lay the fish over the potatoes. Scatter the remaining leeks and sliced potatoes on top of the fish and drizzle with the olive oil. Bake uncovered for 15–20 minutes.

5 Meanwhile, to make the sauce, rapidly boil the reserved stock in a saucepan for 10 minutes or until reduced by two-thirds. Stir in the cream and the remaining dill. Boil for 5 minutes to thicken slightly.

6 Remove the fish from the oven and garnish with dill. Place the individual portions on plates and serve with the sauce.

JANSSON'S TEMPTATION

THIS IS ONE OF SWEDEN'S MOST FAMOUS DISHES. LAYERED WITH ANCHOVIES AND ONIONS AND BAKED WITH CREAM, THE POTATOES TAKE ON A WONDERFUL FLAVOUR.

SERVES SIX

INGREDIENTS
1kg/2¼lb potatoes
2 very large onions
2–3 tins anchovy fillets
ground black pepper
150ml/¼ pint/⅔ cup single cream
25g/1oz/2 tbsp butter, finely diced,
   plus extra for greasing
150ml/¼ pint/⅔ cup double cream

COOK'S TIP
To make this recipe in individual portions, pile all the ingredients except for the double cream on to large squares of buttered foil. Gather up the edges and bring them together. Bake for 40 minutes, then complete according to the recipe.

1 Preheat the oven to 220°C/425°F/ Gas 7. Peel the potatoes and cut into matchsticks. Slice the onions into rings.

2 Grease a 1.75 litre/3 pint/7½ cup casserole dish. Layer half the potatoes and onions in it. Drain the anchovies into a bowl, reserving the oil and lay the fillets over the potatoes, then layer the remaining potatoes and onions. Season.

3 Mix the anchovy oil and single cream together. Then pour evenly over the potatoes. Dot the surface with butter.

4 Cover the potatoes with foil and tightly seal the edges. Bake for 1 hour in the oven. Remove from the oven, taste and adjust the seasonings if necessary. Pour the double cream over and serve immediately.

INDONESIAN PRAWNS
WITH SLICED POTATOES

WITH A FRESH TASTING COMBINATION OF PRAWNS AND THINLY SLICED POTATOES MADE IN INDONESIAN STYLE WITH SATAY SAUCE, THIS DISH IS SURPRISINGLY RICH AND FILLING.

SERVES FOUR

INGREDIENTS
2 large waxy maincrop potatoes,
   peeled and cut in half
120ml/4fl oz/½ cup vegetable oil
1 bunch spring onions, finely sliced
2 red chillies, seeded and diced
450g/1lb peeled cooked prawns
45ml/3 tbsp crunchy peanut butter
200ml/7fl oz/⅞ cup coconut cream
15ml/1 tbsp dark soy sauce
1 bunch chopped fresh coriander
salt

COOK'S TIP
For a more luxurious version, replace the cooked, peeled prawns with fresh raw, shelled king prawns.

1 Cook the potatoes in lightly salted boiling water for 15 minutes until tender. Drain and when cool enough to handle cut into 3mm/⅛in slices. Heat the oil in a frying pan and sauté the potatoes for 10 minutes, turning occasionally until browned. Drain on kitchen paper and keep hot.

2 Drain off almost all of the oil from the pan and fry the spring onions and half the chillies in the pan for 1 minute. Add the prawns and toss for a few seconds.

3 Beat together the peanut butter, coconut cream, soy sauce and remaining chilli. Add this sauce to the prawns and cook for a further minute or two until thoroughly heated through.

4 Lightly grease a large oval platter and arrange the prepared potatoes evenly around the base. Spoon the prawn mixture over until the potatoes are mostly covered over. Top with the coriander.

CLASSIC FISH AND CHIPS

NOTHING BEATS A PIECE OF COD COOKED TO A CRISP WITH FRESHLY MADE CHIPS ON THE SIDE.
THE BATTER SHOULD BE LIGHT AND CRISP, BUT NOT TOO GREASY AND THE FISH SHOULD MELT IN
THE MOUTH. SERVE WITH LEMON WEDGES, OR LIME WEDGES IF YOU REALLY WANT TO TART IT UP.
THE SECRETS OF COOKING FISH AND CHIPS SUCCESSFULLY ARE TO MAKE SURE THE OIL IS FRESH
AND CLEAN. HEAT THE OIL TO THE CORRECT TEMPERATURE BEFORE COOKING THE CHIPS AND AGAIN
BEFORE ADDING THE FISH. SERVE THE DISH IMMEDIATELY, WHILE STILL CRISP AND PIPING HOT.

SERVES FOUR

INGREDIENTS
   450g/1lb potatoes
   groundnut oil for deep fat frying
   4 x 175g/6oz cod fillets, skinned
     and any tiny bones removed
For the batter
   75g/3oz/⅔ cup plain flour
   1 egg yolk
   10ml/2 tsp oil
   175ml/6fl oz/¾ cup water
   salt

1 Cut the potatoes into 5mm/¼in thick slices. Cut each slice again to make 5mm/¼in chips.

2 Heat the oil in a deep fat fryer to 180°C/350°F. Add the chips to the fryer and cook for 3 minutes, then remove from the pan and shake off all fat. Set to one side.

3 To make the batter, sift the flour into a bowl and add the remaining ingredients with a pinch of salt. Beat well until smooth. Set aside until ready to use.

4 Cook the chips again in the fat for a further 5 minutes or so until they are really nice and crisp. Drain on kitchen paper and season with salt. Keep hot in a low oven while you cook the pieces of fish.

VARIATION
Although cod is the traditional choice for fish and chips, you can also use haddock. Rock salmon, sometimes sold as huss or dogfish, also has a good flavour. It has a central bone which cannot be removed before cooking otherwise the pieces of fish will fall apart, but can be easily prized out once the fish is served.

5 Dip the fish into the batter, making sure they are evenly coated and shake off any excess.

6 Carefully lower the fish into the fat and cook for 5 minutes. Drain on kitchen paper. Serve with lemon wedges and the chips.

COOK'S TIP
Use fresh rather than frozen fish for the very best texture and flavour. If you have to use frozen fish, defrost it thoroughly and make sure it is dry before coating with batter.

CARIBBEAN CRAB CAKES

CRAB MEAT MAKES WONDERFUL FISH CAKES, AS EVIDENCED WITH THESE GUTSY MORSELS. SERVED WITH A RICH TOMATO DIP, THEY BECOME GREAT PARTY FOOD TOO, ON "STICKS".

MAKES ABOUT FIFTEEN

INGREDIENTS
225g/8oz white crab meat (fresh,
    frozen or canned)
115g/4oz cooked floury potatoes,
    mashed
30ml/2 tbsp fresh herb seasoning
2.5ml/½ tsp mild mustard
2.5ml/½ tsp ground black pepper
½ fresh hot chilli pepper,
    finely chopped
5ml/1 tsp fresh oregano
1 egg, beaten
plain flour, for dredging
vegetable oil, for frying
lime wedges and coriander sprigs,
    to garnish
fresh whole chilli peppers, to garnish
For the tomato dip
15g/½oz/1 tbsp butter or margarine
½ onion, finely chopped
2 canned plum tomatoes, chopped
1 garlic clove, crushed
150ml/¼ pint/⅔ cup water
5–10ml/1–2 tsp malt vinegar
15ml/1 tbsp chopped fresh coriander
½ hot fresh chilli pepper, chopped

1 To make the crab cakes, mix together the crab meat, potatoes, herb seasoning, mustard, peppers, oregano and egg in a large bowl. Chill the mixture in the bowl for at least 30 minutes.

2 Meanwhile, make the tomato dip to accompany the crab cakes. Melt the butter or margarine in a small pan over a medium heat.

3 Add the onion, tomatoes and garlic and sauté for about 5 minutes until the onion is tender. Add the water, vinegar, coriander and hot chilli pepper. Bring to the boil then reduce the heat and simmer for 10 minutes.

4 Transfer the mixture to a food processor or blender and blend to a smooth purée. Pour into a bowl. Keep warm or chill as wished.

5 Using a spoon, shape the crab into rounds and dredge with flour, shaking off the excess. Heat a little oil in a frying pan and fry, a few at a time, for 2–3 minutes on each side. Drain on kitchen paper and keep warm in a low oven while cooking the remainder.

6 Serve with the tomato dip and garnish with lime wedges, coriander sprigs and whole chillies.

PILCHARD AND LEEK POTATO CAKES

THIS IS A SIMPLE SUPPER USING A SELECTION OF BASIC STORE CUPBOARD INGREDIENTS. USING PILCHARDS IN TOMATO SAUCE GIVES A GREATER DEPTH OF FLAVOUR TO THE FINISHED DISH.

SERVES SIX

INGREDIENTS
    225g/8oz potatoes, diced
    425g/15oz can pilchards in tomato
      sauce, boned and flaked
    1 small leek, very finely diced
    5ml/1 tsp lemon juice
    salt and ground black pepper
For the coating
    1 egg, beaten
    75g/3oz/1½ cups fresh white
      breadcrumbs
    vegetable oil for frying
    salad leaves, cucumber and lemon
      wedges, to garnish
    mayonnaise, to serve

1 Cook the potatoes in lightly salted boiling water for 10 minutes or until tender. Drain, mash, and cool.

2 Add the pilchards and their tomato sauce, leeks and lemon juice. Season with salt and pepper and then beat well until you have formed a smooth paste. Chill for 30 minutes.

3 Divide the mixture into six pieces and shape into cakes. Dip each cake in the egg and then the breadcrumbs.

4 Heat the oil and shallow fry the fish cakes on each side for 5 minutes. Drain on kitchen paper and garnish with salad leaves, cucumber ribbons and lemon wedges. Serve with mayonnaise.

TUNA AND CORN FISH CAKES

DEFINITELY ONE FOR YOUNGER MEMBERS OF THE FAMILY WHO LIKE THE SWEET TASTE OF CORN.
THEY MAY EVEN HELP YOU MAKE SOME FISHY-SHAPED CAKES.

SERVES FOUR

INGREDIENTS
300g/11oz mashed potatoes
200g/7oz can tuna fish in
  soya oil, drained
115g/4oz/¾ cup canned or frozen
  sweetcorn
30ml/2 tbsp chopped fresh parsley
50g/2oz/1 cup fresh white or brown
  breadcrumbs
salt and ground black pepper
grilled baby plum tomatoes and
  salad potatoes, to serve

VARIATIONS
For simple storecupboard variations,
try using canned sardines, red or pink
salmon, or smoked mackerel in place of
the tuna and instant mash when you're
in a real hurry!

1 Preheat the grill. Place the mashed potatoes in a large bowl and stir in the tuna fish, sweetcorn and chopped fresh parsley.

2 Season the mixture to taste with salt and pepper and mix together thoroughly, then shape into eight patty shapes.

3 Lightly coat the fish cakes in the breadcrumbs, pressing to adhere, then place on a baking sheet.

4 Cook the fish cakes under the hot grill until crisp and golden brown on both sides, turning once. Serve hot with grilled baby plum tomatoes and small salad potatoes.

SWEET POTATO, PUMPKIN AND PRAWN CAKES

THIS UNUSUAL ASIAN COMBINATION MAKES A DELICIOUS DISH WHICH NEEDS ONLY A FISH SAUCE OR
SOY SAUCE TO DIP INTO. SERVE WITH NOODLES OR FRIED RICE FOR A LIGHT MEAL.

SERVES FOUR

INGREDIENTS
200g/7oz/1⅔ cups strong white
  bread flour
2.5ml/½ tsp salt
2.5ml/½ tsp dried yeast
175ml/6fl oz/¾ cup warm water
1 egg, beaten
200g/7oz fresh prawn tails, peeled
225g/8oz pumpkin, peeled, seeded
  and grated
150g/5oz sweet potato, grated
2 spring onions, chopped
50g/2oz water chestnuts, chopped
2.5ml/½ tsp chilli sauce
1 garlic clove, crushed
juice of ½ lime
vegetable oil, for deep-frying
lime wedges, to serve

1 Sift together the flour and salt into a large bowl and make a well in the centre. In a separate container dissolve the yeast in the water until creamy then pour into the centre of the flour and salt mixture. Pour in the egg and set aside for a few minutes until bubbles appear. Mix to form a smooth batter.

2 Place the prawns in a saucepan with just enough water to cover. Bring to the boil then reduce the heat and simmer for about 10 minutes. Drain, rinse in cold water and drain again well. Roughly chop then place in a bowl along with the pumpkin and sweet potato.

3 Add the spring onions, water chestnuts, chilli sauce, garlic and lime juice and mix well. Fold into the batter mixture carefully until evenly mixed.

4 Heat a 1cm/½in layer of oil in a large frying pan until really hot. Spoon in the batter in heaps, leaving space between each one, and fry until golden on both sides. Drain on kitchen paper and serve with the lime wedges.

SWEET POTATO FISH ROLLS

THE SWEETNESS OF THE POTATOES IS OFFSET PERFECTLY BY THE TARTNESS OF THE LEMON BUTTER SAUCE SERVED OVER THE FISH ROLLS.

SERVES FOUR

INGREDIENTS
    2 large sweet potatoes
    450g/1lb cod fillet
    300ml/½ pint/1¼ cups milk
    300ml/½ pint/1¼ cups water
    30ml/2 tbsp chopped parsley
    rind and juice of 1 lemon
    2 eggs, beaten
For the coating
    175g/6oz/3 cups fresh white
      breadcrumbs
    5ml/1 tsp Thai 7-spice seasoning
    vegetable oil, for frying
For the sauce
    50g/2oz/4 tbsp butter
    150ml/¼ pint/⅔ cup single cream
    15ml/1 tbsp chopped fresh dill
    lemon zest, to serve

1 Scrub the sweet potatoes and cook them in their skins in plenty of lightly salted boiling water for 45 minutes or until very tender. Drain and cool.

2 When the potatoes are cool, peel the skins and mash the flesh.

3 Place the cod fillet in a large frying pan and pour over the milk and water. Cover and poach for 10 minutes or until the fish starts to flake.

4 Drain and discard the milk, and then remove the skin and the bones from the fish.

5 Flake the fish into the potatoes in a large bowl, stir in the parsley, the rind and juice of ½ of the lemon and 1 egg. Chill for 30 minutes.

COOK'S TIP
Make sure the mixture is chilled thoroughly before you begin shaping and cooking. This helps to hold the ingredients together.

6 Divide and shape the mixture into 8 oval sausages. Dip each in egg. Mix the breadcrumbs with the seasoning. Roll the dipped fish rolls in the breadcrumbs.

7 Heat the oil and shallow fry in batches for about 7 minutes, carefully rolling the rolls to brown evenly. Remove from the pan and drain on kitchen paper. Keep hot.

8 To make the sauce, melt the butter in a small pan and add the remaining lemon juice and rind and allow the mixture to sizzle for a few seconds.

9 Remove from the heat and add the cream and dill. Whisk well to prevent the sauce from curdling and serve with the fish rolls.

Vegetarian Dishes

GIVE THE CLASSIC JACKET POTATO A NEW TWIST WITH A CHOICE OF INTERESTING TOPPINGS. USE POTATOES TO TOP A PIZZA, OR ADD THEM TO A RICH CHEESY BAKE OR A SPICY, GARLIC-FLAVOURED CASSEROLE. MANY COUNTRIES HAVE THEIR OWN SIGNATURE DISHES, SUCH AS GREEK TOMATO AND POTATO BAKE, WHERE CHUNKS OF POTATO ARE SLOW COOKED WITH MEDITERRANEAN RIPENED TOMATOES AND GARLIC — SIMPLY DELICIOUS.

POTATO AND CABBAGE RISSOLES

ORIGINALLY MADE ON MONDAYS WITH LEFTOVER POTATOES AND CABBAGE FROM THE SUNDAY LUNCH, THESE RISSOLES ARE QUICK TO MAKE AND GREAT FOR ANY LIGHT MEAL. OR MAKE THEM FOR BRUNCH TEAMED WITH FRIED EGGS, GRILLED TOMATOES AND MUSHROOMS.

SERVES FOUR

INGREDIENTS
450g/1lb mashed potato
225g/8oz steamed or boiled cabbage
  or kale, shredded
1 egg, beaten
115g/4oz/1 cup Cheddar cheese,
  grated
freshly grated nutmeg
plain flour, for coating
vegetable oil, for frying
salt and ground black pepper
lettuce, to serve

COOK'S TIP
If you want to flavour the rissoles with a stronger tasting cheese, try a blue, such as Stilton or Shropshire Blue.

1 Mix the potato with the cabbage or kale, egg, cheese, nutmeg and seasoning. Divide and shape into eight small sausage shapes.

2 Chill for an hour or so, if possible, as this enables the rissoles to become firm and makes them easier to fry. Dredge them in the flour, shaking off the excess.

3 Heat a 1cm/½in layer of oil in a frying pan until it is really hot. Carefully slide the rissoles into the oil and fry in batches on each side for about 3 minutes until golden and crisp.

4 Remove the rissoles from the pan and drain on kitchen paper. Serve piping hot with fresh lettuce leaves.

POTATO, MOZZARELLA AND GARLIC PIZZA

NEW POTATOES, SMOKED MOZZARELLA AND GARLIC MAKE THIS PIZZA UNIQUE. YOU COULD ADD SLICED SMOKED PORK SAUSAGE OR PASTRAMI TO MAKE IT EVEN MORE SUBSTANTIAL.

SERVES TWO TO THREE

INGREDIENTS
350g/12oz small new or
  salad potatoes
45ml/3 tbsp olive oil
2 garlic cloves, crushed
1 pizza base, 25–30cm/
  10–12 in diameter
1 red onion, thinly sliced
150g/5oz/1¼ cups smoked mozzarella
  cheese, grated
10ml/2 tsp chopped fresh rosemary
  or sage
salt and ground black pepper
30ml/2 tbsp freshly grated Parmesan
  cheese, to garnish

1 Preheat the oven to 220°C/425°F/ Gas 7. Cook the potatoes in boiling salted water for 5 minutes. Drain well and leave to cool. Peel and slice thinly.

2 Heat 30ml/2 tbsp of the oil in a frying pan. Add the sliced potatoes and garlic and fry for 5–8 minutes turning frequently until tender.

3 Brush the pizza base with the remaining oil. Scatter the onion over, then arrange the potatoes on top.

4 Sprinkle over the mozzarella and rosemary or sage and plenty of black pepper. Bake for 15–20 minutes until golden. Remove from the oven, sprinkle with Parmesan and more black pepper.

BAKED POTATOES AND THREE FILLINGS

POTATOES BAKED IN THEIR SKINS UNTIL THEY ARE CRISP ON THE OUTSIDE AND FLUFFY IN THE MIDDLE MAKE AN EXCELLENT AND NOURISHING MEAL ON THEIR OWN. BUT FOR AN EVEN BETTER TREAT, ADD ONE OF THESE DELICIOUS AND EASY TOPPINGS.

SERVES FOUR

INGREDIENTS
    4 medium baking potatoes
    olive oil
    sea salt
    filling of your choice (see below)

COOK'S TIP
Choose potatoes which are evenly sized and have undamaged skins, and scrub them thoroughly. If they are done before you are ready to serve them, take them out of the oven and wrap them up in a warmed cloth until they are needed.

1 Preheat the oven to 200°C/400°F/ Gas 6. Score the potatoes with a cross and rub all over with the olive oil.

2 Place on a baking sheet and cook for 45 minutes to 1 hour until a knife inserted into the centres indicates they are cooked. Or cook in the microwave according to your manufacturer's instructions.

3 Cut the potatoes open along the score lines and push up the flesh. Season and fill with your chosen filling.

STIR-FRY VEG
    45ml/3 tbsp groundnut or sunflower oil
    2 leeks, thinly sliced
    2 carrots, cut into sticks
    1 courgette, thinly sliced
    115g/4oz baby corn, halved
    115g/4oz/1½ cup button mushrooms, sliced
    45ml/3 tbsp soy sauce
    30ml/2 tbsp dry sherry or vermouth
    15ml/1 tbsp sesame oil
    sesame seeds, to garnish

1 Heat the groundnut or sunflower oil in a wok or large frying pan until really hot. Add the leeks, carrots, courgette and baby corn and stir-fry together for about 2 minutes, then add the mushrooms and stir-fry for a further minute. Mix the soy sauce, sherry or vermouth and sesame oil and pour over the vegetables. Heat through until just bubbling and scatter the sesame seeds over.

RED BEAN CHILLIES
    425g/15oz can red kidney beans, drained
    200g/7oz/scant 1 cup low-fat cottage or cream cheese
    30ml/2 tbsp mild chilli sauce
    5ml/1 tsp ground cumin

1 Heat the beans in a pan or microwave and stir in the cottage or cream cheese, chilli sauce and cumin.

2 Serve topped with more chilli sauce.

CHEESE AND CREAMY CORN
    425g/15oz can creamed corn
    115g/4oz/1 cup hard cheese, grated
    5ml/1 tsp mixed dried herbs
    fresh parsley sprigs, to garnish

1 Heat the corn gently with the cheese and mixed herbs until well blended.

2 Use to fill the potatoes and garnish with fresh parsley sprigs.

TRUFFADE

BAKED UNTIL MELTINGLY SOFT, THIS WARMING CHEESE AND POTATO SUPPER IS THE PERFECT SLOW BAKE TO COME HOME TO. IN FRANCE, WHERE IT ORIGINATED, IT WOULD BE MADE WITH A TOMME OR CANTAL CHEESE WHICH ARE NOW READILY AVAILABLE.

SERVES FOUR TO SIX

INGREDIENTS
  a little sunflower oil or melted butter
  1 large onion, thinly sliced
  675g/1½lb baking potatoes, very
    thinly sliced
  150g/5oz/1¼ cups grated hard
    cheese, such as Tomme, Cantal or
    mature Cheddar
  freshly grated nutmeg
  salt and ground black pepper
  mixed salad leaves, to serve

VARIATION
In France, they make a non-vegetarian
version of this dish, which is cooked with
diced streaky bacon (lardons) and the
cheese is chopped, not grated. The
ingredients are mixed and cooked
slowly in a little lard in a pan on top
of the stove.

1 Preheat the oven to 180°C/350°F/
Gas 4. Lightly grease the base of a
shallow baking dish or roasting tin with
the oil or melted butter.

2 Arrange a layer of onions over the
bottom of the dish and then add a
layer of potatoes over them, and a
sprinkling of cheese. Finish with a layer
of potatoes.

3 Brush the top layer of potatoes with
oil or melted butter and season with
nutmeg, salt and pepper.

4 Top the dish with a layer of cheese.
Bake for 1 hour 5 minutes until the
vegetables are tender and the top is
golden brown. Leave the dish to stand
for about 5 minutes, then serve in
wedges with a salad.

POTATOES BAKED WITH TOMATOES

THIS SIMPLE, HEARTY DISH FROM THE SOUTH OF ITALY IS BEST WHEN TOMATOES ARE IN SEASON AND BURSTING WITH FLAVOUR, BUT IT CAN ALSO BE MADE WITH CANNED PLUM TOMATOES.

SERVES SIX

INGREDIENTS
  2 large red or yellow onions,
    thinly sliced
  1kg/2¼lb baking potatoes,
    thinly sliced
  450g/1lb tomatoes, fresh or canned,
    sliced, with their juice
  90ml/6 tbsp olive oil
  115g/4oz/1 cup Parmesan
    or Cheddar cheese,
    freshly grated
  a few fresh basil leaves
  50ml/2fl oz/¼ cup water
  salt and ground black pepper

1 Preheat the oven to 180°C/350°F/
Gas 4. Brush a large baking dish
generously with oil.

2 Arrange a layer of some onions in
the base of the dish, followed by layers
of some potatoes and tomatoes
alternating them to make the dish look
colourful. Pour a little of the oil over the
surface, and sprinkle with some of the
cheese. Season with salt and ground
black pepper.

3 Continue to layer the vegetables in
the dish until they are used up, ending
with an overlapping layer of potatoes
and tomatoes. Tear the basil leaves into
small pieces, and add them here and
there among the vegetables, saving a
few for garnish. Sprinkle the top with
the remaining grated cheese and oil.

4 Pour the water over the dish. Bake in
the oven for 1 hour until the vegetables
are tender.

5 Check the potato dish towards the
end of cooking and if the top begins to
brown too much, place a sheet of foil or
greaseproof paper, or a flat baking tray
on top of the dish. Garnish the dish with
the remaining fresh basil, once it is
cooked, and serve hot.

TURKISH-STYLE NEW POTATO CASSEROLE

HERE'S A MEAL IN A POT THAT'S SUITABLE FOR FEEDING LARGE NUMBERS OF PEOPLE. IT'S LIGHTLY SPICED AND HAS PLENTY OF GARLIC — WHO COULD REFUSE?

SERVES FOUR

INGREDIENTS

60ml/4 tbsp olive oil
1 large onion, chopped
2 small–medium aubergines, cut into
   small cubes
4 courgettes, cut into small chunks
1 green pepper, seeded and chopped
1 red or yellow pepper, seeded
   and chopped
115g/4oz/1 cup fresh or frozen peas
115g/4oz French beans
450g/1lb new or salad
   potatoes, cubed
2.5ml/½ tsp cinnamon
2.5ml/½ tsp ground cumin
5ml/1 tsp paprika
4–5 tomatoes, skinned
400g/14oz can chopped tomatoes
30ml/2 tbsp chopped fresh parsley
3–4 garlic cloves, crushed
350ml/12fl oz/1½ cups
   vegetable stock
salt and ground black pepper
black olives, to garnish
fresh parsley, to garnish

1 Preheat the oven to 190°C/375°F/Gas 5. Heat 45ml/3 tbsp of the oil in a heavy-based pan, add the onion and fry until golden. Add the aubergines, sauté for about 3 minutes and then add the courgettes, green and red or yellow peppers, peas, beans and potatoes, together with the spices and seasoning.

2 Continue to cook for 3 minutes, stirring all the time. Transfer to a shallow ovenproof dish.

3 Halve, seed and chop the fresh tomatoes and mix with the canned tomatoes, parsley, garlic and the remaining olive oil in a bowl.

4 Pour the stock over the aubergine mixture and then spoon over the prepared tomato mixture.

5 Cover and bake the dish for 30–45 minutes until the vegetables are tender. Serve hot, garnished with black olives and parsley.

POTATO GNOCCHI

*GNOCCHI ARE LITTLE ITALIAN DUMPLINGS MADE EITHER WITH MASHED POTATO AND FLOUR, OR WITH
SEMOLINA. TO ENSURE THAT THEY ARE LIGHT AND FLUFFY, TAKE CARE NOT TO OVERMIX THE DOUGH.*

4 Divide the dough into 4 pieces. On
a lightly floured surface, form each into
a roll about 2cm/¾in in diameter. Cut
the rolls crossways into pieces about
2cm/¾in long.

5 Hold an ordinary table fork with tines
sideways, leaning on the board. Then
one by one, press and roll the gnocchi
lightly along the tines of the fork
towards the points, making ridges on
one side, and a depression from your
thumb on the other.

SERVES FOUR TO SIX

INGREDIENTS
  1kg/2¼lb waxy potatoes
  250–300g/9–11oz/2¼–2¾ cups
    plain flour, plus more
    if necessary
  1 egg
  pinch of freshly grated nutmeg
  25g/1oz/2 tbsp butter
  salt
  fresh basil leaves, to garnish
  Parmesan cheese cut in shavings,
    to garnish

COOK'S TIP
Gnocchi are also excellent served with
a heated sauce, such as Bolognese.

1 Cook the potatoes in their skins in a
large saucepan of boiling salted water
until tender but not falling apart.
Drain and peel while the potatoes
are still hot.

2 Spread a layer of flour on a work
surface. Pass the hot potatoes through
a food mill, dropping them directly on to
the flour. Sprinkle with about half of the
remaining flour and mix in very lightly.
Break the egg into the mixture.

3 Finally add the nutmeg to the dough
and knead lightly, adding more flour if
the mixture is too loose. When the
dough is light to the touch and no
longer moist it is ready to be rolled.

6 Bring a large pan of salted water to a
fast boil, then drop in about half the
prepared gnocchi.

7 When the gnocchi rise to the surface,
after 3–4 minutes, they are done. Lift
them out with a slotted spoon, drain
well, and place in a warmed serving
bowl. Dot with butter. Cover to keep
warm while cooking the remainder.
As soon as they are cooked, toss the
gnocchi with the butter, garnish with
Parmesan shavings and fresh basil
leaves, and serve at once.

PUMPKIN GNOCCHI WITH A CHANTERELLE PARSLEY CREAM

ITALIANS LOVE PUMPKIN AND OFTEN INCORPORATE IT INTO THEIR DUMPLINGS AND OTHER TRADITIONAL PASTA DISHES AS IT ADDS A SLIGHT SWEET RICHNESS. THESE GNOCCHI ARE SUPERB ON THEIR OWN BUT THEY ARE ALSO GREAT SERVED WITH MEAT OR GAME.

SERVES FOUR

INGREDIENTS
450g/1lb floury potatoes
450g/1lb pumpkin, peeled, seeded
   and chopped
2 egg yolks
200g/7oz/1¾ cups plain flour, plus
   more if necessary
pinch of ground allspice
1.5ml/¼ tsp cinnamon
pinch of freshly grated nutmeg
finely grated rind of ½ orange
salt and ground pepper
For the sauce
30ml/2 tbsp olive oil
1 shallot, finely chopped
175g/6oz/2½ cups fresh chanterelles,
   sliced, or 15g/½oz/½ cup dried,
   soaked in warm water for
   20 minutes, then drained
10ml/2 tsp almond butter
150ml/¼ pint/⅔ cup crème fraîche
a little milk or water
75ml/5 tbsp chopped fresh parsley
50g/2oz/½ cup Parmesan cheese,
   freshly grated

1 Cook the potatoes in a large saucepan of boiling salted water for 20 minutes. Drain and set aside.

2 Place the pumpkin in a bowl, cover and microwave on full power for 8 minutes. Alternatively, wrap the pumpkin in foil and bake at 180°C/ 350°F/Gas 4 for 30 minutes. Drain well.

3 Pass the pumpkin and potatoes through a food mill into a bowl. Add the egg yolks, flour, spices, orange rind and seasoning and mix well to make a soft dough. If you find that the mixture is too loose you can add a little more flour to stiffen it up.

4 Bring a large pan of salted water to a fast boil. Meanwhile, spread a layer of flour on a clean work surface. Spoon the prepared gnocchi mixture into a piping bag fitted with a 1cm/½in plain nozzle.

VARIATION
Turn these gnocchi into a main meal for vegetarians by serving them with a rich home-made tomato sauce. If you want to make the dish more special, serve the gnocchi with a side dish of ratatouille made from courgettes, peppers and aubergines, cooked gently with tomatoes, plenty of garlic and really good extra virgin olive oil.

5 Pipe directly on to the flour to make a 15cm/6in sausage. Roll in flour and cut crossways into 2.5cm/1in pieces. Repeat to make more sausage shapes and pieces. Mark each lightly with the tines of a fork and drop into the boiling water. When they rise to the surface, after 3–4 minutes, they are done.

6 Meanwhile make the sauce. Heat the oil in a non-stick frying pan, add the shallot and fry until soft but not coloured. Add the chanterelles and cook briefly, then add the almond butter. Stir to melt and stir in the crème fraîche. Simmer briefly and adjust the consistency with milk or water. Add the parsley and season to taste.

7 Lift the gnocchi out of the water with a slotted spoon, drain well, and turn into bowls. Spoon the sauce over the top, sprinkle with grated Parmesan, and serve at once.

COOK'S TIPS
If planning ahead, gnocchi can be shaped, ready for cooking, up to 8 hours in advance. Almond butter is available from health food shops.

POTATO CAKES WITH GOAT'S CHEESE

GRILLED GOAT'S CHEESE MAKES A DELICATELY TANGY AND GENTLY BUBBLING TOPPING FOR THESE HERBY POTATO CAKES. SERVE WITH A FLAVOURSOME SALAD.

SERVES TWO TO FOUR

INGREDIENTS
    450g/1lb floury potatoes
    10ml/2 tsp chopped fresh thyme
    1 garlic clove, crushed
    2 spring onions (including the green
        parts), finely chopped
    30ml/2 tbsp olive oil
    50g/2oz/4 tbsp unsalted butter
    2 x 65g/2½oz firm goat's cheese
    salt and ground black pepper
    salad leaves, such as curly endive,
        radicchio and lamb's lettuce, tossed
        in walnut dressing, to serve
    thyme sprigs, to garnish

COOK'S TIP
These potato cakes make great party
snacks. Make them half the size and
serve warm on a large platter.

1 Coarsely grate the potatoes. Using
your hands, squeeze out as much of
the thick starchy liquid as possible,
then gently combine with the chopped
thyme, garlic, spring onions and
seasoning.

2 Heat half the oil and butter in a non-
stick frying pan. Add two large
spoonfuls of the potato mixture, spacing
them well apart, and press firmly down
with a spatula. Cook for 3–4 minutes on
each side until golden.

3 Drain the potato cakes on kitchen
paper and keep warm in a low oven.
Heat the remaining oil and butter and
fry two more potato cakes in the same
way with the remaining mixture.
Meanwhile preheat the grill.

4 Cut the cheese in half horizontally
and place one half, cut side up, on
each potato cake. Grill for 2–3 minutes
until lightly golden. Serve on plates and
arrange the salad leaves around them.
Garnish with thyme sprigs.

WILD MUSHROOM GRATIN WITH BEAUFORT CHEESE, NEW POTATOES AND WALNUTS

THIS IS ONE OF THE SIMPLEST AND MOST DELICIOUS WAYS OF COOKING MUSHROOMS. SERVE THIS DISH AS THE SWISS DO, WITH NEW POTATOES AND GHERKINS.

SERVES FOUR

INGREDIENTS
    900g/2lb small new or
        salad potatoes
    50g/2oz/4 tbsp unsalted butter or
        60ml/4 tbsp olive oil
    350g/12oz/5 cups assorted wild and
        cultivated mushrooms, thinly sliced
    175g/6oz Beaufort or Fontina cheese,
        thinly sliced
    50g/2oz/½ cup broken walnuts,
        toasted
    salt and ground black pepper
    12 gherkins and mixed green salad
        leaves, to serve

1 Cook the potatoes in boiling salted
water for 20 minutes until tender. Drain
and return to the pan. Add a knob of
butter or oil and cover to keep warm.

2 Heat the remaining butter or the oil
in a frying pan over a medium-high
heat. Add the mushrooms and fry until
their juices appear, then increase the
heat and fry until most of their juices
have cooked away. Season.

3 Meanwhile preheat the grill. Arrange
the cheese on top of the mushroom
slices, place the pan under the grill and
grill until bubbly and golden brown.
Scatter the gratin with walnuts and
serve at once with the buttered
potatoes and sliced gherkins. Serve a
side dish of mixed green salad to
complete this meal.

SPICY POTATO STRUDEL

WRAP UP A TASTY MIXTURE OF VEGETABLES IN A SPICY, CREAMY SAUCE WITH CRISP FILO PASTRY.
SERVE WITH A GOOD SELECTION OF CHUTNEYS OR A YOGURT SAUCE.

SERVES FOUR

INGREDIENTS

1 onion, chopped
2 carrots, coarsely grated
1 courgette, chopped
350g/12oz firm potatoes,
  finely chopped
65g/2½oz/5 tbsp butter
10ml/2 tsp mild curry paste
2.5ml/½ tsp dried thyme
150ml/¼ pint/⅔ cup water
1 egg, beaten
30ml/2 tbsp single cream
50g/2oz/½ cup Cheddar
  cheese, grated
8 sheets filo pastry, thawed if frozen
sesame seeds, for sprinkling
salt and ground black pepper

1 In a large frying pan cook the onion, carrots, courgette and potatoes in 25g/1oz/2 tbsp of the butter for 5 minutes tossing frequently so they cook evenly. Add the curry paste and stir in. Continue to cook, the vegetables for a further minute or so.

2 Add the thyme, water and seasoning. Bring to the boil then reduce the heat and simmer for 10 minutes until tender, stirring occasionally.

3 Remove from the heat and leave to cool. Transfer the mixture into a large bowl and then mix in the egg, cream and cheese. Chill until ready to fill the filo pastry.

4 Melt the remaining butter and lay out four sheets of filo pastry, slightly overlapping them to form a fairly large rectangle. Brush with some melted butter and fit the other sheets on top. Brush again.

5 Preheat the oven to 190°C/375°F/ Gas 5. Spoon the filling along one long side, then roll up the pastry. Form it into a circle and set on a baking sheet. Brush again with the last of the butter and sprinkle over the sesame seeds.

6 Bake the strudel in the oven for about 25 minutes until golden and crisp. Stand for 5 minutes before cutting.

PEPPER AND POTATO TORTILLA

TORTILLA IS TRADITIONALLY A SPANISH DISH LIKE A THICK OMELETTE, BEST EATEN COLD IN CHUNKY WEDGES. IT MAKES IDEAL PICNICKING FOOD. USE A HARD SPANISH CHEESE, LIKE MAHÓN, OR A GOAT'S CHEESE, ALTHOUGH SHARP CHEDDAR MAKES A GOOD SUBSTITUTE.

SERVES FOUR

INGREDIENTS

2 medium firm potatoes
45ml/3 tbsp olive oil, plus more
   if necessary
1 large onion, thinly sliced
2 garlic cloves, crushed
2 peppers, one green and one red,
   seeded and thinly sliced
6 eggs, beaten
115g/4oz/1 cup sharp cheese, grated
salt and ground black pepper

VARIATION
You can add any sliced and lightly cooked vegetable, such as mushrooms, courgette or broccoli, to this tortilla instead of the green and red peppers. Cooked pasta or brown rice are both excellent alternatives to the potatoes.

1 Par-boil the potatoes in boiling water for about 10 minutes. Drain and leave to cool slightly. Slice them thickly. Preheat the grill.

2 In a large non-stick or well-seasoned frying pan, heat the oil over a medium heat. Add the onion, garlic and peppers and cook for 5 minutes until softened.

3 Add the potatoes and continue frying, stirring occasionally, until the potatoes are tender.

4 Pour in half the beaten eggs, sprinkle half the cheese over this and then the remainder of the egg. Season. Finish with a layer of cheese. Reduce the heat to low and continue to cook without stirring, half covering the pan with a lid to help set the eggs.

5 When the tortilla is firm, place the pan under the hot grill to seal the top just lightly. Leave the tortilla in the pan to cool. Serve at room temperature, cut into wedges.

CHINESE POTATOES WITH CHILLI BEANS

EAST MEETS WEST IN THIS AMERICAN-STYLE DISH WITH A CHINESE FLAVOUR – THE SAUCE IS PARTICULARLY TASTY. TRY IT AS A QUICK SUPPER WHEN YOU FANCY A MEAL WITH A LITTLE ZING!

SERVES FOUR

INGREDIENTS
    4 medium firm or waxy potatoes,
        cut into thick chunks
    30ml/2 tbsp sunflower or
        groundnut oil
    3 spring onions, sliced
    1 large fresh chilli, seeded and sliced
    2 garlic cloves, crushed
    400g/14oz can red kidney
        beans, drained
    30ml/2 tbsp soy sauce
    15ml/1 tbsp sesame oil
    15ml/1 tbsp sesame seeds,
        to garnish
    chopped fresh coriander or parsley,
        to garnish
    salt and ground black pepper

1 Cook the potatoes in boiling water until they are just tender. Take care not to overcook them. Drain and reserve.

2 Heat the oil in a large frying pan or wok over a medium-high heat. Add the spring onions and chilli and stir-fry for about 1 minute, then add the garlic and stir-fry for a few seconds longer.

3 Add the potatoes, stirring well, then the beans and finally the soy sauce and sesame oil.

4 Season to taste and continue to cook the vegetables until they are well heated through. Sprinkle with the sesame seeds and the coriander or parsley and serve hot.

GREEK TOMATO AND POTATO BAKE

AN ADAPTATION OF A CLASSIC GREEK DISH, WHICH IS USUALLY COOKED ON THE HOB. THIS RECIPE HAS A RICHER FLAVOUR AS IT IS STOVE COOKED FIRST AND THEN BAKED IN THE OVEN.

SERVES FOUR

INGREDIENTS
    120ml/4fl oz/½ cup olive oil
    1 large onion, finely chopped
    3 garlic cloves, crushed
    4 large ripe tomatoes, peeled,
        deseeded and chopped
    1kg/2¼lb even-size main crop
        waxy potatoes
    salt and freshly ground black pepper
    flat leaf parsley, to garnish

COOK'S TIP
Make sure that the potatoes are completely coated in the oil for even cooking.

1 Preheat the oven to 180°C/350°F/ Gas 4. Heat the oil in a flameproof casserole. Fry the onion and garlic for 5 minutes until softened and just starting to brown.

2 Add the tomatoes to the pan, season and cook for 1 minute. Cut the potatoes into wedges. Add to the pan. Cook for 10 minutes. Season again and cover with a tight fitting lid.

3 Place the covered casserole on the middle shelf of the oven and cook for 45 minutes–1 hour. Garnish with flat leaf parsley.

CHILLI CHEESE TORTILLA <u>WITH</u> FRESH TOMATO SALSA

GOOD WARM OR COLD, THIS IS LIKE A SLICED POTATO QUICHE WITHOUT THE PASTRY BASE, WELL SPIKED WITH CHILLI. THE SALSA CAN BE MADE WITHOUT THE CHILLI IF YOU PREFER.

SERVES FOUR

INGREDIENTS
45ml/3 tbsp sunflower or olive oil
1 small onion, thinly sliced
2–3 fresh green jalapeño chillies,
  seeded and sliced
200g/7oz cold cooked potato,
  thinly sliced
120g/4¼oz/generous 1 cup cheese,
  grated (use a firm but not hard
  cheese, such as Double Gloucester,
  Monterey Jack or Manchego)
6 eggs, beaten
salt and ground black pepper
fresh herbs, to garnish
For the salsa
500g/1¼lb fresh flavoursome
  tomatoes, peeled, seeded and
  finely chopped
1 fresh mild green chilli, seeded and
  finely chopped
2 garlic cloves, crushed
45ml/3 tbsp chopped fresh coriander
juice of 1 lime
2.5ml/½ tsp salt

1 To make the salsa, put the tomatoes in a bowl and add the chopped chilli, garlic, coriander, lime juice and salt. Mix well and set aside.

2 Heat 15ml/1 tbsp of the oil in a large omelette pan and gently fry the onion and jalapeños for 5 minutes, stirring until softened. Add the potato and cook for 5 minutes until lightly browned, keeping the slices whole.

3 Using a slotted spoon, transfer the vegetables to a warm plate. Wipe the pan with kitchen paper, then add the remaining oil and heat until really hot. Return the vegetables to the pan. Scatter the cheese over the top. Season.

4 Pour in the beaten eggs, making sure that they seep under the vegetables. Cook the tortilla over a low heat, without stirring, until set. Serve hot or cold, cut into wedges, garnished with fresh herbs and with the salsa on the side.

POTATO AND RED PEPPER FRITTATA

FRITTATA IS LIKE A LARGE OMELETTE, THIS TASTY VERSION IS FILLED WITH POTATOES AND PLENTY OF HERBS. DO USE FRESH MINT IN PREFERENCE TO DRIED IF YOU CAN FIND IT.

2 Whisk together the eggs, mint and seasoning in a bowl, then set aside. Heat the oil in a large frying pan.

3 Add the onion, garlic, peppers and potatoes to the pan and cook, stirring occasionally, for 5 minutes.

4 Pour the egg mixture over the vegetables in the frying pan and stir gently.

5 Push the mixture towards the centre of the pan as it cooks to allow the liquid egg to run on to the base. Meanwhile preheat the grill.

6 When the frittata is lightly set, place the pan under the hot grill for 2–3 minutes until the top is a light golden brown colour.

7 Serve hot or cold, cut into wedges piled high on a serving dish and garnished with sprigs of mint.

SERVES THREE TO FOUR

INGREDIENTS
  450g/1lb small new or
    salad potatoes
  6 eggs
  30ml/2 tbsp chopped fresh mint
  30ml/2 tbsp olive oil
  1 onion, chopped
  2 garlic cloves, crushed
  2 red peppers, seeded and
    roughly chopped
salt and ground black pepper
mint sprigs, to garnish

1 Cook the potatoes in their skins in boiling salted water until just tender. Drain and leave to cool slightly, then cut into thick slices.

POTATOES WITH BLUE CHEESE AND WALNUTS

FIRM SMALL POTATOES, SERVED IN A CREAMY BLUE CHEESE SAUCE WITH THE CRUNCH OF WALNUTS, MAKE A GREAT SIDE DISH TO A SIMPLE ROAST MEAL. FOR A CHANGE, SERVE IT AS A LUNCH DISH OR A LIGHT SUPPER WITH A GREEN SALAD.

SERVES FOUR

INGREDIENTS
   450g/1lb small new or
      salad potatoes
   1 small head of celery, sliced
   1 small red onion, sliced
   115g/4oz/1 cup blue cheese, mashed
   150ml/¼ pint/⅔ cup single cream
   50g/2oz/½ cup walnut pieces
   30ml/2 tbsp chopped fresh parsley
   salt and ground black pepper

COOK'S TIP
Use a combination of blue cheeses, such as Dolcelatte and Roquefort, or go for the distinctive flavour of Stilton on its own. If walnuts are not available, blue cheeses marry equally well with hazelnuts.

1 Cook the potatoes in their skins in a large saucepan with plenty of boiling water for about 15 minutes or until tender, adding the sliced celery and onion to the pan for the last 5 minutes or so of cooking.

2 Drain the vegetables well through a colander and put them into a shallow serving dish.

3 In a small saucepan, slowly melt the cheese in the cream, stirring occasionally. Do not allow the mixture to boil but heat it until it scalds.

4 Check the sauce and season to taste. Pour it evenly over the vegetables in the dish and scatter over the walnut pieces and fresh parsley. Serve hot, straight from the dish.

RACLETTE WITH NEW POTATOES

TRADITIONAL TO BOTH SWITZERLAND AND FRANCE, RACLETTE MELTS TO A VELVETY CREAMINESS AND WARM GOLDEN COLOUR AND HAS A SAVOURY TASTE WITH A HINT OF SWEETNESS.

SERVES FOUR

INGREDIENTS
For the pickle
   2 red onions, sliced
   5ml/1 tsp sugar
   90ml/6 tbsp red wine vinegar
   2.5ml/½ tsp salt
   generous pinch of dried dill
For the potatoes
   500g/1¼lb new or salad potatoes,
      halved if large
   250g/9oz raclette cheese slices
   salt and ground black pepper

1 To make the pickle spread out the onions in a glass dish, pour over boiling water to cover and leave until cold.

2 Meanwhile mix the sugar, vinegar, salt and dill in a small pan. Heat gently, stirring, until the sugar has dissolved, then set aside to cool.

3 Drain the onions and return them to the dish, pour the vinegar mixture over, cover and leave for at least 1 hour, preferably overnight.

4 Cook the potatoes in their skins in boiling water until tender, then drain and place in a roasting tin. Preheat the grill. Season the potatoes and arrange the raclette on top. Place the tin under the grill until the cheese melts. Serve hot. Drain the excess vinegar from the red onion pickle and serve the pickle with the potatoes.

COOK'S TIP
To speed up the process look for ready-sliced raclette for this dish. It is available from most large supermarkets and specialist cheese shops.

LAYERED VEGETABLE TERRINE

*A COMBINATION OF VEGETABLES AND HERBS LAYERED AND BAKED IN A SPINACH-LINED LOAF TIN.
DELICIOUS SERVED HOT OR WARM WITH A SIMPLE SALAD GARNISH.*

SERVES SIX

INGREDIENTS
  3 red peppers, halved
  450g/1lb main crop waxy potatoes
  115g/4oz spinach leaves, trimmed
  25g/1oz/2 tbsp butter
  pinch grated nutmeg
  115g/4oz/1 cup vegetarian Cheddar
    cheese, grated
  1 medium courgette, sliced
    lengthways and blanched
  salt and ground black pepper

1 Preheat the oven to 180°C/350°F/
Gas 4. Place the peppers in a roasting
tin and roast, cores in place, for 30–45
minutes until charred. Remove from the
oven. Place in a plastic bag to cool.
Peel the skins and remove the cores.
Halve the potatoes and boil in lightly
salted water for 10–15 minutes.

2 Blanch the spinach for a few
seconds in boiling water. Drain and pat
dry on kitchen paper. Line the base and
sides of a 900g/2lb loaf tin, making sure
the leaves overlap slightly.

3 Slice the potatoes thinly and lay one-
third of the potatoes over the base, dot
with a little of the butter and season
with salt, pepper and nutmeg. Sprinkle
a little cheese over.

4 Arrange 3 of the peeled pepper
halves on top. Sprinkle a little cheese
over and then a layer of courgettes. Lay
another one-third of the potatoes on top
with the remaining peppers and some
more cheese, seasoning as you go. Lay
the final layer of potato on top and
scatter over any remaining cheese. Fold
the spinach leaves over. Cover with foil.

5 Place the loaf tin in a roasting tin
and pour boiling water around the
outside, making sure the water comes
halfway up the sides of the tin. Bake for
45 minutes–1 hour. Remove from the
oven and turn the loaf out. Serve sliced
with lettuce and tomatoes.

BAKED SCALLOPED POTATOES WITH FETA CHEESE AND OLIVES

THINLY SLICED POTATOES ARE COOKED WITH GREEK FETA CHEESE AND BLACK AND GREEN OLIVES IN OLIVE OIL. THIS DISH IS A GOOD ONE TO SERVE WITH TOASTED PITTA BREAD.

SERVES FOUR

INGREDIENTS
900g/2lb main crop potatoes
150ml/¼ pint/⅔ cup olive oil
1 sprig rosemary
275g/10oz/2½ cups feta cheese,
  crumbled
115g/4oz/1 cup pitted black and
  green olives
300ml/½ pint/1¼ cups hot
  vegetable stock
salt and ground black pepper

COOK'S TIP
Make sure you choose Greek feta cheese, which has a completely different texture to Danish.

1 Preheat the oven to 200°C/400°F/ Gas 6. Cook the potatoes in plenty of boiling water for 15 minutes. Drain and cool slightly. Peel the potatoes and cut into thin slices.

2 Brush the base and sides of a 1.5 litre/2½ pint/6¼ cup rectangular ovenproof dish with some of the olive oil.

3 Layer the potatoes in the dish with the rosemary, cheese and olives. Drizzle with the remaining olive oil and pour over the stock. Season the whole with salt and plenty of ground black pepper.

4 Cook for 35 minutes, covering with foil to prevent the potatoes from getting too brown. Serve hot, straight from the dish.

Breads and Scones

POTATOES PLAY AN ESSENTIAL PART IN MANY LOCAL
AND REGIONAL BREAD AND SCONE DISHES.
TRY MAKING HERB POTATO
SCONES AND BE SURPRISED AT
THEIR LIGHT TEXTURE AND
WONDERFUL FLAVOUR. FOR A
CONTRAST IN FLAVOURS, SERVE
STEAMING HOT BOWLS OF SOUP
WITH SWEET POTATO AND HONEY
BREAD ROLLS, SPICED WITH THE
DELICATE FLAVOUR OF CUMIN.

GRATED CHEESE AND ONION POTATO BREAD

A PLAITED LOAF WITH A CRISP CHEESE AND ONION TOPPING. IDEALLY YOU SHOULD SERVE THIS BREAD BY PULLING CHUNKS OFF THE LOAF RATHER THAN SLICING, SO THAT YOU GET MASSES OF TOPPING WITH EACH BITE. THIS BREAD IS PARTICULARLY DELICIOUS SERVED WARM.

MAKES A 900G/2LB LOAF

INGREDIENTS
    225g/8oz floury potatoes
    350g/12oz/3 cups strong white flour
    7.5ml/1½ tsp easy-blend dried yeast
    25g/1oz/2 tbsp butter, diced
    50g/2oz/½ cup pitted green or
      black olives
For the topping
    30ml/2 tbsp olive oil
    1 onion, sliced into rings
    50g/2oz/½ cup mature Cheddar
      cheese, grated
    salt and ground black pepper

1 Chop the potatoes and cook in a large saucepan with plenty of salted boiling water for 15–20 minutes or until tender.

2 Meanwhile, sift the flour into a bowl, add the yeast and a little salt. Rub in the butter to form fine crumbs. Drain the potatoes and mash well. Add to the dry ingredients with 300ml/½ pint/1¼ cups lukewarm water.

3 Bring the mixture together with a round-bladed knife and then turn out on to a floured surface. Knead for about 5 minutes. Return the dough to a bowl and cover with a damp cloth. Leave to rise for 1 hour or until doubled in size. Turn the dough out onto a floured surface and knock back to remove any air bubbles. Carefully knead in the olives. Cut the dough into three even pieces.

4 Roll each piece out to a long thick sausage. Twist the sausages over each other to form a plait (see Cook's Tip, below). Lift on to a greased baking sheet. Cover with a damp cloth and leave to rise for 30 minutes or until doubled in size.

COOK'S TIP
To plait a loaf successfully, lay the three lengths of dough side by side. Plait the dough from one end to the centre and repeat with the other end. This will give an even loaf with a professional looking touch to it.

5 Meanwhile, for the topping, preheat the oven to 220°C/425°F/Gas 7. Heat the oil in a saucepan and fry the onions for 10 minutes until golden.

6 Remove the onions from the pan and drain on kitchen paper.

7 Scatter the onions and grated cheese over the bread and bake in the oven for 20 minutes.

SWEET POTATO AND HONEY BREAD ROLLS

A SWEET ROLL THAT TASTES AS DELICIOUS SERVED WITH CONSERVES AS WITH A SAVOURY SOUP.

MAKES TWELVE

INGREDIENTS
1 large sweet potato
225g/8oz/2 cups strong white flour
5ml/1 tsp easy-blend dried yeast
pinch ground nutmeg
pinch cumin seeds
5ml/1 tsp runny honey
200ml/7fl oz/scant 1 cup
  lukewarm milk
oil, for greasing

1 Cook the potato in plenty of boiling water for 45 minutes or until very tender. Preheat the oven to 220°C/425°F/Gas 7.

2 Meanwhile, sift the flour into a large bowl, add the yeast, ground nutmeg and cumin seeds. Give the ingredients a good stir.

3 Mix the honey and milk together. Drain the potato and peel the skin. Mash the potato flesh and add to the flour mixture with the liquid.

4 Bring the mixture together and knead for 5 minutes on a floured surface. Place the dough in a bowl and cover with a damp cloth. Leave to rise for 30 minutes.

5 Turn the dough out and knock back to remove any air bubbles. Divide the dough into 12 pieces and shape each one into a round.

6 Place the rolls on a greased baking sheet. Cover with a damp cloth and leave to rise in a warm place for 30 minutes or until doubled in size.

7 Bake for 10 minutes. Remove from the oven and drizzle with more honey and cumin seeds before serving.

COOK'S TIP
This dough is quite sticky, so use plenty of flour on the surface when you are kneading and rolling it.

SWEET POTATO BREAD <u>WITH</u> CINNAMON <u>AND</u> WALNUTS

A WONDERFUL BRUNCH DISH, AND COMPLETELY DELICIOUS SERVED WITH CRISPY BACON.

3 Drain the potatoes and cool in cold water, then peel the skins. Mash the potatoes with a fork and mix into the dry ingredients with the nuts.

4 Make a well in the centre and pour in the milk. Bring the mixture together with a round-bladed knife, place on to a floured surface and knead for 5 minutes.

MAKES A 900G/2LB LOAF

INGREDIENTS
1 medium sweet potato
5ml/1 tsp ground cinnamon
450g/1lb/4 cups strong white flour
5ml/1 tsp easy-blend dried yeast
50g/2oz/½ cup walnut pieces
300ml/½ pint/1¼ cups warmed milk
salt and ground black pepper
oil, for greasing

COOK'S TIP
For an extra-crispy loaf, after the bread is cooked, remove from the tin and return the bread to the oven placing it upside down on the oven rack. Continue to cook for a further 5 minutes.

1 Boil the whole potato in its skin for 45 minutes or until tender.

2 Meanwhile, sift the cinnamon and flour together into a large bowl. Stir in the dried yeast.

5 Return the dough to a bowl and cover with a damp cloth. Leave to rise for 1 hour or until doubled in size. Turn the dough out and knock back to remove any air bubbles. Knead again for a few minutes. If the dough feels sticky add more flour to the mixture. Shape into a ball and place the bread in an oiled and base-lined 900g/2lb loaf tin. Cover with a damp cloth and leave to rise in a warm place for 1 hour or until doubled in size.

6 Preheat the oven to 200°C/400°F/ Gas 6. Bake on the middle shelf of the oven for 25 minutes. Turn out and tap the base; if it sounds hollow the bread is cooked. Cool on a wire rack.

POTATO BREAD WITH CARAMELISED ONIONS AND ROSEMARY

THE ROSEMARY AND ONIONS INCORPORATED INTO THIS BREAD GIVE IT A MEDITERRANEAN FEEL.
IT IS DELICIOUS SERVED WARM WITH A SIMPLE VEGETABLE SOUP.

MAKES A 900G/2LB LOAF

INGREDIENTS
450g/1lb/4 cups strong white flour
5ml/1 tsp easy-blend dried yeast
a pinch of salt, for the dough
15g/½oz/1 tbsp butter
325ml/11fl oz/1⅓ cups warmed milk
15ml/1 tbsp olive oil
2 medium onions, sliced into rings
115g/4oz maincrop potatoes, grated
1 sprig rosemary, chopped
2.5ml/½ tsp sea salt
oil, for greasing and to serve

1 Sift the flour into a large bowl. Make a well in the centre and stir in the yeast and a pinch of salt. Rub in the butter until the mixture resembles fine breadcrumbs and then gradually pour in the lukewarm milk.

2 Stir the mixture with a round-bladed knife and then once the wet ingredients have become incorporated, bring it together with your fingers.

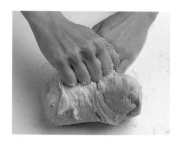

3 Turn the dough out and knead on a surface dusted with flour for 5 minutes or until the dough is smooth and elastic. Return the bread to a clean bowl and cover with a damp cloth. Leave to rise in a warm place for 45 minutes or until the dough has doubled in size.

4 Meanwhile, heat the oil in a saucepan and add the onions, stir over a low heat and cook for about 20 minutes until the onions are golden brown and very soft. Set aside.

5 Bring a saucepan of lightly salted water to the boil and add the grated potatoes to the pan. Cook for 5 minutes or until just tender. Drain and plunge into cold water.

VARIATION
For a more piquant flavour, add some bottled sundried tomatoes, drained of their oil and chopped, and a scattering of pitted black olives to the onion layers. Try fresh thyme for a subtle herby tang.

6 Turn the dough out of the bowl and knock back. Roll out on a lightly floured surface. Drain the potatoes and scatter half over the surface with a little rosemary and half the onions. Carefully roll the dough up into a sausage shape.

7 Lift the dough into an oiled 23 x 23cm/9 x 9in tin. Using the palms of your hands flatten the dough out, making sure that the dough fits the tin neatly. Scatter the remaining potatoes and onions over the top with the sea salt and rosemary.

8 Cover again with a damp cloth and leave to rise for 20 minutes.

9 Meanwhile, preheat the oven to 220°C/425°F/Gas 7. Bake the bread for 15–20 minutes. Serve warm drizzled with a little extra olive oil.

COOK'S TIP
If you don't like your onions very crisp, cover the loaf with foil after 10 minutes to prevent the surface from over-browning. Use the largest grater setting available on the food processor for the potatoes, to keep them from becoming too sticky when blanched.

RUSSIAN POTATO BREAD

POTATOES ARE PART OF THE STAPLE DIET IN RUSSIA AND ARE OFTEN USED TO REPLACE SOME OF THE FLOUR IN BREAD RECIPES. THE RESULT IS A LOVELY, MOIST LOAF WHICH IS DELICIOUS JUST SERVED WITH BUTTER. THIS EASY-TO-MAKE BREAD ALSO KEEPS REALLY WELL.

MAKES ONE LOAF

INGREDIENTS
    butter, for greasing
    225g/8oz floury potatoes, diced
    6g/¼oz sachet easy-blend
        dried yeast
    350g/12oz/3 cups unbleached white
        bread flour
    115g/4oz/1 cup wholemeal
        bread flour, plus extra for sprinkling
    2.5ml/½ tsp caraway seeds, crushed
    10ml/2 tsp salt
    25g/1oz/2 tbsp butter, diced

1 Lightly grease a baking sheet. Cook the potatoes in boiling water until tender. Drain well, reserving 150ml/ ¼ pint/⅔ cup of the cooking water. Mash and sieve the potatoes and leave to cool.

2 Mix together the yeast, white bread flour, wholemeal bread flour, caraway seeds and salt in a large bowl. Add the butter, cut into small pieces and rub in to form a breadcrumb consistency.

3 Mix together the reserved potato water and sieved potatoes. Gradually work this mixture into the flour mixture to form a soft dough.

4 Turn out on to a lightly floured surface and knead for 8–10 minutes until smooth and elastic.

5 Place the dough in a large, lightly oiled bowl, cover with lightly oiled clear film and leave to rise, in a warm place, for about 1 hour, or until it has doubled in size.

VARIATION
Omit the caraway seeds and knead 115g/4oz/1 cup grated or crumbled Cheddar, Red Leicester or blue cheese into the dough before shaping.

6 Turn out on to a lightly floured surface, knock back and knead gently. Shape into a plump oval loaf about 18cm/7in long. Place on the prepared baking sheet and sprinkle with a little wholemeal bread flour.

7 Cover with lightly oiled clear film and leave to rise, in a warm place, for 30 minutes, or until doubled in size.

8 Meanwhile preheat the oven to 200°C/400°F/Gas 6. Using a sharp knife, slash the top with 3–4 diagonal cuts to make a criss-cross effect.

9 Bake for 30–35 minutes until golden and hollow sounding when tapped on the base. Transfer to a wire rack to cool.

KARTOFFELBROT

THIS IS AN ADAPTATION OF THE CLASSIC GERMAN-STYLE BREAD, THIS VERSION IS MADE WITH STRONG WHITE FLOUR AND FLOURY POTATOES.

MAKES A 450G/1LB LOAF

INGREDIENTS
  butter, for greasing
  225g/8oz/2 cups strong white flour
  10ml/2 tsp baking powder
  5ml/1 tsp salt
  175g/6oz potatoes, cooked
  and mashed
  15ml/1 tbsp vegetable oil
  paprika, for dusting
  mustard-flavoured butter, to serve

COOK'S TIP
This bread is best eaten warm with
lashings of mustard-flavoured butter.

1 Preheat the oven to 230°C/450°F/
Gas 8. Grease and line a 450g/1lb loaf tin.

2 Sift the flour into a large bowl and
mix together with baking powder and
the salt.

3 Rub the mashed potato into the dry
ingredients making sure you achieve an
even mixture.

4 Stir in the oil and 200ml/7fl oz/scant
1 cup lukewarm water. Turn the dough
into the tin and dust with the paprika.
Bake in the oven for 25 minutes. Turn
out on to a wire rack to cool. Cut the
bread into thick chunks and serve with
mustard-flavoured butter.

SAVOURY CRANBERRY AND POTATO BREAD SLICE

AN INTERESTING COMBINATION OF CRANBERRIES WITH BACON AND POTATOES. THE CRANBERRIES COLOUR THE BREAD SLICES, GIVING IT A VERY FESTIVE FEEL.

MAKES A 450G/1LB LOAF

INGREDIENTS
    450g/1lb/4 cups strong white flour
    5ml/1 tsp easy-blend dried yeast
    5ml/1 tsp salt
    25g/1oz/2 tbsp butter, diced
    325ml/11fl oz/1⅓ cups
        lukewarm water
    75g/3oz/¾ cup fresh or frozen
        cranberries, thawed
    oil, for greasing
    225g/8oz floury potatoes, halved
    6 rashers rindless streaky
        bacon, chopped
    30ml/2 tbsp runny honey
    salt and ground black pepper

1 Sift the flour into a bowl, stir in the yeast and 5ml/1 tsp salt. Rub in the butter to form breadcrumbs. Make a well in the centre and stir in the water.

2 Bring the mixture together with a round-bladed knife and then turn out on to a floured surface. Knead for 5 minutes. Place the dough in a bowl and cover with a damp cloth. Leave to rise for 1 hour or until doubled in size.

COOK'S TIP
If you can't find fresh or frozen cranberries, substitute them with sweetcorn niblets.

3 Turn the dough out and knock back to remove the air bubbles. Knead for a few minutes. Carefully knead the cranberries into the bread. Roll the dough out to a rectangle and place in an oiled 23 x 23cm/9 x 9in flan tin. Push the dough into the corners and cover with a damp cloth. Leave to rise in a warm place for 30 minutes.

4 Preheat the oven to 220°C/425°F/ Gas 7. Meanwhile, boil the potatoes in plenty of salted water for 15 minutes or until just tender. Drain and when cool enough to handle, slice thinly.

5 Scatter the potatoes and bacon over the risen bread dough, season, then drizzle with the honey and bake for 25 minutes, covering the bread loosely with foil after 20 minutes to prevent burning.

6 Remove the bread from the oven and transfer to a wire rack. Return to the oven for 5 minutes to crisp the base. Leave to cool on the wire rack.

CHEESE AND POTATO BREAD TWISTS

A COMPLETE "PLOUGHMAN'S LUNCH", WITH THE CHEESE COOKED RIGHT IN THE BREAD. IT MAKES AN EXCELLENT BASE FOR A FILLING OF SMOKED SALMON WITH LEMON JUICE.

MAKES EIGHT

INGREDIENTS
225g/8oz potatoes, diced
225g/8oz/2 cups strong
    white flour
5ml/1 tsp easy-blend
    dried yeast
150ml/¼ pint/⅔ cup
    lukewarm water
175g/6oz/1½ cups red Leicester
    cheese, finely grated
10ml/2 tsp olive oil, for greasing
salt

1 Cook the potatoes in a large saucepan with plenty of lightly salted boiling water for 20 minutes or until tender. Drain through a colander and return to the pan. Mash until smooth and set aside to cool.

2 Meanwhile, sift the flour into a large bowl and add the yeast and a good pinch of salt. Stir in the potatoes and rub with your fingers to form a crumb consistency.

3 Make a well in the centre and pour in the lukewarm water. Start by bringing the mixture together with a round-bladed knife, then use your hands. Knead for 5 minutes on a well-floured surface. Return the dough to the bowl. Cover with a damp cloth and leave to rise in a warm place for 1 hour or until doubled in size.

4 Turn the dough out and knock back the air bubbles. Knead again for a few seconds.

5 Divide the dough into 12 pieces and shape into rounds.

6 Scatter the cheese over a baking sheet. Take each ball of dough and roll it in the cheese.

7 Roll each cheese-covered roll on a dry surface to a long sausage shape. Fold the two ends together and twist the bread. Lay the bread twists on an oiled baking sheet.

8 Cover with a damp cloth and leave the bread to rise in a warm place for 30 minutes. Preheat the oven to 220°C/425°F/Gas 7. Bake the bread for 10–15 minutes.

VARIATION
Any hard, well-flavoured cheese can be used. Mature Cheddar is the traditional choice for a ploughman's lunch, or you could try a smoked cheese, or a variety with added herbs, such as sage Lancashire. For a substantial filling, use slices of ham from the bone, rashers of crisply grilled streaky bacon with avocado slices, or a helping of egg mayonnaise.

COOK'S TIP
These bread twists stay moist and fresh for up to 3 days if stored in airtight food bags.

SWEET POTATO SCONES

THESE ARE SCONES WITH A DIFFERENCE. A SWEET POTATO GIVES THEM A PALE ORANGE COLOUR AND THEY ARE MELTINGLY SOFT IN THE CENTRE, JUST WAITING FOR A KNOB OF BUTTER.

2 In a separate bowl, mix the mashed sweet potatoes with the milk and melted butter or margarine. Beat well to blend.

3 Add the flour to the sweet potato mixture and stir to make a dough. Turn out on to a lightly floured surface and knead until soft and pliable.

MAKES ABOUT TWENTY-FOUR

INGREDIENTS
  butter, for greasing
  150g/5oz/1¼ cups plain flour
  20ml/4 tsp baking powder
  5ml/1 tsp salt
  15g/½oz/1 tbsp soft light
    brown sugar
  150g/5oz mashed sweet potatoes
  150ml/¼ pint/⅔ cup milk
  50g/2oz/4 tbsp butter or margarine,
    melted

1 Preheat the oven to 230°C/450°F/ Gas 8. Grease a baking sheet. Sift together the flour, baking powder and salt into a bowl. Mix in the sugar.

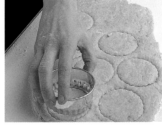

4 Roll or pat out the dough to a 1cm/½in thickness. Cut into rounds using a 4cm/1½in cutter.

5 Arrange the rounds on the baking sheet. Bake for about 15 minutes until risen and lightly golden. Serve warm.

IRISH GRIDDLE SCONES

THESE ARE ALSO CALLED POTATO CAKES OR GRIDDLE CAKES, BUT WHATEVER YOU CALL THEM THEY ARE DELICIOUS SERVED HOT WITH BUTTER AND JAM, OR WITH BACON FOR A HEARTY BREAKFAST.

MAKES SIX

INGREDIENTS
    225g/8oz floury potatoes, cut into
        uniform chunks
    115g/4oz/1 cup plain flour
    2.5ml/½ tsp salt
    2.5ml/½ tsp baking powder
    50g/2oz/4 tbsp butter, diced
    25ml/1½ tbsp milk
    bacon rashers, to serve
    butter, for greasing

1 Cook the potatoes in a saucepan of boiling water until tender.

2 Drain the potatoes and return them to the pan over a high heat. Using a wooden spoon, stir the potatoes for 1 minute until all traces of moisture have evaporated. Remove from the heat. Mash well, making sure there are no lumps.

3 Sift together the flour, salt and baking powder into a bowl. Rub in the butter with your fingertips until it has the consistency of fine breadcrumbs.

4 Add the mashed potatoes and mix thoroughly with a fork. Make a well in the centre and pour in the milk. Mix to form a smooth dough.

5 Turn out on to a lightly floured surface and knead gently for about 5 minutes until soft and pliable. Roll out to a round 5mm/¼ in thick. Cut in half, then cut each half into three wedges.

6 Before you cook the scones, fry a batch of bacon rashers to serve with them. Keep warm in a low oven, until the scones are ready.

7 Grease a griddle or frying pan with a little butter and heat until very hot. Add the cakes and fry for 3–4 minutes until golden brown on both sides turning once. Serve hot with the bacon rashers.

DILL AND POTATO SCONES

POTATO SCONES FLAVOURED WITH DILL ARE QUITE SCRUMPTIOUS AND CAN BE SERVED WARM JUST WITH BUTTER. OR IF YOU WANT TO MAKE THEM SUBSTANTIAL ENOUGH FOR A LIGHT SUPPER, SERVE THEM TOPPED WITH FLAKED SALMON, KIPPER OR MACKEREL.

MAKES ABOUT TEN

INGREDIENTS
  oil, for greasing
  225g/8oz/2 cups self-raising flour
  40g/1½oz/3 tbsp butter, softened
  pinch of salt
  15ml/1 tbsp finely chopped fresh dill
  175g/6oz mashed potato,
    freshly made
  30–45ml/2–3 tbsp milk

COOK'S TIP
If you don't have any dill you can replace it with the herb of your choice. Try fresh parsley or basil as an alternative.

1 Preheat the oven to 230°C/450°F/ Gas 8. Grease a baking sheet. Sift the flour into a bowl, and rub in the butter with your fingertips. Add the salt and dill and stir.

2 Add the mashed potato to the mixture and enough milk to make a soft, pliable dough.

3 Turn out the dough on to a well-floured surface and roll out until it is fairly thin. Cut into rounds using a 7.5cm/3in cutter.

4 Place the scones on the prepared baking sheet, leaving space between each one, and bake for 20–25 minutes until risen and golden. Serve warm.

SAVOURY POTATO DROP SCONES

A LIGHT SCONE WITH A MILD MUSTARD AND CHEESE FLAVOUR, THESE MAKE A DELICIOUS BREAKFAST DISH SERVED WITH SCRAMBLED EGGS AND GRILLED TOMATOES.

MAKES SIXTEEN

INGREDIENTS
  175g/6oz floury potatoes, diced
  115g/4oz/1 cup self-raising flour
  5ml/1 tsp mustard powder
  1 egg, beaten
  25g/1oz/¼ cup Cheddar cheese,
    grated
  150ml/¼ pint/⅔ cup milk
  oil, for frying and greasing
  salt and freshly ground black pepper
  butter, to serve

COOK'S TIP
It is best to use a flat griddle rather than a ridged one for this recipe as the scones are quite small and thin.

1 Cook the potatoes in plenty of boiling salted water for 20 minutes or until tender. Drain the potatoes and then mash them well.

2 Spoon the mashed potato from the saucepan into a large mixing bowl and then add the flour, mustard powder, egg, cheese and milk.

3 Beat well until the mixture comes together. Season.

4 Heat a griddle pan and brush with oil. Drop tablespoonfuls of the mixture on to the griddle and cook for 1–2 minutes. Flip the scones over and cook the second side. Repeat to make 16 scones. Serve warm with butter.

SWEET POTATO MUFFINS WITH RAISINS

MUFFINS HAVE BEEN A PART OF THE AMERICAN BREAKFAST FOR MANY YEARS. THIS VARIETY MIXES THE GREAT COLOUR AND FLAVOUR OF SWEET POTATOES WITH THE MORE USUAL INGREDIENTS.

2 Meanwhile, preheat the oven to 220°C/425°F/Gas 7. Sift the flour and baking powder over the potatoes with a pinch of salt and beat in the egg.

3 Stir the butter and milk together and pour into the bowl. Add the raisins and sugar and mix the ingredients until everything has just come together.

MAKES TWELVE

INGREDIENTS
  1 large sweet potato
  350g/12oz/3 cups plain flour
  15ml/1 tbsp baking powder
  1 egg, beaten
  225g/8oz/1 cup butter, melted
  250ml/8fl oz/1 cup milk
  50g/2oz/scant ½ cup raisins
  50g/2oz/¼ cup caster sugar
  salt
  12 paper muffin cases
  icing sugar, for dusting

1 Cook the sweet potato in plenty of boiling water for 45 minutes or until very tender. Drain the potato and when cool enough to handle peel off the skin. Place in a large bowl and mash well.

4 Spoon the mixture into muffin cases set in a muffin tin.

5 Bake for 25 minutes until golden. Dust with icing sugar and serve warm.

THREE HERB POTATO SCONES

THESE FLAVOURSOME SCONES ARE PERFECT SERVED WARM AND SPLIT IN TWO WITH HAND-CARVED HAM AND PARMESAN SHAVINGS AS A FILLING.

MAKES TWELVE

INGREDIENTS
    225g/8oz/2 cups self-raising flour
    5ml/1 tsp baking powder
    pinch of salt
    50g/2oz/4 tbsp butter, diced
    25g/1oz potato flakes
    15ml/1 tbsp chopped fresh parsley
    15ml/1 tbsp chopped fresh basil
    15ml/1 tbsp chopped fresh oregano
    150ml/¼ pint/⅔ cup milk
    oil, for greasing

1 Preheat the oven to 180°C/350°F/ Gas 4. Sift the flour into a bowl with the baking powder. Add a pinch of salt. Rub in the butter with your fingertips to form crumbs. Place the potato flakes in bowl and pour over 200ml/7fl oz/scant 1 cup boiling water. Beat well and cool slightly.

2 Stir the potatoes into the dry ingredients with the herbs and milk.

3 Bring the mixture together to form a soft dough. Turn out on to a floured surface and knead the dough very gently for a few minutes, until soft and pliable.

COOK'S TIP
Don't be tempted to overseason the mixture, as once cooked the baking powder can also increase the salty flavour of the finished scone and this can overpower the taste of the herbs.

4 Roll the dough out on a floured surface to about 4cm/1½in thickness and stamp out rounds using a 7.5cm/3in cutter. Reshape any remaining dough and re-roll for more scones. Place the scones on to a greased baking dish and brush the surfaces with a little more milk.

5 Cook for 15–20 minutes and serve warm. They can be eaten plain, or with a filling.

CHOCOLATE POTATO CAKE

THIS IS A VERY RICH, MOIST CHOCOLATE CAKE, TOPPED WITH A THIN LAYER OF CHOCOLATE ICING.
USE A GOOD-QUALITY DARK CHOCOLATE FOR BEST RESULTS AND SERVE WITH WHIPPED CREAM.

MAKES A 23CM/9IN CAKE

INGREDIENTS
  oil, for greasing
  200g/7oz/1 cup sugar
  250g/9oz/1 cup and 2 tbsp butter
  4 eggs, separated
  275g/10oz dark chocolate
  75g/3oz/¾ cup ground almonds
  165g/5½oz mashed potato
  225g/8oz/2 cups self-raising flour
  5ml/1 tsp cinnamon
  45ml/3 tbsp milk
  white and dark chocolate shavings,
    to garnish
  whipped cream, to serve

1 Preheat the oven to 180°C/350°F/
Gas 4. Grease and base-line a
23cm/9in round cake tin with a circle of
baking parchment.

2 In a large bowl, cream together
the sugar and 225g/8oz/1 cup of the
butter until light and fluffy. Then beat
the egg yolks into the creamed
mixture one at a time until it is smooth
and creamy.

3 Finely chop or grate 175g/6oz of the
chocolate and stir it into the creamed
mixture with the ground almonds. Pass
the mashed potato through a sieve or
ricer and stir it into the creamed
chocolate mixture.

4 Sift together the flour and cinnamon
and fold into the mixture with the milk.

COOK'S TIP
Chocolate can be melted very
successfully in the microwave. Place
the pieces of chocolate in a plastic
measuring jug or bowl. The chocolate
may scorch if placed in a glass bowl.
Microwave on high for 1 minute, stir,
and then heat again for up to
1 minute, checking halfway through
to see if it is done.

5 Whisk the egg whites until they hold
stiff but not dry peaks, and fold into the
cake mixture.

6 Spoon into the prepared tin and
smooth over the top, but make a slight
hollow in the middle to help keep the
surface of the cake level during
cooking. Bake in the oven for 1¼ hours
until a wooden toothpick inserted in the
centre comes out clean. Allow the cake
to cool slightly in the tin, then turn out
and cool on a wire rack.

7 Meanwhile break up the remaining
chocolate into a heatproof bowl and
stand it over a saucepan of hot water.
Add the remaining butter in small
pieces and stir well until the chocolate
has melted and the mixture is smooth
and glossy.

8 Peel off the lining paper and trim
the top of the cake so that it is level.
Smooth over the chocolate icing and
allow to set. Decorate with white and
dark chocolate shavings and serve with
lashings of whipped cream.

RICE

INTRODUCTION

*The rice grain is famous for its
versatility and has been valued as
a hard-working food crop since the
earliest days of its cultivation
some 8,000 years ago. A look
at the history of rice opens this
second half of the book to explain
the mystical reverence with which
some cultures regard rice, even
today. Included in the introduction
is a photographic directory of
world rices and rice products,
with a comprehensive section on
preparation and cooking techniques.
The world's most distinctive
cuisines each have their own way of
dealing with rice, and to complete
the book we feature the very best
of them, to help you explore and
appreciate this highly important
staple food.*

THE STORY OF RICE

RICE IS A SUPREMELY important crop. It is a food that feeds half the population of the world, and is the grain that has sculpted the cultures of Asia, linking Heaven and Earth, mortal to gods. In Bangladesh, Thailand and China, a common greeting, instead of "How are you?", is "Have you eaten rice today?". And at New Year, the traditional saying is "May your world never burn". To upset a bowl of rice is a sign of bad luck, while deliberately upending a fellow diner's rice bowl is a deadly insult.

Festivals and traditions all over South-east Asia celebrate the importance of rice. In Cambodia, for instance, where people believe the rice spirit, Yiey Tep, lives on in the rice fields, farmers show their devotion by praying and making offerings of sweet rice. The Balinese have numerous rice rituals, from laying pinches of rice along the edges of fields to keep away evil spirits, to fabulous celebrations in the island's many temples.

There are two distinct attitudes to rice and two distinct types of rice eater. For many of us in the West, rice is just another grain, albeit a valued one.

We view rice as a pleasant alternative to potatoes, pasta or bread; we make pilaffs and risottos, or use rice to serve as a salad or to accompany a curry.

But for the peoples of Indonesia, Thailand and other South-east Asian countries, rice is central to life itself. Many Asians eat rice three times a day and in some languages, such as Thai, the phrase for eating rice is the same as for eating food. For many Chinese or Malays, for instance, rice is the food that you eat; the rest is merely relish. On average, in the West, we each consume 1.8kg/4lb of rice a year, compared with the 150kg/330lb a year average annual consumption per person in Asia. In this book we suggest cooking 225g/8oz of rice – a generous cupful – to serve four people, yet that would scarcely satisfy a single hungry Indonesian or Chinese adult. The world produces about 350 million tonnes of rice each year and over half of this amount is consumed within 48km/ 30 miles of where it was grown.

Paddy fields are one of the most defining images of South-east Asia. The sight of the two-thousand-year-old

terraces of the Ifugao of Luzon in the northern Philippines is one of the wonders of the world. Rice that is growing in the field is called paddy, which comes from the word *padi*, meaning "rice growing in deep water". Rice is known as paddy until it has been threshed.

In Asia, most rice is still planted, tended and harvested by hand. By direct contrast, in the USA and Australia the process is highly mechanized and involves lasers, low-flying aircraft, combine harvesters and computers.

Yet the lack of technology in the Asian paddy fields belies the complex organization that is rice farming. Entire families are involved in the growing and harvesting of the rice they eat, and each member has a specific role to play in the process. Rice provides the family with a living, so long as the weather is predictable and the rains forthcoming, and rice cultivation shapes their way of life.

Below: Rice is farmed throughout France, including here in Provence, although the country is not a major exporter.

The myths of these rich cultures tell us a great deal about the history of rice, and highlight its central role in people's lives. How and when it was first grown is more difficult to discover. What is certain is that it is native to South-east Asia and has been cultivated there for perhaps 8000 years. Evidence from a cave in northern Thailand proves that rice was being cultivated from around 6000 BC.

Rice, which is a member of the grass family, grew extensively in Thailand. It is likely that early man first grew wild rice, and only later began cultivating local species. Some scholars believe that this first rice would have been dry and that wet rice was a later development. Others say that people grew whatever rice was best suited to their particular environment. Certainly rice is adaptable, and will accommodate itself to the habitat; some varieties tolerate floods and cold nights, while others survive hot temperatures and relatively little water.

Gradually, people realised the value of this sustaining crop, and rice began to travel. From north-east India and Thailand, rice spread first through South-east Asia, and then further afield.

THE HISTORY OF RICE

Study the history of rice and you will discover that it is bound up with many strange and fascinating myths. Rice has fed more people than any other crop, and the story of its cultivation must rank as one of the most important developments in history. Almost every culture in the East has its own rice legend, and in many Asian countries these stories are still celebrated today.

In Bali and other parts of Indonesia, puppets act out a creation myth, which tells of how Lord Vishnu caused the Earth to give birth to rice, and the god Indra taught the people how it should be grown. From China comes the story of a devastating flood, which left all the crops destroyed. Facing certain starvation, the people of the town one day saw a dog with strange yellow seeds hanging from its tail. Rice grew when the seeds were planted in the waterlogged soil.

In the many myths from around Indonesia, Thailand and Japan, the rice spirit is always feminine. She is young and tender – a beautiful maiden, dusted with rice powder to emphasize her perfect white skin. In almost all of the many Asian cultures, the femininity of rice is reflected in the way it is grown. Men prepare the land, build the dykes and attend to irrigation, but it is the women who plant the rice, tend it in the fields, cut it and, finally, cook it.

There are numerous signs all over South-east Asia that rice is still highly revered today. A family will traditionally store its rice in a rice barn. These beautiful and elaborate buildings are where the rice spirit is said to reside until the time of the next planting, and there are often strict rules about who may enter these barns. Usually, only the women are allowed inside, and even then only once a day.

Above: Famine in the streets of Bombay in 1900. Rice is given to the starving.

Rice cultivation is believed to have begun in China in the Yangtze River delta around 4000 BC, although the rice may at first have been considered nothing more than a weed, as taro root was cultivated in parts of this region around this time. Rice isn't thought to have become an important part of the Chinese diet until around 800 BC.

By the 9th century AD, rice was widely eaten in southern China, but in the north, where it could not be grown, it was food only for the wealthy. Remarkably, rice was not cultivated in Japan until the second century BC and even then, millet remained the principal cereal for most Japanese. Twelve hundred years later, in spite of famine, rice was still mainly a food for the rich and was not to be consumed in any large quantity for another 800 years.

THE REST OF THE WORLD

It is difficult to chart exactly how and when the cultivation of rice spread beyond Asia. In the Middle East and the Mediterranean, wheat was initially the main crop, while in America, maize was by far the most important cereal. Rice was not known here until the Spanish introduced it in the late 16th century.

Rice is enjoyed in many Middle Eastern countries, and basmati rice, in particular, has a special place in people's affections. Today, the Middle Eastern repertoire of rice dishes is wide-ranging,

but it clearly wasn't always so. Rice was probably introduced via northern India and Afghanistan through conquest, expansion and trading. However, even in the 13th century, rice was still regarded as a luxury item in Baghdad.

Rice came to Europe by various routes. Its popularity was determined not so much by its versatility, but by whether or not the crop could be cultivated. Unless rice could be produced locally, the cost of transporting it made the price high, and limited supply and demand. By the middle of this century, the cost of transporting foodstuffs became relatively cheap and foods such as rice, once thought of as exotic, became affordable to the majority and not just the élite.

In Spain, rice was introduced by the Moors, who ruled that country for about 300 years, from the beginning of the 8th century. It was the Moors who built the irrigation canals around Valencia and in the hills around Murcia, which are still used today for rice growing.

The Arabs introduced a dry or upland rice to Sicily, and shortly afterwards there is evidence of paddy fields in northern Italy, around Piedmont and on the Lombardy plains. Here, a wet short grain rice was cultivated, which most scholars believe was introduced not via the south of the country, but from Spain, where another short grain variety of rice had long been

Above: Rice irrigation in China, during the Yuan Dynasty, 13–14th century.

grown. Either way, from around the 14th century onwards, rulers around Pisa and Milan became aware that rice was a good alternative to wheat as a staple food. After a series of devastating famines, they began in earnest to encourage the cultivation of rice. In the 18th century, Piedmont rice was of such high quality that Thomas Jefferson, then US Minister in France, smuggled some out of Italy and sent it to friends in Charleston with instructions for its cultivation. (This was the same Thomas Jefferson who had written the Declaration of Independence and who was later to become the third president of the United States.)

In parts of Europe where cultivation was not an option, rice was often regarded with suspicion, and there appears to have been some resistance to eating it. In Britain at least, it has taken many years, notwithstanding the ubiquitous rice pudding, for rice to become truly accepted. However, rice was not totally unknown in England; in the 13th century, knights returning from the Crusades brought back rice along with other Arabian products such as sugar and lemons.

For a long time in Britain, rice was regarded in the same way as the newly arrived spices. Expensive to buy, it was used by chefs to the aristocracy to make delicate sweets and desserts,

Left: Men and women harvesting rice in China during the 13–14th century: threshing, winnowing and sorting rice.

Above: A flooded rice field in Queensland, Australia. The water will be drained from the field before the rice is harvested.

but was not considered a food for working people. Apart from rice pudding, its most famous appearance was in the savoury breakfast dish, kedgeree, developed in India during 19th-century colonnial rule. Based on the Indian dish *kitchiri*, kedgeree is a creamy mixture of smoked haddock, eggs and basmati rice, flavoured with nutmeg and often lightly curried. It gained great popularity in Victorian England and is now an established national favourite.

Rice was introduced to the Americas by the conquering Spanish and Portuguese, and it has flourished ever since. Nowadays, rice is a hugely important crop in many South American countries, most notably Brazil, which grows as much rice as Japan yet still cannot meet its own needs. Brazil is second only to Europe as the world's largest importer of rice.

Some scholars believe rice came to North America with the slaves, who brought the seeds with them from West Africa. It was said that only they had the knowledge of how to grow rice. Another story talks of a ship from Madagascar that was blown off course and put into harbour in Charleston, South Carolina. As a gift of thanks, the captain presented the town with some "seeds of gold", which is a type of rice named for its colour. The reality is probably a combination of these legendary stories.

The first Spanish colonists in Florida brought rice with them from the Old World, along with wheat and bread. While Florida proved a congenial environment for growing rice, it was South Carolina which became the main focus for rice cultivation. Attempts to grow upland rice in North Carolina had failed but Carolina Gold, grown in the freshwater island swamps of South Carolina, proved successful. By the late 17th century Carolina Gold was being produced in large quantities.

South Carolina's rice fields were worked entirely by slaves, and it was this situation that contributed directly to the collapse of the rice industry in the Carolinas. When the slaves were freed after the American Civil War in the 1860s, the rice fields were left empty. The war put an end to large scale rice cultivation in the Carolinas and Georgia, but it did continue along the Mississippi River, in Louisiana, Arkansas and Texas. In the early 20th century rice cultivation spread to California, where rice is still a major crop today. The United States is now the world's second major rice exporter.

Left: The combine harvester has a central role in the modern-day rice harvest.

THE RICE FIELD

Just before harvest time, the paddy fields of Asia are a spectacular sight. On the mountain sides and in the valleys, the land is a sea of soft, luminescent shades of green, and from a distance seems to sway as if in perpetual motion. View it from the air, and you'll notice that some fields are flooded, but many are dry. These are the fields ready for harvest, where the farmer has drained the paddy while the grain continues to ripen, so that the ground is easy to walk upon. It is a mistake to think that the rice plant spends its entire life under water. Water is used to flood the fields, and the plant will remain under water for some weeks or months, but the careful farmer will always regulate this flooding.

Classification

There are numerous varieties of rice although all stem from a single species. In simple terms, each of these varieties can be classified as one of three main types of grain: indica, japonica and javonica. Indica, as the name suggests, is the rice of India. The grains are long and tend to remain separate after cooking. Japonica, which is grown in other parts of Asia, has short grains that are sticky or glutinous when cooked. The third group, javonica, is long-grained but has sticky properties.

Cultivation

Rice is the only important cereal to grow in water. The water brings nutrients to the plant, insulates it against extreme heat and cold and, some believe, helps to keep down weeds, although weeding is still required.

In America the rice checks (rice fields) are flooded through a system of canals, which introduce fresh water from a nearby river wherever it is needed. In much of South-east Asia, water for the paddy fields flows constantly, but relying on Nature for the supply can be problematic. Either there is too much or too little, or the water flows too quickly or not at all. The plant will survive wet or dry periods, and can grow in still water, but ideally the paddy should be flooded after the plant has flowered, and drained dry before harvest.

Rice today is grown throughout the world, but the principal growing regions are the southern United States, Brazil, Egypt, Spain and Italy. The biggest rice-producing area is South-east Asia, from Pakistan in the east to Japan and the Philippines in the west.

In the West, as you would expect, mechanization has taken over the jobs that in Asia are still carried out by manual labour. The rice fields of Texas and Louisiana look very different from those of Bali or Thailand. It is only in Asia where you will find the traditional images associated with rice growing: water buffalo harrowing the paddy fields, men hoeing the flooded fields before planting, and women in conical hats, planting rice seeds.

In many parts of Asia, farmers aim to achieve two crops a year, and the first job is to prepare the land. A hoe is used to break up the soil, which is then flooded prior to planting. In mountainous areas, rice is planted in the highest fields first, and the water is allowed to flow downhill to the lower terraces once the first fields are soaked. Oxen or water buffalo may be used for harrowing the flooded field, which is then planted, often by women. It can take several days to plant one paddy field, and during the growing season all members of the family are needed to help with the ongoing work of adding fertilizers and pesticides, and weeding.

Harvesting

In many Asian countries, come harvest, the women once again move back into the fields to cut the rice stalks, using a small, sharp knife. Rice is so central to people's lives here that people continue to honour the old traditions; women will conceal the cutting knife in order to protect the rice spirit from the knowledge that she must die.

Once they have been cut, the rice stalks are stacked in bundles and threshed – beaten over hard ground with flails or drawn over spikes to release the rice grains. Mechanization is creeping in, predominantly in the developed world, but you may still see hand threshing in parts of Java and Bali. Here, the grain is manually husked and winnowed to dispel the straw and chaff before being stored in the traditional family rice barn, the highly elaborate shrine to the rice spirit.

Below: Modern rice production in Spain. The milled grains are laid out to dry under the hot summer sun (bottom) before being bagged and weighed (top).

Milling

Unless it has been threshed and husked manually, paddy, once cut, is taken to the mill where the bran and husk is removed to give fully milled or "polished" white rice. Unmilled rice that has had only the husk removed is known as cargo rice. It is in this form that rice is imported into Europe from both Asia and America, so that the milling process can be completed at one of the modern mills that exist in Europe, most notably in the Netherlands.

In Europe, milling is a mechanized procedure, although the basic principle is much the same as in the small, noisy mills of Asia. The brown rice passes between rubber rollers that rub away the brown outer skin, leaving the white grain. Once fully milled this is known as "polished" rice, and while once this did imply that the grain had been treated with glycerine or talc to make the grains glossy, this operation is now fairly rare.

Marketing

Until recently, all the rice grown on a typical Asian plot would have been for the family's own consumption, and even today less than 4 per cent is traded between countries. Demand for rice is growing worldwide, however, and as agriculture and jobs diversify, a greater proportion of the rice farmer's annual crop will be sold either for the local market or for export.

Europe is the biggest importer of rice, followed by Brazil and the Middle East. Many rice-growing countries import rice to supplement their own crop, as in the case of Brazil, or so that the home-grown rice can be exported. In order to earn foreign currency, China exports the greater part of its high grade rice and imports a low grade rice for its own population. In parts of the Punjab where basmati rice is grown, almost the entire crop is exported. The price that basmati can fetch means that there is a huge incentive to sell this quality rice. Paradoxically, within the region, bread is more commonly eaten than rice.

NUTRITION

Rice is a non-allergenic food, rich in complex carbohydrates and low in salts and fats. Because brown rice retains the bran, it has twice the nutritional content of white rice and is therefore considered the healthy choice. This shouldn't deter you from eating white rice, however, as all rice is known to be good for you.

Starch/Carbohydrate Rice contains two main starches. It is these starches that determine how sticky or glutinous a rice is. Rice is an excellent carbohydrate food, supplying energy without increasing fat intake.

Protein Brown and white rice contain a small amount of easily digestible protein.

Minerals Rice contains small amounts of phosphorous, magnesium, potassium and zinc. Since these minerals are contained in the bran, they are mostly found in brown rice and, to a lesser extent, in par-boiled rice, the production of which involves a process that "glues" nutrients into the grain.

Fibre The rice bran in brown rice provides some fibre. Little fibre remains in white rice after the bran has been taken out.

Vitamins Rice contains small amounts of Vitamin E, B vitamins, Thiamine, Riboflavin, Niacin, Vitamin B6 and folic acid, although since most of the vitamins are contained in the bran, brown rice is a richer source. Par-boiled rice also contains a higher proportion of vitamins than white rice.

TYPES OF RICE

There are thousands of varieties of rice. In the world's major rice-growing areas, it is not unknown for each paddy field to yield its own particular strain. This does not mean, however, that people who live in these areas are faced with a bewildering choice; on the contrary, most only eat the rice that is grown locally. It is said that, with just one or two exceptions worldwide, 65 per cent of rice is eaten within 500 metres of where it is grown.

There are several possible ways of classifying rice: by region; by colour; by cooking properties; even by price. Visit an ethnic store and you are likely to find rice grouped in one of these ways, but the most common classification, and the one most supermarkets favour, is by the length of the grain, which can be long, medium or short. As a general rule long and medium grain rices are used for savoury dishes, while short grain is used for desserts, although there are exceptions: risotto is only ever made with special short grain rices, for example. In America the terms Patna, rose and pearl are used by millers to describe long, medium and short grain rice respectively.

Left: From left, white and brown long grain rices.

Below: Organic rice is grown entirely free of chemicals.

Organic Rice

This is rice that has been grown without the use of pesticides or fertilizers. It can be long, medium or short grain.

Long Grain Rices

Long grain rice is three or four times as long as it is wide. When cooked, the individual grains separate. Long grain rice can be used in a variety of recipes. **White Long Grain Rice** This is the most commonly available white rice and may come from any of a number of countries. America is the most significant producer of long grain rice sold in Europe. China, India, Malaysia and Thailand, among others, produce far greater amounts of this rice than does America, but their production is principally used for the home market and is not exported.

In China long grain rice is called simply *xian* or *indica* (*oryza indica* is the generic name for all long grain rice). In the rice eating areas of China it is the cheapest and most widely available rice for everyday consumption.

The white variety of long grain rice has been fully milled, and all of the bran and outer coating has been removed. The grains are white and slightly shiny, a feature often described by the expression "polished", although strictly speaking, this would mean that glycerine or talc has been used to polish the grains, giving them a smooth and glossy appearance. This practice is relatively rare these days, although the term "polished rice" still persists in some quarters. While white rice hasn't the flavour of basmati or Thai fragrant rice, it is still a firm favourite and is a good choice for a large number of Western-style and oriental dishes.

Below: From left, white and brown basmati rices, admired for their fragrance and for the slender grains, which provide such a unique texture.

Brown Long Grain Rice Sometimes called wholegrain rice, this is the whole of the grain complete with bran – the rice equivalent of wholemeal bread. In countries where rice is a staple food and thus eaten in large quantities, brown rice is generally disliked and is seldom eaten. Most brown rice is consumed in the West, where it is considered a healthier alternative to white rice, and is enjoyed for its pleasant texture and nutty flavour. Almost all brown rice is long or medium grain. Short grain rice, perhaps because it is generally used for sweet puddings and desserts, is almost always milled first to remove the bran, although it is possible to buy brown short grain rice from health food shops.

Right: American long grain rice

Basmati Rice

This rice is grown in northern India, in the Punjab, in parts of Pakistan adjacent to West Punjab and in the foothills of the Himalayas. The particular soil and climate of this region is thought to account for basmati's unique taste and texture. The word "basmati" means "the fragrant one" in Hindi, and it is rightly considered by most rice lovers around the world to be the prince of rice. Basmati has a fine aromatic flavour. The grains are long and slender and become even longer during cooking, which partly accounts for its wonderful texture. There are various grades of basmati, but it is impossible for the shopper to differentiate between them except by trying the brands to discover the variety with the best fragrance and flavour. Basmati is excellent in almost any savoury rice dish and is perfect for pilaffs or for serving with curries. It is also an essential ingredient in biryani.
Brown Basmati Like all types of brown rice, brown basmati comes with the bran. It has all the flavour of white basmati with the texture typical of brown rice. It would not be used in Indian dishes but is superb in any number of Western-style meals.

*Above: Thai
fragrant rice*

Patna Rice

At one time, most of the long grain rice sold in Europe came from Patna in India, and the term was used loosely to mean any long grain rice. The custom persists in parts of America, but elsewhere Patna is used to describe a specific variety of long grain rice from the Bihar region of India.

Dehra Dun

A long grain, non-sticky Indian rice. It is not generally available outside India, except from specialist stores.

Domsiah Rice

A fine grained, Persian rice, available from Middle Eastern stores.

Thai Fragrant Rice or Jasmine Rice

This fragrant long grain rice is cultivated in Thailand and is widely used in South-east Asian and oriental cooking. The rice has a faintly scented, almost milky aroma that is a perfect match for the exotic flavours of oriental cuisine. Once cooked, the grains are slightly sticky. Thai fragrant rice is excellent both for savoury dishes and for sweet ones. To fully appreciate its fragrance, it is best cooked by the absorption method.

American Aromatic Rice

America grows several familiar aromatic rices, including Jasmine, and has developed several of its own.

Texmati, an American version of basmati, is not sold outside the United States, although it can often be found in specialist American stores.

Medium Grain Rices

Medium grain rice is about twice as long as it is wide. After cooking, the grains are moist and tender, and tend to cling together more than long grain. Medium grain rice is sold in both brown and white varieties. In Spain, white medium grain rice is often used for making paella.

Short Grain Rices

Mention short grain rice and most people will either think of risotto or creamy, slow-cooked puddings. Both these dishes owe their success to the ability of short grain rice to absorb liquid, becoming soft and sticky in the process. Short grain rice is almost as broad as it is long and is sometimes described as round grain. The grains stick together when cooked.

Pudding Rice

This is a catch-all name for any short grain rice. Virtually all pudding rice is white, with short, plump grains. Carolina rice was the original name for American short grain rice, taking its name from the state where it was first grown. The name is seldom used today, although you may occasionally find cookbooks calling for Carolina rice.

Italian Rice

Italy produces more rice, and in greater variety, than any other country in Europe. Most is grown in the north of the country, in the Po Valley around Piedmont. Italian rice is classified by size, ranging from the shortest grain, *ordinario*, to *semi-fino*, *fino* and *superfino*. Most of the varieties of risotto rice are either *fino* or *superfino*.

*Right: Short grain
pudding rice*

rice grown is a medium short grain variety, which has a slightly sticky consistency when cooked. It is particularly popular for making paella. A longer grain rice is also grown and is generally added to soups.

Within Spain, rice is graded by the amount of whole grains included in the weight: *Categoria Extra* (red label) is the finest rice, with 95 per cent whole grains, *Categoria Uno* (green label) has 87 per cent whole grains, while *Categoria Dos* (yellow label) has 80 per cent whole grains. *Calasperra* is a top quality short grain rice that is quite easy to locate outside Spain, unlike most Spanish rices, which must be bought from specialist stores.

Grano Largo or Variedad Americana A long grain white rice. The brown equivalent is called *arroz integral*.

Bahia A medium grain rice used for making paella.

Bomba Another paella rice. Like an Italian risotto rice, the plump grain absorbs a lot of liquid.

Oriental Rices

In Japan, two basic types of rice are eaten: glutinous rice (see separate entry) and a plump short grained rice, called *uruchimai* and often sold simply as Japanese rice. Although not a glutinous rice, even the ordinary rice has sticky properties – a non-sticky rice would be difficult to eat with chopsticks.

Sushi Rice In the West, a packet labelled sushi rice will almost inevitably contain a short grain rice that will need to be cooked before you can use it to make sushi. Typical examples are Japanese Rose, Kokuho Rose and Calrose. Ask for sushi rice in Japan, however, and you are likely to be offered rice that has been cooked with vinegar, sugar and salt, and is thus ready for making sushi.

Shinmai This is a highly esteemed Japanese rice that is sold in Japan in late summer. It is the first rice of the season. Because of its high moisture content, it needs less water for cooking.

Arborio This is one of the best known varieties of Italian risotto rice, and takes its name from a town in the Vercelli region of north-west Italy. Unlike the finer risotto rices such as Carnaroli, Arborio has a comparatively large plump grain with a high proportion of amylopectin. This is the starch that dissolves during cooking to give *risotti* their creamy texture. However, because of the length of the grain and because it contains less amylose (the firm inner starch) it is easy to overcook Arborio rice. Recipes often recommend turning off the heat when the risotto is almost cooked and "resting" it for a few minutes. The rice will continue to cook, due to its own heat, without becoming pappy.

Vialone Nano This is another popular risotto rice. It has a plump grain. Vialone Nano contains less amylopectin than Arborio and has a higher proportion of amylose, so retains a firm "bite" at the centre of the grain when the rest of the rice has cooked to a creamy consistency. Risottos made using this rice tend to be of a rippling consistency, which is described in Italian as *all' onda*. Vialone Nano is especially popular for making Venetian- and Verona-style risottos.

Carnaroli This is considered the premium risotto rice. It was developed by a Milanese rice grower who crossed Vialone Nano with a Japanese rice. The outer part of the grain is made up of a soft starch that dissolves during cooking to leave the inner grain, which has a satisfying, firm "bite".

Spanish Rices

Rice is grown extensively in Spain, particularly in the swampy regions outside Valencia. The most common

Left: Sushi rices. Clockwise from top, a sweetened variety, Kokuho and sushi rice.

Wild Rice

This is not a true rice at all, but a grass that grows in the marshy areas around the American Great Lakes. Wild rice was once a favourite food of the Native American Indians, and today much of America's wild rice is harvested by Native Americans, who have treaty agreements to harvest this rice.

Wild rice needs to be soaked for several hours before cooking, and must be cooked for about 40 minutes until the inner grain breaks through the husk. Wild rice has acquired a fashionable status throughout the West, but its greatest popularity is still in the United States. It is used at Thanksgiving for stuffing the turkey, a symbol of the fact that wild rice was an important staple food for the early settlers when the wheat and barley they had brought with them failed to thrive in the New World.

Below: Canadian wild rice

Glutinous Rice

There are several types of glutinous rice. The name is misleading – the grains contain no gluten – but they are renowned for the way they stick together after cooking. Often known as sticky or sweet rice, glutinous rice is not usually eaten with savoury dishes, but is sweetened and served, hot or cold, with fruit as a dessert.

Japanese Glutinous Rice This short-grained rice is sticky when cooked, a characteristic that makes it perfect for shaping. It has a slightly sweet taste.

Chinese Glutinous Rice In China, glutinous rice is called *geng* rice. It is also known by the generic name for short grain rice (*oryza japonica*). There are white and black varieties, and also a pinkish red rice that grows along the Yangtze river. Glutinous rice is used for puddings and dim sum.

Above: Short-grained white Chinese glutinous rice.

Thai Glutinous Rice Also available in white and black grains, Thai glutinous rice is very popular in puddings and desserts. The cooked black rice grain is really a deep blue-purple colour.

Red Rice

Red rice is not unheard of in rice growing areas, but its presence is not always welcome as it means the rice is reverting to a wild strain, and is likely to be brittle, shatter easily and prove difficult to harvest. In the Camargue region of France, however, a red rice has been developed that is the result of cross pollination between the local white rice and an indigenous wild red rice. The uncooked grain is a reddish brown, and as it cooks the colour intensifies and the water turns a distinct shade of red. Like most wholegrain rice, red rice needs to be cooked for longer than white rice. It has a nutty flavour and a good firm texture. Use in place of brown rice or long grain white rice.

Above: The semi-wild hybrid, red rice.

Giant Canadian Wild Rice

Canadian wild rice is similar to the variety from the United States, but the grains are longer and the Canadian rice is considered to have a superior flavour. The rice is grown on lakes in the north and on the west coast of Canada, where it is harvested by local Indians, who traditionally beat the overhanging grass stems with canoe paddles. The grain that falls into their canoes is theirs to keep, while the remainder, which settles in the shallow water, is for next year's harvest. Like all wild rice, this giant version should be soaked in water for several hours and rinsed, before being cooked for at least 40 minutes, until the tough outer husk has burst open.

Wild Rice and Basmati

This is simply a mixture of two popular and well flavoured grains. Because wild rice normally takes much longer to cook than plain basmati, the makers of this product balance the equation by using a par-boiled basmati, which has a longer cooking time, matching it with a strain of wild rice that requires less cooking than usual. Check the packet for exact cooking times.

Par-boiled or Easy-cook Rice

In spite of its name, par-boiled rice (sometimes labelled "easy-cook") is not a quick cooking rice; indeed, it takes almost half as long again to cook as most long grain rices. Par-boiling is an ancient technique that was developed in India. The whole grain rice is soaked in water and then steamed, which has the effect of locking in the nutrients that are in the bran layer. For white rice, the bran is then removed.

In parts of India and the Middle East, par-boiled rice is very popular. In the West it is mainly – and mistakenly – perceived to be an easy-to-cook rice, although a better description might be "difficult to ruin" as it can stand up to quite a bit of abuse during cooking.

The par-boiled rice grains are more yellow than those of normal rice, although this coloration disappears during cooking; when fully cooked, par-boiled white rice is a brilliant white. Par-boiled rice does take longer to cook than normal rice, but the advantage, for those who enjoy this rice, is that the rice grains stay noticeably separate and slightly chewy. Some people, however, dislike the over-assertive texture and complain that the flavour is bland.

If you're not sure, try both types and compare the results. There are par-boiled versions of white and brown basmati and white and brown long grain rice.

Right: Nowadays, there is a wide choice of convenience rices on the market. Some are ready-mixed with flavourings or vegetables for an instant side dish.

Below: Wild and basmati rices

Quick-cook Rices

Boil-in-the-bag Rice This is a called a convenience rice, although it takes just as long to cook as regular rice; the main convenience is that the pan doesn't have to be washed afterwards. Most boil-in-the-bag rices are prepared with par-boiled (easy-cook) rice.

Pre-cooked and Quick-cook Rice

Not to be confused with par-boiled, pre-cooked rice is just that – rice that has been fully cooked in advance and only needs to be rehydrated and heated in order to be ready to serve. There are a number of different brands available, each with different rehydrating and reheating instructions, so it is important to check the packet carefully before cooking.

Frozen Rice Also a pre-cooked rice, this needs only to be thawed and reheated, which can often be done in the microwave; check the instructions on the packet.

Canned Rice This type of rice really couldn't be simpler to use; just open the can, tip into a bowl and reheat in the microwave or in a conventional oven. For single people with little time for cooking, canned rice may be a handy standby, but it is a hugely expensive way to eat rice, and the flavour is severely diminished.

RICE PRODUCTS

Flaked Rice

Flaked rice is commonly used in Chinese, Thai and Vietnamese cooking for stuffings and desserts. The par-boiled rice is flattened with heavy rollers, so the rice cooks quickly and evenly. In the West, flaked rice is used by the food trade for breakfast cereals and snacks but it is seldom used in recipes. Flaked rice is available from oriental stores.

Ground Rice

More granulate than rice flour, this is used for milk puddings, and was once particularly popular in England. Ground rice is also widely used for biscuits and baking and is a good substitute for wheat flour, especially for people who cannot tolerate gluten.

Rice Flour

Finer than ground rice, this is also used in both oriental and Western cooking for cakes, biscuits and desserts.

Glutinous Rice Flour

This is made from glutinous rice and is normally labelled rice powder. It is used for sweet puddings.

Shiratamo-Ko

A Japanese version of glutinous rice flour.

White Rice Vinegar

Made from glutinous rice, Japanese rice wine vinegar has a subtle, delicate flavour. It is excellent not only in oriental cooking but for any dressing where you need a mild, unassuming flavour. Chinese rice wine vinegar is not as delicate but it makes a good alternative to wine vinegar.

From left: Flaked rice and ground rice. Both cook quickly and evenly, which makes them good for puddings, desserts and baking.

Black Rice Vinegar

Though dark in colour, black rice vinegar has a surprisingly mild taste. It can be used for oriental soups and for dipping sauces.

Red Rice Vinegar

Much spicier than other rice vinegars, Chinese red rice vinegar is used mainly in hot dipping sauces to be served with seafood.

Shaoxing

This Chinese rice wine, which is made from glutinous rice, yeast and water, has a rich, mellow flavour. It is popular throughout China for cooking and drinking, and is available in Chinese groceries and some wine stores. Although both are rice wines, do not confuse Shaoxing with sake, which has a completely different taste.

Left: Glutinous rice flours. The top product is made from cooked glutinous rice, while the bottom product is made from uncooked rice. The difference between the two will affect recipe cooking times and flavours.

Above: From left, Japanese seasoned rice vinegar, Chinese red rice vinegar and Japanese sweetened vinegar. The mild Japanese vinegars are used for a variety of cooking purposes; the spicy Chinese vinegar is generally only used for sharper-flavoured dishes and dipping sauces.

Sake

This Japanese rice wine is quite sweet with a mild flavour that belies its potency. It is served in small cups – about the size of egg cups – and can be chilled but is more often served warm. Nowadays, sake is often drunk with a meal, which is a shift in emphasis; traditionally, sake was the central attraction, and the small portions of food that accompanied it were there to enhance the flavour of this celebrated drink.

Mirin

A sweet cooking sake with a light, delicate flavour, mirin is normally stirred into Japanese dishes during the final stages of cooking. It adds a mild sweetness to sauces or dips. Combined with soy sauce, it is the basis of teriyaki sauce, which is popular for basting grilled foods. Mirin is available from any Japanese food store and from many of the larger supermarkets.

Rice-stick Noodles

These flat noodles vary in thickness; each is roughly the same length as a chopstick. To cook rice-stick noodles, soak them in warm water or stock for 20 minutes to soften before draining.

The noodles are used to thicken soups and casseroles, and for stir-fries.

Rice Vermicelli Noodles

These hair-like noodles are very popular in Thai, Vietnamese and Indonesian cooking. Don't confuse them with bean thread noodles (which look similar and are confusingly called vermicelli noodles) as these are made from ground mung beans. Soak rice vermicelli noodles in warm water for 5–10 minutes to soften, then use according to the recipe.

Japanese Harusame Noodles

Similar to rice vermicelli noodles, these are also made from ground rice and are sold in fragile-looking loops. Prepare the noodles in the same way as rice vermicelli noodles.

Below: Round and triangular rice papers. Clockwise from top, Thai, Chinese and Vietnamese varieties.

Above: Chinese and Thai rice-stick and rice vermicelli noodles.

Rice Paper

Sometimes called rice wrappers, these wafer thin papers are made from rice flour, salt and water. They are sold dried in oriental stores and supermarkets, and can be round or triangular in shape. Before use, dip the rice papers into hot water for a few seconds to soften them. They are used in Vietnamese cooking to make spring rolls, and are popular in some Chinese dishes. Don't confuse them with spring roll wrappers, which are made from wheat flour and water, nor with the edible rice paper used for lining baking sheets.

Below: From left, Japanese sake and Shaoxing rice wine.

COOKING PERFECT RICE

BOILED RICE

Choosing the Rice

Which rice you choose will depend largely on the meal you intend to cook. Basmati, with its wonderful fragrance and flavour, is for many the only rice to serve with an Indian meal. For a Chinese, Thai or Indonesian meal, Thai fragrant rice, with its pleasant aroma and slightly sticky texture (important if you intend to use chopsticks) is excellent, while the versatile American long grain rice is great for stir-fries, pilaffs, jambalayas and gumbos.

There are a few instances where only a specific type of rice will do – risottos, for example, can only be made successfully with risotto rice – but in general, providing you know a little about the qualities of the rice, there are no hard and fast rules. Although tradition demands rice puddings be made with a short grain rice, there's no reason why you shouldn't use long grain. Thai fragrant rice and basmati make delicious puddings too.

Quantities

There are no absolute rules. In the West, 450g/1lb/2⅓ cups of uncooked rice is the quantity recommended for eight people as an accompaniment, but would barely be enough for two Javanese workmen. The following quantities of uncooked rice apply to basmati rice, Thai fragrant rice and brown and white long grain rices.
• For side dishes allow 50–75g/2–3oz rice per person or 225–350g/8–12oz rice to serve four.
• For pilaffs allow 50g/2oz rice per person or 225g/8oz to serve four,
• For salads allow 25–40g/1–1½oz per person or 115–175g/4–6oz to serve four.
• For short grain rice puddings allow 15–20g/½–¾oz per person or 50–75g/2–3oz to serve four.
The weight of rice doubles in weight after cooking, although this depends on the type of rice, the amount of liquid and the cooking time. As a basic rule, when a recipe calls for cooked rice, use just under half the weight in uncooked rice.

Preparing Rice

Some types of rice benefit from being rinsed in cold water, while others should be left to soak before use. Precisely which procedure to follow will be outlined in individual recipes.

Rinsing

• Suitable for: basmati, brown basmati, Thai fragrant rice, brown and white long grain, sushi, glutinous and short grain rice.

Rinsing rice before it is cooked is not essential but it does help to remove excess starch and any dust that may have accumulated in storage. Most types of rice benefit from being rinsed. Do not rinse if using rice in a risotto. If you rinse rice which is to be used in a paella or any other dish where it is fried at the beginning of the recipe, be sure to drain it thoroughly first.

1 Cover the rice with cold water and swirl the grains between your fingers. The water will become slightly cloudy.

2 Allow the rice to settle, then tip the bowl so that the water drains away. Cover the rice once more with cold water, then rinse. Repeat several times until the water runs clear.

COOK'S TIP

In Japan, it is common practice for rice to be rinsed and then left to drain for 30 minutes or longer.

Soaking

• Suitable for: basmati, brown basmati, glutinous rice and sometimes American long grain, brown long grain rice, short grain rice and Thai fragrant rice.

Soaking is seldom essential but it does increase the moisture content of the grains, which means the rice will cook more quickly and will be less sticky. Soaking is particularly beneficial for basmati rice; less so for Thai fragrant rice, where a slight stickiness is an advantage. Risotto rice must not be soaked. Occasionally, rice that has been soaked will be fried; if this is the case, drain it very thoroughly first.

1 To soak rice, simply place it in a large bowl and cover with double the volume of cold water.

2 Leave the rice in the bowl for about 30 minutes or for the time suggested in the recipe, then drain it thoroughly in a sieve or colander.

Making Perfect Boiled Rice

Pan-of-water method

• Suitable for: most types of rice, but particularly for basmati, brown basmati, American long grain, red Camargue and brown rice. Not recommended for Thai fragrant rice.

In Asia, cooks often add a few drops of vegetable oil as well as salt when cooking rice by this method.

1 Put the rice in a large saucepan. Pour in a large amount of boiling water or stock (about 1.2 litres/2 pints/5 cups for every 200g/7oz/1 cup rice) and add a pinch of salt. Bring back to the boil, then lower the heat and simmer, uncovered, for the time indicated on the packet, until just tender.

2 Strain the cooked rice in a sieve or colander and rinse thoroughly with plenty of hot water.

3 Either return the rice to the pan or set the sieve over the pan. Cover with the pan lid or a dish towel and leave the rice to stand for 5 minutes. Fork through before serving, adding butter or oil if you like.

Adding flavourings Stock can be used instead of water, and flavourings such as bay leaves, curry leaves or whole spices can be added if you like, especially if the rice is to be used for a salad, a fried rice dish or a stuffing.

Absorption method

• Suitable for: basmati, Thai fragrant rice, short grain rice and glutinous rice. Sometimes used for brown basmati and American long grain rice.

This is also known as the covered pan method. The rice is cooked in a measured amount of water in a pan with a tightly fitting lid until the water has been absorbed. The proportion of rice to water, and the cooking time, will depend on the type of rice used. Use this method if you need cooked rice for stir-frying, or for a rice salad. It is also used when making some rice puddings.

1 Put the rice into a pan and pour in the measured liquid. Bring back to the boil, then reduce the heat to the lowest possible setting.

2 Cover and cook until the liquid has been absorbed. This can take up to 25 minutes, depending on the type of rice.

3 Remove the pan from the heat and leave to stand, covered with the lid or with foil or a dish towel, for 5 minutes. Steam holes will have appeared on the surface of the rice. If the grains are not completely tender, replace the cover tightly and leave the rice to stand for 5 minutes more.

Adding flavourings If you want to flavour the rice, the absorption method provides the perfect opportunity. Lemon grass, curry leaves and whole spices can be added with the liquid, which can be water, stock, coconut milk or a mixture. This method of cooking rice is the basis of several pilaff-style dishes, where onions, garlic and other ingredients, such as spices, are fried before the rice and liquid are added.

COOK'S TIP

It is vital that the pan is covered tightly and that the rice is cooked at as low a heat as possible. If the lid of the pan is loose, cover the pan with foil or a dish towel before fitting the lid, making sure that any excess fabric is kept well away from the heat source. White rice will cook however low the heat. If, after bringing the liquid back to the boil, the pan is removed entirely from the heat, the rice would continue to cook but would just take longer.

The absorption method is the best way to cook Thai fragrant rice, and basmati rice will retain its excellent flavour when cooked by this method.

Microwave method

- Suitable for: basmati, brown basmati, Thai fragrant and white and brown long grain rice.

Although no faster than conventional cooking, using the microwave is very convenient. It frees a burner on the hob, and the rice can be served in the dish in which it is cooked.

1 Using the same quantities of rice and liquid as for the absorption method, put the rice in a deep glass bowl or microwave container and stir in the boiling water or stock.

2 Cover the bowl with a lid or with microwave-proof clear film and cook on 100% Full Power. Check your microwave instruction book for timings. Leave the rice to stand for 10 minutes before using.

Adding flavourings Cooking in the microwave is essentially the same as when following the absorption method and simple flavourings can be added. If using a large number of additional ingredients, consult your microwave instruction book as the cooking times may differ.

Oven method

- Suitable for: basmati, brown basmati, American long grain, brown long grain, and red Camargue rice.

This is a combination of two methods: the rice is partially cooked first in a pan on the hob, before being finished in the oven. It produces a slightly dry rice, with separate grains.

1 Cook the rice by the pan-of-water method or the absorption method for three-quarters of the normal cooking time. Drain, if necessary, then spoon the rice into a baking dish.

2 Dot with butter or ghee, then cover tightly and cook in a moderate oven for 10–20 minutes. The oven temperature can be between 160°C/325°F/Gas 3 and 190°C/375°F/Gas 5 but the cooking time will need to be adjusted accordingly.

Adding flavourings Flavourings can be added to the rice during the first stage of cooking, or part of the cooked rice can be coloured and flavoured with a saffron or spice, if you like. Fried onions, garlic or cardamoms can be dotted over the partly cooked rice before it is placed in the oven.

Steaming

- Suitable for: white basmati, American long grain and Thai fragrant rice.

This method is also combined. The rice is partially cooked first in a pan of simmering liquid, before being steamed. This method of cooking is used for plain boiled rice and some glutinous rice dishes.

1 Cook the rice by the pan-of-water method or the absorption method for about three-quarters of the normal cooking time. Tip the part-cooked rice into a sieve or colander.

2 Transfer the cooked rice to a muslin bag set inside a pan of simmering water. Cover and steam for 5–10 minutes for white rice; 15 minutes for brown rice. If the grains of rice still feel hard, steam for a little longer.

Adding flavourings The rice can be flavoured during the first stage of cooking, in the same way as for the pan-of-water or absorption methods. Replace the cooking water with stock, coconut milk or a mixture, if you like, and add bay leaves, curry leaves, lemon grass or whole spices with the liquid.

Electric rice cooker

• Suitable for: all types of rice.

1 Put the rice into the cooker and add the required amount of water as indicated in your instruction booklet. Do not add salt. Cover the cooker with the lid and switch it on. The cooker will switch itself off automatically when the rice is ready, and will keep the rice hot until you are ready to serve.

Quick-cook method

Rice can be soaked in boiling water and then quickly cooked at the last minute. This works particularly well with basmati rice that is to be cooked by the pan-of-water method. It is a useful cooking method if you are entertaining and want the rice to cook quickly, and with as little fuss as possible.

1 Put the measured rice into a large bowl and pour over boiling water to cover. Leave to stand, uncovered, for at least 30 minutes or up to 1 hour.

2 Bring a saucepan of lightly salted stock or water to the boil. Drain the rice, add it to the pan and cook for 3–4 minutes until tender.

Adding flavourings Flavourings can be added in the same way as for boiled rice.

Cooking Brown Rice

Brown rice takes longer to cook than white rice, but how much longer will depend on the type of rice; always check the packet instructions. Soaking brown rice in a bowl of water first will soften the grains but it will not shorten the cooking time.

Cooking Glutinous Rice

Glutinous rice should be soaked before cooking, for at least 1 hour and up to 4 hours. After being drained, the rice can then be simmered with coconut milk and sugar if it is to be served as a dessert. For a savoury accompaniment, steam the drained rice for about 10–15 minutes, until it is tender.

Cooking Wild Rice

Although this is not strictly a rice, wild rice can be treated in the same way. It takes a lot of cooking, and for best results, should be soaked in water for 1 hour before being boiled in lightly salted water for 45–60 minutes. Check the instructions on the packet as cooking times differ according to the size of the grains. Wild rice is cooked when the inner white grain bursts out of the black husk.

Cooking Par-boiled or Easy-cook Rice

This takes longer to cook than regular rice. Check the packet for instructions. Easy-cook rice can be cooked by the pan-of-water or the absorption method. It can also be cooked in the microwave or in a rice cooker. This type of rice is fine for accompanying a meal, but is not as good for fried rice dishes.

Cooking/Heating Frozen or Canned Rice

Follow the instructions on the packet or can. Most can be reheated or cooked on the hob or in the microwave.

Storing Rice

Raw (uncooked) rice can be kept in a cool, dark place for up to three years in the unopened packet or in an airtight container. It should be kept perfectly dry; if the moisture content creeps up, the rice will turn mouldy. If the rice is very old, it may need more water or longer cooking. Check the packet for "best before" dates.

Cooked rice can be stored for up to 24 hours if cooled, covered and kept in the fridge. You can also freeze the cooled rice; reheat it in a covered casserole in the oven or thaw it and use for fried rice or in a salad. Reheated rice should be piping hot all the way through.

Above: Cooked, cooled rice freezes well.

RISOTTO

This simple Italian dish is very much a peasant food and it says a great deal about the changing attitudes towards food and healthy eating that in the last decade or so, this dish, like much *cucina povera*, has come to be so widely appreciated. Nowadays you will see risotto on the menu at some of the classiest restaurants in town, enjoyed for the same reasons it has always been valued, because it is healthy, satisfying and extremely good to eat. Yet what could be simpler than a risotto? Although there are complicated and elaborate versions, some of the best risottos are made using little more than rice, a good stock and a few fresh herbs or cheeses. These simple risottos, like *Risi e Bisi* (Rice and Peas) or *Risotto alla Parmigiana* (Rice with Cheese) are probably the most traditional of all, and are no less tasty for their plain ingredients.

Since the first risottos were the food of poorer people, there is no long line of recipes that chart the popularity of this dish. Recipe books written in Italy during risotto's infancy tended to concern themselves with costly meats or spices and were written for the wealthy who could afford these expensive ingredients. Peasants and poor farmers had neither the time, the ability nor the inclination to read what they knew already: that rice was a cheap and sustaining food that was also delicious when cooked with care.

Short grain rice, which is the central ingredient in risotto, has been grown in Italy for several hundred years. The Arabs introduced rice into Italy during the Middle Ages, but this early rice was a longer grained variety and was grown in Sicily and the south of the country.

At some point though, rice was introduced to Lombardy in northern Italy, and by the 15th century, rice cultivation had become an established part of the Italian way of life. It was around this time that the custom of cultivating rice in fields flooded with water was adopted in Italy; this method of growing rice followed the process used in Asia, as opposed to the method of dry cultivation favoured by the Arabs.

Today, Italy shares with Spain the honour of being Europe's leading rice producer. Risotto rices are still grown in the north of the country, where the rice fields are irrigated with water running down from the Alps. The varieties of rice grown today have been improved and refined since earlier times, yet the characteristic starchy short grain has remained the same.

The method of cooking rice in stock may have been influenced by cooking styles in France and Spain but, whether by accident or design, it is difficult to imagine a better way of doing justice to fine rice than to serve it as a risotto.

Risotto is traditionally eaten as a separate course before the meat and vegetables. Only rice and stock are the essential ingredients, but you should choose these carefully. The stock must be home-made (or the very best you can afford) and the rice must be one of those recommended for the purpose. Have the stock simmering in a pan adjacent to the risotto pan, and add it slowly and lovingly. Observe the standing time at the end, as this allows the rice to rest and reach perfection. Do all this – and it is not difficult – and you'll find risotto one of the most simple and rewarding rice dishes you can make.

Types of Risotto Rice

It is essential to use a risotto rice, but precisely which one is up to you. Named risotto rices are becoming more widely available, but you will often find packages labelled simply Italian risotto rice. Of the named varieties, Arborio is the most widely available, with Carnaroli and Vialone Nano becoming increasingly easy to find in Italian delicatessens and good supermarkets. Other specific types of risotto rice include Baldo, Vialone Nano Gigante and Roma. Each has its own particular qualities, which will be familiar to those who specialize in cooking *risotti*. Some recipes call for a named risotto rice, but most are non-specific and any risotto rice will give a good result.

INSTANT RISOTTOS

There are several instant risottos on the market, available from supermarkets and delicatessens. They are easy to make, all you need to do is add water, heat and stir. Packets give simple instructions and recommend simmering for about 10 minutes – roughly half the time required for making a classic risotto. Instant risottos come in several flavours, including four cheeses, spinach, saffron, tomato and black cuttlefish. They are handy for a quick meal, and the colours supplied by the flavourings make them pretty to serve. More importantly, these risottos taste surprisingly good.

Left: Clockwise from top, instant risottos flavoured with cuttlefish, tomatoes, saffron and spinach.

Making Perfect Risotto

1 In a large, deep saucepan, fry the onion, garlic and any other vegetable(s) in extra virgin olive oil over a medium heat for a few minutes, stirring all the time. Unless the recipe specifies otherwise, the onion and other vegetables should be softened but not browned.

2 If using any uncooked meat or poultry, add these ingredients to the onions in the pan, unless the recipe specifies otherwise. Turn up the heat to high and cook, stirring frequently, until browned on all sides.

3 Tip the risotto rice into the pan, and stir, so that every grain is coated in the oil. Fry the rice over a high heat for 3–4 minutes, stirring all the time. You will notice that the grains of rice become transparent as they are stirred into the hot oil, except for the very centre of the grain, which remains opaque.

4 Add a little wine, if this is what is called for in the recipe, or a ladleful of hot stock. Stir the rice until all the liquid has been absorbed.

5 Lower the heat to moderate, then add another ladleful of hot stock and stir it into the rice. Keep the pan over a moderate heat so that the liquid bubbles but the rice is in no danger of burning. Stir the rice frequently.

6 Add the remaining stock a ladleful at a time, making sure that each ladleful is used up before adding the next. This process will take about 20 minutes. As the risotto cooks, the grains of rice will begin to soften and merge together.

7 When the risotto begins to look creamy, grate in the cheese or add extra butter. The rice should be virtually tender, but still a little hard in the centre. At this point remove the pan from the heat, cover with a dish towel and leave to rest for about 5 minutes. The risotto will cook to perfection in the residual heat.

RISOTTO TIPS

• To begin, fry the rice in hot oil, stirring all the time, until the grains are coated and begin to turn translucent.

• Add any wine or sherry to the risotto before adding the stock. The alcohol will evaporate, but the flavour will remain.

• Use a good quality, home-made stock for your risotto. Alternatively, buy cartons of fresh stock, which are available from delicatessens and large supermarkets.

• The stock added to a risotto must always be hot. Have it simmering in a separate pan adjacent to the pan in which you are cooking the risotto.

• Add the hot stock slowly, ladleful by ladleful. Make sure all the liquid has been absorbed before adding the next ladleful.

• Avoid overcooking the risotto. Remove the pan from the heat while the rice is still slightly undercooked.

• For best results, season the risotto after cooking but before leaving it to rest. Stock, salted butter and Parmesan cheese will all contribute some saltiness, as may other ingredients, so always taste the risotto before adding any extra salt.

• Don't use ready-grated Parmesan. For the best flavour, buy good quality Parmesan in one piece and grate it yourself.

Equipment

There are only three essential pieces of equipment needed for cooking a risotto, and with luck you'll have them already.

• A heavy-based pan. Ideally, this should be a wide, straight-sided pot, deep enough to contain the cooked risotto. A deep frying pan can be used for smaller quantities.

• A wooden spoon.

• A saucepan for the simmering stock.

Adding Risotto Ingredients

Recipes will tell you when to stir in any additional ingredients needed for the risotto, but this guide may be helpful when devising your own risotto recipes.

Vegetables Onions and garlic are fried until soft at the beginning, before the rice is added. Most other vegetables, such as aubergines, carrots, courgettes and pepper, are sautéed with the onions. Vegetables that require little cooking, such as spinach and asparagus, should be stirred in towards the end of cooking. Mushrooms are usually fried at the same time or just after the onions, before adding the rice.

Above: Onions and garlic are essential ingredients in a good risotto. Use red onions or shallots for variations in flavour.

Above: Fresh green vegetables, such as courgettes, spinach and asparagus, add texture to the risotto. They retain their shape and colour during cooking, and always look impressive.

Fish and shellfish These are generally cooked before being added to the risotto. It is usual for fillets of fish, such as salmon, plaice or sea bass to be poached, then flaked. Scallops should be lightly cooked, then sliced. Stir fish or shellfish into the risotto about three-quarters of the way through cooking.

Above: Almost any fresh fish and seafood can be used in a risotto, including salmon fillets, haddock, plaice and tiger prawns.

Meat and poultry These are usually added at an early stage, at the same time as the onions; the rice is added later, so that both ingredients cook together. The exception is cooked meats, such as sausage or ham, which tend to be stirred into the risotto towards the end of cooking.

Above: Chicken fillets and gammon are both very successful ingredients for risottos, but the choice really is endless. Cut the meat into small pieces and brown with the onions before stirring in the rice.

Herbs Robust herbs are sometimes cooked with the onions, but more delicate herbs, such as parsley or coriander, are usually added at the end of cooking, at the same time as the Parmesan cheese or butter.

Above: Delicate-flavoured herbs, such as thyme, sage, coriander and tarragon, can all be stirred into the cooked rice for a simple risotto.

Cheese Where cheese is the dominant flavouring, as in a four-cheese risotto, it can be added halfway through cooking, but it is more usual for grated Parmesan to be added just before the risotto is left to rest.

Above: Most cheeses can be used in risottos but the one essential cheese is Parmesan. Use it either on its own as a simple flavouring or to complement other ingredients in the recipe. Fresh shavings of Parmesan can be used to garnish the risotto, or supply a bowl of Parmesan, grated fresh from the block, to be passed separately when serving.

MAKING STOCKS

Chicken Stock

MAKES ABOUT 1.5 LITRES/2½ PINTS/6¼ CUPS

INGREDIENTS
1 onion, quartered
2 celery sticks, chopped
1 carrot, roughly chopped
about 675g/1½lb fresh chicken,
   either ½ whole chicken or 2–3
   chicken quarters
1 fresh thyme or marjoram sprig
2 fresh parsley sprigs
8 whole peppercorns
salt

1 Put the prepared vegetables in a large, heavy-based saucepan and lay the chicken on top. Pour over cold water to cover the chicken (about 1.5 litres/2½ pints/6¼ cups).

2 Bring to the boil slowly. Do not cover the pan. When bubbling, skim off any fat that has risen to the surface.

3 Add the herbs, peppercorns and a pinch of salt. Lower the heat, cover the pan and simmer the stock gently for 2–2½ hours, until the chicken is tender.

4 Using a slotted spoon, transfer the chicken or chicken pieces to a plate. Remove any skin or bones; the chicken can be used in another recipe. Strain the stock into a clean bowl, leave it to cool, then chill in the fridge.

5 A layer of fat will form on the surface of the chilled stock. Remove this just before use. The stock can be kept in the fridge for up to 3 days or frozen for up to 6 months.

Fish Stock

MAKES ABOUT 2.5 LITRES/4 PINTS/10 CUPS

INGREDIENTS
900g/2lb white fish bones and
   trimmings, but not gills
2.5 litres/4 pints/10 cups water
1 onion, roughly chopped
1 celery stick, chopped
1 carrot, chopped
1 bay leaf
3 fresh parsley sprigs
6 peppercorns
5cm/2in piece of pared lemon rind
75ml/5 tbsp/⅓ cup dry white wine

1 Put the fish bones and fish heads in a large, heavy-based saucepan. Pour in the water.

2 Bring the liquid to the boil, using a spoon to skim off any scum that rises to the surface. Add the onion, celery, carrot, bay leaf, parsley, peppercorns, lemon rind and white wine.

3 Lower the heat, and cover the pan with the lid. Simmer the stock gently for 20–30 minutes, then leave to cool.

4 Strain the cooled stock through a muslin bag into a clean bowl. Keep the stock in the fridge for up to 2 days or freeze it for up to 3 months.

COOK'S TIP

Do not allow the fish stock to boil for a prolonged period or the bones will begin to disintegrate and the stock will acquire an unpleasant, bitter flavour.

Vegetable Stock

MAKES ABOUT 1.2 LITRES/2 PINTS/5 CUPS

INGREDIENTS
3–4 shallots, halved
2 celery sticks or 75g/3oz celeriac,
   chopped
2 carrots, roughly chopped
3 tomatoes, halved
3 fresh parsley stalks
1 fresh tarragon sprig
1 fresh marjoram or thyme sprig
2.5cm/1in piece of pared orange rind
6 peppercorns
2 allspice berries
1.5 litres/2½ pints/6¼ cups water

1 Put all the vegetables into a heavy-based saucepan. Add the fresh herbs, orange rind and spices. Pour in the water.

2 Bring the liquid to the boil, then lower the heat and simmer the stock gently for 30 minutes. Leave it to cool completely.

3 Strain the stock through a sieve into a large bowl, pressing out all the liquid from the vegetables using the back of a spoon. Store the cold stock in the fridge for up to 3 days or in the freezer for up to 6 months.

PAELLA

In Spain, paella is not just a meal, it is an occasion. Come fiestas and holidays (and there are many of these in Spain), it is not unknown for someone to say, "how about a paella", and, the weather being good, and the company convivial, ingredients, utensils and plenty of red wine will then be gathered up and the party will head outdoors, to the beach or into the mountains. The ingredients can be many and various. Rice – the short grain variety – is an obvious essential, but saffron, garlic and olive oil will inevitably be included, too. Everyone will help to gather wood and light a fire, after which one of the men will prepare and cook the paella. Other men will doubtless make their contribution. There will be advice for the chef on when to add the rice, how much stock to use and whether to add herbs early or late, but the principle is that men do the cooking.

Traditionally, a paella should always be cooked out of doors, over a wood fire by a man. The indoor version, cooked more conventionally over a stove, and by a woman, is strictly speaking not a paella at all but an *arroz* – a rice.

There are other conventions concerning paella, some more imperative than others. Short grain rice and saffron are essential ingredients. Purists believe that an authentic paella should contain only eels, snails and beans, the ingredients used in the original Valencian paella, but most Spanish people today are fairly relaxed about using other ingredients. Fish, shellfish, meat and poultry are routinely used, sometimes together.

More important in Spain is the manner in which the paella is eaten. For the Spanish, paella is the epitome of convivial eating: it is always served with generous amounts of wine and is inevitably made for a large party of people. The paella dish – the *paellera* – is placed on the table as a spectacular centrepiece, and everyone helps themselves to the food, while the conversation, lubricated by the wine, is, in true Spanish fashion, animated and lively.

For all these reasons, paella has become one of the world's best loved rice dishes. There are hundreds of variations, with restaurants up and down the country producing their own speciality. Although tradition dictates that paella should be cooked out of doors, superb paellas can be made in conventional kitchens, albeit on a more modest scale. A paella can be simple or elaborate and you can vary the combination of meat, poultry, fish and shellfish to suit your taste, your pocket and the occasion.

Making Perfect Paella

1 Cut the meat or joint the poultry into large pieces; season if the recipe requires. Fry the meat or poultry in olive oil in the paella pan or in a large frying pan until it turns an even, deep golden brown. Transfer the cooked meat or poultry to a plate. Slice the sausage.

2 Prepare any fish and shellfish that is to be included according to type: steam mussels (discarding any that fail to open), prepare squid and peel prawns. Fry the fish and shellfish briefly, if required by the recipe, and transfer to a plate.

3 In a paella pan, fry the onions in olive oil until golden. Add the garlic, tomatoes and any firm vegetables. Stir in cooked dried beans, if using. Stir briefly, then add water or stock and any seasonings. Bring to the boil.

4 Tip in the rice, stirring so that it is evenly distributed, then add the meat or poultry, and any sausage. Cook, uncovered, over a medium heat (so that the liquid simmers nicely) for 15 minutes.

5 Lower the heat, and add any softer vegetables, fish or shellfish. Add saffron to give the paella its distinctive colour. Cook over a low heat for 10 minutes until the liquid has been absorbed, then cover and rest for 5–10 minutes.

To Stir or Not to Stir

Read any guide to making paella, and you'll be told that the paella mustn't be stirred or disturbed in any way. This is fine advice for a true paella – cooked over an open fire so that the heat is distributed evenly over the base of the pan. But if you're using a gas or electric flame, the uneven heat distribution will mean that the centre will cook more quickly than the outside. To get around this problem, you can either break the rules and stir occasionally, or cook the paella in the oven. That way it will cook evenly, although technically, in Spain, it would be a "rice" (*arroz*) and not a paella.

A GUIDE TO PAELLA QUANTITIES

Individual paella recipes will usually specify quantities of rice, liquid and other ingredients, although the following can be used as a rough guide.

Amount of rice	Amount of liquid	Servings
200g/7oz/1 cup	550ml/18fl oz/2¼ cups	2–3
350g/12oz/1¾ cups	900ml/1½ pints/3¾ cups	4–6
450g/1lb/2⅓ cups	1.2 litres/2 pints/5 cups	6
500g/1¼lb/3 cups	1.3 litres/2¼ pints/5½ cups	8

Allow between 65–75g/2½–3oz/⅓–½ cup rice per person

PAELLA TIPS

• Use the right type of rice. The Spanish will occasionally use a medium grain rice, although the traditional choice is a short grain rice that absorbs liquid well. The round grained and stubby Spanish rice Calasperra would be ideal, or use Italian Arborio risotto rice.
• It is important to use a large pan. The rice needs to be cooked in a shallow layer so there should be plenty of room to spread it out. If at all possible use a paella pan (called a *paellera*), which is a wide flat metal pan. If you don't have a paella pan, you can use a frying pan – the largest you have – but this will probably only be large enough for a paella for three or four people.
• Always use fresh ingredients, especially the fish and seafood. Paella is not a dish for leftovers.
• Cook other ingredients carefully before you start to cook the paella. Meats should be cooked until golden brown, as should onions, as this will add flavour to the dish. Fish should be seared lightly, and added to the rice towards the end of cooking, to avoid overcooking it.

Below: The width and shallow depth of the paella pan allow an even distribution of heat when the rice is cooking.

• Less tender cuts of meat or larger pieces of poultry may require longer cooking. Always check instructions in the recipe for timings.
• Use a well-flavoured stock – preferably home-made chicken, meat, fish or vegetable.
• Bring the stock or other liquid in the pan to a fierce boil before tipping in the rice. (This is the opposite of the technique used when making a risotto, where the stock is added slowly to the rice.)
• Use saffron strands rather than turmeric or any other colouring.
• Once the liquid has been absorbed by the rice, cover the paella with a dampened dish towel and allow it to rest for a few minutes before serving, to complete the cooking.

SUSHI

Sushi is wonderful food. Sushi bars, or *sushiya*, are to be found everywhere in Tokyo and are now a familiar sight in London, New York, Sydney and other large cities. The little snacks are a superb treat – clean tasting yet surprisingly filling. They are not difficult to prepare at home and make an attractive and impressive snack or starter.

A Japanese short grain rice should be used for sushi. Some supermarkets and delicatessens sell a rice labelled sushi rice, which takes the guesswork out of the process. Japanese short grain rice is slightly sticky, which makes it easy to pick up with chopsticks and ideal for sushi, as the grains of rice cling together. Glutinous rice is not suitable for making sushi, as it is too sticky.

The rice should be rinsed and left to drain for 30 minutes before being cooked by the absorption method. You can use an electric rice cooker but don't be tempted to use the pan-of-water method as the results will be disastrous.

Nori This dried seaweed is sold in paper-thin sheets. It is dark green to black in colour and almost transparent in places. Some nori comes ready-toasted (yaki-nori), often seasoned with soy sauce and sesame oil. Alternatively, toast the nori under a hot grill before use.
Gari Pale pink ginger pickles, which are excellent for serving with sushi.
Shoyu This Japanese soy sauce is milder than Chinese soy sauce. Serve with sushi.
Wasabi A hot green horseradish to serve with fish. It is sold as a paste or as a powder, to which water is added.

Above: Clockwise from top, bamboo rolling mat, gari, wasabi paste, shoyu and nori sheet.

Making Perfect Sushi

1 Rinse the rice and drain for 30–60 minutes, then put in a heavy pan and add a piece of dried kelp (kombu). Add water (see Quantities below), and bring to the boil. Remove the kelp, cover the pan and cook gently over a low heat for about 15 minutes. Increase to high for 10 seconds, then remove from the heat and let stand for 10 minutes. Lift the lid. Steam holes will have appeared in the rice and it will be tender.

2 Prepare the sushi vinegar. For every 450g/1lb/2⅓ cups rice, mix together 60ml/4 tbsp rice vinegar, 15ml/1 tbsp granulated sugar and 2.5ml/½ tsp salt.

3 Stir the sushi vinegar into the rice, cover with a damp cloth and leave to cool. Do not put the rice in the fridge as this will make it go hard.

Quantities

Use between 600ml/1 pint/2½ cups and 750ml/1¼ pints/3 cups water for every 450g/1lb/2⅓ cups sushi rice, depending on the type of rice; always check the instructions on the packet. If you prefer, you could use sake instead of 30ml/2 tbsp of the water.

Rolled Sushi with Smoked Salmon

MAKES 24 SLICES

1 Line a bamboo mat with clear film. Arrange the smoked salmon across the mat, overlapping if necessary, so that there are no gaps or holes. Spread a generous layer of the dressed rice over the salmon.

2 Roll the mat away from you so that the salmon rolls up around the rice. Do not roll up the clear film with the fish. Make more rolls in the same way.

3 Chill the rolls in the fridge for about 10 minutes, then unwrap and cut each roll into six slices, using a wet knife. Cover with a damp cloth and keep cool.

Rolled Sushi with Nori and Filling

MAKES 24 SLICES

To make this sushi you will need
sheets of yaki-nori (toasted seaweed).
Two sheets will make four long rolls.

1 Cut the yaki-nori in half lengthways
and place a half-sheet, shiny side
down, on the bamboo mat.

2 Spread a layer of the dressed rice
over the yaki-nori, leaving a 1cm/½in
clear edge at the top and bottom.

3 Arrange a line of filling horizontally
across the middle of the rice. The
filling could be raw salmon or raw tuna,
cut into 1cm/½in square long sticks,
sliced raw scallops, Japanese omelette,
roasted pepper, spring onions,
cucumber or a selection of two or
three of these.

4 Using the rolling mat as a guide, and
working from the nearest edge of yaki-
nori, roll up the yaki-nori and rice into
a cigar (do not include the mat in the
roll). Roll the mat in the palms of your
hands so that the edges stick together.

5 Wrap the rolls in clear film and chill
in the fridge for 10 minutes, then
unwrap the rolls. Use a wet knife to
cut each roll into six slices, rinsing the
knife occasionally.

Shaped Sushi

1 Wet your hands. Take about 15–20g/
½–¾oz/2–3 tbsp dressed sushi rice at
a time and shape it into a rectangle,
measuring about 2 x 5cm/¾ x 2in and
1cm/½in high.

2 Repeat this process until all the rice
is used up. Gently spread a little wasabi
paste in the middle of each of the
rectangles of rice, then add your
chosen topping.

Sushi Toppings

Make plain rolled sushi and top them
with any one of these suggestions.

**Raw sushi-grade salmon, raw sushi-
grade tuna, salmon roe or other fish roe**
Cut the salmon and tuna into pieces
that are roughly the same size as the
rice portions.

Peeled raw prawn tails Cook the
prawns for about 1 minute in a pan of
simmering water, then drain. Slit each
prawn along the belly and remove the
dark vein, then carefully open out each
prawn like a book. Mix together 15ml/
1 tbsp rice vinegar and 5ml/1 tsp
granulated sugar in a small bowl. Add
the prawns, turn to coat, and leave to
marinate in a cool place for about
10 minutes.

Blanched squid and boiled octopus
Slice the squid and octopus into strips
that are roughly the same size as the
rice portions.

Rolled omelette slices Beat together
1 egg, 15ml/1 tbsp sake, 15ml/1 tbsp
granulated sugar, 15ml/1 tbsp water
and a pinch of salt. Heat a little
groundnut oil in a small frying pan,
then pour in the egg mixture. Fry over
a medium to high heat until the egg is
just set but not browned. Roll up the
omelette and slice.

Garnishes

Fish sushi can be garnished with
fresh chives, fresh coriander or toasted
sesame seeds. Omelette sushi can be
decorated by wrapping strips of yaki-
nori around the moulded rice.

COOK'S TIP
Sushi rice should be cooked either by
the absorption method or in an electric
rice cooker. The pan-of-water method
should not be used.

Sushi rice is very sticky when cooked.
If you find it becomes unmanageable,
rinse your hands in a bowl of water to
which 5ml/1 tsp oil has been added.
Pat your hands dry; they will be slightly
oily and the rice will no longer stick
to them.

BIRYANI

This is one of India's most famous rice dishes. Perfect for parties and other festivities, biryani is served with other vegetables and meats, but essentially takes centre stage itself. It is basically an all-in-one dish. The rice is piled on top of a meat or vegetable curry, with saffron milk dribbled over the top to give the rice a splash of golden colour.

Although biryani takes a little time to prepare, it is straightforward and simple. The only rule is to use basmati rice, which should be soaked for 3 hours, preferably in lightly salted water, a technique which the Persians, who are credited with inventing this dish, believed made the rice a brilliant white.

Lamb, chicken and beef are commonly used in biryanis, but duck and game work well, and vegetarian biryanis are popular, too. Biryanis should never be very hot, but are traditionally flavoured with fragrant spices. They can be made using coconut milk, but natural yogurt is more common. The sauce should be sweet and fragrant, with a creamy consistency.

Making Perfect Chicken Biryani

1 First make the saffron milk. Crumble a generous pinch (about 5ml/1 tsp) of saffron strands into 30ml/2 tbsp of warm milk in a small bowl. Stir, then leave to soak for about 3 hours.

2 Meanwhile, wash 275g/10oz/1½ cups basmati rice in cold water. Drain the rice thoroughly, then tip it into a large bowl and cover with more cold water. Stir in 10ml/2 tsp salt and leave to soak for 3 hours.

3 Prepare a chicken curry. Heat 45ml/ 3 tbsp oil in a frying pan and add 3 sliced onions. Cook until soft. Add 175g/6oz cubed chicken breasts, along with any spices you are using. Stir to coat the chicken in the spices, then add 2.5ml/½ tsp salt, 2–3 chopped garlic cloves and lemon juice to taste. Stir-fry for 5 minutes more, until the chicken is browned. Drain the rice and cook it in boiling salted water for 4–5 minutes until three-quarters cooked.

4 Spoon a little drained rice into a flameproof dish, just enough to cover the bottom, then add the curry. Spoon 150ml/¼ pint/⅔ cup natural yogurt evenly over the curry. Preheat the oven to 150°C/300°F/Gas 2.

5 Pile the remaining rice in a hillock on top of the curry, then, using the handle of a wooden spoon, make a 2.5cm/1in hole down from the peak to the bottom.

6 Dribble the saffron milk and 50ml/ ¼ pint/⅔ cup hot chicken stock over the rice, and dot with butter or ghee. Scatter over fried onions, sultanas and toasted almonds. Cover the dish tightly with a double piece of foil held in place by the lid. Cook in the oven for 40 minutes.

Spices for Chicken Biryani

For 175g/6oz chicken use 10 whole green cardamom pods; 1.5ml/¼ tsp ground cloves; 2–3 whole cloves; 5cm/2in cinnamon stick; 5ml/1 tsp ground cumin; 2.5ml/½ tsp ground black pepper; 5ml/1 tsp ground coriander; 5ml/1 tsp finely chopped fresh root ginger; 1.5ml/¼ tsp chilli powder.

LONTONG (COMPRESSED RICE)

This is a speciality of Indonesia and Malaysia. The rice is cooked in a confined space for longer than normal to form a compact solid mass, which when cooled, can be cut into squares. Lontong is eaten cold, usually with salads and satay, when it absorbs the spicy dressings and sauces.

Lontong is traditionally cooked in a banana leaf, although a muslin bag is generally easier to use.

Thai fragrant rice, basmati or any other long grain rice can be used for lontong. Do not be tempted to use par-boiled (easy-cook) rice, as it will not form a solid mass.

Making Perfect Lontong

1 You will need several muslin bags, each about 15cm/6in square. Leave the top of each bag open. Spoon in enough long grain rice to fill each bag one-third full (about 115g/4oz/generous ½ cup), then sew the opening closed.

2 Bring a pan of salted water to the boil, lower in the bags of rice and allow to simmer gently, uncovered, for about 75 minutes, making sure the pan doesn't boil dry and adding more water if necessary.

3 Remove the bags from the water and drain them thoroughly. Each bag should feel like a rather hard and solid lump.

4 When the lontong is completely cold, open the muslin bags, remove the blocks of compressed rice and cut each block into squares or oblongs, using a wet, sharp knife.

FRIED RICE TIPS

• Rice must be cooked and completely cold before frying. Warm rice will become soggy and oily if fried. If you are cooking rice especially for frying, spread it out on a baking sheet as soon as it has been cooked so that it cools rapidly. Leave it for at least 2–3 hours.

• Use long grain white or brown rice for frying.

• Other ingredients should be cooked before the rice is added.

• Always cook the rice over a low heat. It is important to heat the rice through completely, but take care not to overcook it.

FRIED RICE

Wherever rice is a staple food, every region, even every family, has its own fried rice recipe. When rice is served at almost every meal, there are inevitably leftovers, and it's a simple matter to fry these with other ingredients for breakfast, for a lunchtime snack or for a more elaborate evening meal.

There are several classic fried rice dishes – Nasi Goreng, one of the most famous, comes from Indonesia, but is more commonly associated with the Dutch *Rijstafel* (rice table). There are also several well known Chinese fried rices, Egg Fried Rice and Special Fried Rice being two of the most popular. Recipes for any of these dishes are extremely flexible. Provided you follow a few simple rules, the best way with any rice dish is to make up your own favourite mixture.

The choice of ingredients is up to the individual cook, but here are some suggestions.

Aromatics Sliced spring onions or shallots; red or yellow onions, sliced or cut into wedges; sliced or crushed garlic. Stir-fry in oil for 3–4 minutes, then add the meat, fish, vegetables and/or eggs. If choosing two or more different ingredients, stir-fry them individually before stirring together.

Meat Any tender cut of poultry or meat, such as chicken, duck, beef, lamb or pork fillet can be used. Slice meat thinly so that it cooks quickly. Meats can be marinated for 30 minutes before cooking (see individual recipes for marinade ingredients). Stir-fry with onions until cooked. Cooked meats only require heating through.

Fish Raw fish and shellfish work well and should be stir-fried after any meat. Cooked fish or prawns can be stirred in at the end.

Vegetables Choose colourful vegetables such as carrots, peppers, courgettes and mushrooms. Cut them into julienne strips so that they cook quickly and evenly. Stir-fry until just tender.

Eggs Beat together and scramble with the onions. Or use the eggs to make an omelette; roll it up, cut into slices and use to garnish the rice.

Making Perfect Fried Rice

1 Stir-fry any uncooked meat in oil in a wok or large, deep frying pan, then add onions. Transfer the meat to a plate.

2 Add beaten egg to the frying pan and scramble with sliced spring onions.

3 Add spices and flavourings such as soy sauce, rice wine, fresh chillies, tomato purée or spices.

4 Tip the cold rice into the frying pan and mix with the scrambled egg. Return any cooked meats, cooked fish or cooked vegetables to the pan at this stage, or add chopped herbs. Cook over a low heat, stirring occasionally, to warm the rice through completely.

RICE PUDDING

In one form or another, rice pudding is enjoyed all over the world. It is England's best known rice dish, and most other European countries have at least one favourite rice pudding to call their own.

Perhaps the popularity of rice pudding in the past arose from the fact that it is difficult to overcook it. In the eighteenth century, food was often badly cooked, and overcooked, stodgy savoury rice dishes were probably despised then as they are now. Rice pudding was one of the few foods that could stand up to such abuse. With its meltingly tender grains slowly cooked in creamy milk, flavoured with vanilla or nutmeg and sweetened with sugar, rice pudding quickly became a firm favourite in Britain and beyond.

English rice pudding is made with short grain rice but this is not essential. Thai fragrant rice and basmati rice can be used equally successfully. In Asia, glutinous rice, which is stickier than our short grain, is the favoured rice for making puddings.

Making Perfect English Rice Pudding

Oven method

1 Preheat the oven to 150°C/300°F/Gas 2. Following your chosen recipe, put the rice and sugar in a shallow baking dish and pour in cold milk. Stir well to mix and then dot the surface with a little butter.

2 Bake in the preheated oven for about 45 minutes, by which time a thick skin will have formed on top of the pudding.

3 Stir the skin into the pudding and bake the pudding for about 1¼ hours more, stirring once or twice.

Pan method

1 Place the rice in a large saucepan. Add the quantity of milk and sugar as specified in the recipe and stir to mix.

2 Bring to the boil, then lower the heat, cover the pan and simmer very gently for 1¼ hours, stirring frequently.

3 Remove the lid and simmer for 15–20 minutes more until the rice mixture is thick and creamy.

Combination method

1 Partially cook the rice using the absorption method. Put the rice in a pan and add a third of the measured liquid. Simmer gently over a low heat.

2 When the liquid has been absorbed, stir in half the remaining liquid and simmer for about 6 minutes more.

3 Stir in the sugar, any flavourings and the remaining milk, then pour the mixture into a buttered baking dish.

4 Dot with butter and bake for 1–1½ hours at a temperature between 150°C/300°F/Gas 2 and 180°C/350°F/Gas 4. The lower temperature cooks slower but will give the pudding a creamier taste.

Making Perfect Glutinous Rice Pudding

1 Place the rice in a large bowl, add cold water to cover and leave to soak for 3–4 hours.

2 Drain the rice, put it in a saucepan and pour in coconut milk or cow's milk. Bring to the boil, then lower the heat, cover the saucepan and simmer gently for 25–30 minutes, stirring frequently.

3 Add sugar, creamed coconut and any flavourings, and cook for 5–10 minutes more, uncovered, until the rice reaches the consistency you like. Serve with slices of exotic fruits such as mango, papaya and pineapple, if you like.

Making Perfect Thai Rice Pudding

This is quick, easy and quite delicious. Cook Thai fragrant rice in boiling water using the absorption method. Leave it to stand for a few minutes, then stir in milk and sugar to taste, and creamed coconut, if you like. Serve the pudding hot, with fresh fruit.

Quantities

• For short grain rice pudding, use 600ml/1 pint/2½ cups milk for every 50g/2oz/generous ¼ cup rice. Stir in 45ml/3 tbsp granulated sugar. This should be sufficient to serve four.
• For glutinous rice pudding, use 300ml/½ pint/1¼ cups liquid for every 75g/3oz/scant ½ cup rice to serve four.
• For Thai rice pudding, use 475ml/ 16 fl oz/2 cups water, 120ml/4 fl oz/ ½ cup milk and 60ml/4 tbsp creamed coconut for every 50g/2oz/generous ¼ cup rice to serve four.

COOK'S TIPS

To give an English rice pudding a richer flavour, try any one of the following suggestions.
• Replace half the liquid with evaporated milk and add demerara sugar.
• If using the pan method, stir in a little cream just before serving.
• Beaten eggs can be stirred into the hot, cooked rice, or added to the part-cooked rice (see combination method).

Flavourings

Vanilla Give the milk a delicate vanilla flavour by heating it with a vanilla pod until the milk is hot but not boiling. Remove from the heat and leave to infuse for 1–2 hours. Strain the flavoured milk over the rice.
Nutmeg This is another very popular addition. Either grate it over the surface of a rice pudding that is to be baked, or stir grated nutmeg into the mixture in the pan. Ground cinnamon could be used instead.

Above: Aromatic nutmeg will add sweetness and warmth to the pudding.

Raisins or sultanas Stir into the rice or scatter at the bottom of the dish.
Spices Add lemon grass, cardamom pods, or pared orange, lemon or lime rind to the rice as it is cooking.
Nuts Chopped pistachios or almonds can be added during cooking to a rice pudding which is being cooked by the combination or pan method.

Above: Pistachios stirred into the pudding with shreds of fresh mint will provide texture and a slightly sweet flavour.

EQUIPMENT

Electric Rice Cooker

In Japan and other more affluent rice-eating countries, electric rice cookers have now replaced more conventional means of cooking rice. In the West they are also becoming increasingly popular, and cooks who use them often swear by them. The cookers cook rice perfectly and have the added advantage of keeping it warm throughout the meal, without it drying or becoming soggy. Another bonus of the rice cooker is that it frees hob space.

Saucepans

Even if you have invested in a rice cooker, you will always need saucepans. For plain boiled rice and for risottos, a heavy-based pan is the best choice – the actual size will depend on the quantities you are likely to be making but in general, bigger is better; small amounts of rice can be cooked in a large pan but you'll run into difficulties if you try cooking lots of rice in a pan that is too small. For risottos, some

Below: Saucepans

Left: Electric rice cooker

Right: Colander and sieve

cooks prefer to use a deep frying pan. A small frying pan or crêpe pan will be useful for frying the omelettes often used to garnish oriental rice dishes.

Colanders and Sieves

A colander or sieve is essential for draining boiled rice. Buy a good quality colander with a long handle, so that you can stand well back to pour the steaming rice out of the saucepan.

Measuring Jugs and Scales

It is important to measure rice accurately, and to add the correct quantity of water or other liquid, as specified in the recipe or on the packet, especially when cooking by the absorption method. In most recipes the rice is measured by weight, although it can also be measured by volume. Use measuring jug when adding stocks and other liquids.

Flameproof Casserole

Several rice dishes are started off on the hob, then finished in the oven. A flameproof casserole is perfect for this, and will also prove useful for dishes that are entirely oven-baked. Casseroles should have well-fitting lids; if lids are at all loose, cover the casserole with foil before fitting the lid in place.

Earthenware Casserole

These cannot be used on the hob, but are very useful for oven-cooked pilaffs. It is essential for the casserole to have a well-fitting lid.

Parmesan Grater

Freshly grated Parmesan cheese is an essential ingredient in risottos. Although many supermarkets now stock freshly grated Parmesan, it is fairly expensive, and buying Parmesan as one whole piece and grating it yourself is a much better option. Small metal Parmesan graters are available, but the graters where you pop the cheese in the top and turn the handle allow you to grate precisely the amount you need.

Left: Earthenware and flameproof casseroles

Left: Bamboo steamer

Above: Chopsticks and chopstick stands

Left: Japanese bamboo sushi mat

Mortar and Pestle

Spices are not necessary for cooking rice, but if for interesting meals, particularly those with an oriental flavour, they are essential.

The advantage of grinding your own spices is that you can be sure they are absolutely fresh; you'll notice the difference at once compared with ready ground spices. A mortar and pestle is the traditional piece of equipment for grinding spices, and has the advantage that you can grind very small quantities. The mortar is the container, while the pestle is used to pulverize spices, seeds, garlic or herbs. Mortar and pestle sets can be made of stone, wood or marble.

Spice Mill

A spice mill can be used instead of a mortar and pestle. It will grind spices very finely with very little effort.

Cooking Knives

Not specifically required for cooking rice, but good quality kitchen knives in a range of sizes and weights are essential for preparing other ingredients.

Paella Pan

If you are likely to make paella on a regular basis – or fancy bringing back a useful souvenir of your Spanish holiday – do invest in a paella pan. Bigger pans obviously make bigger paellas, but very large pans will inevitably turn out to be bigger than the ring on your cooker, meaning that the food will cook unevenly.

Wok

You will need a wok for any stir-fried rice dish and will find one useful for many curries, and for making stir-fries to accompany rice dishes. Buy the appropriate wok for your cooker. Round-bottomed woks can only be used on gas hobs; a flat-bottomed wok should be used on an electric hob.

Steamers

You can use a rice steamer to cook rice and for "finishing" rice if you do not have an electric rice cooker.

Japanese Bamboo Rolling Mat

Essential for rolling rice when making sushi, this simple but very useful piece of equipment is flexible in one direction but rigid in the other.

Muslin Bag

This is not essential, but is useful for making your own lontong (compressed rice). If you don't have a bamboo steamer, the bag containing the rice can be set inside a pan of boiling water. You can make your own muslin bag by cutting two 25cm/10in squares of muslin and sewing them together around three sides, leaving one edge open.

Chopsticks and Chopstick Rests

Oriental cooks use long chopsticks for manipulating foods when stir-frying. You may like to have good quality chopsticks to use when serving a Chinese or Thai meal, as they add authenticity. Chopstick stands are used for chopsticks at the table; less elaborate ones can be used when cooking.

Rice Bowls

Not essential pieces of equipment, but very attractive accessories: Chinese or Japanese rice bowls will make a huge difference to the look of an oriental meal. Buy genuine sets from oriental markets, or when travelling, for use on special occasions.

Right: Rice bowls

Rice Recipes

India

WE HAVE INDIA TO THANK FOR A LARGE NUMBER OF OUR FAVOURITE RICE DISHES. WHETHER SIDE DISHES OR MAIN MEALS, THERE ARE COUNT-LESS RICE RECIPES FROM INDIA. SOME, SUCH AS CHICKEN BIRYANI, ARE KNOWN AND LOVED ACROSS THE WORLD. OTHERS, SUCH AS SAFFRON RICE WITH CARDAMOMS, MADE WITH FRAGRANT BASMATI RICE, ARE THE ESSENTIAL ACCOMPANIMENT TO CURRIES.

CHICKEN BIRYANI

EASY TO MAKE AND VERY TASTY, THIS IS THE IDEAL DISH FOR A FAMILY SUPPER.

SERVES FOUR

INGREDIENTS

10 whole green cardamom pods
275g/10oz/1½ cups basmati rice,
   soaked and drained
2.5ml/½ tsp salt
2–3 whole cloves
5cm/2in cinnamon stick
45ml/3 tbsp vegetable oil
3 onions, sliced
4 chicken breasts, each about
   175g/6oz, cubed
1.5ml/¼ tsp ground cloves
1.5ml/¼ tsp hot chilli powder
5ml/1 tsp ground cumin
5ml/1 tsp ground coriander
2.5ml/½ tsp ground black pepper
3 garlic cloves, chopped
5ml/1 tsp finely chopped fresh
   root ginger
juice of 1 lemon
4 tomatoes, sliced
30ml/2 tbsp chopped fresh coriander
150ml/¼ pint/⅔ cup natural yogurt
4–5 saffron strands, soaked in
   10ml/2 tsp hot milk
150ml/¼ pint/⅔ cup water
toasted flaked almonds and fresh
   coriander sprigs, to garnish
natural yogurt, to serve

1 Preheat the oven to 190°C/375°F/
Gas 5. Remove the seeds from half the
cardamom pods and grind them finely,
using a pestle and mortar. Set them
aside. Bring a pan of water to the boil
and add the rice, salt, whole cardamom
pods, cloves and cinnamon stick. Boil
for 2 minutes, then drain, leaving the
whole spices in the rice.

2 Heat the oil in a frying pan and fry
the onions for 8 minutes, until softened
and browned. Add the chicken and the
ground spices, including the ground
cardamom seeds. Mix well, then add
the garlic, ginger and lemon juice.
Stir-fry for 5 minutes.

3 Transfer the chicken mixture to a
casserole and arrange the tomatoes on
top. Sprinkle on the fresh coriander,
spoon the yogurt evenly on top and
cover with the drained rice.

4 Drizzle the saffron milk over the rice
and pour over the water. Cover tightly
and bake for 1 hour. Transfer to a
warmed serving platter and remove the
whole spices from the rice. Garnish with
toasted almonds and fresh coriander
sprigs and serve with the natural yogurt.

BASMATI AND NUT PILAFF

VEGETARIANS WILL LOVE THIS SIMPLE PILAFF. ADD WILD OR CULTIVATED MUSHROOMS, IF YOU LIKE.

SERVES FOUR

INGREDIENTS

15–30ml/1–2 tbsp sunflower oil
1 onion, chopped
1 garlic clove, crushed
1 large carrot, coarsely grated
225g/8oz/generous 1 cup basmati
    rice, soaked
5ml/1 tsp cumin seeds
10ml/2 tsp ground coriander
10ml/2 tsp black mustard seeds
    (optional)
4 green cardamom pods
450ml/¾ pint/scant 2 cups vegetable
    stock or water
1 bay leaf
75g/3oz/¾ cup unsalted walnuts and
    cashew nuts
salt and freshly ground black pepper
fresh parsley or coriander sprigs,
    to garnish

1 Heat the oil in a large, shallow frying pan and gently fry the onion, garlic and carrot for 3–4 minutes. Drain the rice and then add to the pan with the spices. Cook for 1–2 minutes more, stirring to coat the grains in oil.

2 Pour in the stock or water, add the bay leaf and season well. Bring to the boil, lower the heat, cover and simmer very gently for 10–12 minutes.

3 Remove the pan from the heat without lifting the lid. Leave to stand for about 5 minutes, then check the rice. If it is cooked, there will be small steam holes on the surface of the rice. Remove and discard the bay leaf and the cardamom pods.

4 Stir in the nuts and check the seasoning. Spoon on to a platter, garnish with the parsley or coriander and serve.

COOK'S TIP
Use whichever nuts you prefer in this dish – even unsalted peanuts taste good, although almonds, cashew nuts or pistachios are more exotic.

SAVOURY RICE WITH MADRAS CURRY

BITE-SIZE CUBES OF STEWING BEEF SIMMER GENTLY WITH SPICES UNTIL THEY ARE TENDER ENOUGH TO MELT IN THE MOUTH. THEY ARE SERVED WITH BASMATI RICE, COOKED UNTIL LIGHT AND FLUFFY.

SERVES FOUR

INGREDIENTS
    225g/8oz/generous 1 cup basmati
        rice
    15ml/1 tbsp sunflower oil
    30ml/2 tbsp ghee or butter
    1 onion, finely chopped
    1 garlic clove, crushed
    5ml/1 tsp ground cumin
    2.5ml/½ tsp ground coriander
    4 green cardamom pods
    1 cinnamon stick
    1 small red pepper, seeded and diced
    1 small green pepper, seeded and diced
    300ml/½ pint/1¼ cups chicken stock
    salt and freshly ground black pepper
For the curry
    30ml/2 tbsp vegetable oil
    30ml/2 tbsp ghee or butter
    675g/1½lb stewing beef, cut into
        bite-size cubes
    1 onion, chopped
    3 green cardamom pods
    2 fresh green chillies, seeded and
        finely chopped
    2.5cm/1in piece of fresh root ginger,
        grated
    2 garlic cloves, crushed
    15ml/1 tbsp Madras curry paste
    5ml/1 tsp ground cumin
    5ml/1 tsp ground coriander
    150ml/¼ pint/⅔ cup beef stock

1 Start by making the curry. Heat half the oil and ghee or butter in a frying pan and fry the meat, in batches if necessary, until browned on all sides. Transfer to a plate and set aside.

2 Heat the remaining oil and ghee or butter and fry the onion for about 3–4 minutes until softened. Add the cardamom pods and fry for 1 minute, then add the chillies, ginger and garlic and fry for 2 minutes more.

3 Stir in the curry paste, ground cumin and coriander, then add the meat and stock. Season with salt, bring to the boil, then lower the heat and simmer very gently for 1–1½ hours, until the meat is tender.

4 When the curry is almost ready, prepare the rice. Put it in a bowl and pour over boiling water to cover. Set aside for 10 minutes, then drain, rinse under cold water and drain again. The rice will still be uncooked but should have lost its brittleness.

5 Heat the oil and ghee or butter in a flameproof casserole and fry the onion and garlic gently for 3–4 minutes until softened and lightly browned.

6 Stir in the cumin and ground coriander, cardamom pods and cinnamon stick. Fry for 1 minute, then add the diced peppers.

7 Add the rice, stirring to coat the grains in the spice mixture, and pour in the stock. Bring to the boil, then lower the heat, cover the pan tightly and simmer for about 8–10 minutes, or until the rice is tender and the stock has been absorbed. Spoon into a bowl and serve with the curry. Offer a little mango chutney, if you like.

COOK'S TIP
The curry should be fairly dry, but take care that it does not catch on the bottom of the pan. If you want to leave it unattended, cook it in a heavy-based pan or flameproof casserole, either on the hob or in an oven preheated to 180°C/350°F/Gas 4.

LAMB PARSI

THIS IS SIMILAR TO BIRYANI, BUT HERE THE LAMB IS MARINATED WITH THE YOGURT, A TECHNIQUE WHICH IS A PARSI SPECIALITY. SERVE WITH A DHAL OR WITH SPICED MUSHROOMS.

SERVES SIX

INGREDIENTS
    900g/2lb lamb fillet, cut into
        2.5cm/1in cubes
    60ml/4 tbsp ghee or butter
    2 onions, sliced
    450g/1lb potatoes, cut into large
        chunks
    chicken stock or water (see method)
    450g/1lb/2⅓ cups basmati rice,
        soaked
    generous pinch of saffron strands,
        dissolved in 30ml/2 tbsp warm milk
    fresh coriander sprigs, to garnish
For the marinade
    475ml/16fl oz/2 cups natural yogurt
    3–4 garlic cloves, crushed
    10ml/2 tsp cayenne pepper
    20ml/4 tsp garam masala
    10ml/2 tsp ground cumin
    5ml/1 tsp ground coriander

1 Make the marinade by mixing all the ingredients in a large bowl. Add the meat, stir to coat, then cover and leave to marinate for 3–4 hours in a cool place or overnight in the fridge.

2 Melt 30ml/2 tbsp of the ghee or butter in a large saucepan and fry the onions for 6–8 minutes until lightly golden. Transfer to a plate.

3 Melt a further 25ml/1½ tbsp of the ghee or butter in the pan. Fry the marinated lamb cubes in batches until evenly brown, transferring each batch in turn to a plate. When all the lamb has been browned, return it to the pan and scrape in the remaining marinade.

4 Stir in the potatoes and add about three-quarters of the fried onions. Pour in just enough chicken stock or water to cover the mixture. Bring to the boil, then cover and simmer over a very low heat for 40–50 minutes until the lamb is tender and the potatoes are cooked. Preheat the oven to 160°C/325°F/Gas 3.

5 Drain the rice. Cook it in a pan of boiling stock or water for 5 minutes. Meanwhile, spoon the lamb mixture into a casserole. Drain the rice and mound it on top of the lamb, then, using the handle of a wooden spoon, make a hole down the centre. Top with the remaining fried onions, pour the saffron milk over the top and dot with the remaining ghee or butter.

6 Cover the pan with a double layer of foil and a lid. Cook in the oven for 30–35 minutes or until the rice is completely tender. Garnish with fresh coriander sprigs and serve.

COOK'S TIP
Take care not to overcook the rice when parboiling it. The grains should still be quite hard, but should have a slightly powdery consistency.

GOAN PRAWN CURRY WITH SOUTHERN-STYLE RICE

MAKE THIS CURRY AS MILD OR AS FIERY AS YOU WISH. GOANS TRADITIONALLY LIKE THEIR SEAFOOD DISHES FAIRLY HOT, BUT A MILDER CURRY IS JUST AS DELICIOUS, FLAVOURED WITH HERBS AND SPICES.

SERVES FOUR

INGREDIENTS
15g/½oz/1 tbsp ghee or butter
2 garlic cloves, crushed
450g/1lb small raw prawns, peeled
  and deveined
4 cardamom pods
4 cloves
1 cinnamon stick
15ml/1 tbsp mustard seeds
about 15ml/1 tbsp groundnut oil
1 large onion, chopped
½–1 fresh red chilli, seeded and
  finely sliced
4 tomatoes, peeled, seeded and
  chopped
175ml/6fl oz/¾ cup fish stock or
  water
350ml/12fl oz/1½ cups coconut milk
45ml/3 tbsp fragrant spice mix (see
  Cook's Tip)
10–20ml/2–4 tsp cayenne pepper
salt
For the rice
350g/12oz/1¾ cups basmati rice,
  soaked and drained
5ml/1 tsp coriander seeds
5ml/1 tsp cumin seeds
30ml/2 tbsp urad dhal, rinsed
  (optional)
2.5ml/½ tsp ground turmeric
5ml/1 tsp brown mustard seeds
115g/4oz/1 cup unroasted cashew
  nuts
15ml/1 tbsp groundnut oil
15ml/1 tbsp ghee or butter

COOK'S TIP
To make a fragrant spice mix, dry-fry
25ml/1½ tbsp coriander seeds, 15ml/
1 tbsp mixed peppercorns, 5ml/1 tsp
cumin seeds, 1.5ml/¼ tsp fenugreek
seeds and 1.5ml/¼ tsp fennel seeds
until aromatic, then grind finely in a
spice mill. Alternatively, use ready-
ground spices, in which case 15ml/
1 tbsp ground coriander will be required.

1 Melt the ghee or butter in a
flameproof casserole, add the garlic
and stir over a low heat for a few
seconds. Add the prawns and stir-fry
briefly to coat. Transfer to a plate.

2 Dry-fry the cardamom pods, cloves
and cinnamon stick for 2 minutes. Add
the mustard seeds and fry for 1 minute.
Heat the oil and fry the onion and chilli
for 3–4 minutes. Add the remaining
curry ingredients. Set aside.

3 Preheat the oven to 180°C/350°F/
Gas 4. Cook the rice for 5 minutes.
Drain well. Meanwhile, dry-fry the
coriander and cumin seeds with the
urad dhal, if using, for a few minutes.
Add the turmeric and grind the mixture
finely in a spice mill.

4 Fry the mustard seeds and cashews
in oil for a few minutes and stir into the
rice with the ground spice mix.

5 Spoon the rice mixture into a large
casserole and dot with ghee or butter.
Cover tightly with foil or a muslin cloth
before fitting the lid securely. Cook in
the oven for 20 minutes.

6 About 10 minutes before the rice is
ready, reheat the curry sauce and add
the prawns. Simmer gently for 5–8
minutes until the prawns are cooked
through. Spoon into a dish and serve
with the rice.

CHICKEN KORMA <u>WITH</u> SAFFRON RICE

MILD AND FRAGRANT, THIS DISH IS — QUITE UNDERSTANDABLY — AN OLD FAVOURITE.

SERVES FOUR

INGREDIENTS
75g/3oz/¾ cup flaked almonds
15ml/1 tbsp ghee or butter
about 15ml/1 tbsp sunflower oil
675g/1½lb skinless, boneless
   chicken breasts, cut into bite-size
   pieces
1 onion, chopped
4 green cardamom pods
2 garlic cloves, crushed
10ml/2 tsp ground cumin
5ml/1 tsp ground coriander
1 cinnamon stick
good pinch of chilli powder
300ml/½ pint/1¼ cups canned
   coconut milk
175ml/6fl oz/¾ cup chicken stock
5ml/1 tsp tomato purée (optional)
75ml/5 tbsp single cream
15–30ml/1–2 tbsp fresh lime or
   lemon juice
10ml/2 tsp grated lime or lemon rind
5ml/1 tsp garam masala
salt and freshly ground black pepper
fresh coriander sprigs, to garnish
   (optional)
poppadums, to serve (optional)
For the saffron rice
275g/10oz/1½ cups basmati rice,
   soaked
750ml/1¼ pints/3 cups chicken stock
generous pinch of saffron strands,
   crushed, then soaked in hot water
   (see Cook's Tip)

1 Dry-fry the flaked almonds in a small frying pan until pale golden. Transfer about two-thirds of the almonds to a plate and continue to dry-fry the remainder until they are slightly deeper in colour. Transfer the darker almonds to a separate plate and set them aside for the garnish. Let the paler almonds cool, then grind them in a spice grinder or coffee mill.

2 Heat the ghee or butter and oil in a large frying pan or wok and fry the chicken pieces, in batches if necessary, until evenly brown. Transfer the chicken to a plate.

3 Add a little more oil if necessary and fry the onion for 2 minutes, then stir in the cardamom pods and garlic and fry for 3–4 minutes more, until the onion is lightly flecked with brown.

4 Stir in the ground flaked almonds, cumin, coriander, cinnamon stick and chilli powder and fry for 1 minute. Stir in the coconut milk, chicken stock and tomato purée, if using.

5 Bring to simmering point, then add the chicken and season. Cover and cook over a gentle heat for 10 minutes until the chicken is tender. Set aside, covered, while cooking the rice.

6 Drain the rice and put it in a saucepan. Add the seasoned stock and the saffron. Bring to the boil over a medium heat, then cover tightly and cook over a low heat for 10 minutes or according to the instructions on the packet.

7 Just before the rice is ready, reheat the korma until it is simmering gently. Stir in the cream, the citrus juice and rind and the garam masala. Taste and season as necessary. Pile the rice into a warmed serving dish and spoon the korma into a separate dish. Garnish with the reserved browned almonds and fresh coriander sprigs, and serve with poppadums, if you like.

COOK'S TIP
Saffron should always be soaked before use. Soak the strands for about an hour in either warm water or milk, according to the recipe.

BEEF BIRYANI

THE MOGULS INTRODUCED THIS DRY, SPICY RICE DISH TO CENTRAL INDIA. IT IS A MEAL IN ITSELF.

SERVES FOUR

INGREDIENTS

2 large onions
2 garlic cloves, chopped
2.5cm/1in piece of fresh root ginger, peeled and roughly chopped
½–1 fresh green chilli, seeded and roughly chopped
small bunch of fresh coriander
60ml/4 tbsp flaked almonds
30–45ml/2–3 tbsp water
15ml/1 tbsp ghee or butter, plus 25g/1oz/2 tbsp butter, for the rice
45ml/3 tbsp sunflower oil
30ml/2 tbsp sultanas
500g/1¼lb braising or stewing steak, cubed
5ml/1 tsp ground coriander
15ml/1 tbsp ground cumin
2.5ml/½ tsp ground turmeric
2.5ml/½ tsp ground fenugreek
good pinch of ground cinnamon
175ml/6fl oz/¾ cup natural yogurt
275g/10oz/1½ cups basmati rice
about 1.2 litres/2 pints/5 cups hot chicken stock or water
salt and freshly ground black pepper
2 hard-boiled eggs, quartered, to garnish

1 Roughly chop 1 onion and place it in a food processor or blender. Add the garlic, ginger, chilli, fresh coriander and half the flaked almonds. Pour in the water and process to a smooth paste.

2 Finely slice the remaining onion into rings or half rings. Heat half the ghee or butter with half the oil in a heavy-based, flameproof casserole and fry the onion rings over a medium heat for 10–15 minutes until they are a deep golden brown. Transfer to a plate with a slotted spoon. Fry the remaining flaked almonds briefly until golden and set aside with the onion rings, then quickly fry the sultanas until they swell. Transfer to the plate.

3 Heat the remaining ghee or butter in the casserole with a further 15ml/1 tbsp of the oil. Fry the meat, in batches, until evenly brown. Transfer to a plate and set aside.

4 Wipe the casserole clean with kitchen paper, heat the remaining oil and pour in the onion and ginger paste. Cook over a medium heat for 2–3 minutes, stirring all the time, until the mixture begins to brown lightly. Stir in all the spices, season with salt and pepper and cook for 1 minute more.

5 Lower the heat, then stir in the yogurt, a little at a time. When all of it has been incorporated into the spice mixture, return the meat to the casserole. Stir to coat, cover tightly and simmer over a gentle heat for 40–45 minutes until the meat is tender. Soak the rice in a bowl of cold water for 15–20 minutes.

6 Preheat the oven to 160°C/325°F/ Gas 3. Drain the rice, place in a saucepan and add the hot chicken stock or water, together with a little salt. Bring back to the boil, cover and cook for 5–6 minutes.

7 Drain the rice, and pile it in a mound on top of the meat in the casserole. Using the handle of a spoon, make a hole through the rice and meat mixture, to the bottom of the pan. Scatter the fried onions, almonds and sultanas over the top and dot with butter. Cover the casserole tightly with a double layer of foil and secure with a lid.

8 Cook the biryani in the oven for 30–40 minutes. To serve, spoon the mixture on to a warmed serving plate and garnish with the quartered hard-boiled eggs. Serve with parathas, naan bread or chapatis, if liked.

SPICY LAMB AND APRICOTS WITH PEA RICE

THE SLIGHTLY DRY FLAVOUR OF THE SPLIT PEAS AND BASMATI CONTRASTS WELL WITH THE SWEETNESS OF THE LAMB.

SERVES FOUR

INGREDIENTS

675g/1½lb lamb leg fillet
15ml/1 tbsp ghee or butter
1 onion, finely chopped
5ml/1 tsp ground coriander
10ml/2 tsp ground cumin
5ml/1 tsp fenugreek
2.5ml/½tsp turmeric
pinch of cayenne pepper
1 cinnamon stick
120ml/4fl oz/½ cup chicken stock
175g/6oz ready-to-eat apricots,
  halved or quartered
salt and freshly ground black pepper
fresh coriander, to garnish

For the marinade
120ml/4fl oz/½ cup natural yogurt
15ml/1 tbsp sunflower oil
juice of half a lemon
2.5cm/1in pieces fresh root ginger,
  grated

For the rice
175g/6oz/½ cup chana dhal or yellow
  split peas, soaked for 1–2 hours
225g/8oz/generous 1 cup basmati
  rice, soaked and drained
15ml/1 tbsp sunflower oil
1 large onion, finely sliced
1 garlic clove, crushed
10ml/2 tsp finely grated fresh root
  ginger
60ml/4 tbsp natural yogurt
15ml/1 tbsp chopped fresh coriander
15ml/1 tbsp ghee or butter
salt

1 Trim the meat and cut into bite-size pieces. Make the marinade by blending together the yogurt, oil, lemon juice and ginger. Add the meat, stir to coat, then cover with clear film and leave in a cool place for 2–4 hours to marinate.

2 Put the chana dhal or yellow split peas in a large saucepan, cover with boiling water and boil for 20–30 minutes until tender. Drain and set aside. Cook the drained rice in boiling salted water until it is three-quarters cooked and almost tender. Drain and set aside.

3 Heat the oil in a frying pan and fry the onion rings until golden. Transfer to a plate. Stir in the garlic and ginger and fry for a few seconds, then add the yogurt and cook for a few minutes, stirring. Add the dhal, coriander and salt. Stir well, then remove from the heat and set aside. Preheat the oven to 180°C/350°F/Gas 4.

4 Drain the meat, reserving the marinade. Melt the ghee or butter in a flameproof casserole and fry the onion for 3–4 minutes until soft. Add the coriander, cumin, fenugreek, turmeric, cayenne pepper and cinnamon stick, and fry over a medium heat until the spices are sizzling.

5 Fry the meat until browned, then spoon in the remaining marinade, add the chicken stock and apricots, and season well. Slowly bring to the boil, then cover and cook in the oven for 45–55 minutes until the meat is tender.

6 Meanwhile, finish cooking the rice. Spoon the dhal mixture into a casserole and stir in the rice. Dot the top with ghee or butter and sprinkle with the onion rings. Cover with a double layer of foil, secured with the lid. Place in the oven 30 minutes before the lamb is ready. The rice and dhal should be tender but the grains should be separate. Serve the rice and spiced lamb together, garnished with fresh coriander.

INDIAN RICE WITH TOMATOES AND SPINACH

THIS TASTY RICE DISH CAN BE SERVED WITH A MEAT CURRY OR AS PART OF A VEGETARIAN MEAL.

SERVES FOUR

INGREDIENTS
- 30ml/2 tbsp sunflower oil
- 15ml/1 tbsp ghee or butter
- 1 onion, chopped
- 2 garlic cloves, crushed
- 3 tomatoes, peeled, seeded and chopped
- 225g/8oz/generous 1 cup brown basmati rice, soaked
- 10ml/2 tsp dhana jeera powder or 5ml/1 tsp ground coriander and 5ml/1 tsp ground cumin
- 2 carrots, coarsely grated
- 900ml/1½ pints/3¾ cups vegetable stock
- 275g/10oz baby spinach leaves, washed
- 50g/2oz/½ cup unsalted cashew nuts, toasted
- salt and freshly ground black pepper

1 Heat the oil and ghee or butter in a flameproof casserole and gently fry the onion and garlic for 4–5 minutes until soft. Add the chopped tomatoes and cook for 3–4 minutes, stirring, until slightly thickened.

2 Drain the rice, add it to the casserole and cook gently for 1–2 minutes, stirring, until the rice is coated with the tomato and onion mixture.

COOK'S TIP
If you can't get baby spinach leaves, use larger fresh spinach leaves. Remove any tough stalks and chop the leaves roughly.

3 Stir in the dhana jeera powder or coriander and cumin, then add the carrots and season with salt and pepper. Pour in the stock and stir well to mix.

4 Bring to the boil, then cover tightly and simmer over a very gentle heat for 20–25 minutes until the rice is tender. Lay the spinach on the surface of the rice, cover again and cook for 2–3 minutes until the spinach has wilted. Fold the spinach into the rest of the rice and check the seasoning. Sprinkle with cashews and serve.

SWEET RICE WITH HOT SOUR CHICK-PEAS

MUCH MORE THAN US IN THE WEST, INDIANS ENJOY DISHES THAT COMBINE SWEET FLAVOURS WITH HOT OR SOUR ONES. HERE, THE RICE IS DISTINCTLY SWEET BUT GOES WELL WITH THE HOT SOUR TASTE OF THE CHICK-PEAS.

SERVES SIX

INGREDIENTS
350g/12oz/1⅔ cups dried chick-peas, soaked overnight
60ml/4 tbsp vegetable oil
1 large onion, very finely chopped
225g/8oz tomatoes, peeled and finely chopped
15ml/1 tbsp ground coriander
15ml/1 tbsp ground cumin
5ml/1 tsp ground fenugreek
5ml/1 tsp ground cinnamon
1–2 fresh hot green chillies, seeded and finely sliced
2.5cm/1in piece of fresh root ginger, grated
60ml/4 tbsp lemon juice
15ml/1 tbsp chopped fresh coriander
salt and freshly ground black pepper
For the rice
40g/1½oz/3 tbsp ghee or butter
4 green cardamom pods
4 cloves
650ml/22fl oz/2¾ cups boiling water
350g/12oz/1¾ cups basmati rice, soaked and drained
5–10ml/1–2 tsp granulated sugar
5–6 saffron strands, soaked in warm water

1 Drain the chick-peas well and place them in a large saucepan. Pour in water to cover, bring to the boil, then simmer, covered, for 1–1¼ hours until tender, topping up the liquid from time to time. Drain the chick-peas, reserving the cooking liquid.

2 Heat the oil in a saucepan. Reserve about 30ml/2 tbsp of the chopped onion and add the remainder to the pan. Fry over a medium heat for 4–5 minutes, stirring frequently.

3 Add the tomatoes. Cook over a moderately low heat for 5–6 minutes, until they are very soft, stirring and mashing them frequently.

4 Stir in the coriander, cumin, fenugreek and cinnamon. Cook for 30 seconds, then add the chick-peas and 350ml/12fl oz/1½ cups of the reserved cooking liquid. Season with salt, then cover and simmer very gently for 15–20 minutes, stirring occasionally and adding more liquid if the chick-peas begin to dry out.

5 While the chick-peas are cooking, melt the ghee or butter in a saucepan and fry the cardamom pods and cloves for a few minutes. Remove the pan from the heat, and when the fat has cooled a little, pour in the boiling water and stir in the basmati rice. Cover tightly and cook by the absorption method for 10 minutes.

6 When the rice is cooked, add the sugar and saffron liquid and stir thoroughly. Cover again. The rice will keep warm while you finish cooking the chick-peas.

7 Mix the reserved onion with the sliced chillies, ginger and lemon juice, and stir the mixture into the chick-peas. Add the chopped coriander, adjust the seasoning and serve with the rice.

SAFFRON RICE WITH CARDAMOMS

THE ADDITION OF AROMATIC GREEN CARDAMOM PODS, CLOVES, MILK AND SAFFRON GIVES THIS DISH BOTH A DELICATE FLAVOUR AND COLOUR.

2 Add the cardamoms, cloves and salt. Stir, then bring to the boil. Lower the heat, cover the pan tightly and simmer for about 5 minutes.

3 Meanwhile, place the milk in a small saucepan. Add the saffron strands and heat gently.

4 Add the saffron milk to the rice and stir. Cover again and continue cooking over a low heat for 5–6 minutes. Remove from the heat without lifting the lid. Leave the rice to stand for 5 minutes before serving.

SERVES SIX

INGREDIENTS
  450g/1lb/2⅓ cups basmati rice,
    soaked
  750ml/1¼ pints/3 cups water
  3 green cardamom pods
  2 cloves
  5ml/1 tsp salt
  45ml/3 tbsp semi-skimmed milk
  2.5ml/½ tsp saffron strands, crushed

1 Drain the rice and place it in a saucepan. Pour in the water.

COOK'S TIP
The saffron milk can be heated in the microwave. Mix the milk and saffron strands in a suitable jug or bowl and warm them for 1 minute on Low.

PILAU RICE WITH WHOLE SPICES

THIS FRAGRANT RICE DISH MAKES A PERFECT ACCOMPANIMENT TO ANY INDIAN MEAL.

SERVES FOUR

INGREDIENTS
generous pinch of saffron
   strands
600ml/1 pint/2½ cups hot
   chicken stock
50g/2oz/¼ cup butter
1 onion, chopped
1 garlic clove, crushed
½ cinnamon stick
6 green cardamom pods
1 bay leaf
250g/9oz/1⅓ cups basmati rice
50g/2oz/⅓ cup sultanas
15ml/1 tbsp sunflower oil
50g/2oz/½ cup cashew nuts
naan bread and tomato and onion
   salad, to serve (optional)

1 Stir the saffron strands into a jug of hot stock and set aside.

2 Heat the butter in a saucepan and fry the onion and garlic for 5 minutes. Stir in the cinnamon stick, cardamoms and bay leaf and cook for 2 minutes.

3 Add the rice and cook, stirring, for 2 minutes more. Pour in the saffron-flavoured stock and add the sultanas. Bring to the boil, stir, then lower the heat, cover and cook gently for about 10 minutes or until the rice is tender and the liquid has all been absorbed.

4 Meanwhile, heat the oil in a frying pan and fry the cashew nuts until browned. Drain on kitchen paper. Scatter the cashew nuts over the rice. Serve with naan bread and a tomato and onion salad, if you like.

COOK'S TIP
Don't be tempted to use black cardamoms in this dish. They are coarser and more strongly flavoured than green cardamoms and are only used in highly spiced dishes that are cooked for a long time.

MUSHROOM PILAU

THIS DISH IS SIMPLICITY ITSELF. SERVE WITH ANY INDIAN DISH OR WITH ROAST LAMB OR CHICKEN.

SERVES FOUR

INGREDIENTS
   30ml/2 tbsp vegetable oil
   2 shallots, finely chopped
   1 garlic clove, crushed
   3 green cardamom pods
   25g/1oz/2 tbsp ghee or butter
   175g/6oz/2½ cups button
     mushrooms, sliced
   225g/8oz/generous 1 cup basmati
     rice, soaked
   5ml/1 tsp grated fresh root ginger
   good pinch of garam masala
   450ml/¾ pint/scant 2 cups water
   15ml/1 tbsp chopped fresh coriander
   salt

1 Heat the oil in a flameproof casserole and fry the shallots, garlic and cardamom pods over a medium heat for 3–4 minutes until the shallots have softened and are beginning to brown.

2 Add the ghee or butter. When it has melted, add the mushrooms and fry for 2–3 minutes more.

3 Add the rice, ginger and garam masala. Stir-fry over a low heat for 2–3 minutes, then stir in the water and a little salt. Bring to the boil, then cover tightly and simmer over a very low heat for 10 minutes.

4 Remove the casserole from the heat. Leave to stand, covered, for 5 minutes. Add the chopped coriander and fork it through the rice. Spoon into a serving bowl and serve at once.

Asia

RICE IS BY FAR THE MOST IMPORTANT CEREAL
OF SOUTH-EAST ASIA, YET EACH COUNTRY HAS
ITS OWN FAVOURITE STYLE OF COOKING RICE,
AND EACH ITS OWN DISTINGUISHING RICE-
BASED CUISINE. FRIED RICE FROM CHINA,
NASI GORENG FROM INDONESIA OR SUSHI FROM
JAPAN ARE JUST SOME OF THE CLASSIC ASIAN RICE
DISHES NOW ENJOYED ALL OVER THE WORLD.

SUSHI

ONCE BARELY KNOWN OUTSIDE JAPAN, THESE TASTY ROLLS OF FLAVOURED RICE AND PAPER-THIN SEAWEED HAVE BECOME VERY POPULAR, PARTLY DUE TO THE PROLIFERATION OF SUSHI BARS THAT HAVE SPRUNG UP IN MANY MAJOR CITIES.

SERVES FOUR TO SIX

INGREDIENTS
For the tuna sushi
  2–3 baby carrots, blanched
  3 sheets nori (paper-thin seaweed),
    cut in half
  115g/4oz fresh tuna fillet, cut into
    fingers
  5ml/1 tsp thin wasabi paste
    (Japanese horseradish mustard)
For the salmon sushi
  2 eggs
  10ml/2 tsp granulated sugar
  2.5ml/½ tsp salt
  10ml/2 tsp butter
  3 sheets nori
  150g/5oz fresh salmon fillet, cut into
    fingers
  ½ small cucumber, cut into strips
  5ml/1 tsp thin wasabi paste
For the sushi rice
  450g/1lb/4 cups sushi rice, rinsed
  about 650ml/22fl oz/2¾ cups water
For the sushi dressing
  60ml/4 tbsp rice vinegar
  15ml/1 tbsp sugar
  2.5ml/½ tsp salt
To serve
  sliced pickled ginger, cut in strips
  wasabi paste, thinned with water
  Japanese sushi soy sauce

1 Place the rice in a heavy pan and add 650ml/22fl oz/2¾ cups water or according to the instructions on the packet. Bring to the boil, cover tightly and cook over a very low heat for 15 minutes. Increase the heat to high for 10 seconds, then remove from the heat and let stand for 10 minutes. Meanwhile, blend together the rice vinegar, sugar and salt.

2 Stir the sushi dressing into the rice, then cover with a damp cloth and cool. Do not put in the fridge as this will make the rice go hard.

3 To make the tuna sushi, cut the carrots into thin strips. Cut one nori sheet in half and lay one half, shiny side down, on a bamboo rolling mat. Lay strips of tuna across the length of the nori and spread with a little wasabi. Place a line of carrots next to the tuna and, using the mat as a guide, roll up tightly. Repeat with the other half of nori. Set aside any extra tuna or carrot.

4 Place a square of greaseproof paper on the bamboo mat and spread with a little of the cooled sushi rice, leaving a 1cm/½in edge at the top and bottom.

5 Place the tuna-filled nori roll on top, about 2.5cm/1in from the edge of the rice, and roll up, using the paper as a guide (and making sure it doesn't get rolled up with the rice). Wrap the roll in greaseproof paper and chill for about 10 minutes. Make another sushi roll using the other tuna-filled nori roll.

6 To make the salmon sushi, beat together the eggs with 30ml/2 tbsp water and the sugar and salt. Melt about one-third of the butter in a small frying pan and add one-third of the egg mixture to make an omelette. Repeat until you have three small omelettes.

7 Place a nori sheet, shiny side down, on a bamboo rolling mat, cover with an omelette and spread with sushi rice, leaving a 1cm/½in edge at the top and bottom. Lay strips of salmon across the width and lay cucumber strips next to the salmon. Spread a little wasabi paste over the salmon. Roll the nori around the filling. Wrap in clear film and chill for 10 minutes. Repeat to make three rolls.

8 When the rolls are cool, remove the greaseproof paper and clear film. Using a wet knife, cut the rolls into six slices. Serve with pickled ginger, wasabi and Japanese sushi soy sauce.

RICE OMELETTE

*RICE OMELETTES MAKE A GREAT SUPPER DISH. IN JAPAN, THEY ARE A FAVOURITE WITH CHILDREN,
WHO USUALLY TOP THEM WITH A LIBERAL HELPING OF TOMATO KETCHUP.*

2 Melt a further 10ml/2 tsp butter in the frying pan, add the rice and stir well. Mix in the fried ingredients, ketchup and pepper. Stir well, adding salt to taste, if necessary. Keep the mixture warm. Beat the eggs with the milk in a bowl. Stir in the measured salt and add pepper to taste.

3 Melt 5ml/1 tsp of the remaining butter in an omelette pan. Pour in a quarter of the egg mixture and stir it briefly with a fork, then allow it to set for 1 minute. Top with a quarter of the rice mixture.

SERVES FOUR

INGREDIENTS
1 skinless, boneless chicken thigh, about 115g/4oz, cubed
40ml/8 tsp butter
1 small onion, chopped
½ carrot, diced
2 shiitake mushrooms, stems removed and chopped
15ml/1 tbsp finely chopped fresh parsley
225g/8oz/2 cups cooked long grain white rice
30ml/2 tbsp tomato ketchup
6 eggs, lightly beaten
60ml/4 tbsp milk
5ml/1 tsp salt, plus extra to season
freshly ground black pepper
tomato ketchup, to serve

1 Season the chicken with salt and pepper. Melt 10ml/2 tsp butter in a frying pan. Fry the onion for 1 minute, then add the chicken and fry until the cubes are white and cooked. Add the carrot and mushrooms, stir-fry over a medium heat until soft, then add the parsley. Set this mixture aside. Wipe the frying pan with kitchen paper.

4 Fold the omelette over the rice and slide it to the edge of the pan to shape it into a curve. Slide it on to a warmed plate, cover with kitchen paper and press neatly into a rectangular shape. Keep hot while cooking three more omelettes from the remaining ingredients. Serve immediately, with tomato ketchup.

CHICKEN AND MUSHROOM DONBURI

"DONBURI" MEANS A ONE-DISH MEAL THAT IS EATEN FROM A BOWL, AND TAKES ITS NAME FROM THE EPONYMOUS JAPANESE PORCELAIN FOOD BOWL. AS IN MOST JAPANESE DISHES, THE RICE HERE IS COMPLETELY PLAIN BUT IS NEVERTHELESS AN INTEGRAL PART OF THE DISH.

SERVES FOUR

INGREDIENTS

    10ml/2 tsp groundnut oil
    50g/2oz/4 tbsp butter
    2 garlic cloves, crushed
    2.5cm/1in piece of fresh root ginger,
      grated
    5 spring onions, diagonally sliced
    1 green fresh chilli, seeded and
      finely sliced
    3 skinless, boneless chicken breasts,
      cut into thin strips
    150g/5oz tofu, cut into small cubes
    115g/4oz/1¾ shiitake mushrooms,
      stalks discarded and cups sliced
    15ml/1 tbsp Japanese rice wine
    30ml/2 tbsp light soy sauce
    10ml/2 tsp granulated sugar
    400ml/14fl oz/1⅔ cups chicken stock
For the rice
    225–275g/8–10oz/generous
      1–1½ cups Japanese rice or Thai
      fragrant rice

1 Cook the rice by the absorption method or by following the instructions on the packet.

2 While the rice is cooking, heat the oil and half the butter in a large frying pan. Stir-fry the garlic, ginger, spring onions and chilli for 1–2 minutes until slightly softened. Add the strips of chicken and fry, in batches if necessary, until all the pieces are evenly browned.

3 Transfer the chicken mixture to a plate and add the tofu to the pan. Stir-fry for a few minutes, then add the mushrooms. Stir-fry for 2–3 minutes over a medium heat until the mushrooms are tender.

4 Stir in the rice wine, soy sauce and sugar and cook briskly for 1–2 minutes, stirring all the time. Return the chicken to the pan, toss over the heat for about 2 minutes, then pour in the stock. Stir well and cook over a gentle heat for 5–6 minutes until bubbling.

5 Spoon the rice into individual serving bowls and pile the chicken mixture on top, making sure that each portion gets a generous amount of chicken sauce.

COOK'S TIP
Once the rice is cooked, leave it covered until ready to serve. It will stay warm for about 30 minutes. Fork through lightly just before serving.

CHINESE FRIED RICE

THIS DISH, A VARIATION ON SPECIAL FRIED RICE, IS MORE ELABORATE THAN THE MORE FAMILIAR EGG FRIED RICE, AND IS ALMOST A MEAL IN ITSELF.

SERVES FOUR

INGREDIENTS
    50g/2oz cooked ham
    50g/2oz cooked prawns, peeled
    3 eggs
    5ml/1 tsp salt
    2 spring onions, finely chopped
    60ml/4 tbsp vegetable oil
    115g/4oz/1 cup green peas, thawed
      if frozen
    15ml/1 tbsp light soy sauce
    15ml/1 tbsp Chinese rice wine or dry
      sherry
    450g/1lb/4 cups cooked white long
      grain rice

1 Dice the cooked ham finely. Pat the cooked prawns dry on kitchen paper.

2 In a bowl, beat the eggs with a pinch of salt and a few spring onion pieces.

VARIATIONS
This is a versatile recipe and is ideal for using up leftovers. Use cooked chicken or turkey instead of the ham, doubling the quantity if you omit the prawns.

3 Heat about half the oil in a wok, stir-fry the peas, prawns and ham for 1 minute, then add the soy sauce and rice wine or sherry. Transfer to a bowl and keep hot.

4 Heat the remaining oil in the wok and scramble the eggs lightly. Add the rice and stir to make sure that the grains are separate. Add the remaining salt, the remaining spring onions and the prawn mixture. Toss over the heat to mix. Serve hot or cold.

STIR-FRIED RICE AND VEGETABLES

THE GINGER GIVES THIS ORIENTAL DISH A WONDERFUL FLAVOUR. SERVE IT AS A VEGETARIAN MAIN COURSE OR AS AN UNUSUAL VEGETABLE ACCOMPANIMENT.

SERVES FOUR AS AN ACCOMPANIMENT

INGREDIENTS
115g/4oz/generous ½ cup brown
  basmati rice, rinsed and drained
350ml/12fl oz/1½ cups vegetable stock
2.5cm/1in piece of fresh root ginger,
  finely sliced
1 garlic clove, halved
5cm/2in piece of pared lemon rind
115g/4oz/1½ cups shiitake mushrooms
15ml/1 tbsp groundnut oil
15ml/1 tbsp ghee or butter
175g/6oz baby carrots, trimmed
225g/8oz baby courgettes, halved
175-225g/6-8oz/about 1½ cups
  broccoli, broken into florets
6 spring onions, diagonally sliced
15ml/1 tbsp light soy sauce
10ml/2 tsp toasted sesame oil

1 Put the rice in a saucepan and pour in the stock. Add the ginger, garlic and lemon rind. Slowly bring to the boil, then cover and cook very gently for 20–25 minutes until the rice is tender. Discard the flavourings and keep the pan covered so that the rice stays warm.

2 Slice the mushrooms, discarding the stems. Heat the oil and ghee or butter in a wok and stir-fry the carrots for 4–5 minutes until partially tender. Add the mushrooms and courgettes, stir-fry for 2–3 minutes, then add the broccoli and spring onions and cook for 3 minutes more, by which time all the vegetables should be tender but should still retain a bit of "bite".

3 Add the cooked rice to the vegetables, and toss briefly over the heat to mix and heat through. Toss with the soy sauce and sesame oil. Spoon into a bowl and serve immediately.

CRACKLING RICE PAPER FISH ROLLS

THE RICE IN THIS DISH IS IN THE RICE PAPER WRAPPERS, WHICH MANAGE TO HOLD THEIR SHAPE DURING COOKING, YET ALMOST MAGICALLY DISSOLVE IN YOUR MOUTH WHEN IT COMES TO EATING.

MAKES TWELVE

INGREDIENTS
12 Vietnamese rice paper sheets
  (bahn trang), each about 20 x
  10cm/8 x 4in
45ml/3 tbsp plain flour mixed to
  a paste with 45ml/3 tbsp water
vegetable oil, for deep-frying
fresh herbs, to garnish
For the filling
24 young asparagus spears, trimmed
225g/8oz raw prawns, peeled and
  deveined
25ml/1½ tbsp olive oil
6 spring onions, finely chopped
1 garlic clove, crushed
2cm/¾in piece of fresh root ginger,
  grated
30ml/2 tbsp chopped fresh coriander
5ml/1 tsp five-spice powder
5ml/1 tsp finely grated lime or lemon
  rind
salt and freshly ground black pepper

1 Make the filling. Bring a saucepan of lightly salted water to the boil and cook the asparagus for 3–4 minutes until tender. Drain, refresh under cold water and drain again. Cut the prawns into 2cm/¾in pieces.

2 Heat half of the oil in a small frying pan or wok and stir-fry the spring onions and garlic over a low heat for 2–3 minutes until soft. Using a slotted spoon, transfer the vegetables to a bowl and set aside.

3 Heat the remaining oil in the pan and stir-fry the prawns over a brisk heat for just a few seconds until they start to go pink. Add to the spring onion mixture with the ginger, coriander, five-spice powder, lime or lemon rind and a little pepper. Stir to mix.

4 To make each roll, brush a sheet of rice paper liberally with water and lay it on a clean surface. Place two asparagus spears and a spoonful of the prawn mixture just off centre. Fold in the sides and roll up to make a fat cigar. Seal the ends with a little of the flour paste.

5 Heat the oil in a wok or deep-fryer and fry the rolls in batches until pale golden in colour. Drain well, garnish with herbs and serve.

MALACCA FRIED RICE

THERE ARE MANY VERSIONS OF THIS DISH THROUGHOUT ASIA, ALL BASED UPON LEFTOVER COOKED RICE. INGREDIENTS VARY ACCORDING TO WHAT IS AVAILABLE, BUT PRAWNS ARE A POPULAR ADDITION.

SERVES FOUR TO SIX

INGREDIENTS

2 eggs
45ml/3 tbsp vegetable oil
4 shallots or 1 onion, finely chopped
5ml/1 tsp chopped fresh root ginger
1 garlic clove, crushed
225g/8oz raw prawns, peeled and
  deveined
5ml/1 tsp chilli sauce (optional)
3 spring onions, green part only,
  roughly chopped
225g/8oz/2 cups frozen peas
225g/8oz thickly sliced roast pork,
  diced
45ml/3 tbsp light soy sauce
350g/12oz/3 cups cooked white long
  grain rice, cooled
salt and freshly ground black pepper

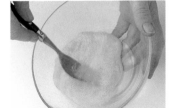

1 In a bowl, beat the eggs well with salt and freshly ground black pepper to taste. Heat 15ml/1 tbsp of the oil in a large, non-stick frying pan, pour in the eggs and cook until set, without stirring. This will take less than a minute. Roll up the pancake, slide it on to a plate, cut into thin strips and set aside.

2 Heat the remaining vegetable oil in a preheated wok, add the shallots or onion, ginger, garlic and prawns, and cook for 1–2 minutes, taking care that the garlic does not burn.

3 Add the chilli sauce, if using, the spring onions, peas, pork and soy sauce. Stir to heat through, then add the rice. Fry over a medium heat for 6–8 minutes. Spoon into a dish, decorate with the pancake strips and serve immediately.

COOK'S TIP
You don't have to wait until the day after you've served a Sunday roast to try this. Most delicatessens sell sliced roast pork.

CHINESE JEWELLED RICE

*ANOTHER FRIED RICE MEDLEY, THIS TIME WITH CRAB MEAT AND WATER CHESTNUTS, PROVIDING
CONTRASTING TEXTURES AND FLAVOURS.*

SERVES FOUR

INGREDIENTS

350g/12oz/1¾ cups white long grain
  rice
45ml/3 tbsp vegetable oil
1 onion, roughly chopped
4 dried black Chinese mushrooms,
  soaked for 10 minutes in warm
  water to cover
115g/4oz cooked ham, diced
175g/6oz drained canned white crab
  meat
75g/3oz/½ cup drained canned water
  chestnuts
115g/4oz/1 cup peas, thawed if
  frozen
30ml/2 tbsp oyster sauce
5ml/1 tsp granulated sugar
salt

1 Rinse the rice, then cook for about
10–12 minutes in a saucepan of lightly
salted boiling water. Drain, refresh
under cold water, drain again and allow
to cool. Heat half the oil in a wok. When
very hot, stir-fry the rice for 3 minutes.
Transfer the cooked rice to a bowl and
set aside.

2 Heat the remaining oil in the wok
and cook the onion until softened but
not coloured. Drain the mushrooms,
cut off and discard the stems, then
chop the caps.

3 Add the chopped mushrooms to the
wok, with all the remaining ingredients
except the rice. Stir-fry for 2 minutes,
then add the rice and stir-fry for about
3 minutes more. Serve at once.

COOK'S TIP
When adding the oil to the hot wok,
drizzle it in a "necklace" just below
the rim. As it runs down, it will coat
the inner surface as it heats.

THAI RICE

THIS IS A LOVELY, SOFT, FLUFFY RICE DISH, PERFUMED WITH FRESH LEMON GRASS AND LIMES.

SERVES FOUR

INGREDIENTS

2 limes
1 lemon grass stalk
225g/8oz/generous 1 cup brown long
   grain rice
15ml/1 tbsp olive oil
1 onion, chopped
2.5cm/1in piece of fresh root ginger,
   peeled and finely chopped
7.5ml/1½ tsp coriander seeds
7.5ml/1½ tsp cumin seeds
750ml/1¼ pints/3 cups vegetable stock
60ml/4 tbsp chopped fresh coriander
spring onion green, toasted coconut
   strips and lime wedges, to serve

1 Pare the limes using a canelle knife or a fine grater, taking care to avoid cutting the bitter pith. Set aside the rind. Finely chop the lower portion of the lemon grass stalk and set aside.

2 Rinse the rice in plenty of cold water until the water runs clear. Tip into a sieve and drain thoroughly.

3 Heat the oil in a saucepan. Add the onion, ginger, spices, lemon grass and lime rind and fry gently over a low heat for 2–3 minutes.

4 Add the drained rice and cook for 1 minute, then pour in the stock and bring to the boil. Reduce the heat to very low and cover the pan. Cook gently for 30 minutes, then check the rice. If it is still crunchy, cover the pan and leave for 3–5 minutes more. Remove from the heat.

5 Stir in the fresh coriander, fluff up the grains, cover and leave for about 10 minutes. Garnish with spring onion green and toasted coconut strips, and serve with lime wedges.

THAI FRIED RICE

THIS SUBSTANTIAL DISH IS BASED ON THAI FRAGRANT RICE, WHICH IS SOMETIMES KNOWN AS JASMINE RICE. CHICKEN, RED PEPPER AND SWEETCORN ADD COLOUR AND EXTRA FLAVOUR.

SERVES FOUR

INGREDIENTS
    475ml/16fl oz/2 cups water
    50g/2oz/½ cup coconut milk powder
    350g/12oz/1¾ cups Thai fragrant
       rice, rinsed
    30ml/2 tbsp groundnut oil
    2 garlic cloves, chopped
    1 small onion, finely chopped
    2.5cm/1in piece of fresh root ginger,
       grated
    225g/8oz skinless, boneless chicken
       breasts, cut into 1cm/½in dice
    1 red pepper, seeded and sliced
    115g/4oz/1 cup drained canned
       sweetcorn kernels
    5ml/1 tsp chilli oil
    5ml/1 tsp hot curry powder
    2 eggs, beaten
    salt
    spring onion shreds, to garnish

3 Push the vegetables to the sides of the wok, add the chicken to the centre and stir-fry for 2 minutes. Add the rice and stir-fry over a high heat for about 3 minutes more.

4 Stir in the sliced red pepper, sweetcorn, chilli oil and curry powder, with salt to taste. Toss over the heat for 1 minute. Stir in the beaten eggs and cook for 1 minute more. Garnish with spring onion shreds and serve.

1 Pour the water into a saucepan and whisk in the coconut milk powder. Add the rice, bring to the boil. Lower the heat, cover and cook for 12 minutes or until the rice is tender and the liquid has been absorbed. Spread the rice on a baking sheet and leave until cold.

2 Heat the oil in a wok, add the garlic, onion and ginger and stir-fry over a medium heat for 2 minutes.

COOK'S TIP
It is important that the rice is completely cold before being fried and the oil is very hot, or the rice will absorb too much oil.

EXOTIC FRUIT AND VEGETABLE SALAD

THIS IS A VARIATION ON THE FAMOUS INDONESIAN SALAD KNOWN AS GADO GADO. CHOOSE SOME OR ALL OF THE SUGGESTED FRUITS AND VEGETABLES TO MAKE AN ATTRACTIVE CENTREPIECE FOR AN INDONESIAN OR THAI MEAL.

SERVES SIX TO EIGHT

INGREDIENTS

115g/4oz green beans, trimmed
2 carrots, cut into batons
115g/4oz/2 cups bean sprouts
¼ head Chinese leaves, shredded
½ small cucumber, cut into thin strips
8 spring onions, sliced diagonally
6 cherry tomatoes or small tomatoes, halved
12–16 cooked tiger prawns
1 small mango
1 small papaya
1 quantity Lontong (compressed rice)
4 hard-boiled eggs, quartered
fresh coriander

For the peanut dressing
120ml/8 tbsp crunchy or smooth peanut butter, preferably unsalted
1 garlic clove, crushed
300ml/½ pint/1¼ cups coconut milk
15ml/1 tbsp tamarind water (see Cook's Tip) or juice of ½ lemon
15–30ml/1–2 tbsp light soy sauce
hot chilli sauce, to taste

1 First, make the peanut dressing. Place all the ingredients except the chilli sauce in a pan and heat the mixture, stirring all the time, until it is very hot and smooth. Stir in chilli sauce to taste. Keep the dressing warm, or allow to cool and reheat before serving.

2 Cook the beans and carrots in boiling water for 3–4 minutes until just tender but still firm. Drain, then refresh under cold water and drain again. Cook the bean sprouts in boiling water for 2 minutes, then drain and refresh.

3 Arrange the carrots, beans and bean sprouts on a large, attractive platter, with the shredded Chinese leaves, cucumber strips, spring onions, tomatoes, and prawns.

4 Peel the mango and cut the flesh into cubes. Quarter the papaya, remove the skin and seeds, then slice the flesh. Add to the salad platter, with the lontong. Garnish with the egg quarters and fresh coriander.

5 Reheat the peanut dressing, if necessary. As soon as it is warm, pour it into a serving bowl. Place the bowl in the centre of the salad and serve. Guests help themselves to the salad, adding as much dressing as they like.

COOK'S TIP
To make tamarind water, break off a 2.5cm/1in cube of tamarind and put it in a bowl. Pour in 150ml/¼ pint/⅔ cup warm water. Using your fingers, squeeze the tamarind so that the juices dissolve into the water. Strain, discarding the solid tamarind, and use as directed in the recipe. Any unused tamarind water can be kept in a container in the fridge for up to 1 week.

FESTIVE RICE

THIS PRETTY THAI DISH IS TRADITIONALLY SHAPED INTO A CONE AND SURROUNDED BY A VARIETY OF ACCOMPANIMENTS BEFORE BEING SERVED.

SERVES EIGHT

INGREDIENTS

450g/1lb/2⅓ cups Thai fragrant rice
60ml/4 tbsp oil
2 garlic cloves, crushed
2 onions, finely sliced
2.5ml/½ tsp ground turmeric
750ml/1¼ pints/3 cups water
400ml/14fl oz can coconut milk
1–2 lemon grass stalks, bruised
For the accompaniments
omelette strips
2 fresh red chillies, shredded
cucumber chunks
tomato wedges
deep-fried onions
prawn crackers

1 Put the rice in a strainer and rinse thoroughly under cold water. Drain well.

2 Heat the oil in a frying pan which has a lid. Fry the garlic, onions and turmeric over a low heat for a few minutes, until the onions are softened but not browned. Add the rice and stir well so that each grain is coated in oil.

3 Pour in the water and coconut milk and add the lemon grass. Bring to the boil, stirring well. Cover the pan and cook gently for 12 minutes, or until all the liquid has been absorbed.

COOK'S TIP
Look out for fresh turmeric at Asian markets or food stores.

4 Remove the pan from the heat and lift the lid. Cover with a clean dish towel, replace the lid and leave to stand in a warm place for 15 minutes. Remove the lemon grass, mound the rice mixture in a cone on a serving platter and garnish with the accompaniments. Serve immediately.

THAI CRISPY NOODLES WITH BEEF

RICE VERMICELLI ARE VERY FINE, DRY, WHITE NOODLES BUNDLED IN LARGE FRAGILE LOOPS AND SOLD IN PACKETS. THEY ARE DEEP-FRIED BEFORE BEING ADDED TO THIS DISH, AND IN THE PROCESS THEY EXPAND TO AT LEAST FOUR TIMES THEIR ORIGINAL SIZE.

SERVES FOUR

INGREDIENTS
about 450g/1lb rump or sirloin steak
teriyaki sauce, for sprinkling
175g/6oz rice vermicelli
groundnut oil for deep-frying and
  stir-frying
8 spring onions, diagonally sliced
2 garlic cloves, crushed
4–5 carrots, cut into julienne strips
1–2 fresh red chillies, seeded and
  finely sliced
2 small courgettes, diagonally sliced
5ml/1 tsp grated fresh root ginger
60ml/4 tbsp white or yellow rice
  vinegar
90ml/6 tbsp light soy sauce
about 475ml/16fl oz/2 cups spicy
  stock

1 Beat out the steak, if necessary, to about 2.5cm/1in thick. Place in a shallow dish, brush generously with the teriyaki sauce and set aside for 2–4 hours to marinate.

2 Separate the rice vermicelli into manageable loops and spread several layers of kitchen paper on a very large plate. Add the oil to a depth of about 5cm/2in in a large wok, and heat until a strand of vermicelli cooks as soon as it is lowered into the oil.

3 Carefully add a loop of vermicelli to the oil. It should immediately expand and become opaque. Turn the noodles over so that the strands cook on both sides and then transfer the cooked noodles to the plate. Repeat the process until all the noodles are cooked. Transfer the cooked noodles to a separate wok or deep serving bowl and keep them warm while you cook the steak and vegetables.

4 Strain the oil from the wok into a heatproof bowl and set it aside. Heat 15ml/1 tbsp groundnut oil in the clean wok. When it sizzles, fry the steak for about 30 seconds on each side until browned. Transfer to a board and cut into thick slices. The meat should be well browned on the outside but still pink inside. Set aside.

5 Add a little extra oil to the wok and stir-fry the spring onions, garlic and carrots over a medium heat for 5–6 minutes until the carrots are slightly soft and have a glazed appearance. Add the chillies, courgettes and ginger and stir-fry for 1–2 minutes more.

6 Stir in the rice vinegar, soy sauce and stock. Cook for about 4 minutes until the sauce has slightly thickened. Add the steak and cook for a further 1–2 minutes (or longer, if you prefer your meat well done).

7 Pour the steak, vegetables and all the mixture over the noodles and toss lightly and carefully to mix. Serve at once.

COOK'S TIP
As soon as you add the meat mixture to the noodles, they will soften. If you wish to keep a few crispy noodles, stir some to the surface so they do not come into contact with the hot liquid.

RICE NOODLES WITH PORK

RICE NOODLES HAVE LITTLE FLAVOUR THEMSELVES BUT THEY HAVE A WONDERFUL ABILITY TO TAKE ON THE FLAVOUR OF OTHER INGREDIENTS.

SERVES FOUR TO SIX

INGREDIENTS
    450g/1lb pork fillet
    225g/8oz dried rice noodles
    115g/4oz/1 cup broccoli florets
    1 red pepper, quartered and seeded
    about 45ml/3 tbsp groundnut oil
    2 garlic cloves, crushed
    10 spring onions, trimmed and cut
        into 5cm/2in diagonal slices
    1 lemon grass stalk, finely chopped
    1–2 fresh red chillies, seeded and
        finely chopped
    300ml/½ pint/1¼ cups coconut milk
    15ml/1 tbsp tomato purée
    3 kaffir lime leaves (optional)
For the marinade
    45ml/3 tbsp light soy sauce
    15ml/1 tbsp rice wine
    30ml/2 tbsp groundnut oil
    2.5cm/1in piece of fresh root ginger

1 Cut the pork into thin strips, about 2.5cm/1in long and 1cm/½in wide. Mix all the marinade ingredients in a bowl, add the pork, stir to coat and leave to marinate for about 1 hour.

2 Spread out the noodles in a shallow dish, pour over hot water to cover and soak for 20 minutes until soft. Drain. Blanch the broccoli in a small pan of boiling water for 2 minutes, then drain and refresh under cold water. Set aside.

3 Place the pepper pieces under a hot grill for a few minutes until the skin blackens and blisters. Put in a plastic bag for about 10 minutes and then, when cool enough to handle, peel away the skin and slice the flesh thinly.

4 Drain the pork, reserving the marinade. Heat 30ml/2 tbsp of the oil in a large frying pan. Stir-fry the pork, in batches if necessary, for 3–4 minutes until the meat is tender. Transfer to a plate and keep warm.

5 Add a little more oil to the pan if necessary and fry the garlic, spring onions, lemon grass and chillies over a low to medium heat for 2–3 minutes. Add the broccoli and pepper and stir-fry for a few minutes more.

6 Stir in the reserved marinade, coconut milk and tomato purée, with the kaffir lime leaves, if using. Simmer gently until the broccoli is nearly tender, then add the pork and noodles. Toss over the heat, for 3–4 minutes until completely heated through.

CHICKEN AND BASIL COCONUT RICE

FOR THIS DISH, THE RICE IS PARTIALLY BOILED BEFORE BEING SIMMERED WITH COCONUT SO THAT IT FULLY ABSORBS THE FLAVOUR OF THE CHILLIES, BASIL AND SPICES.

SERVES FOUR

INGREDIENTS

350g/12oz/1¾ cups Thai fragrant rice, rinsed
30–45ml/2–3 tbsp groundnut oil
1 large onion, finely sliced into rings
1 garlic clove, crushed
1 fresh red chilli, seeded and finely sliced
1 fresh green chilli, seeded and finely sliced
generous handful of basil leaves
3 skinless, boneless chicken breasts, about 350g/12oz, finely sliced
5mm/¼in piece of lemon grass, pounded or finely chopped
50g/2oz piece of creamed coconut dissolved in 600ml/1 pint/2½ cups boiling water
salt and freshly ground black pepper

1 Bring a saucepan of lightly salted water to the boil. Add the rice to the pan and boil for about 6 minutes, until partially cooked. Drain.

2 Heat the oil in a frying pan and fry the onion rings for 5–10 minutes until golden and crisp. Lift out, drain on kitchen paper and set aside.

3 Fry the garlic and chillies in the oil remaining in the pan for 2–3 minutes, then add the basil leaves and fry briefly until they begin to wilt. Remove a few leaves and set them aside for the garnish, then add the chicken slices with the lemon grass and fry for 2–3 minutes until golden.

4 Add the rice. Stir-fry for a few minutes to coat the grains, then pour in the coconut liquid. Cook for 4–5 minutes or until the rice is tender, adding a little more water if necessary. Adjust the seasoning. Pile the rice into a warmed serving dish, scatter with the fried onion rings and basil leaves, and serve immediately.

INDONESIAN PINEAPPLE RICE

THIS WAY OF PRESENTING RICE NOT ONLY LOOKS SPECTACULAR, IT ALSO TASTES SO GOOD THAT IT CAN EASILY BE SERVED SOLO.

SERVES FOUR

INGREDIENTS

75g/3oz/¾ cup natural peanuts
1 large pineapple
45ml/3 tbsp groundnut or sunflower oil
1 onion, chopped
1 garlic clove, crushed
2 chicken breasts, about 225g/8oz, cut into strips
225g/8oz/generous 1 cup Thai fragrant rice, rinsed
600ml/1 pint/2½ cups chicken stock
1 lemon grass stalk, bruised
2 thick slices of ham, cut into julienne strips
1 fresh red chilli, seeded and very finely sliced
salt

1 Dry-fry the peanuts in a non-stick frying pan until golden. When cool, grind one-sixth of them in a coffee or herb mill and chop the remainder.

2 Cut a lengthways slice of pineapple, slicing through the leaves, then cut out the flesh to leave a neat shell. Chop 115g/4oz of the pineapple into cubes; saving the remainder for another dish.

3 Heat the oil in a saucepan and fry the onion and garlic for 3–4 minutes until soft. Add the chicken strips and stir-fry over a medium heat for a few minutes until evenly brown.

4 Add the rice to the pan. Toss with the chicken mixture for a few minutes, then pour in the stock, with the lemon grass and a little salt. Bring to just below boiling point, then lower the heat, cover the pan and simmer gently for 10–12 minutes until both the rice and the chicken pieces are tender.

5 Stir the chopped peanuts, the pineapple cubes and the ham into the rice, then spoon the mixture into the pineapple shell. Sprinkle the ground peanuts and the sliced chilli over the top and serve.

NASI GORENG

ONE OF THE MOST POPULAR AND BEST-KNOWN INDONESIAN DISHES, THIS IS A MARVELLOUS WAY TO USE UP LEFTOVER RICE, CHICKEN AND MEATS SUCH AS PORK.

SERVES FOUR TO SIX

INGREDIENTS
350g/12oz/1¾ cups basmati rice (dry
    weight), cooked and cooled
2 eggs
30ml/2 tbsp water
105ml/7 tbsp sunflower oil
225g/8oz pork fillet or fillet of beef
2–3 fresh red chillies
10ml/2 tsp Thai fish paste
2 garlic cloves, crushed
1 onion, sliced
115g/4oz cooked, peeled prawns
225g/8oz cooked chicken, chopped
30ml/2 tbsp dark soy sauce
salt and freshly ground black pepper
deep-fried onions, to garnish

1 Separate the grains of the cold, cooked rice with a fork. Cover and set aside until needed.

VARIATION
If preferred, replace the Thai fish paste with blachan, found in Oriental stores.

2 Beat the eggs with the water and a little seasoning. Heat 15ml/1 tbsp of the oil in a frying pan, pour in about half the mixture and cook until set, without stirring. Roll up the omelette, slide it on to a plate, cut into strips and set aside. Make another omelette in the same way.

3 Cut the pork or beef fillet into neat strips. Finely shred one of the chillies and set aside. Put the terasi into a food processor, add the remaining chilli, the garlic and the onion. Process to a paste.

4 Heat the remaining oil in a wok. Fry the paste, without browning, until it gives off a spicy aroma. Add the strips of pork or beef and toss the meat over the heat, to seal in the juices. Cook the meat in the wok for about 2 minutes, stirring constantly.

5 Add the prawns, cook for 2 minutes, then add the chicken, rice, and soy sauce, with salt and pepper to taste, stirring constantly. Serve in individual bowls, garnished with omelette strips, shredded chilli and deep-fried onions.

INDONESIAN COCONUT RICE

THIS WAY OF COOKING RICE IS VERY POPULAR THROUGHOUT THE WHOLE OF SOUTH-EAST ASIA.
COCONUT RICE GOES PARTICULARLY WELL WITH FISH, CHICKEN AND PORK.

SERVES FOUR TO SIX

INGREDIENTS
   350g/12oz/1¾ cups Thai fragrant rice
   400ml/14fl oz can coconut milk
   300ml/½ pint/1¼ cups water
   2.5ml/½ tsp ground coriander
   5cm/2in cinnamon stick
   1 lemon grass stalk, bruised
   1 bay leaf
   salt
   deep-fried onions, to garnish

1 Put the rice in a strainer and rinse thoroughly under cold water. Drain well, then put in a pan. Pour in the coconut milk and water. Add the coriander, cinnamon stick, lemon grass and bay leaf. Season with salt. Bring to the boil, then lower the heat, cover and simmer for 8–10 minutes.

2 Lift the lid and check that all the liquid has been absorbed, then fork the rice through carefully, removing the cinnamon stick, lemon grass and bay leaf.

3 Cover the pan with a tight-fitting lid and continue to cook over the lowest possible heat for 3–5 minutes more.

4 Pile the rice on to a warm serving dish and serve garnished with the crisp, deep-fried onions.

COOK'S TIP
When bringing the rice to the boil, stir it frequently to prevent it from settling on the bottom of the pan. Once the rice is nearly tender, continue to cook over a very low heat or just leave to stand for 5 minutes. The important thing is to cover the pan tightly.

LEMON GRASS AND COCONUT RICE WITH GREEN CHICKEN CURRY

USE ONE OR TWO FRESH GREEN CHILLIES IN THIS DISH, ACCORDING TO HOW HOT YOU LIKE YOUR CURRY. THE MILD AROMATIC FLAVOUR OF THE RICE OFFSETS THE SPICINESS OF THE CURRY.

SERVES THREE TO FOUR

INGREDIENTS

4 spring onions, trimmed and roughly chopped
1–2 fresh green chillies, seeded and roughly chopped
2cm/¾in piece of fresh root ginger, peeled
2 garlic cloves
5ml/1 tsp Thai fish sauce
large bunch of fresh coriander
small handful of fresh parsley
30–45ml/2–3 tbsp water
30ml/2 tbsp sunflower oil
4 skinless, boneless chicken breasts, cubed
1 green pepper, seeded and finely sliced
75g/3oz piece of creamed coconut dissolved in 400ml/14fl oz/1⅔ cups boiling water
salt and freshly ground black pepper
For the rice
225g/8oz/generous 1 cup Thai fragrant rice, rinsed
75g/3oz piece of creamed coconut dissolved in 400ml/14fl oz/1⅔ cups boiling water
1 lemon grass stalk, quartered and bruised

1 Put the spring onions, chillies, ginger, garlic, fish sauce and fresh herbs in a food processor or blender. Pour in the water and process to a smooth paste.

2 Heat half the oil in large frying pan. Fry the chicken cubes until evenly browned. Transfer to a plate.

3 Heat the remaining oil in the pan. Stir-fry the green pepper for 3–4 minutes, then add the chilli and ginger paste. Fry, stirring, for 3–4 minutes until the mixture becomes fairly thick.

4 Return the chicken to the pan and add the coconut liquid. Season and bring to the boil, then lower the heat; half cover the pan and simmer for 8–10 minutes.

5 When the chicken is cooked, transfer it with the peppers to a plate. Boil the cooking liquid remaining in the pan for 10–12 minutes until it is well reduced and fairly thick.

6 Meanwhile, put the rice in a large saucepan. Add the coconut liquid and the bruised pieces of lemon grass. Stir in a little salt, bring to the boil, then lower the heat, cover and simmer very gently for 10 minutes, or for the time recommended on the packet. When the rice is tender, discard the pieces of lemon grass and fork the rice on to a warmed serving plate.

7 Return the chicken and peppers to the green curry sauce, stir well and cook gently for a few minutes to heat through. Spoon the curry over the rice, and serve.

COOK'S TIP
Lemon grass features in many Asian dishes, and makes the perfect partner for coconut, especially when used with chicken. In this recipe, bruise the tough, top end of the lemon grass stem in a pestle and mortar before use.

COCONUT CREAM DESSERT

USE THAI FRAGRANT RICE FOR THIS DISH. DESSERTS LIKE THESE ARE SERVED IN COUNTRIES ALL OVER THE FAR EAST, OFTEN WITH MANGOES, PINEAPPLE OR GUAVAS. ALTHOUGH COMMERCIALLY GROUND RICE CAN BE USED FOR THIS DISH, GRINDING THE RICE YOURSELF — IN A FOOD PROCESSOR — GIVES A MUCH BETTER RESULT.

SERVES FOUR TO SIX

INGREDIENTS

75g/3oz/scant ½ cup Thai fragrant rice, soaked overnight in 175ml/ 6fl oz/¾ cup water
350ml/12fl oz/1½ cups coconut milk
150ml/¼ pint/⅔ cup single cream
50g/2oz/¼ cup caster sugar
fresh raspberries and mint leaves, to decorate
For the coulis
75g/3oz/¾ cup blackcurrants, stalks removed
30ml/2 tbsp caster sugar
75g/3oz/½ cup fresh or frozen raspberries

1 Put the rice and its soaking water into a food processor and process for a few minutes until the mixture is soupy.

2 Heat the coconut milk and cream in a non-stick saucepan. When the mixture is on the point of boiling, stir in the rice mixture.

3 Cook over a very gentle heat for 10 minutes, stirring constantly, then stir in the sugar and continue cooking for 10–15 minutes more, or until the mixture is thick and creamy.

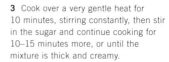

4 Pour the rice mixture into a rectangular pan that has been lined with non-stick baking paper. Cool, then chill in the fridge until the pudding is firm.

5 To make the coulis, put the blackcurrants in a bowl and sprinkle with the sugar. Set aside for about 30 minutes. Tip into a wire sieve with the raspberries and press the fruit against the sides of the sieve so that the juices collect in a bowl underneath. Taste and add more sugar if necessary.

6 Carefully cut the coconut cream into diamonds. Spoon a little of the coulis on to each dessert plate, arrange the coconut cream diamonds on top and decorate with fresh raspberries and mint leaves.

THAI RICE CAKE

NOT A DRY SNACK FROM THE HEALTH FOOD SHOP, BUT A SUMPTUOUS CELEBRATION GATEAU, MADE FROM THAI FRAGRANT RICE, TANGY CREAM AND WITH A FRESH FRUIT TOPPING.

SERVES EIGHT TO TEN

INGREDIENTS

225g/8oz/generous 1 cup Thai
    fragrant rice, rinsed
1 litre/1¾ pints/4 cups milk
115g/4oz/scant ½ cup caster sugar
6 green cardamom pods, crushed
2 bay leaves
300ml/½ pint/1¼ cups whipping
    cream
6 eggs, separated
red and white currants, sliced star
    fruit and kiwi fruit, to decorate
For the topping
250ml/8fl oz/1 cup double cream
150g/5oz/⅔ cup Quark or low-fat soft
    cheese
5ml/1 tsp vanilla essence
grated rind of 1 lemon
40g/1½oz/3 tbsp caster sugar

1 Grease and line a 25cm/10in round, deep cake tin. Cook the rice in a pan of boiling unsalted water for 3 minutes, then drain, return to the pan and pour in the milk. Stir in the caster sugar, cardamoms and bay leaves. Bring to the boil, then lower the heat and simmer the rice for 20 minutes, stirring occasionally. Allow the mixture to cool, then remove the bay leaves and cardamom husks.

2 Preheat the oven to 180°C/350°F/ Gas 4. Spoon the rice mixture into a bowl. Beat in the cream and then the egg yolks. Whisk the egg whites until they form soft peaks, then fold them into the rice mixture.

3 Spoon into the prepared tin and bake for 45–50 minutes until risen and golden brown. Chill overnight in the tin. Turn the cake out on to a large serving plate.

4 Whip the cream until stiff, then gently fold in the Quark or soft cheese, vanilla essence, lemon rind and sugar.

5 Cover the top of the cake with the cream mixture, swirling it attractively. Decorate with red and white currants, sliced star fruit and kiwi fruit.

COOK'S TIP
Do not worry if the centre of the cake is slightly wobbly when you take it out of the oven. It will firm up as the cake starts to cool.

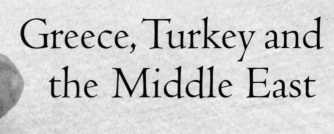

Greece, Turkey and the Middle East

THE PEOPLE OF THE MIDDLE EAST
LEARNED ABOUT RICE FROM THEIR
EASTERN NEIGHBOURS AND HAVE
LOVED IT EVER SINCE: RICE IS
ALMOST AS MUCH OF A STAPLE HERE
AS IT IS IN PARTS OF ASIA. RICH ARABIAN
SPICES AND LUSCIOUS MEDITERRANEAN
PRODUCE ARE THE INSPIRATION FOR THE
FEAST OF DISHES FROM THIS REGION —
MANY OF WHICH ARE NOW WORLD CLASSICS.

AVGOLEMONO

THIS IS A GREAT FAVOURITE IN GREECE AND IS A FINE EXAMPLE OF HOW A FEW INGREDIENTS CAN MAKE A MARVELLOUS DISH IF CAREFULLY CHOSEN AND COOKED. IT IS ESSENTIAL TO USE A WELL-FLAVOURED STOCK. ADD AS LITTLE OR AS MUCH RICE AS YOU LIKE.

2 Whisk the egg yolks in a bowl, then add about 30ml/2 tbsp of the lemon juice, whisking constantly until the mixture is smooth and bubbly. Add a ladleful of soup and whisk again.

3 Remove the soup from the heat and slowly add the egg mixture, whisking all the time. The soup will turn a pretty lemon colour and will thicken slightly.

4 Taste and add more lemon juice if necessary. Stir in the parsley. Serve at once, without reheating, garnished with lemon slices and parsley sprigs.

SERVES FOUR

INGREDIENTS
900ml/1½ pints/3¾ cups chicken stock, preferably home-made
50g/2oz/generous ⅓ cup long grain rice
3 egg yolks
30–60ml/2–4 tbsp lemon juice
30ml/2 tbsp finely chopped fresh parsley
salt and freshly ground black pepper
lemon slices and parsley sprigs, to garnish

1 Pour the stock into a pan, bring to simmering point, then add the drained rice. Half cover and cook for about 12 minutes until the rice is just tender. Season with salt and pepper.

COOK'S TIP
The trick here is to add the egg mixture to the soup without it curdling. Avoid whisking the mixture into boiling liquid. It is safest to remove the soup from the heat entirely and then whisk in the mixture in a slow but steady stream. Do not reheat as curdling would be almost inevitable.

DOLMADES

NOW POPULAR THE WORLD OVER, THESE STUFFED VINE LEAVES ORIGINATED IN GREECE. IF YOU CAN'T LOCATE FRESH VINE LEAVES, USE A PACKET OR CAN OF BRINED VINE LEAVES. SOAK THE LEAVES IN HOT WATER FOR 20 MINUTES, THEN RINSE AND DRY WELL ON KITCHEN PAPER BEFORE USE.

MAKES 20 TO 24

INGREDIENTS

24–28 fresh young vine leaves,
  soaked
30ml/2 tbsp olive oil
1 large onion, finely chopped
1 garlic clove, crushed
225g/8oz/2 cups cooked long grain
  rice, or mixed white and wild rice
about 45ml/3 tbsp pine nuts
15ml/1 tbsp flaked almonds
40g/1½oz/¼ cup sultanas
15ml/1 tbsp snipped fresh chives
15ml/1 tbsp finely chopped fresh
  mint
juice of ½ lemon
150ml/¼ pint/⅔ cup white wine
hot vegetable stock
salt and freshly ground black pepper
fresh mint sprig, to garnish
garlic yogurt and pitta bread,
  to serve (optional)

1 Bring a large pan of water to the boil and cook the vine leaves for about 2–3 minutes. They will darken and go limp after about 1 minute and simmering for a further minute or so will ensure they are pliable. If using leaves from a packet or can, place them in a large bowl, cover with boiling water and leave for a few minutes until the leaves can be easily separated. Rinse them under cold water and drain on kitchen paper.

2 Heat the oil in a small frying pan and fry the onion and garlic for 3–4 minutes over a gentle heat until soft. Spoon the mixture into a large bowl and add the cooked rice.

3 Stir in 30ml/2 tbsp of the pine nuts, the almonds, sultanas, chives and mint. Squeeze in the lemon juice. Add salt and pepper to taste and mix well.

4 Set aside four large vine leaves. Lay a vine leaf on a clean work surface, veined side uppermost. Place a spoonful of filling near the stem, fold the lower part of the vine leaf over it and roll up, folding in the sides as you go. Stuff the rest of the vine leaves in the same way.

5 Line the base of a deep frying pan with the reserved vine leaves. Place the dolmades close together in the pan, seam side down, in a single layer. Pour over the wine and enough stock to just cover. Anchor the dolmades by placing a plate on top of them, then cover the pan and simmer gently for 30 minutes.

6 Transfer the dolmades to a plate. Cool, chill, then garnish with the remaining pine nuts and the mint. Serve with a little garlic yogurt and pitta bread, if you like.

COOK'S TIP
Check the pan frequently when cooking the dolmades, to make sure that the pan does not boil dry.

GREEK PICNIC PIE

AUBERGINES LAYERED WITH SPINACH, FETA CHEESE AND RICE MAKE A MARVELLOUS FILLING FOR A PIE THAT IS PERFECT FOR PICNICS. IT CAN BE SERVED WARM OR COLD AND MAKES A GOOD VEGETARIAN DISH FOR A BUFFET LUNCH.

SERVES SIX

INGREDIENTS

375g/13oz shortcrust pastry, thawed
  if frozen
45–60ml/3–4 tbsp olive oil
1 large aubergine, sliced into rounds
1 onion, chopped
1 garlic clove, crushed
175g/6oz spinach, washed
4 eggs
75g/3oz/½ cup crumbled feta cheese
40g/1½oz/½ cup freshly grated
  Parmesan cheese
60ml/4 tbsp natural yogurt
90ml/6 tbsp creamy milk
225g/8oz/2 cups cooked white or
  brown long grain rice
salt and freshly ground black pepper

2 Heat 30–45ml/2–3 tbsp of the oil in a frying pan and fry the aubergine slices for 6–8 minutes on each side until golden. You may need to add a little more oil at first, but this will be released as the flesh softens. Lift out and drain on kitchen paper.

3 Add the onion and garlic to the oil remaining in the pan and fry over a gentle heat for 4–5 minutes until soft, adding a little extra oil if necessary.

5 Spread the rice in an even layer over the bottom of the part-baked pie. Reserve a few aubergine slices for the top, and arrange the rest in an even layer over the rice.

1 Preheat the oven to 180°C/350°F/ Gas 4. Roll out the pastry thinly and line a 25cm/10in flan ring. Prick the base all over and bake in the oven for 10–12 minutes until the pastry is pale golden. (Alternatively, bake blind, having lined the pastry with baking parchment and weighted it with a handful of baking beans.)

4 Chop the spinach finely, by hand or in a food processor. Beat the eggs in a large mixing bowl, then add the spinach, feta, Parmesan, yogurt, milk and the onion mixture. Season well with salt and pepper and stir thoroughly to mix.

6 Spoon the spinach and feta mixture over the aubergines and place the remaining slices on top. Bake for 30–40 minutes until lightly browned. Serve the pie warm, or cool completely before transferring to a serving plate or wrapping and packing for a picnic.

VARIATION
Courgettes could be used in place of aubergines, if you prefer. Fry the sliced courgettes in a little oil for 3–4 minutes until golden. You will need three to four medium-size courgettes, or use baby courgettes and slice them horizontally: these would look particularly attractive arranged on top of the pie.

COOK'S TIP
If making your own pastry, add 5ml/1 tsp dried basil to the flour before rubbing in the butter, margarine or lard.

TURKISH LAMB ON A BED OF RICE

IN TURKEY, THE TRADITIONAL WAY OF COOKING MEAT — OVER HOT CHARCOAL OR IN A WOOD-BURNING STOVE — RESULTS IN A CRUSTY, ALMOST CHARRED EXTERIOR ENCLOSING BEAUTIFULLY MOIST, TENDER MEAT. IN THIS RECIPE, THE MEAT JUICES FLAVOUR THE RICE BENEATH.

SERVES SIX

INGREDIENTS

half leg of lamb, about
  1.5kg/3–3½lb, boned
bunch of fresh parsley
small bunch of fresh coriander
50g/2oz/½ cup cashew nuts
2 garlic cloves
15ml/1 tbsp sunflower oil
1 small onion, finely chopped
200g/7oz/1¾ cups cooked white long
  grain rice
75g/3oz/scant ½ cup ready-to-eat
  dried apricots, finely chopped
salt and freshly ground black pepper
fresh parsley or coriander sprigs, to
  garnish
tzatziki, black olives and pitta bread,
  to serve (optional)

1 Preheat the oven to 200°C/400°F/Gas 6. Remove the excess fat from the lamb, then trim the joint, if necessary, so that it lies flat. (If the leg has been tunnel boned, you will need to cut the meat before it will lie flat.)

2 Put the parsley and coriander in a food processor or blender and process until finely chopped. Add the cashew nuts and pulse until roughly chopped.

3 Crush 1 of the garlic cloves. Heat the oil in a frying pan and fry the onion and crushed garlic for 3–4 minutes until softened but not browned.

4 Put the rice in a bowl. Using a spatula, scrape all the parsley and cashew nut mixture into the rice. Add the fried onion mixture and the chopped apricots. Season with salt and pepper, stir well, then spoon into the bottom of a roasting tin, which is just large enough to hold the lamb.

COOK'S TIP
In Turkey, the meat would be cooked until very well done, but it can also be served slightly pink, in the French style. For a doner kebab, split warmed pitta breads (preferably home-made) and stuff with meat, yogurt and a spicy tomato sauce. Alternatively, serve this dish with rice and a broad bean salad.

5 Cut the remaining garlic clove in half and rub the cut sides over the meat. Season with pepper, then lay the meat on top of the rice, tucking all the rice under the meat, so that no rice is visible.

6 Roast the lamb for 30 minutes, then lower the oven temperature to 180°C/350°F/Gas 4. Cook for 35–45 minutes more or until the meat is cooked to your taste.

7 Cover the lamb and rice with foil and leave to rest for 5 minutes, then lift the lamb on to a board and slice it thickly. Spoon the rice mixture on to a platter, arrange the meat slices on top and garnish with fresh parsley or coriander. Serve at once, with a bowl of tzatziki, black olives and pitta bread, if liked.

YOGURT CHICKEN AND RICE CAKE

THIS MIDDLE-EASTERN SPECIALITY IS TRADITIONALLY FLAVOURED WITH SMALL, DRIED BERRIES CALLED ZERESHK, BUT IS JUST AS DELICIOUS WITH FRESH CRANBERRIES.

SERVES SIX

INGREDIENTS
40g/1½oz/3 tbsp butter
1 chicken, about 1.5kg/3–3½lb, cut
    into pieces
1 large onion, chopped
250ml/8fl oz/1 cup chicken stock
2 eggs, beaten
475ml/16fl oz/2 cups natural yogurt
2–3 saffron strands, dissolved in
    15ml/1 tbsp warm water
5ml/1 tsp ground cinnamon
450g/1lb/2⅓ cups basmati rice,
    soaked
1.2 litres/2 pints/5 cups boiling
    water
75g/3oz/¾ cup cranberries or zereshk
    (see Cook's Tip)
50g/2oz/½ cup flaked almonds
salt and freshly ground black pepper

1 Melt two-thirds of the butter in a flameproof casserole. Fry the chicken pieces with the onion for 4–5 minutes, until the onion is softened and the chicken has browned. Add the stock and season with salt and pepper. Bring to the boil, lower the heat and simmer for 45 minutes, or until the chicken is cooked and the stock has reduced by half.

2 Drain the chicken, reserving the stock. Cut the flesh into large pieces, discarding the skin and bones, and place in a large bowl. In a separate bowl, mix the eggs with the yogurt. Add the saffron water and cinnamon. Season lightly. Pour over the chicken and stir to coat. Cover and leave to marinate for up to 2 hours.

3 Preheat the oven to 160°C/325°F/ Gas 3. Grease a large baking dish, about 10cm/4in deep. Drain the rice and put it in a saucepan. Add the boiling water and a little salt, bring back to the boil and then lower the heat and simmer gently for 10 minutes. Drain, rinse thoroughly in warm water and drain once more.

4 Using a slotted spoon, lift the chicken pieces out of the yogurt marinade and put them on a plate. Mix half the rice into the marinade. Spread the mixture on the bottom of the baking dish. Arrange the chicken pieces in a single layer on top, then cover evenly with about half the plain rice. Sprinkle over the cranberries or zereshk, then cover with the rest of the rice.

COOK'S TIP
If you are lucky enough to locate zereshk, wash them thoroughly before use. Heat the berries before layering them with the rice.

5 Pour the reserved chicken stock over the rice. Sprinkle with flaked almonds and dot with the remaining butter. Cover tightly with foil and bake in the oven for 35–45 minutes.

6 Leave the dish to cool for a few minutes, then place it on a cold, damp dish towel (this will help to lift the rice from the bottom of the dish). Run a knife around the inside rim of the dish. Invert a large, flat plate over the dish and turn out the rice "cake". Cut into six wedges and serve hot, with a herb and radicchio salad, if you like.

STUFFED VEGETABLES

COLOURFUL, EASY TO PREPARE AND UTTERLY DELICIOUS, THIS MAKES A POPULAR SUPPER DISH, AND WITH A CHOICE OF VEGETABLES INCLUDED IN THE RECIPE, THERE'S BOUND TO BE SOMETHING TO APPEAL TO EVERY MEMBER OF THE FAMILY.

SERVES FOUR

INGREDIENTS

1 aubergine
1 green pepper
2 beefsteak tomatoes
45ml/3 tbsp olive oil
1 onion, chopped
2 garlic cloves, crushed
115g/4oz/1–1½ cups button
  mushrooms, chopped
1 carrot, grated
225g/8oz/2 cups cooked white long
  grain rice
15ml/1 tbsp chopped fresh dill
90g/3½oz/scant ½ cup feta cheese,
  crumbled
75g/3oz/¾ cup pine nuts, lightly
  toasted
30ml/2 tbsp currants
salt and freshly ground black pepper

1 Preheat the oven to 190°C/375°F/ Gas 5. Lightly grease a shallow baking dish. Cut the aubergine in half, through the stalk, and scoop out the flesh from each half to leave two hollow "boats". Dice the aubergine flesh. Cut the pepper in half lengthways and remove the cores and seeds.

2 Cut off the tops from the tomatoes and hollow out the centres with a spoon. Chop the flesh and add it to the diced aubergine. Place the tomatoes upside down on kitchen paper to drain.

3 Bring a pan of water to the boil, add the aubergine halves and blanch for 3 minutes. Add the pepper halves to the boiling water and blanch for 3 minutes more. Drain the vegetables, then place, hollow up, in the baking dish.

4 Heat 30ml/2 tbsp oil in a saucepan and fry the onion and garlic for about 5 minutes. Stir in the diced aubergine and tomato mixture with the mushrooms and carrot. Cover, cook for 5 minutes until softened, then mix in the rice, dill, feta, pine nuts and currants. Season to taste.

5 Divide the mixture among the vegetable shells, sprinkle with the remaining olive oil and bake for 20 minutes until the topping has browned. Serve hot or cold.

PERSIAN RICE WITH A TAHDEEG

PERSIAN OR IRANIAN CUISINE IS EXOTIC AND DELICIOUS, AND THE FLAVOURS ARE INTENSE. A TAHDEEG IS THE GLORIOUS, GOLDEN RICE CRUST OR "DIG" THAT FORMS ON THE BOTTOM OF THE SAUCEPAN AS THE RICE COOKS.

SERVES SIX TO EIGHT

INGREDIENTS

450g/1lb/2⅓ cups basmati rice,
  soaked
150ml/¼ pint/⅔ cup sunflower oil
2 garlic cloves, crushed
2 onions, 1 chopped, 1 finely sliced
150g/5oz/⅔ cup green lentils, soaked
600ml/1 pint/2½ cups stock
50g/2oz/⅓ cup raisins
10ml/2 tsp ground coriander
45ml/3 tbsp tomato purée
a few saffron strands
1 egg yolk, beaten
10ml/2 tsp natural yogurt
75g/3oz/6 tbsp melted ghee or
  clarified butter
salt and freshly ground black pepper

1 Drain the rice, then cook it in plenty of boiling salted water for 10–12 minutes or until tender. Drain again.

2 Heat 30ml/2 tbsp of the oil in a large saucepan and fry the garlic and the chopped onion for 5 minutes. Stir in the lentils, stock, raisins, ground coriander and tomato purée, with salt and pepper to taste. Bring to the boil, then lower the heat, cover and simmer for about 20 minutes.

3 Soak the saffron strands in a little hot water. Mix the egg yolk and yogurt in a bowl. Spoon in about 120ml/4 fl oz/ ½ cup of the cooked rice and mix thoroughly. Season well.

4 Heat about two-thirds of the remaining oil in a large saucepan. Scatter the egg and yogurt rice evenly over the bottom of the pan.

COOK'S TIP
In Iran, aromatic white basmati rice would traditionally be used for this dish, but you could use any long grain rice, or a brown rice, if you prefer.

5 Scatter the remaining rice into the pan, alternating it with the lentil mixture. Build up in a pyramid shape away from the sides of the pan, finishing with a layer of plain rice. With a long wooden spoon handle, make three holes down to the bottom of the pan; drizzle over the melted ghee or butter. Bring to a high heat, then wrap the pan lid in a clean, wet dish towel and place firmly on top. When a good head of steam appears, turn the heat down to low. Cook slowly for about 30 minutes.

6 Meanwhile, fry the onion slices in the remaining oil until browned and crisp. Drain well. Remove the rice pan from the heat, keeping it covered, and plunge the base briefly into a sink of cold water to loosen the rice on the bottom. Strain the saffron water into a bowl and stir in a few spoons of the white rice.

7 Toss the rice and lentils together in the pan and spoon out on to a serving dish, mounding the mixture. Scatter the saffron rice on top. Break up the rice crust on the bottom of the pan and place pieces of it around the mound. Scatter over the crispy fried onions and serve.

ROASTED SQUASH

GEM SQUASH HAS A SWEET, SUBTLE FLAVOUR THAT CONTRASTS WELL WITH OLIVES AND SUN-DRIED TOMATOES IN THIS RECIPE. THE RICE ADDS SUBSTANCE WITHOUT CHANGING ANY OF THE FLAVOURS.

2 Mix the rice, tomatoes, olives, cheese, half the olive oil and basil in a bowl.

3 Oil a shallow baking dish with the remaining oil, just large enough to hold the squash side by side. Divide the rice mixture among the squash and place them in the dish.

SERVES FOUR AS A STARTER

INGREDIENTS
   4 whole gem squashes
   225g/8oz/2 cups cooked white
      long grain rice
   75g/3oz/1½ cups sun-dried tomatoes,
      chopped
   50g/2oz/½ cup pitted black olives,
      chopped
   60ml/4 tbsp soft goat's cheese
   30ml/2 tbsp olive oil
   15ml/1 tbsp chopped fresh basil
      leaves, plus basil sprigs, to serve
   yogurt and mint dressing or green
      salad, to serve (optional)

1 Preheat the oven to 180°C/350°F/ Gas 4. Trim away the base of each squash, slice off the top and scoop out and discard the seeds.

4 Cover with foil and bake for 45–50 minutes until the squash is tender when pierced with a skewer. Garnish with basil sprigs and serve with a yogurt and mint dressing or with a green salad.

AUBERGINE ROLLS

AS WELL AS MAKING AN ORIGINAL STARTER, THESE LITTLE ROLLS OF AUBERGINE WRAPPED AROUND A FILLING OF RICOTTA AND RICE ARE TASTY SERVED AS PART OF A BUFFET OR FOR A TURKISH-STYLE MEZE.

SERVES FOUR

INGREDIENTS

    2 aubergines
    olive oil, for shallow frying
    75g/3oz/scant ½ cup ricotta cheese
    75g/3oz/scant ½ cup soft goat's
      cheese
    225g/8oz/2 cups cooked white long
      grain rice
    15ml/1 tbsp chopped fresh basil
    5ml/1 tsp chopped fresh mint, plus
      mint sprigs, to garnish
    salt and freshly ground black pepper
For the tomato sauce
    15ml/1 tbsp olive oil
    1 red onion, finely chopped
    1 garlic clove, crushed
    400g/14oz can chopped tomatoes
    120ml/4fl oz/½ cup chicken stock
      or white wine or a mixture
    15ml/1 tbsp chopped fresh parsley

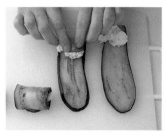

2 Meanwhile, cut the aubergines lengthways into four or five slices. Heat the oil in a large frying pan and fry the aubergine slices in batches until they are golden brown on both sides. Drain on kitchen paper. Mix the ricotta, goat's cheese, rice, basil and mint in a bowl. Season well with salt and pepper.

3 Place a generous spoonful of the cheese and rice mixture at one end of each aubergine slice and roll up. Arrange the rolls side by side in a shallow baking dish. Pour the tomato sauce over the top and bake for 10–15 minutes until heated through. Garnish with the mint sprigs and serve.

1 Preheat the oven to 190°C/375°F/ Gas 5. Make the tomato sauce. Heat the oil in a small saucepan and fry the onion and garlic for 3–4 minutes until softened. Add the tomatoes, chicken stock and wine, if using, and sprinkle in the parsley. Season with salt and pepper. Bring to the boil, then lower the heat and simmer for 10–12 minutes until slightly thickened, stirring.

COOK'S TIP
Cut off and discard the skin on the two outer slices of aubergine. If you prefer to use less oil for the aubergines, brush each slice with a little oil, then grill until evenly browned.

RICE WITH DILL AND BROAD BEANS

THIS IS A FAVOURITE RICE DISH IN IRAN, WHERE IT IS CALLED BAGHALI POLO. THE COMBINATION OF BROAD BEANS, DILL AND WARM SPICES WORKS VERY WELL, AND THE SAFFRON RICE ADDS A SPLASH OF BRIGHT COLOUR.

SERVES FOUR

INGREDIENTS
275g/10oz/1½ cups basmati rice,
   soaked
750ml/1¼ pints/3 cups water
40g/1½oz/3 tbsp melted butter
175g/6oz/1½ cups frozen baby broad
   beans, thawed and peeled
90ml/6 tbsp finely chopped fresh
   dill, plus 1 fresh dill sprig, to
   garnish
5ml/1 tsp ground cinnamon
5ml/1 tsp ground cumin
2–3 saffron strands, soaked in
   15ml/1 tbsp boiling water
salt

1 Drain the rice, tip it into a saucepan and pour in the water. Add a little salt. Bring to the boil, then lower the heat and simmer very gently for 5 minutes. Drain, rinse well in warm water and drain once again.

2 Melt the butter in a non-stick saucepan. Pour two-thirds of the melted butter into a small jug and set aside. Spoon enough rice into the pan to cover the bottom. Add a quarter of the beans and a little dill. Spread over another layer of rice, then a layer of beans and dill. Repeat the layers until all the beans and dill have been used up, ending with a layer of rice. Cook over a gentle heat for 8 minutes until nearly tender.

3 Pour the reserved melted butter over the rice. Sprinkle with the ground cinnamon and cumin. Cover the pan with a clean dish towel and a tight-fitting lid, lifting the corners of the cloth back over the lid. Cook over a low heat for 25–30 minutes.

4 Spoon about 45ml/3 tbsp of the cooked rice into the bowl of saffron water; mix well. Mound the remaining rice mixture on a large serving plate and spoon the saffron rice on one side to decorate. Serve at once, decorated with the sprig of dill.

SWEET AND SOUR RICE

THIS POPULAR MIDDLE EASTERN RICE DISH IS FLAVOURED WITH FRUIT AND SPICES. IT IS OFTEN SERVED WITH LAMB OR CHICKEN.

SERVES FOUR

INGREDIENTS

50g/2oz/½ cup zereshk (see Cook's Tip)
45g/1½oz/3 tbsp butter
50g/2oz/⅓ cup raisins
50g/2oz/¼ cup granulated sugar
5ml/1 tsp ground cinnamon
5ml/1 tsp ground cumin
350g/12oz/1¾ cups basmati rice, soaked
2–3 saffron strands, soaked in 15ml/1 tbsp boiling water
pinch of salt

1 Thoroughly wash the zereshk in cold water at least four or five times to rinse off any bits of grit. Drain well.

2 Melt 15g/½oz/1 tbsp of the butter in a frying pan and fry the raisins for about 1–2 minutes.

3 Add the zereshk, fry for a few seconds, and then add the sugar, with half of the cinnamon and cumin. Cook briefly and then set aside.

4 Drain the rice, then put it in a pan with plenty of boiling, lightly salted water. Bring back to the boil, reduce the heat and simmer for 4 minutes. Drain and rinse once again, if you like.

COOK'S TIP
Zereshk are small dried berries. Look for them in Middle Eastern markets and shops. If you cannot locate them, use fresh cranberries instead.

5 Melt half the remaining butter in the clean pan, add 15ml/1 tbsp water and stir in half the cooked rice. Sprinkle with half the raisin and zereshk mixture and top with all but 45ml/3 tbsp of the rice. Sprinkle over the remaining raisin and zereshk mixture.

6 Mix the remaining cinnamon and cumin with the reserved rice, and scatter this mixture evenly over the layered mixture. Melt the remaining butter, drizzle it over the surface, then cover the pan with a clean dish towel. Cover with a tight-fitting lid, lifting the corners of the cloth back over the lid. Steam the rice over a very low heat for about 20–30 minutes.

7 Just before serving, mix 45ml/3 tbsp of the rice with the saffron water. Spoon the sweet and sour rice on to a large, flat serving dish and scatter the saffron rice over the top, to garnish.

SWEET RICE

IN IRAN, SWEET RICE IS A TRADITIONAL DISH WHICH IS SERVED AT WEDDING BANQUETS AND ON OTHER SPECIAL FEASTING OCCASIONS. IT CAN BE SERVED SOLO OR TO ACCOMPANY A MEAT DISH.

3 Melt 15g/½oz/1 tbsp of the butter in a pan and fry the carrots for 2–3 minutes. Add the remaining sugar and 60ml/4 tbsp water. Simmer for 10 minutes, shaking the pan frequently, until most of the liquid has evaporated.

4 Stir the carrots and half of the nuts into the orange peel in the pan and set aside. Drain the rice and cook in salted water for about 5 minutes. Drain once more and rinse thoroughly in plenty of cold water.

SERVES FOUR TO SIX

INGREDIENTS
 2 oranges
 45ml/3 tbsp granulated sugar
 40g/1½oz/3 tbsp butter
 3 carrots, cut into julienne strips
 50g/2oz/½ cup mixed chopped
  pistachios, almonds and pine nuts
 350g/12oz/1¾ cups basmati rice,
  soaked
 2–3 saffron strands, soaked in
  15ml/1 tbsp warm water
 salt, to taste

1 Pare the rind from the oranges in wide strips, using a potato peeler and taking care to avoid including the white pith. Cut the rind into thin shreds. Place in a saucepan with enough water to cover and bring to the boil. Simmer for a few minutes, then drain. Repeat until the rind no longer tastes bitter.

2 Return the orange rind to the pan. Add half the sugar, then pour in 60ml/4 tbsp water. Bring to the boil, then simmer until the syrup is reduced by half. Set aside.

5 Melt half the remaining butter in the clean pan. Add 45ml/3 tbsp water. Fork a little of the rice into the pan and spoon on some of the carrot mixture. Repeat these layers until all the mixture has been used up. Cook gently for 10 minutes. Melt the remaining butter, pour it over the sweet rice and cover the pan with a clean dish towel and a tight-fitting lid. Steam for 30–45 minutes. Mound on plates, garnish with the remaining nuts, drizzle with the saffron water, and serve.

ALMA-ATA

THIS DISH COMES FROM CENTRAL ASIA AND IS A SPECTACULAR COMBINATION OF THE FRUITS AND NUTS FROM THAT REGION.

SERVES FOUR

INGREDIENTS

75g/3oz/¾ cup blanched almonds
60ml/4 tbsp sunflower oil
225g/8oz carrots, cut into julienne
   strips
2 onions, chopped
115g/4oz/½ cup ready-to-eat dried
   apricots, chopped
50g/2oz/⅓ cup raisins
350g/12oz/1¾ cups basmati rice,
   soaked
600ml/1 pint/2½ cups vegetable stock
150ml/¼ pint/⅔ cup orange juice
grated rind of 1 orange
25g/1oz/⅓ cup pine nuts
1 red eating apple, chopped
salt and freshly ground black pepper

3 Pour in the vegetable stock and orange juice, stirring constantly, then stir in the orange rind. Reserve a few toasted almonds for the garnish and stir in the remainder with the pine nuts. Cover the pan with a double piece of foil and fit the casserole lid securely. Transfer to the oven and bake for 30–35 minutes, until the rice is tender and all the liquid has been absorbed.

4 Remove from the oven, season to taste and stir in the chopped apple. Serve from the casserole or spoon into a warmed serving dish. Garnish with the reserved almonds.

1 Preheat the oven to 160°C/325°F/ Gas 3. Toast the almonds in a dry frying pan for 4–5 minutes until golden.

2 Heat the oil in a heavy, flameproof casserole and fry the carrots and onions over a moderately high heat for 6–8 minutes until both are slightly glazed. Add the apricots, raisins and rice and cook over a medium heat for a few minutes, stirring all the time, until the grains of rice are coated in the oil.

VARIATION

For a one-dish meal, add 450g/1lb lamb, cut into cubes. Brown in the casserole in a little oil, then transfer to a dish while you cook the onion and carrots. Stir the meat back into the casserole when you add the stock and orange juice.

SWEET BASMATI DESSERT

YOU WILL FIND VARIATIONS ON THIS SWEET AND CREAMY DESSERT IN TURKEY, EGYPT, LEBANON AND SYRIA. THE BASMATI AROMA IS DISTINCTIVE WITHOUT BEING INTRUSIVE.

SERVES SIX TO EIGHT

INGREDIENTS

275g/10oz/1½ cups basmati rice, soaked
1.2 litres/2 pints/5 cups milk
pinch of saffron strands dissolved in warm milk or water
about 2.5ml/½ tsp ground cardamom seeds
75–115g/3–4oz/½ cup granulated sugar
400g/14oz can evaporated milk
To serve
1 papaya
25g/1oz/¼ cup flaked almonds (optional)

1 Drain the rice and cook it in plenty of water, using a non-stick saucepan.

2 Drain the rice again, return to the pan and pour in the milk. Heat very gently until barely simmering and cook for 30–45 minutes, stirring occasionally.

3 Stir in the saffron milk or water, the ground cardamom seeds and the sugar. Cook for 3–4 minutes more, then stir in the evaporated milk.

4 Cut the papaya in half, remove the skin and scoop out the seeds. Slice the flesh and arrange it on a platter. Spoon the sweet basmati rice into individual bowls, sprinkle with flaked almonds and top each portion with two small slices of papaya, if you like. Serve the dessert at once.

COOK'S TIP
If you cook the pudding on top of the stove, it is essential to use a non-stick pan. If you haven't got one, bake the pudding instead. Spoon the cooked rice into a baking dish. Bring the milk to the boil, pour it over the rice, stir and cover tightly. Bake at 150°C/300°F/Gas 2 for 45 minutes, then stir in the remaining ingredients and bake for 15 minutes more. Cool slightly before serving.

FRUITED RICE RING

THIS UNUSUAL RICE PUDDING LOOKS BEAUTIFUL TURNED OUT OF A RING MOULD, BUT IF YOU PREFER, YOU CAN STIR THE FRUIT INTO THE RICE AND SERVE IT IN INDIVIDUAL DISHES.

SERVES FOUR

INGREDIENTS

65g/2½oz/⅓ cup short grain pudding rice
900ml/1½ pints/3¾ cups semi-skimmed milk
5cm/2in cinnamon stick
175g/6oz/1½ cups dried fruit salad
175ml/6fl oz/¾ cup orange juice
45ml/3 tbsp caster sugar
finely grated rind of 1 small orange
sunflower oil, for greasing

1 Mix the rice and milk in a saucepan. Add the cinnamon stick and bring to the boil. Lower the heat, cover the saucepan and simmer, stirring occasionally, for about 1½ hours, until all the liquid has been absorbed.

2 Meanwhile, put the dried fruit salad in a separate pan, pour over the orange juice and bring to the boil. Lower the heat, cover and simmer very gently for about 1 hour, until the fruit is tender and no liquid remains.

3 Remove the cinnamon stick from the rice and gently stir in the caster sugar and grated orange rind.

COOK'S TIP
When spooning the dried fruit into the tin, bear in mind that this will be the topping when the ring is turned out. Try to balance colours and varieties of fruit.

4 Lightly oil a 1.5 litre/2½ pint/6¼ cup ring tin. Spoon in the fruit so that it covers the bottom of the tin evenly. Top with the rice, smooth it down firmly, then chill until firm.

5 Run a knife around the edge of the ring tin, then invert a serving plate on top. Turn tin and plate over together, then lift off the tin. Serve in slices.

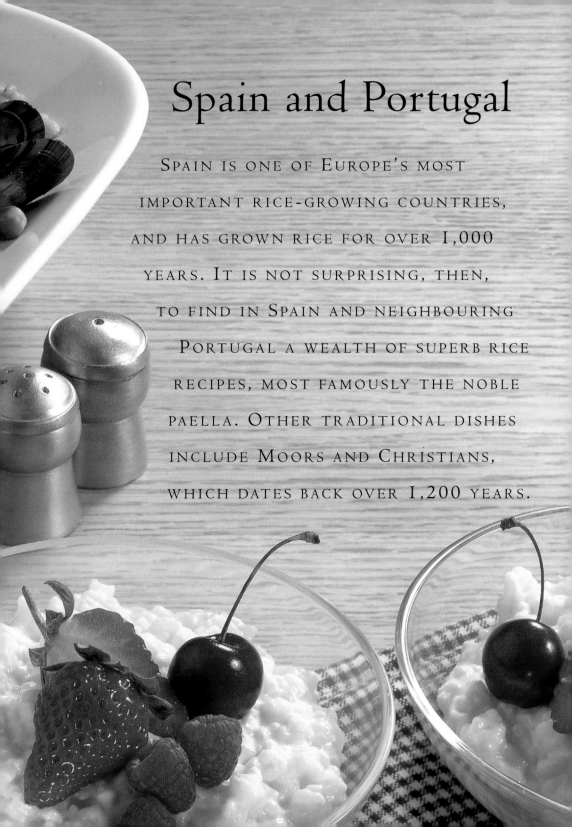

Spain and Portugal

SPAIN IS ONE OF EUROPE'S MOST
IMPORTANT RICE-GROWING COUNTRIES,
AND HAS GROWN RICE FOR OVER 1,000
YEARS. IT IS NOT SURPRISING, THEN,
TO FIND IN SPAIN AND NEIGHBOURING
PORTUGAL A WEALTH OF SUPERB RICE
RECIPES, MOST FAMOUSLY THE NOBLE
PAELLA. OTHER TRADITIONAL DISHES
INCLUDE MOORS AND CHRISTIANS,
WHICH DATES BACK OVER 1,200 YEARS.

FLAMENCO EGGS

THIS ADAPTATION OF A CLASSIC SPANISH RECIPE WORKS VERY WELL WITH CAMARGUE RED RICE, ALTHOUGH ANY LONG GRAIN RICE — BROWN OR WHITE — COULD BE USED.

SERVES FOUR

INGREDIENTS
   175g/6oz/scant 1 cup Camargue red rice
   chicken or vegetable stock or water
   45ml/3 tbsp olive oil
   1 Spanish onion, chopped
   1 garlic clove, crushed
   350g/12oz lean minced beef
   75g/3oz chorizo sausage, cut into small cubes
   5ml/1 tsp paprika, plus extra for dusting
   10ml/2 tsp tomato purée
   15–30ml/1–2 tbsp chopped fresh parsley
   2 red peppers, seeded and sliced
   3 tomatoes, peeled, seeded and chopped
   120ml/4fl oz/½ cup passata or tomato juice
   4 eggs
   40ml/8 tsp single cream
   salt and freshly ground black pepper

1 Preheat the oven to 180°C/350°F/Gas 4. Cook the rice in stock or water, following the instructions on the packet. Heat 30ml/2 tbsp of oil and fry the onion and garlic for 5 minutes until the onion is tinged with brown, stirring occasionally.

2 Add the minced beef and cook, stirring occasionally, until browned. Stir in the chorizo and paprika and continue cooking over a low heat for 4–5 minutes. Stir in the tomato purée and parsley and season with salt and pepper.

3 Heat the remaining oil in a saucepan and fry the peppers until they begin to sizzle. Cover and cook over a moderate heat, shaking the pan occasionally, for 4–5 minutes until the peppers are singed in places. Add the tomatoes and continue cooking for 3–4 minutes until they are very soft. Remove the pan from the heat, stir in the passata or tomato juice and add salt to taste.

4 Drain the rice, and divide it among four shallow ovenproof dishes. Spread the meat mixture over the rice and top with the peppers and tomatoes. Make a hole in the centre of each portion and break in an egg. Spoon 10ml/2 tsp of the cream over each egg yolk, dust with paprika, and bake for about 12–15 minutes until the whites of the eggs are set. Serve at once.

ORANGE CHICKEN SALAD

*WITH THEIR TANGY FLAVOUR, ORANGE SEGMENTS ARE THE PERFECT PARTNER FOR TENDER CHICKEN IN
THIS TASTY RICE SALAD. TO APPRECIATE ALL THE FLAVOURS FULLY, SERVE IT AT ROOM TEMPERATURE.*

SERVES FOUR

INGREDIENTS

3 large seedless oranges
175g/6oz/scant 1 cup white long
   grain rice
475ml/16fl oz/2 cups water
10ml/2 tsp Dijon mustard
2.5ml/½ tsp caster sugar
175ml/6fl oz/¾ cup vinaigrette
   dressing (see Cook's Tip)
450g/1lb cooked chicken, diced
45ml/3 tbsp snipped fresh chives
75g/3oz/¾ cup cashew nuts, toasted
salt and freshly ground black pepper
mixed salad leaves, to serve

1 Pare 1 of the oranges thinly, taking
care to remove only the coloured part of
the rind and avoiding the bitter pith.

2 Put the pieces of orange rind in a
saucepan and add the rice. Pour in the
water, add a pinch of salt and bring to
the boil. Cover and steam over a very
low heat for about 15 minutes, or until
the rice is tender and all the water has
been absorbed.

3 Meanwhile, peel all the oranges.
Working over a plate to catch the
juices, cut them into segments. Add
the orange juice, mustard and sugar
to the vinaigrette dressing and whisk
to combine well. Taste and add more
salt and pepper if needed.

4 When the rice is cooked, remove it
from the heat and discard the orange
rind. Spoon the rice into a bowl, let it
cool slightly, then add half the dressing.
Toss well and cool completely.

5 Add the chicken, chives, cashew
nuts and orange segments to the rice
in the bowl. Add the remaining dressing
and toss gently. Serve on a bed of
mixed salad leaves.

COOK'S TIP
To make the dressing, whisk 45ml/3 tbsp
red wine vinegar with salt and pepper to
taste. Gradually whisk in 90ml/6 tbsp
corn oil and 60ml/4 tbsp olive oil.

MOORS AND CHRISTIANS

THIS DISH IS THE TRADITIONAL CENTREPIECE OF THE MOYOS E CRISTIANOS FESTIVAL, WHICH IS HELD IN SPAIN EVERY YEAR TO REMEMBER THE CONQUEST OF THE CHRISTIANS OVER THE MOORS. THE BLACK BEANS REPRESENT THE DARK-SKINNED MOORS, AND THE WHITE RICE THE WHITE CHRISTIANS.

SERVES SIX

INGREDIENTS
400g/14oz/2 cups black beans,
  soaked overnight
1 onion, quartered
1 carrot, sliced
1 stalk celery, sliced
1 garlic clove, crushed
1 bay leaf
5ml/1 tsp paprika
45ml/3 tbsp olive oil
juice of 1 orange
300g/11oz/1¾ cups long grain rice
salt and cayenne pepper
For the garnish
  chopped fresh parsley, sliced orange,
  sliced red onion, 2 hard-boiled
  eggs, cut into wedges

1 Put the beans in a saucepan with the onion, carrot, celery, garlic and bay leaf and 1.75 litres/3 pints/7½ cups water. Bring to the boil and cook rapidly for 10 minutes, then reduce the heat and simmer for 1 hour, topping up the water if necessary. When the beans are almost tender, drain, discarding the vegetables. Return the beans to a clean saucepan.

2 Blend together the paprika, oil and cayenne pepper and stir into the beans with the orange juice. Top up with a little extra water, if necessary. Heat gently until barely simmering, then cover and cook for 10–15 minutes until the beans are completely tender. Remove from the heat and allow to stand in the liquid for 15 minutes. Add salt to taste.

3 Meanwhile, cook the rice until tender, either by boiling or by the absorption method. Drain, then pack into a buttered bowl and allow to stand for 10 minutes.

4 Unmould the rice onto a serving plate, placing the black beans around the edge of the plate. Garnish with chopped parsley, orange slices, red onion and egg wedges.

ALICANTE OMELETTE RICE

THIS IS A REALLY UNUSUAL DISH, FLAVOURED WITH GARLICKY SPANISH SAUSAGE AND TOPPED WITH BEATEN EGG SO THAT THE EFFECT SUGGESTS AN OMELETTE OR EVEN A SOUFFLE. IF YOU CANNOT GET BUTIFARRA, USE CHORIZO OR ANY SIMILAR SPANISH SAUSAGE INSTEAD.

SERVES SIX

INGREDIENTS
45ml/3 tbsp sunflower oil
200g/7oz butifarra or other Spanish
  sausage, sliced
2 tomatoes, peeled, seeded and
  chopped
175g/6oz lean pork, cut into bite-
  size pieces
175g/6oz skinless, boneless chicken
  breast or rabbit, cut into chunks
350g/12oz/1¾ cups Spanish rice or
  risotto rice
900ml–1 litre/1½–1¾ pints/
  3¾–4 cups hot chicken stock
pinch of saffron strands, crushed
115g/4oz/⅔ cup cooked chick-peas
6 eggs
salt and freshly ground black pepper

1 Preheat the oven to 190°C/375°F/ Gas 5. Heat the oil in a flameproof casserole and fry the sausage for a few minutes. Transfer to a plate.

2 Add the tomatoes and fry for a few minutes until slightly thickened. Stir in the pork and chicken or rabbit pieces and cook for 2–3 minutes until the meat has browned lightly, stirring frequently. Add the rice, stir over the heat for about a minute, then pour in the hot stock. Add the saffron, with salt and pepper to taste, and stir well.

3 Bring to the boil, then lower the heat and add the sausage and chick-peas. Cover tightly with the lid and cook over a low heat for about 15 minutes until the rice is tender.

4 Beat the eggs with a little water and a pinch of salt and pour over the rice. Place the casserole, uncovered, in the oven and cook for about 10 minutes, until the eggs have set and browned slightly on top.

BAKED TROUT WITH RICE, SUN-DRIED TOMATOES AND NUTS

TROUT IS VERY POPULAR IN SPAIN, PARTICULARLY IN THE NORTH. IF YOU FILLET THE TROUT BEFORE YOU COOK IT, IT COOKS MORE EVENLY, AND IS EASIER TO SERVE BECAUSE THERE ARE NO BONES TO GET IN THE WAY OF THE STUFFING.

SERVES FOUR

INGREDIENTS

2 fresh trout, each about 500g/1¼lb
75g/3oz/¾ cup mixed unsalted
  cashew nuts, pine nuts, almonds or
  hazelnuts
25ml/1½ tbsp olive oil, plus extra for
  drizzling
1 small onion, finely chopped
10ml/2 tsp grated fresh root ginger
175g/6oz/1½ cups cooked white long
  grain rice
4 tomatoes, peeled and very finely
  chopped
4 sun-dried tomatoes in oil, drained
  and chopped
30ml/2 tbsp chopped fresh tarragon
2 fresh tarragon sprigs
salt and freshly ground black pepper
dressed green leaves, to serve

1 Unless the fishmonger has already filleted the trout, use a sharp knife to do so, leaving as little flesh on the bones as possible. Check the cavity for any tiny bones remaining and remove these with tweezers.

2 Preheat the oven to 190°C/375°F/ Gas 5. Spread out the nuts in a shallow baking tin and bake for 3–4 minutes until golden, shaking the tin occasionally. Chop the nuts roughly.

3 Heat the oil in a small frying pan and fry the onion for 3–4 minutes until soft. Stir in the ginger, cook for 1 minute more, then spoon into a mixing bowl.

4 Stir in the rice, chopped tomatoes, sun-dried tomatoes, toasted nuts and tarragon. Season the stuffing well.

5 Place each of the two trout in turn on a large piece of oiled foil and spoon the stuffing into the cavity. Add a sprig of tarragon and a drizzle of olive oil.

6 Fold the foil over to enclose each trout completely, and put the parcels in a large roasting tin. Bake for 20–25 minutes until the fish is just tender. Cut the fish into thick slices. Serve with dressed green leaves.

SEVILLE CHICKEN

ORANGES AND ALMONDS ARE A FAVOURITE INGREDIENT IN SOUTHERN SPAIN, ESPECIALLY AROUND SEVILLE, WHERE THE ORANGE AND ALMOND TREES ARE A FAMILIAR AND WONDERFUL SIGHT.

SERVES FOUR

INGREDIENTS
 1 orange
 8 chicken thighs
 plain flour, seasoned with salt and
   pepper
 45ml/3 tbsp olive oil
 1 large Spanish onion, roughly
   chopped
 2 garlic cloves, crushed
 1 red pepper, seeded and sliced
 1 yellow pepper, seeded and sliced
 115g/4oz chorizo sausage, sliced
 50g/2oz/½ cup flaked almonds
 225g/8oz/generous 1 cup brown
   basmati rice
 about 600ml/1 pint/2½ cups chicken
   stock
 400g/14oz can chopped tomatoes
 175ml/6fl oz/¾ cup white wine
 generous pinch of dried thyme
 salt and freshly ground black pepper
 fresh thyme sprigs, to garnish

1 Pare a thin strip of peel from the orange and set it aside. Peel the orange, then cut it into segments, working over a bowl to catch the juice. Dust the chicken thighs with seasoned flour.

2 Heat the oil in a large frying pan and fry the chicken pieces on both sides until nicely brown. Transfer to a plate. Add the onion and garlic to the pan and fry for 4–5 minutes until the onion begins to brown. Add the red and yellow peppers and fry, stirring occasionally, until slightly softened.

3 Add the chorizo, stir-fry for a few minutes, then sprinkle over the almonds and rice. Cook, stirring, for 1–2 minutes.

4 Pour in the chicken stock, tomatoes and wine and add the orange strip and thyme. Season well. Bring to simmering point, stirring, then return the chicken pieces to the pan.

5 Cover tightly and cook over a very low heat for 1–1¼ hours until the rice and chicken are tender. Just before serving, add the orange segments and allow to cook briefly to heat through. Garnish with fresh thyme and serve.

COOK'S TIP
Cooking times for this dish will depend largely on the heat. If the rice seems to be drying out too quickly, add a little more stock or wine and reduce the heat. If, after 40 minutes or so, the rice is still barely cooked, increase the heat a little. Make sure the rice is kept below the liquid (the chicken can lie on the surface) and stir the rice occasionally if it seems to be cooking unevenly.

CELEBRATION PAELLA

THIS PAELLA IS A MARVELLOUS MIXTURE OF SOME OF THE FINEST SPANISH INGREDIENTS. CHICKEN AND RABBIT, SEAFOOD AND VEGETABLES ARE MIXED WITH RICE TO MAKE A COLOURFUL PARTY DISH.

SERVES SIX TO EIGHT

INGREDIENTS

    450g/1lb fresh mussels
    90ml/6 tbsp white wine
    150g/5oz French beans, cut into
      2.5cm/1in lengths
    115g/4oz/1 cup frozen broad beans
    6 small skinless, boneless chicken
      breasts, cut into large pieces
    30ml/2 tbsp plain flour, seasoned
      with salt and pepper
    about 90ml/6 tbsp olive oil
    6–8 large raw prawns, tailed and
      deveined, or 12 smaller raw prawns
    150g/5oz pork fillet, cut into bite-
      size pieces
    2 onions, chopped
    2–3 garlic cloves, crushed
    1 red pepper, seeded and sliced
    2 ripe tomatoes, peeled, seeded and
      chopped
    900ml/1½ pints/3¾ cups well-
      flavoured chicken stock
    good pinch of saffron, dissolved in
      30ml/2 tbsp hot water
    350g/12oz/1¾ cups Spanish rice or
      risotto rice
    225g/8oz chorizo sausage, thickly
      sliced
    115g/4oz/1 cup frozen peas
    6–8 stuffed green olives, thickly
      sliced

COOK'S TIP

Ideally, you need to use a paella pan for this dish and, strictly speaking, the paella shouldn't be stirred during cooking. You may find, though, that – because of the distribution of heat – the rice cooks in the centre but not around the outside. (This doesn't happen if paella is cooked traditionally – outdoors, on a large wood fire.) To make sure your paella cooks evenly, you could break the rule and stir occasionally, or cook the paella on the sole of a hot 190°C/375°F/ Gas 5 oven for about 15–18 minutes. The result should be practically identical, but in Spain this would be termed an *arroz* – a rice – rather than paella.

1 Scrub the mussels, discarding any that do not close when sharply tapped. Place in a large saucepan with the wine, bring to the boil, then cover the pan tightly and cook for 3–4 minutes until all the mussels have opened, shaking the pan occasionally. Drain, reserving the liquid and discarding any mussels that have not opened.

2 Briefly cook the green beans and broad beans in separate pans of boiling water for 2–3 minutes. Drain. As soon as the broad beans are cool enough to handle, pop them out of their skins.

3 Dust the chicken with the seasoned flour. Heat half the oil in a paella pan or deep frying pan and fry the chicken until evenly browned. Transfer to a plate. Fry the prawns briefly, adding more oil if needed, then use a slotted spoon to transfer them to a plate. Heat a further 30ml/2 tbsp of the oil in the pan and brown the pork evenly. Transfer to a separate plate.

4 Heat the remaining oil and fry the onions and garlic for 3–4 minutes until golden brown. Add the red pepper, cook for 2–3 minutes, then add the chopped tomatoes and cook until the mixture is fairly thick.

5 Stir in the chicken stock, the reserved mussel liquid and the saffron liquid. Season well with salt and pepper and bring to the boil. When the liquid is bubbling, throw in all the rice. Stir once, then add the chicken pieces, pork, prawns, beans, chorizo and peas. Cook over a moderately high heat for 12 minutes, then lower the heat and leave to cook for 8–10 minutes more, until all the liquid has been absorbed.

6 Add the mussels and olives and continue cooking for a further 3–4 minutes to heat through. Remove the pan from the heat, cover with a clean damp dish towel and leave to stand for 10 minutes before serving from the pan.

SEAFOOD PAELLA

THIS IS A GREAT DISH TO SERVE TO GUESTS ON A SPECIAL OCCASION BECAUSE IT LOOKS SPECTACULAR.
BRING THE PAELLA PAN TO THE TABLE AND LET EVERYONE HELP THEMSELVES.

SERVES FOUR

INGREDIENTS
60ml/4 tbsp olive oil
225g/8oz monkfish or cod fillets,
  skinned and cut into chunks
3 prepared baby squid, body cut into
  rings and tentacles chopped
1 red mullet, filleted, skinned and
  cut into chunks (optional)
1 onion, chopped
3 garlic cloves, finely chopped
1 red pepper, seeded and sliced
4 tomatoes, peeled and roughly
  chopped
225g/8oz/generous 1 cup risotto rice
450ml/¾ pint/scant 2 cups fish stock
150ml/¼ pint/⅔ cup white wine
4–5 saffron strands soaked in
  30ml/2 tbsp hot water
115g/4oz cooked, peeled prawns,
  thawed if frozen
75g/3oz/¾ cup frozen peas
8 fresh mussels, scrubbed
salt and freshly ground black pepper
4 Mediterranean prawns, in the shell,
  and fresh parsley sprigs, to garnish
lemon wedges, to serve

1 Heat half the oil in paella pan or a
large frying pan and add the monkfish
or cod, the squid and the red mullet, if
using. Stir-fry for 2 minutes, then tip
the contents of the pan into a bowl and
set aside.

2 Heat the remaining oil in the pan
and add the onion, garlic and pepper.
Fry for 6–7 minutes, stirring frequently,
until softened.

3 Stir in the tomatoes and fry for
2 minutes, then add the rice. Stir to
coat the grains with oil, then cook for
2–3 minutes. Pour over the fish stock,
wine and saffron water. Season with
salt and freshly ground black pepper,
and mix well.

COOK'S TIP
Before adding the mussels to the rice
mixture, check that they are all closed.
Any that are open should close when
sharply tapped; any that fail to do this
must be discarded.

4 Gently stir in the reserved cooked fish
(with all the juices), then the peeled
prawns and the peas. Push the mussels
into the rice. Cover and cook over a
gentle heat for about 30 minutes, or
until the stock has been absorbed but
the rice mixture is still relatively moist.
All the mussels should have opened;
discard any that remain closed.

5 Remove from the heat, and leave the
paella to stand, covered, for 5 minutes.
Arrange the whole prawns on top.
Sprinkle the paella with parsley and
serve with the lemon wedges.

CHICKEN PIRI-PIRI

THIS IS A CLASSIC PORTUGUESE DISH, BASED ON A HOT SAUCE MADE FROM ANGOLAN CHILLIES. IT IS POPULAR WHEREVER THERE ARE PORTUGUESE COMMUNITIES, AND IS OFTEN SERVED IN SOUTH AFRICA.

SERVES FOUR

INGREDIENTS
    4 chicken breast portions
    30–45ml/2–3 tbsp olive oil
    1 large onion, finely sliced
    2 carrots, cut into thin strips
    1 large parsnip or 2 small parsnips,
      cut into thin strips
    1 red pepper, seeded and sliced
    1 yellow pepper, seeded and sliced
    1 litre/1¾ pints/4 cups chicken stock
    3 tomatoes, peeled, seeded and
      chopped
    generous dash of piri-piri sauce
    15ml/1 tbsp tomato purée
    ½ cinnamon stick
    1 fresh thyme sprig, plus extra fresh
      thyme, to garnish
    1 bay leaf
    275g/10oz/1½ cups white long grain
      rice
    15ml/1 tbsp lime or lemon juice
    salt and freshly ground black pepper

3 Pour in the chicken stock, then add the tomatoes, piri-piri sauce, tomato purée and cinnamon stick. Stir in the thyme and bay leaf. Season to taste and bring to the boil. Using a ladle, spoon off 300ml/½ pint/1¼ cups of the liquid and set aside in a small pan.

4 Put the rice in the bottom of a casserole. Using a slotted spoon, scoop the vegetables out of the pan and spread them over the rice. Arrange the chicken pieces on top. Pour over the spicy chicken stock from the pan, cover the casserole tightly and cook in the oven for about 45 minutes, until both the rice and chicken are completely tender.

5 Meanwhile, heat the reserved chicken stock, adding a few more drops of piri-piri sauce and the lime or lemon juice.

6 To serve, spoon the piri-piri chicken and rice on to warmed serving plates. Serve the remaining sauce separately or poured over the chicken.

1 Preheat the oven to 180°C/350°F/ Gas 4. Rub the chicken skin with a little salt and pepper. Heat 30ml/2 tbsp of the oil in a large frying pan and brown the chicken portions on all sides. Transfer to a plate.

2 Add some more oil if necessary and fry the onion for 2–3 minutes until slightly softened. Add the carrots, parsnip and peppers, stir-fry for a few minutes and then cover and sweat for 4–5 minutes until quite soft.

SPANISH RICE SALAD

RICE AND A CHOICE OF CHOPPED SALAD VEGETABLES ARE SERVED IN A WELL-FLAVOURED DRESSING.

SERVES SIX

INGREDIENTS

275g/10oz/1½ cups white long grain rice
1 bunch spring onions, finely sliced
1 green pepper, seeded and finely diced
1 yellow pepper, seeded and finely diced
225g/8oz tomatoes, peeled, seeded and chopped
30ml/2 tbsp chopped fresh coriander
For the dressing
75ml/5 tbsp mixed sunflower and olive oil
15ml/1 tbsp rice vinegar
5ml/1 tsp Dijon mustard
salt and freshly ground black pepper

COOK'S TIP
Cooked garden peas, cooked diced carrot and drained, canned sweetcorn can be added to this versatile salad.

1 Cook the rice in plenty of boiling water for 10–12 minutes until tender but still *al dente*. Do not overcook. Drain, rinse under cold water and drain again. Leave to cool completely.

2 Place the rice in a large serving bowl. Add the spring onions, peppers, tomatoes and coriander.

3 Make the dressing. Mix all the ingredients in a jar with a tight-fitting lid and shake vigorously until well mixed. Stir 60–75ml/4–5 tbsp of the dressing into the rice and adjust the seasoning.

4 Cover and chill for about 1 hour before serving. Offer the remaining dressing separately.

PRAWN, MELON AND CHORIZO SALAD

THIS IS A RICH AND COLOURFUL SALAD. IT TASTES BEST WHEN MADE WITH FRESH PRAWNS.

SERVES FOUR

INGREDIENTS

450g/1lb/4 cups cooked white long grain rice
1 avocado
15ml/1 tbsp lemon juice
½ small melon, cut into wedges
15g/½oz/1 tbsp butter
½ garlic clove
115g/4oz raw prawns, peeled and deveined
25g/1oz chorizo sausage, finely sliced
flat leaf parsley, to garnish
For the dressing
75ml/5 tbsp natural yogurt
45ml/3 tbsp mayonnaise
15ml/1 tbsp olive oil
3 fresh tarragon sprigs
freshly ground black pepper

1 Put the cooked rice in a large salad bowl, breaking it up with your fingers if necessary.

2 Peel the avocado and cut it into chunks. Place in a mixing bowl and toss lightly with the lemon juice. Slice the melon off the rind, cut the flesh into chunks and add to the avocado.

3 Melt the butter in a small pan and fry the garlic for 30 seconds. Add the prawns and cook for about 3 minutes until evenly pink. Add the chorizo and stir-fry for 1 minute more, then tip the mixture into the bowl with the avocado and melon chunks. Mix lightly, then leave to cool.

4 Make the dressing by whizzing together all the ingredients in a food processor or blender. Stir half of the mixture into the rice and the remainder into the prawn and avocado mixture. Pile the salad on top of the rice. Chill for about 30 minutes before serving, garnished with flat leaf parsley sprigs.

PORTUGUESE RICE PUDDING

THIS IS POPULAR ALL OVER PORTUGAL AND IF YOU VISIT THAT COUNTRY YOU'RE LIKELY TO FIND IT ON MOST MENUS. TRADITIONALLY IT IS SERVED COLD, BUT IS ACTUALLY DELICIOUS WARM AS WELL.

2 Drain well, then return to the clean pan. Add the milk, lemon rind and butter. Bring to the boil over a moderately low heat, then cover, reduce the heat to the lowest setting and simmer for about 20 minutes or until the rice is thick and creamy.

3 Remove the pan from the heat and allow the rice to cool a little. Remove and discard the lemon rind, then stir in the sugar and the egg yolks. Mix well.

SERVES FOUR TO SIX

INGREDIENTS
 175g/6oz/scant 1 cup short grain
  pudding rice
 600ml/1 pint/2½ cups creamy milk
 2 or 3 strips pared lemon rind
 65g/2½oz/5 tbsp butter, in pieces
 115g/4oz/½ cup caster sugar
 4 egg yolks
 salt
 ground cinnamon, for dusting
 lemon wedges, to serve

1 Cook the rice in plenty of lightly salted water for about 5 minutes, by which time it will have lost its brittleness.

4 Divide among four to six serving bowls and dust with ground cinnamon. Serve cool, with lemon wedges for squeezing.

RICE CONDE SUNDAE

COOKING RICE PUDDING ON TOP OF THE HOB INSTEAD OF IN THE OVEN GIVES IT A LIGHT, CREAMY TEXTURE, ESPECIALLY IF YOU REMEMBER TO STIR IT FREQUENTLY. IT IS PARTICULARLY GOOD SERVED COLD WITH A TOPPING OF FRUIT AND TOASTED NUTS OR A TRICKLE OF HOT CHOCOLATE SAUCE.

SERVES FOUR

INGREDIENTS
  50g/2oz/generous ¼ cup short grain
    pudding rice
  5ml/1 tsp vanilla essence
  2.5ml/½ tsp ground cinnamon
  45ml/3 tbsp granulated sugar
  600ml/1 pint/2½ cups milk
For the toppings
  soft berry fruits such as
    strawberries, raspberries and
    cherries
  chocolate sauce and flaked toasted
    almonds (optional)

3 When the grains are soft, remove the pan from the heat. Allow the rice to cool, stirring it occasionally, then chill.

4 Before serving, stir the rice pudding and spoon it into four sundae dishes. Top with fresh fruits, and with chocolate sauce and almonds, if using.

VARIATION
For a special occasion, use single cream instead of milk, and glaze the fruit with a little melted redcurrant jelly. (Add a splash of port if you like.)

1 Mix the rice, vanilla essence, cinnamon and sugar in a saucepan. Pour in the milk. Bring to the boil, stirring constantly, then reduce the heat so that the mixture barely simmers.

2 Cook the rice over a low heat for 30–40 minutes, stirring frequently. Add extra milk to the rice if it begins to dry out.

Italy

In Italy, especially in the north, rice is more than just a useful accompaniment to meat and fish. Risottos are one of the few rice dishes that are entirely native to Europe, and, like the rice eaten in the east, the rice here is loved for its own merits. Other ingredients are added for flavour, but the star of the risotto is the rice itself.

FRIED RICE BALLS STUFFED WITH MOZZARELLA

THESE DEEP-FRIED BALLS OF RISOTTO GO BY THE NAME OF SUPPLI AL TELEFONO *IN THEIR NATIVE ITALY. STUFFED WITH MOZZARELLA CHEESE, THEY ARE VERY POPULAR SNACKS, WHICH IS HARDLY SURPRISING AS THEY ARE QUITE DELICIOUS.*

SERVES FOUR

INGREDIENTS
1 quantity Risotto with Parmesan
Cheese or Mushroom Risotto
3 eggs
breadcrumbs and plain flour, to coat
115g/4oz/⅔ cup mozzarella cheese,
cut into small cubes
oil, for deep-frying
dressed curly endive and cherry
tomatoes, to serve

1 Put the risotto in a bowl and allow it to cool completely. Beat two of the eggs, and stir them into the cold risotto until well mixed.

2 Use your hands to form the rice mixture into balls the size of a large egg. If the mixture is too moist to hold its shape well, stir in a few tablespoons of breadcrumbs. Poke a hole into the centre of each ball with your finger, then fill it with a few small cubes of mozzarella, and close the hole over again with the rice mixture.

3 Heat the oil for deep-frying until a small piece of bread sizzles as soon as it is dropped in.

4 Spread some flour on a plate. Beat the remaining egg in a shallow bowl. Sprinkle another plate with breadcrumbs. Roll the balls in the flour, then in the egg, and finally in the breadcrumbs.

5 Fry them a few at a time in the hot oil until golden and crisp. Drain on kitchen paper while the remaining balls are being fried. Serve hot, with a simple salad of dressed curly endive leaves and cherry tomatoes.

COOK'S TIP
These provide the perfect solution as to what to do with leftover risotto, as they are best made with a cold mixture, cooked the day before.

SPINACH AND RICE SOUP

USE VERY YOUNG SPINACH LEAVES TO PREPARE THIS LIGHT AND FRESH-TASTING SOUP.

SERVES FOUR

INGREDIENTS

675g/1½lb fresh spinach leaves,
  washed
45ml/3 tbsp extra virgin olive oil
1 small onion, finely chopped
2 garlic cloves, finely chopped
1 small fresh red chilli, seeded and
  finely chopped
225g/8oz/generous 1 cup risotto rice
1.2 litres/2 pints/5 cups vegetable
  stock
salt and freshly ground black pepper
shavings of pared Parmesan or
  Pecorino cheese, to serve

1 Place the spinach in a large pan with just the water that clings to its leaves after washing. Add a large pinch of salt. Heat gently until the spinach has wilted, then remove from the heat and drain, reserving any liquid.

2 Either chop the spinach finely using a large kitchen knife or place in a food processor and process the leaves to a fairly coarse purée.

COOK'S TIP
Buy Parmesan or Pecorino cheese in the piece from a reputable supplier, and it will be full of flavour and easy to grate or shave with a vegetable peeler.

3 Heat the oil in a large saucepan and gently cook the onion, garlic and chilli for 4–5 minutes until softened. Stir in the rice until well coated, then pour in the stock and reserved spinach liquid. Bring to the boil, lower the heat and simmer for 10 minutes.

4 Add the spinach, with salt and pepper to taste. Cook for 5–7 minutes, until the rice is tender. Check the seasoning. Serve in heated bowls, topped with the shavings of cheese.

TROUT AND PARMA HAM RISOTTO ROLLS

THIS MAKES A DELICIOUS AND ELEGANT MEAL. THE RISOTTO — MADE WITH PORCINI MUSHROOMS AND PRAWNS — IS A FINE MATCH FOR THE ROBUST FLAVOUR OF THE TROUT ROLLS.

SERVES FOUR

INGREDIENTS
4 trout fillets, skinned
4 slices Parma ham
caper berries, to garnish
For the risotto
30ml/2 tbsp olive oil
8 large raw prawns, peeled and
deveined
1 medium onion, chopped
225g/8oz/generous 1 cup risotto
rice
about 105ml/7 tbsp white wine
about 750ml/1¼ pints/3 cups
simmering fish or chicken stock
15g/½oz/2 tbsp dried porcini or
chanterelle mushrooms, soaked
for 10 minutes in warm water to
cover
salt and freshly ground black pepper

2 Add the chopped onion to the oil remaining in the pan and fry over a gentle heat for 3–4 minutes until soft. Add the rice and stir for 3–4 minutes until the grains are evenly coated in oil. Add 75ml/5 tbsp of the wine and then the stock, a little at a time, stirring over a gentle heat and allowing the rice to absorb the liquid before adding more.

4 Remove the pan from the heat and stir in the prawns. Preheat the oven to 190°C/375°F/Gas 5.

5 Take a trout fillet, place a spoonful of risotto at one end and roll up. Wrap each fillet in a slice of Parma ham and place in a greased ovenproof dish.

1 First make the risotto. Heat the oil in a heavy-based saucepan or deep frying pan and fry the prawns very briefly until flecked with pink. Lift out on a slotted spoon and transfer to a plate.

3 Drain the mushrooms, reserving the liquid, and cut the larger ones in half. Towards the end of cooking, stir the mushrooms into the risotto with 15ml/ 1 tbsp of the reserved mushroom liquid. If the rice is not yet *al dente*, add a little more stock or mushroom liquid and cook for 2–3 minutes more. Season to taste with salt and pepper.

COOK'S TIP
There are no hard and fast rules about which type of risotto to use for this dish. Almost any risotto recipe could be used, although a vegetable or seafood risotto would be particularly suitable.

6 Spoon any remaining risotto around the fish fillets and sprinkle over the rest of the wine. Cover loosely with foil and bake for 15–20 minutes until the fish is tender. Spoon the risotto on to a platter, top with the trout rolls and garnish with caper berries. Serve at once.

STUFFED CHICKEN ROLLS

THESE DELICIOUS CHICKEN ROLLS ARE SIMPLE TO MAKE, BUT SOPHISTICATED ENOUGH TO SERVE AT A DINNER PARTY, ESPECIALLY IF YOU ARRANGE SLICES ON A BED OF TAGLIATELLE TOSSED WITH FRIED WILD MUSHROOMS.

SERVES FOUR

INGREDIENTS
  25g/1oz/2 tbsp butter
  1 garlic clove, chopped
  150g/5oz/1¼ cups cooked white long
    grain rice
  45ml/3 tbsp ricotta cheese
  10ml/2 tsp chopped fresh flat leaf
    parsley
  5ml/1 tsp chopped fresh tarragon
  4 skinless, boneless chicken breasts
  3–4 slices Parma ham
  15ml/1 tbsp olive oil
  120ml/4fl oz/½ cup white wine
  salt and freshly ground black pepper
  fresh flat leaf parsley sprigs, to
    garnish
  cooked tagliatelle and sautéed blewit
    mushrooms, to serve (optional)

2 Add the rice, ricotta, parsley and tarragon and season with salt and pepper. Stir to mix.

3 Place each chicken breast in turn between two sheets of clear film and flatten by beating lightly, but firmly, with a rolling pin.

5 Place a spoonful of the rice stuffing at the wider end of each ham-topped breast. Roll up carefully and tie in place with cooking string or secure with a cocktail stick.

6 Heat the oil and the remaining butter in a frying pan and lightly fry the chicken rolls until browned on all sides. Place side by side in a shallow baking dish and pour over the white wine.

7 Cover the dish with greaseproof paper and cook in the oven for 30–35 minutes until the chicken is tender.

8 Cut the rolls into slices and serve on a bed of tagliatelle with sautéed blewit mushrooms and a generous grinding of black pepper, if you like. Garnish with sprigs of flat leaf parsley.

1 Preheat the oven to 180°C/350°F/ Gas 4. Melt about 10g/¼oz/2 tsp of the butter in a small pan and fry the garlic for a few seconds without browning. Spoon into a bowl.

4 Divide the slices of Parma ham between the chicken breasts, trimming the ham to fit, if necessary.

COOK'S TIP
Risotto rice could be used in place of white long grain in this dish. Risotto rice has a different consistency to long grain, and will make a much denser stuffing for the chicken rolls.

PUMPKIN AND PISTACHIO RISOTTO

VEGETARIANS TIRED OF THE STANDARD DINNER PARTY FARE WILL LOVE THIS ELEGANT COMBINATION OF CREAMY, GOLDEN RICE AND ORANGE PUMPKIN, AND SO WILL EVERYONE ELSE. IT WOULD LOOK PARTICULARLY IMPRESSIVE SERVED IN THE HOLLOWED-OUT PUMPKIN SHELL.

SERVES FOUR

INGREDIENTS

1.2 litres/2 pints/5 cups vegetable
  stock or water
generous pinch of saffron strands
30ml/2 tbsp olive oil
1 onion, chopped
2 garlic cloves, crushed
900g/2lb pumpkin, peeled, seeded
  and cut into 2cm/¾in cubes (about
  7 cups)
400g/14oz/2 cups risotto rice
200ml/7fl oz/scant 1 cup dry white
  wine
30ml/2 tbsp freshly grated Parmesan
  cheese
50g/2oz/½ cup pistachios, coarsely
  chopped
45ml/3 tbsp chopped fresh marjoram
  or oregano, plus leaves to garnish
salt, freshly grated nutmeg and
  freshly ground black pepper

1 Bring the stock or water to the boil and reduce to a low simmer. Ladle a little of it into a small bowl. Add the saffron strands and leave to infuse.

2 Heat the oil in a large, heavy-based saucepan or deep frying pan. Add the onion and garlic and cook gently for about 5 minutes until softened. Add the pumpkin and rice and stir to coat everything in oil. Cook for a few more minutes until the rice looks transparent.

3 Pour in the wine and allow it to bubble hard. When it has been absorbed, add a quarter of the hot stock or water and the saffron liquid. Stir until all the liquid has been absorbed. Gradually add the remaining stock or water, a little at a time, allowing the rice to absorb the liquid before adding more, and stirring constantly. After 20–30 minutes the rice should be golden yellow, creamy and *al dente*.

4 Stir in the Parmesan cheese, cover the pan and leave the risotto to stand for 5 minutes. To finish, stir in the pistachios and marjoram or oregano. Season to taste with a little salt, nutmeg and pepper, scatter over a few marjoram or oregano leaves and serve.

RISOTTO WITH PARMESAN

THIS TRADITIONAL RISOTTO IS SIMPLY FLAVOURED WITH GRATED PARMESAN CHEESE AND GOLDEN, FRIED CHOPPED ONION.

SERVES THREE TO FOUR

INGREDIENTS

1 litre/1¾ pints/4 cups beef,
  chicken or vegetable stock
65g/2½oz/5 tbsp butter
1 small onion, finely chopped
275g/10oz/1½ cups risotto rice
120ml/4fl oz/½ cup dry white wine
75g/3oz/1 cup freshly grated Parmesan
  cheese, plus extra to garnish
basil leaves, to garnish
salt and freshly ground black pepper

1 Heat the stock in a saucepan, and leave to simmer until needed.

2 Melt two-thirds of the butter in a large heavy-based saucepan or deep frying pan. Stir in the onion, and cook gently until soft and golden.

3 Add the rice and stir to coat the grains with butter. After 1–2 minutes, pour in the white wine. Raise the heat slightly, and cook until the wine evaporates. Add one small ladleful of the hot stock. Cook until the stock has been absorbed, stirring constantly.

4 Gradually add the remaining stock, a little at a time, allowing the rice to absorb the liquid before adding more, and stirring constantly. After 20–30 minutes the rice should be creamy and *al dente*. Season to taste.

5 Remove the pan from the heat. Stir in the remaining butter and the Parmesan cheese. Taste again for seasoning. Allow the risotto to rest for 3–4 minutes before serving, garnished with basil leaves and shavings of Parmesan, if you like.

COOK'S TIP

If you run out of stock when cooking the risotto, use hot water, but do not worry if the rice is done before you have used up all the stock.

RISOTTO WITH RICOTTA AND BASIL

THIS IS A WELL-FLAVOURED RISOTTO, WHICH BENEFITS FROM THE DISTINCT PUNGENCY OF BASIL, MELLOWED WITH SMOOTH RICOTTA.

SERVES THREE TO FOUR

INGREDIENTS

45ml/3 tbsp olive oil
1 onion, finely chopped
275g/10oz/1½ cups risotto rice
1 litre/1¾ pints/4 cups hot chicken
  or vegetable stock
175g/6oz/¾ cup ricotta cheese
50g/2oz/generous 1 cup fresh basil
  leaves, finely chopped, plus extra
  to garnish
75g/3oz/1 cup freshly grated
  Parmesan cheese
salt and freshly ground black pepper

1 Heat the oil in a large saucepan or flameproof casserole and fry the onion over a gentle heat until soft.

2 Tip in the rice. Cook for a few minutes, stirring, until the rice is coated with oil and is slightly translucent.

3 Pour in about a quarter of the stock. Cook, stirring, until all the stock has been absorbed, then add another ladleful. Continue in this manner, adding more stock when the previous ladleful has been absorbed, until the risotto has been cooking for about 20 minutes and the rice is just tender.

4 Spoon the ricotta into a bowl and break it up a little with a fork. Stir into the risotto along with the basil and Parmesan. Taste and adjust the seasoning, then cover and let stand for 2–3 minutes before serving, garnished with basil leaves.

RISOTTO FRITTATA

*HALF OMELETTE, HALF RISOTTO, THIS MAKES A DELIGHTFUL LIGHT LUNCH OR SUPPER DISH.
IF POSSIBLE, COOK EACH FRITTATA SEPARATELY, AND PREFERABLY IN A SMALL, CAST IRON PAN,
SO THAT THE EGGS COOK QUICKLY UNDERNEATH BUT STAY MOIST ON TOP.*

SERVES FOUR

INGREDIENTS

30–45ml/2–3 tbsp olive oil
1 small onion, finely chopped
1 garlic clove, crushed
1 large red pepper, seeded and cut
  into thin strips
150g/5oz/¾ cup risotto rice
400–475ml/14–16fl oz/1⅔–2 cups
  simmering chicken stock
25–40g/1–1½oz/2–3 tbsp butter
175g/6oz/2½ cups button
  mushrooms, finely sliced
60ml/4 tbsp freshly grated Parmesan
  cheese
6–8 eggs
salt and freshly ground black pepper

1 Heat 15ml/1 tbsp oil in a large frying pan and fry the onion and garlic over a gentle heat for 2–3 minutes until the onion begins to soften but does not brown. Add the pepper and cook, stirring, for 4–5 minutes, until soft.

2 Stir in the rice and cook gently for 2–3 minutes, stirring all the time, until the grains are evenly coated with oil.

3 Add a quarter of the chicken stock and season. Stir over a low heat until the stock has been absorbed. Continue to add more stock, a little at a time, allowing the rice to absorb the liquid before adding more. Continue cooking in this way until the rice is *al dente*.

4 In a separate small pan, heat a little of the remaining oil and some butter and quickly fry the mushrooms until golden. Transfer to a plate.

5 When the rice is tender, remove from the heat and stir in the mushrooms and Parmesan cheese.

6 Beat together the eggs with 40ml/ 8 tsp cold water and season well. Heat the remaining oil and butter in an omelette pan and add the risotto mixture. Spread the mixture out in the pan, then immediately add the beaten egg, tilting the pan so that the omelette cooks evenly. Fry over a moderately high heat for 1–2 minutes, then transfer to a warmed plate and serve.

COOK'S TIP
This will make a more substantial dish for two, using five or six eggs. If preferred, the frittata could be cooked as individual portions.

PORCINI AND PARMESAN RISOTTO

THE SUCCESS OF A GOOD RISOTTO DEPENDS ON BOTH THE QUALITY OF THE RICE USED AND THE TECHNIQUE. ADD THE STOCK GRADUALLY AND STIR CONSTANTLY TO COAX A CREAMY TEXTURE FROM THE STARCH GRAINS. THIS VARIATION ON THE CLASSIC RISOTTO ALLA MILANESE INCLUDES SAFFRON, PORCINI MUSHROOMS AND PARMESAN.

SERVES FOUR

INGREDIENTS
15g/½oz/2 tbsp dried porcini
    mushrooms
150ml/¼ pint/⅔ cup warm water
1 litre/1¾ pints/4 cups vegetable stock
generous pinch of saffron strands
30ml/2 tbsp olive oil
1 onion, finely chopped
1 garlic clove, crushed
350g/12oz/1¼ cups Arborio or
    Carnaroli rice
150ml/¼ pint/⅔ cup dry white wine
25g/1oz/2 tbsp butter
50g/2oz/⅔ cup freshly grated
    Parmesan cheese
salt and freshly ground black pepper
pink and yellow oyster mushrooms,
    to serve (optional)

1 Put the dried porcini in a bowl and pour over the warm water. Leave the mushrooms to soak for 20 minutes, then lift out with a slotted spoon. Filter the soaking water through a layer of kitchen paper in a sieve, then place it in a saucepan with the stock. Bring the liquid to a gentle simmer.

2 Spoon about 45ml/3 tbsp of the hot stock into a cup and stir in the saffron strands. Set aside. Finely chop the porcini. Heat the oil in a separate pan and lightly sauté the onion, garlic and mushrooms for 5 minutes. Gradually add the rice, stirring to coat the grains in oil. Cook for 2 minutes, stirring constantly. Season with salt and pepper.

3 Pour in the white wine. Cook, stirring, until it has been absorbed, then ladle in a quarter of the stock. Cook, stirring, until the stock has been absorbed. Gradually add the remaining stock, a little at a time, allowing the rice to absorb the liquid before adding more, and stirring constantly.

4 After about 20 minutes, when all the stock has been absorbed and the rice is cooked but still has a "bite", stir in the butter, saffron water (with the strands) and half the Parmesan. Serve, sprinkled with the remaining Parmesan. Garnish with pink and yellow oyster mushrooms, if you like.

VARIATIONS
There are endless variations on this delectable dish. The proportion of stock to rice, onions, garlic and butter must remain constant but you can ring the changes with the flavourings and cheese.

RISOTTO WITH FOUR VEGETABLES

THIS IS ONE OF THE PRETTIEST RISOTTOS, ESPECIALLY WHEN MADE WITH ACORN SQUASH.

SERVES THREE TO FOUR

INGREDIENTS
115g/4oz/1 cup shelled fresh peas
115g/4oz/1 cup green beans, cut
  into short lengths
30ml/2 tbsp olive oil
75g/3oz/6 tbsp butter
1 acorn squash, skin and seeds
  removed, flesh cut into matchsticks
1 onion, finely chopped
275g/10oz/1½ cups risotto rice
120ml/4fl oz/½ cup Italian dry white
  vermouth
1 litre/1¾ pints/4 cups boiling
  chicken stock
75g/3oz/1 cup freshly grated
  Parmesan cheese
salt and freshly ground black pepper

1 Bring a saucepan of lightly salted water to the boil, add the peas and beans and cook for 2–3 minutes, until the vegetables are just tender. Drain, refresh under cold running water, drain again and set aside.

2 Heat the oil with 25g/1oz/2 tbsp of the butter in a medium saucepan until foaming. Add the squash and cook gently for 2–3 minutes or until just softened. Remove with a slotted spoon and set aside. Add the onion to the pan and cook gently for about 3 minutes, stirring frequently, until softened.

3 Stir in the rice until the grains start to swell and burst, then add the vermouth. Stir until the vermouth stops sizzling and most of it has been absorbed by the rice, then add a few ladlefuls of the stock, with salt and pepper to taste. Stir over a low heat until the stock has been absorbed.

4 Gradually add the remaining stock, a few ladlefuls at a time, allowing the rice to absorb the liquid before adding more, and stirring all the time.

VARIATIONS
Shelled broad beans can be used instead of the peas, and asparagus tips instead of the green beans. Use courgettes if acorn squash is not available.

5 After about 20 minutes, when all the stock has been absorbed and the rice is cooked and creamy but still has a "bite", gently stir in the vegetables, the remaining butter and about half the grated Parmesan. Heat through, then taste for seasoning and serve with the remaining grated Parmesan served separately.

GREEN RISOTTO

YOU COULD USE SPINACH-FLAVOURED RISOTTO RICE TO GIVE THIS STUNNING DISH EVEN GREATER DRAMATIC IMPACT. HOWEVER, WHITE RISOTTO RICE MAKES A PRETTY CONTRAST TO THE SPINACH.

SERVES THREE TO FOUR

INGREDIENTS
  30ml/2 tbsp olive oil
  1 onion, finely chopped
  275g/10oz/1½ cups risotto rice
  1 litre/1¾ pints/4 cups hot chicken
    stock
  75ml/5 tbsp white wine
  about 400g/14oz tender baby
    spinach leaves
  15ml/1 tbsp chopped fresh basil
  5ml/1 tsp chopped fresh mint
  60ml/4 tbsp freshly grated Parmesan
    cheese
  salt and freshly ground black pepper
  knob of butter or more grated
    Parmesan cheese, to serve

1 Heat the oil and fry the onion for 3–4 minutes until soft. Add the rice and stir to coat each grain. Pour in the stock and wine, a little at a time, stirring constantly over a gentle heat until all the liquid has been absorbed.

2 Stir in the spinach leaves and herbs with the last of the liquid, and add a little seasoning. Continue cooking until the rice is tender and the spinach leaves have wilted. Stir in the Parmesan cheese, with a knob of butter, if you like, or serve with extra Parmesan.

COOK'S TIP
The secret with risotto is to add the hot liquid gradually, about a ladleful at a time, and to stir constantly until the liquid has been absorbed before adding more.

RISOTTO WITH BACON, BABY COURGETTES AND PEPPERS

THIS WOULD MAKE THE PERFECT DISH TO COME HOME TO AFTER AN EARLY SHOW AT THE THEATRE. CREAMY RISOTTO TOPPED WITH VEGETABLES AND CRISP BACON IS IRRESISTIBLE AND EASY TO MAKE.

SERVES FOUR

INGREDIENTS
  30ml/2 tbsp olive oil
  115g/4oz rindless streaky bacon
    rashers, cut into thick strips
  350g/12oz/1¾ cups risotto rice
  1.2 litres/2 pints/5 cups hot
    vegetable or chicken stock
  30ml/2 tbsp single cream
  45ml/3 tbsp dry sherry
  50g/2oz/⅔ cup freshly grated
    Parmesan cheese
  50g/2oz/⅔ cup chopped fresh parsley
  salt and freshly ground black pepper
For the vegetables
  1 small red pepper, seeded
  1 small green pepper, seeded
  25g/1oz/2 tbsp butter
  75g/3oz horse mushrooms, sliced
  225g/8oz baby courgettes, halved
  1 onion, halved and sliced
  1 garlic clove, crushed

1 Heat half the oil in a frying pan. Add the bacon and heat gently until the fat runs. Increase the heat and fry until crisp, then drain on kitchen paper and set aside.

2 Heat the remaining oil in a heavy-based saucepan. Add the rice, stir to coat the grains, then ladle in a little of the hot stock. Stir until it has been absorbed. Gradually add the rest of the stock, stirring constantly.

3 Cut the peppers into chunks. Melt the butter in a separate pan and fry the peppers, mushrooms, courgettes, onion and garlic until the onion is just tender. Season well, then stir in the bacon.

4 When all the stock has been absorbed by the rice, stir in the cream, sherry, Parmesan, parsley and seasoning. Spoon the risotto on to individual plates and top each portion with fried vegetables and bacon. Serve immediately.

RISOTTO WITH ASPARAGUS

FRESH FARM ASPARAGUS ONLY HAS A SHORT SEASON, SO IT IS SENSIBLE TO MAKE THE MOST OF IT. THIS ELEGANT RISOTTO IS ABSOLUTELY DELICIOUS.

SERVES THREE TO FOUR

INGREDIENTS

225g/8oz fresh asparagus
750ml/1¼ pints/3 cups vegetable or
    chicken stock
65g/2½oz/5 tbsp butter
1 small onion, finely chopped
275g/10oz/1½ cups risotto rice, such
    as Arborio or Carnaroli
75g/3oz/1 cup freshly grated
    Parmesan cheese
salt and freshly ground black pepper

1 Bring a pan of water to the boil. Cut off any woody pieces on the ends of the asparagus stalks, peel the lower portions, then cook in the water for 5 minutes. Drain the asparagus, reserving the cooking water, refresh under cold water and drain again. Cut the asparagus diagonally into 4cm/1½in pieces. Keep the tip and next-highest sections separate from the stalks.

2 Place the stock in a saucepan and add 450ml/¾ pint/scant 2 cups of the asparagus cooking water. Heat to simmering point, and keep it hot.

3 Melt two-thirds of the butter in a large, heavy-based saucepan or deep frying pan. Add the onion and fry until it is soft and golden. Stir in all the asparagus except the top two sections. Cook for 2–3 minutes. Add the rice and cook for 1–2 minutes, mixing well to coat it with butter. Stir in a ladleful of the hot liquid. Using a wooden spoon, stir until the stock has been absorbed.

4 Gradually add the remaining stock, a little at a time, allowing the rice to absorb the liquid before adding more, and stirring all the time.

5 After 10 minutes, add the remaining asparagus sections. Continue to cook as before, for about 15 minutes, until the rice is *al dente* and the risotto is creamy. Off the heat, stir in the remaining butter and the Parmesan. Grind in a little black pepper, and taste again for salt. Serve at once.

RISOTTO WITH FOUR CHEESES

THIS IS A VERY RICH DISH. SERVE IT FOR A SPECIAL DINNER-PARTY FIRST COURSE, WITH A LIGHT, DRY SPARKLING WHITE WINE.

SERVES FOUR

INGREDIENTS

40g/1½oz/3 tbsp butter
1 small onion, finely chopped
1.2 litres/2 pints/5 cups chicken
  stock, preferably home-made
350g/12oz/1¾ cups risotto rice
200ml/7fl oz/scant 1cup dry white
  wine
50g/2oz/½ cup grated Gruyère cheese
50g/2oz/½ cup diced taleggio cheese
50g/2oz/½ cup diced Gorgonzola
  cheese
50g/2oz/⅔ cup freshly grated
  Parmesan cheese
salt and freshly ground black pepper
chopped fresh flat leaf parsley, to
  garnish

1 Melt the butter in a large, heavy-based saucepan or deep frying pan and fry the onion over a gentle heat for about 4–5 minutes, stirring frequently, until softened and lightly browned. Pour the stock into another pan and heat it to simmering point.

2 Add the rice to the onion mixture, stir until the grains start to swell and burst, then add the wine. Stir until it stops sizzling and most of it has been absorbed by the rice, then pour in a little of the hot stock. Add salt and pepper to taste. Stir over a low heat until the stock has been absorbed.

3 Gradually add the remaining stock, a little at a time, allowing the rice to absorb the liquid before adding more, and stirring constantly. After 20–25 minutes the rice will be *al dente* and the risotto creamy.

4 Turn off the heat under the pan, then add the Gruyère, taleggio, Gorgonzola and 30ml/2 tbsp of the Parmesan cheese. Stir gently until the cheeses have melted, then taste for seasoning. Spoon into a serving bowl and garnish with parsley. Serve the remaining Parmesan separately.

TIMBALLO OF RICE WITH PEAS

THE TIMBALLO GETS ITS NAME FROM THE FACT THAT IT LOOKS LIKE AN INVERTED KETTLEDRUM (TIMBALLO OR TIMPANO). IT IS MADE LIKE A RISOTTO, BUT IS GIVEN A FINAL BAKING IN THE OVEN.

SERVES THREE TO FOUR

INGREDIENTS
75g/3oz/6 tbsp butter
30ml/2 tbsp olive oil
1 small onion, finely chopped
50g/2oz ham, cut into small dice
45ml/3 tbsp finely chopped fresh
  parsley, plus a few sprigs to garnish
2 garlic cloves, very finely chopped
225g/8oz/2 cups shelled peas,
  thawed if frozen
60ml/4 tbsp water
1.3 litres/2¼ pints/5½ cups chicken
  or vegetable stock
350g/12oz/1¾ cups risotto rice,
  preferably Arborio
75g/3oz/1 cup freshly grated
  Parmesan cheese
175g/6oz fontina cheese, very
  thinly sliced

1 Preheat the oven to 180°C/350°F/ Gas 4. Heat half the butter and all the oil in a large, heavy-based pan. Cook the onion until soft, then add the ham and stir over a medium heat for 3–4 minutes. Stir in the parsley and garlic. Cook for 2 minutes. Add the peas, then season and add the water.

2 Cover the pan, and cook for 8 minutes for fresh peas, or 4 minutes for frozen peas. Remove the lid and cook until the liquid has evaporated. Spoon half the mixture into a dish. Heat the stock and keep it simmering. Butter a flat-based baking dish and line with non-stick baking paper.

3 Stir the rice into the pea mixture in the pan. Heat through, then add a ladleful of stock. Cook until this has been absorbed, stirring constantly. Add the remaining stock in the same way, adding more liquid only when the previous quantity has been absorbed.

4 After about 20 minutes, when the rice is just tender, remove it from the heat. Season and mix in most of the remaining butter and half the Parmesan.

5 Assemble the timballo. Sprinkle the bottom of the dish with Parmesan, and spoon in half the rice. Add a layer of fontina slices and spoon over the reserved pea and ham mixture. Smooth level, and sprinkle with Parmesan.

6 Cover with the remaining fontina slices and end with the remaining rice. Sprinkle with the last of the Parmesan, and dot with butter. Bake for 10–15 minutes. Remove from the oven, and allow to stand for 10 minutes.

7 To unmould, slip a knife around the timballo between the rice and the dish. Place a serving plate upside down on top. Wearing oven gloves, turn over dish and plate together. Peel off the lining paper. Serve by cutting into wedges.

LEMON AND HERB RISOTTO CAKE

THIS UNUSUAL DISH CAN BE SERVED AS A MAIN COURSE WITH SALAD, OR AS A SATISFYING SIDE DISH. IT IS ALSO GOOD SERVED COLD, AND PACKS WELL FOR PICNICS.

SERVES FOUR

INGREDIENTS
1 small leek, finely sliced
600ml/1 pint/2½ cups chicken stock
225g/8oz/generous 1 cup risotto rice
finely grated rind of 1 lemon
30ml/2 tbsp snipped fresh chives
30ml/2 tbsp chopped fresh parsley
75g/3oz/¾ cup grated mozzarella
  cheese
salt and freshly ground black pepper

1 Preheat the oven to 200°C/400°F/ Gas 6. Lightly oil a 21cm/8½in round loose-based cake tin.

2 Put the leek in a large pan with 45ml/3 tbsp of the stock. Cook over a medium heat, stirring occasionally, until softened. Stir in the rice, then add the remaining stock.

3 Bring to the boil. Lower the heat, cover the pan and simmer gently, stirring occasionally, for about 20 minutes, or until all the liquid has been absorbed.

4 Stir in the lemon rind, herbs, cheese, and seasoning. Spoon the mixture into the tin, cover with foil and bake for 30–35 minutes or until lightly browned. Leave to stand for 5 minutes, then turn out. Serve hot or cold, in slices.

COOK'S TIP
This risotto uses less liquid than normal and therefore has a drier consistency.

RISOTTO WITH PRAWNS

THIS PRAWN RISOTTO IS GIVEN A SOFT PINK COLOUR BY THE ADDITION OF A LITTLE TOMATO PURÉE.

SERVES THREE TO FOUR

INGREDIENTS

350g/12oz large raw prawns, in
   the shells
1 litres/1¾ pints/4 cups water
1 bay leaf
1–2 fresh parsley sprigs
5ml/1 tsp whole peppercorns
2 garlic cloves, peeled and left whole
65g/2½oz/5 tbsp butter
2 shallots, finely chopped
275g/10oz/1½ cups risotto rice
15ml/1 tbsp tomato purée softened
   in 120ml/4fl oz/½ cup dry white
   wine
salt and freshly ground black pepper

1 Put the prawns in a large saucepan and add the water, herbs, peppercorns and garlic. Bring to the boil over a medium heat. As soon as the prawns turn pink, lift them out, peel them and return the shells to the saucepan. Boil the stock with the shells for 10 minutes more, then strain. Return the stock to the clean pan, and simmer gently until needed.

2 Slice the prawns in half lengthways, removing the dark vein along the back. Set four halves aside for the garnish, and roughly chop the rest.

3 Heat two-thirds of the butter in a flameproof casserole and fry the shallots until golden. Add the rice, mixing well to coat it with butter. Pour in the tomato purée and wine and cook until it has been absorbed. Add the simmering stock, a ladleful at a time, allowing it to be absorbed before adding more.

4 When all the stock has been absorbed and the rice is creamy, stir in the chopped prawns, the remaining butter and seasoning. Cover and let the risotto rest for 3–4 minutes. Spoon into a bowl, garnish with the reserved prawns and serve.

MUSHROOM RISOTTO

*MUSHROOM RISOTTO IS EASY TO MAKE AND APPEALS TO ALMOST EVERYONE. WILD MUSHROOMS WILL
GIVE A MORE INTENSE FLAVOUR, BUT YOU CAN USE WHATEVER MUSHROOMS ARE AVAILABLE.*

SERVES THREE TO FOUR

INGREDIENTS

25g/1oz/⅓ cup dried wild
   mushrooms, preferably porcini
350ml/12fl oz/1½ cups warm water
900ml/1½ pints/3¾ cups beef or
   chicken stock
175g/6oz/1½–2 cups button
   mushrooms, sliced
juice of ½ lemon
75g/3oz/6 tbsp butter
30ml/2 tbsp finely chopped fresh
   parsley
30ml/2 tbsp olive oil
1 small onion, finely chopped
275g/10oz/1½ cups risotto rice
120ml/4fl oz/½ cup dry white wine
45ml/3 tbsp freshly grated Parmesan
   cheese
salt and freshly ground black pepper
fresh herbs, to garnish

1 Put the dried mushrooms in a bowl with the warm water. Soak them for at least 40 minutes, then lift them out and rinse them thoroughly. Filter the soaking water through a strainer lined with kitchen paper, and pour into a saucepan. Add the stock to the pan and bring to simmering point.

2 Toss the button mushrooms with the lemon juice in a bowl. Melt a third of the butter in a saucepan and fry the button mushrooms until they give up their juices and begin to brown. Stir in the parsley, cook for 30 seconds more, then transfer to a bowl.

3 Heat the olive oil and half the remaining butter in the saucepan and fry the onion until soft. Add the rice and stir constantly, so that the grains are evenly coated in the oil.

4 Stir in all of the mushrooms, add the wine, and cook over a medium heat until it has been absorbed. Add the stock, a ladleful at a time, making sure each is absorbed before adding more. When all the liquid has been absorbed, remove the pan from the heat, stir in the remaining butter, the Parmesan and seasoning. Cover the pan and allow to rest for 3–4 minutes before serving.

RISOTTO ALLA MILANESE

*THIS CLASSIC RISOTTO IS ALWAYS SERVED WITH THE HEARTY BEEF STEW, OSSO BUCO, BUT ALSO MAKES
A DELICIOUS FIRST COURSE OR LIGHT SUPPER DISH IN ITS OWN RIGHT.*

SERVES THREE TO FOUR

INGREDIENTS
about 1.2 litres/2 pints/5 cups beef
    or chicken stock
good pinch of saffron strands
75g/3oz/6 tbsp butter
1 onion, finely chopped
275g/10oz/1½ cups risotto rice
75g/3oz/1 cup freshly grated
    Parmesan cheese
salt and freshly ground black pepper

1 Bring the stock to the boil, then
reduce to a low simmer. Ladle a little
stock into a small bowl. Add the saffron
strands and leave to infuse.

2 Melt 50g/2oz/4 tbsp of the butter
in a large saucepan until foaming. Add
the onion and cook gently for about
3 minutes, stirring frequently, until
softened but not browned.

3 Add the rice. Stir until the grains
start to swell and burst, then add a few
ladlefuls of the stock, with the saffron
liquid and salt and pepper to taste. Stir
over a low heat until the stock has been
absorbed. Add the remaining stock, a
few ladlefuls at a time, allowing the rice
to absorb all the liquid before adding
more, and stirring constantly. After
20–25 minutes, the rice should be just
tender and the risotto golden yellow,
moist and creamy.

4 Gently stir in about two-thirds of the
grated Parmesan and the remaining
butter. Heat through until the butter
has melted, then taste for seasoning.
Transfer the risotto to a warmed serving
bowl or platter and serve hot, with the
remaining grated Parmesan served
separately.

RISI Ḙ BISI

A CLASSIC PEA AND HAM RISOTTO FROM THE VENETO. ALTHOUGH THIS IS TRADITIONALLY SERVED AS A STARTER IN ITALY, IT ALSO MAKES AN EXCELLENT SUPPER DISH WITH HOT, CRUSTY BREAD.

SERVES FOUR

INGREDIENTS
75g/3oz/6 tbsp butter
1 small onion, finely chopped
about 1 litre/1¾ pints/4 cups
  simmering chicken stock
275g/10oz/1½ cups risotto rice
150ml/¼ pint/⅔ cup dry white wine
225g/8oz/2 cups frozen petits pois,
  thawed
115g/4oz cooked ham, diced
salt and freshly ground black pepper
50g/2oz/⅔ cup freshly grated
  Parmesan cheese, to serve

1 Melt 50g/2oz/4 tbsp of the butter in a saucepan until foaming. Add the onion and cook gently for about 3 minutes, stirring frequently, until softened. Have the hot stock ready in an adjacent pan.

2 Add the rice to the onion mixture. Stir until the grains start to swell, then pour in the wine. Stir until it stops sizzling and most of it has been absorbed, then pour in a little hot stock, with salt and pepper to taste. Stir continuously, over a low heat, until all the stock has been absorbed.

3 Add the remaining stock, a little at a time, allowing the rice to absorb all the liquid before adding more, and stirring constantly. Add the peas after about 20 minutes. After 25–30 minutes, the rice should be *al dente* and the risotto moist and creamy.

4 Gently stir in the diced cooked ham and the remaining butter. Heat through until the butter has melted, then taste for seasoning. Transfer to a warmed serving bowl. Grate or shave a little Parmesan over the top and serve the rest separately.

COOK'S TIP
Always use fresh Parmesan cheese, grated off a block. It has a far superior flavour to the ready-grated Parmesan.

RISOTTO-STUFFED AUBERGINES
WITH SPICY TOMATO SAUCE

AUBERGINES ARE A CHALLENGE TO THE CREATIVE COOK AND ALLOW FOR SOME UNUSUAL RECIPE IDEAS.
HERE, THEY ARE FILLED WITH A RICE STUFFING AND BAKED WITH A CHEESE AND PINE NUT TOPPING.

SERVES FOUR

INGREDIENTS
   4 small aubergines
   105ml/7 tbsp olive oil
   1 small onion, chopped
   175g/6oz/scant 1 cup risotto rice
   750ml/1¼ pints/3 cups hot vegetable
      stock
   15ml/1 tbsp white wine vinegar
   25g/1oz/⅓ cup freshly grated
      Parmesan cheese
   15g/½oz/2 tbsp pine nuts
For the tomato sauce
   300ml/½ pint/1¼ cups thick passata
      or puréed tomatoes
   5ml/1 tsp mild curry paste
   pinch of salt

1 Preheat the oven to 200°C/400°F/
Gas 6. Cut the aubergines in half
lengthways, and remove the flesh with
a small knife. Brush the shells with
30ml/2 tbsp of the oil and bake on a
baking sheet, supported by crumpled
foil, for 6–8 minutes.

2 Chop the aubergine flesh. Heat the
remaining oil in a medium pan. Add
the aubergine flesh and the onion, and
cook over a gentle heat for 3–4 minutes
until soft. Add the rice and stock, and
leave to simmer, uncovered, for about
15 minutes. Add the vinegar.

COOK'S TIP
If the aubergine shells do not stand
level, cut a thin slice from the bottom.

3 Increase the oven temperature to
230°C/450°F/Gas 8. Spoon the rice
mixture into the aubergine skins, top
with the cheese and pine nuts, return
to the oven and brown for 5 minutes.

4 To make the sauce, mix the passata
or puréed tomatoes with the curry paste
in a small pan. Heat through and add
salt to taste. Spoon the sauce on to four
individual serving plates and arrange
two aubergine halves on each one.

LEEK, MUSHROOM AND LEMON RISOTTO

*LEEKS AND LEMON GO TOGETHER BEAUTIFULLY IN THIS LIGHT RISOTTO, WHILE MUSHROOMS ADD
TEXTURE AND EXTRA FLAVOUR.*

SERVES FOUR

INGREDIENTS

225g/8oz trimmed leeks
225g/8oz/2–3 cups brown cap
  mushrooms
30ml/2 tbsp olive oil
3 garlic cloves, crushed
75g/3oz/6 tbsp butter
1 large onion, roughly chopped
350g/12oz/1¾ cups risotto rice
1.2 litres/2 pints/5 cups simmering
  vegetable stock
grated rind of 1 lemon
45ml/3 tbsp lemon juice
50g/2oz/⅔ cup freshly grated
  Parmesan cheese
60ml/4 tbsp mixed chopped fresh
  chives and flat leaf parsley
salt and freshly ground black pepper

1 Slice the leeks in half lengthways,
wash them well and then slice them
evenly. Wipe the mushrooms with
kitchen paper and chop them roughly.

2 Heat the oil in a large saucepan and
cook the garlic for 1 minute. Add the
leeks, mushrooms and plenty of
seasoning and cook over a medium
heat for about 10 minutes, or until the
leeks have softened and browned.
Spoon into a bowl and set aside.

3 Add 25g/1oz/2 tbsp of the butter to
the pan. As soon as it has melted, add
the onion and cook over a medium heat
for 5 minutes until it has softened and
is golden.

4 Stir in the rice and cook for about
1 minute until the grains begin to look
translucent and are coated in the fat.
Add a ladleful of stock and cook gently,
stirring occasionally, until the liquid has
been absorbed.

5 Continue to add stock, a ladleful at
a time, until all of it has been absorbed,
and stirring constantly. This should take
about 25–30 minutes. The risotto will
turn thick and creamy and the rice
should be tender but not sticky.

6 Just before serving, add the leeks
and mushrooms, with the remaining
butter. Stir in the grated lemon rind and
juice. Add the grated Parmesan cheese
and the herbs. Adjust the seasoning
and serve immediately.

RISOTTO WITH CHICKEN

*THIS IS A CLASSIC COMBINATION OF CHICKEN AND RICE, COOKED WITH PARMA HAM, WHITE WINE
AND PARMESAN CHEESE.*

SERVES SIX

INGREDIENTS

   30ml/2 tbsp olive oil
   225g/8oz skinless, boneless chicken
     breasts, cut into 2.5cm/1in cubes
   1 onion, finely chopped
   1 garlic clove, finely chopped
   450g/1lb/2⅓ cups risotto rice
   120ml/4fl oz/½ cup dry white wine
   1.5ml/¼ tsp saffron threads
   1.75 litres/3 pints/7½ cups
     simmering chicken stock
   50g/2oz Parma ham, cut into thin
     strips
   25g/1oz/2 tbsp butter, cubed
   25g/1oz/⅓ cup freshly grated
     Parmesan cheese, plus extra to
     serve
   salt and freshly ground black pepper
   flat leaf parsley, to garnish

1 Heat the oil in a frying pan over a
moderately high heat. Add the chicken
cubes and cook, stirring, until they start
to turn white.

2 Reduce the heat to low and add the
onion and garlic. Cook, stirring, until
the onion is soft. Stir in the rice. Sauté
for 1–2 minutes, stirring constantly,
until all the rice grains are coated in oil.

3 Add the wine and cook, stirring,
until the wine has been absorbed.
Stir the saffron into the simmering
stock, then add ladlefuls of stock to
the rice, allowing each ladleful to be
absorbed before adding the next.

4 When the rice is three-quarters
cooked, add the Parma ham and
continue cooking until the rice is just
tender and the risotto creamy.

5 Add the butter and the Parmesan
and stir in well. Season with salt and
pepper to taste. Serve the risotto hot,
sprinkled with a little more Parmesan,
and garnish with parsley.

RISOTTO WITH SMOKED BACON AND TOMATO

A CLASSIC RISOTTO, WITH PLENTY OF ONIONS, SMOKED BACON AND SUN-DRIED TOMATOES. YOU'LL WANT TO KEEP GOING BACK FOR MORE!

SERVES FOUR TO SIX

INGREDIENTS

8 sun-dried tomatoes in olive oil
275g/10oz good-quality rindless
  smoked back bacon
75g/3oz/6 tbsp butter
450g/1lb onions, roughly chopped
2 garlic cloves, crushed
350g/12oz/1¾ cups risotto rice
300ml/½ pint/1¼ cups dry white wine
1 litre/1¾ pints/4 cups simmering
  vegetable stock
50g/2oz/⅔ cup freshly grated
  Parmesan cheese
45ml/3 tbsp mixed chopped fresh
  chives and flat leaf parsley
salt and freshly ground black pepper

1 Drain the sun-dried tomatoes and reserve 15ml/1 tbsp of the oil. Roughly chop the tomatoes and set aside. Cut the bacon into 2.5cm/1in pieces.

2 Heat the oil from the sun-dried tomatoes in a large saucepan. Fry the bacon until well cooked and golden. Remove with a slotted spoon and drain on kitchen paper.

3 Heat 25g/1oz/2 tbsp of the butter in a saucepan and fry the onions and garlic over a medium heat for 10 minutes, until soft and golden brown.

4 Stir in the rice. Cook for 1 minute, until the grains turn translucent. Stir the wine into the stock. Add a ladleful of the mixture to the rice and cook gently until the liquid has been absorbed.

5 Stir in another ladleful of the stock and wine mixture and allow it to be absorbed. Repeat this process until all the liquid has been used up. This should take 25–30 minutes. The risotto will turn thick and creamy, and the rice should be tender but not sticky.

6 Just before serving, stir in the bacon, sun-dried tomatoes, Parmesan, half the herbs and the remaining butter. Adjust the seasoning (remember that the bacon may be quite salty) and serve sprinkled with the remaining herbs.

SHELLFISH RISOTTO WITH MIXED MUSHROOMS

THIS IS A QUICK AND EASY RISOTTO, WHERE ALL THE LIQUID IS ADDED IN ONE GO. THE METHOD IS WELL-SUITED TO THIS SHELLFISH DISH, AS IT MEANS EVERYTHING COOKS TOGETHER UNDISTURBED.

SERVES SIX

INGREDIENTS
225g/8oz live mussels
225g/8oz live Venus or carpet shell clams
45ml/3 tbsp olive oil
1 onion, chopped
450g/1lb/2⅓ cups risotto rice
1.75 litres/3 pints/7½ cups simmering chicken or vegetable stock
150ml/¼ pint/⅔ cup white wine
225g/8oz/2–3 cups assorted wild and cultivated mushrooms, trimmed and sliced
115g/4oz raw peeled prawns, deveined
1 medium or 2 small squid, cleaned, trimmed and sliced
3 drops truffle oil (optional)
75ml/5 tbsp chopped mixed fresh parsley and chervil
celery salt and cayenne pepper

1 Scrub the mussels and clams clean and discard any that are open and do not close when tapped with a knife. Set aside. Heat the oil in a large frying pan and fry the onion for 6–8 minutes until soft but not browned.

2 Add the rice, stirring to coat the grains in oil, then pour in the stock and wine and cook for 5 minutes. Add the mushrooms and cook for 5 minutes more, stirring occasionally.

3 Add the prawns, squid, mussels and clams and stir into the rice. Cover the pan and simmer over a low heat for 15 minutes until the prawns have turned pink and the mussels and clams have opened. Discard any of the shellfish that remain closed.

4 Switch off the heat. Add the truffle oil, if using, and stir in the herbs. Cover tightly and leave to stand for 5–10 minutes to allow all the flavours to blend. Season to taste with celery salt and a pinch of cayenne, pile into a warmed dish, and serve immediately.

SALMON RISOTTO WITH CUCUMBER AND TARRAGON

THIS SIMPLE RISOTTO IS COOKED ALL IN ONE GO, AND IS THEREFORE SIMPLER THAN THE USUAL RISOTTO. IF YOU PREFER TO COOK THE TRADITIONAL WAY, ADD THE LIQUID GRADUALLY, ADDING THE SALMON ABOUT TWO-THIRDS OF THE WAY THROUGH COOKING.

SERVES FOUR

INGREDIENTS

25g/1oz/2 tbsp butter
small bunch of spring onions, white
  parts only, chopped
½ cucumber, peeled, seeded and
  chopped
350g/12oz/1¾ cups risotto rice
1.2 litres/2 pints/5 cups hot chicken
  or fish stock
150ml/¼ pint/⅔ cup dry white wine
450g/1lb salmon fillet, skinned and
  diced
45ml/3 tbsp chopped fresh tarragon
salt and freshly ground black pepper

1 Heat the butter in a large saucepan and add the spring onions and cucumber. Cook for 2–3 minutes without letting the spring onions colour.

2 Stir in the rice, then pour in the stock and wine. Bring to the boil, then lower the heat and simmer, uncovered, for 10 minutes, stirring occasionally.

3 Stir in the diced salmon and season to taste with salt and freshly ground black pepper. Continue cooking for a further 5 minutes, stirring occasionally, then switch off the heat. Cover and leave to stand for 5 minutes.

4 Remove the lid, add the chopped tarragon and mix lightly. Spoon into a warmed bowl and serve.

VARIATION
Carnaroli risotto rice would be excellent in this risotto, although if it is not available, Arborio can be used instead.

TRUFFLE AND LOBSTER RISOTTO

To capture the precious qualities of the fresh truffle, partner it with lobster and serve in a silky smooth risotto. Both truffle shavings and truffle oil are added towards the end of cooking to preserve their flavour.

SERVES FOUR

INGREDIENTS

  50g/2oz/4 tbsp unsalted butter
  1 medium onion, chopped
  350g/12oz/1¾ cups risotto rice,
    preferably Carnaroli
  1 fresh thyme sprig
  150ml/¼ pint/⅔ cup dry white wine
  1.2 litres/2 pints/5 cups simmering
    chicken stock
  1 freshly cooked lobster
  45ml/3 tbsp chopped mixed fresh
    parsley and chervil
  3–4 drops truffle oil
  2 hard-boiled eggs
  1 fresh black or white truffle
  salt and freshly ground black pepper

1 Melt the butter, add the onion and fry until soft. Add the rice and stir well to coat with fat. Add the thyme, then the wine, and cook until it has been absorbed. Add the chicken stock a little at a time, stirring. Let each ladleful be absorbed before adding the next.

2 Twist off the lobster tail, cut the underside with scissors and remove the white tail meat. Carefully break open the claws with a small kitchen hammer and remove the flesh. Cut half the meat into big chunks, then roughly chop the remainder.

3 Stir in the chopped lobster meat, half the chopped herbs and the truffle oil. Remove the rice from the heat, cover and leave to stand for 5 minutes.

4 Divide among warmed plates and centre the lobster chunks on top. Cut the hard-boiled eggs into wedges and arrange them around the lobster meat. Finally, shave fresh truffle over each portion and sprinkle with the remaining herbs. Serve immediately.

COOK'S TIP
To make the most of the aromatic truffle scent, keep the tuber in the rice jar for a few days before use.

PANCETTA AND BROAD BEAN RISOTTO

THIS DELICIOUS RISOTTO MAKES A HEALTHY AND FILLING MEAL, SERVED WITH COOKED FRESH SEASONAL VEGETABLES OR A MIXED GREEN SALAD.

SERVES FOUR

INGREDIENTS
    15ml/1 tbsp olive oil
    1 onion, chopped
    2 garlic cloves, finely chopped
    175g/6oz smoked pancetta, diced
    350g/12oz/1¾ cups risotto rice
    1.5 litres/2½ pints/6¼ cups
      simmering chicken stock
    225g/8oz/2 cups frozen baby broad
      beans
    30ml/2 tbsp chopped fresh mixed
      herbs, such as parsley, thyme and
      oregano
    salt and freshly ground black pepper
    shavings of Parmesan cheese, to
      serve

1 Heat the oil in a large saucepan. Add the onion, garlic and pancetta and cook gently for about 5 minutes, stirring occasionally. Do not allow the onion and garlic to brown.

2 Add the rice to the pan and cook for 1 minute, stirring. Add a ladleful of stock and cook, stirring all the time, until the liquid has been absorbed.

3 Continue adding the stock, a ladleful at a time, until the rice is tender, and almost all the liquid has been absorbed. This will take 30–35 minutes.

4 Meanwhile, cook the broad beans in a saucepan of lightly salted, boiling water for about 3 minutes until tender. Drain well and stir into the risotto, with the mixed herbs. Add salt and pepper to taste. Spoon into a bowl and serve, sprinkled with shavings of fresh Parmesan cheese.

COOK'S TIP
If the broad beans are large, or if you prefer skinned beans, remove the outer skin after cooking.

BROWN RICE RISOTTO WITH MUSHROOMS AND PARMESAN

A CLASSIC RISOTTO OF MIXED MUSHROOMS, HERBS AND FRESH PARMESAN CHEESE, BUT MADE USING BROWN LONG GRAIN RICE. SERVE SIMPLY, WITH A MIXED LEAF SALAD TOSSED IN A LIGHT DRESSING.

SERVES FOUR

INGREDIENTS
15ml/1 tbsp olive oil
4 shallots, finely chopped
2 garlic cloves, crushed
15g/½oz/2 tbsp dried porcini
  mushrooms, soaked in 150ml/
  ¼ pint/⅔ cup hot water for 20
  minutes
250g/9oz/1⅓ cups brown long grain
  rice
900ml/1½ pints/3¾ cups
  well-flavoured vegetable stock
450g/1lb/6 cups mixed mushrooms,
  such as closed cup, chestnut and
  field mushrooms, sliced if large
30–45ml/2–3 tbsp chopped fresh flat
  leaf parsley
50g/2oz/⅔ cup freshly grated
  Parmesan cheese
salt and freshly ground black pepper

1 Heat the oil in a large saucepan, add the shallots and garlic and cook gently for 5 minutes, stirring. Drain the porcini, reserving their liquid, and chop roughly. Add the brown rice to the shallot mixture and stir to coat the grains in oil.

2 Stir the vegetable stock and the porcini soaking liquid into the rice mixture in the saucepan. Bring to the boil, lower the heat and simmer, uncovered, for about 20 minutes or until most of the liquid has been absorbed, stirring frequently.

3 Add all the mushrooms, stir well, and cook the risotto for 10–15 minutes more until the liquid has been absorbed.

4 Season with salt and pepper to taste, stir in the chopped parsley and grated Parmesan and serve immediately.

CRAB RISOTTO

THIS IS A FRESH-FLAVOURED RISOTTO WHICH MAKES A WONDERFUL MAIN COURSE OR STARTER.
YOU WILL NEED TWO CRABS FOR THIS RECIPE, AND IT IS THEREFORE A GOOD DISH TO FOLLOW
A VISIT TO THE SEASIDE, WHERE CRABS ARE CHEAP AND PLENTIFUL.

SERVES THREE TO FOUR

INGREDIENTS
    2 large cooked crabs
    15ml/1 tbsp olive oil
    25g/1oz/2 tbsp butter
    2 shallots, finely chopped
    275g/10oz/1½ cups risotto rice,
        preferably Carnaroli
    75ml/5 tbsp Marsala or brandy
    1 litre/1¾ pints/4 cups simmering
        fish stock
    5ml/1 tsp chopped fresh tarragon
    5ml/1 tsp chopped fresh parsley
    60ml/4 tbsp double cream
    salt and freshly ground black pepper

1 First remove the crab meat from each of the shells in turn. Hold the crab firmly in one hand and hit the back underside firmly with the heel of your hand. This should loosen the shell from the body. Using your thumbs, push against the body and pull away from the shell. From the inside of the shell, remove and discard the intestines.

2 Discard the grey gills (dead man's fingers). Break off the claws and legs from the body, then use a small hammer or crackers to break them open. Using a pick, remove the meat from the claws and legs. Place the meat on a plate.

3 Using a pick or a skewer, pick out the white meat from the body cavities and place on the plate with the meat from the claws and legs, reserving some white meat to garnish. Scoop out the brown meat from inside the shell and set aside with the white meat on the plate.

4 Heat the oil and butter in a pan and gently fry the shallots until soft but not browned. Add the rice. Cook for a few minutes, stirring, until the rice is slightly translucent, then add the Marsala or brandy, bring to the boil, and cook, stirring, until the liquid has evaporated.

5 Add a ladleful of hot stock and cook, stirring, until all the stock has been absorbed. Continue cooking in this way until about two-thirds of the stock has been added, then carefully stir in all the crab meat and the herbs.

6 Continue to cook the risotto, adding the remaining stock. When the rice is almost cooked but still has a slight "bite", remove it from the heat, stir in the cream and adjust the seasoning. Cover and leave to stand for 3 minutes to finish cooking. Serve garnished with the reserved white crab meat.

MONKFISH RISOTTO

MONKFISH IS A VERSATILE, FIRM-TEXTURED FISH WITH A SUPERB FLAVOUR, WHICH IS ACCENTUATED WITH LEMON GRASS IN THIS SOPHISTICATED RISOTTO.

SERVES THREE TO FOUR

INGREDIENTS
    seasoned flour
    about 450g/1lb monkfish, cut into
      cubes
    30ml/2 tbsp olive oil
    40g/1½oz/3 tbsp butter
    2 shallots, finely chopped
    1 lemon grass stalk, finely chopped
    275g/10oz/1½ cups risotto rice,
      preferably Carnaroli
    175ml/6fl oz/¾ cup dry white wine
    1 litre/1¾ pints/4 cups simmering
      fish stock
    30ml/2 tbsp chopped fresh parsley
    salt and white pepper
    dressed salad leaves, to serve

4 Tip in the rice. Cook for 2–3 minutes, stirring, until the rice is coated with oil and is slightly translucent. Gradually add the wine and the hot stock, stirring and waiting until each ladleful has been absorbed before adding the next.

5 When the rice is about three-quarters cooked, stir in the monkfish. Continue to cook the risotto, adding the remaining stock and stirring constantly until the grains of rice are tender, but still retain a bit of "bite". Season with salt and white pepper.

6 Remove the pan from the heat, stir in the parsley and cover with the lid. Leave the risotto to stand for a few minutes before serving with a garnish of dressed salad leaves.

COOK'S TIP
Lemon grass adds a subtle flavour to this dish. Remove the tough outer skin and chop the inner flesh finely.

1 Spoon the seasoned flour over the monkfish cubes in a bowl. Toss the monkfish until coated.

2 Heat 15ml/1 tbsp of the oil with half the butter in a frying pan. Fry the monkfish cubes over a medium to high heat for 3–4 minutes until cooked, turning occasionally. Transfer to a plate and set aside.

3 Heat the remaining oil and butter in a saucepan and fry the shallots over a low heat for about 4 minutes until soft but not brown. Add the lemon grass and cook for 1–2 minutes more.

SCALLOP RISOTTO

TRY TO BUY FRESH SCALLOPS FOR THIS DISH, WHICH TASTE MUCH BETTER THAN FROZEN ONES.
FRESH SCALLOPS COME WITH THE CORAL ATTACHED, WHICH ADDS FLAVOUR, TEXTURE AND COLOUR.

SERVES THREE TO FOUR

INGREDIENTS

about 12 scallops, with their corals
50g/2oz/4 tbsp butter
15ml/1 tbsp olive oil
30ml/2 tbsp Pernod
2 shallots, finely chopped
275g/10oz/1½ cups risotto rice
1 litre/1¾ pints/4 cups simmering
 fish stock
generous pinch of saffron strands,
 dissolved in 15ml/1 tbsp warm milk
30ml/2 tbsp chopped fresh parsley
60ml/4 tbsp double cream
salt and freshly ground black pepper

1 Separate the scallops from their corals. Cut the white flesh in half or into 2cm/¾in slices.

2 Melt half the butter with 5ml/1 tsp oil. Fry the white parts of the scallops for 2–3 minutes. Pour over the Pernod, heat for a few seconds, then ignite and allow to flame for a few seconds. When the flames have died down, remove the pan from the heat.

3 Heat the remaining butter and olive oil in a pan and fry the shallots for about 3–4 minutes, until soft but not browned. Add the rice and cook for a few minutes, stirring, until the rice is coated with oil and is beginning to turn translucent around the edges.

4 Gradually add the hot stock, a ladleful at a time, stirring constantly and waiting for each ladleful of stock to be absorbed before adding the next.

5 When the rice is very nearly cooked, add the scallops and all the juices from the pan, together with the corals, the saffron milk, parsley and seasoning. Stir well to mix. Continue cooking, adding the remaining stock and stirring occasionally, until the risotto is thick and creamy.

6 Remove the pan from the heat, stir in the double cream and cover. Leave the risotto to rest for about 3 minutes to complete the cooking, then pile it into a warmed bowl and serve.

SQUID RISOTTO WITH CHILLI AND CORIANDER

SQUID NEEDS TO BE COOKED EITHER VERY QUICKLY OR VERY SLOWLY. HERE THE SQUID IS MARINATED IN LIME AND KIWI FRUIT – A POPULAR METHOD IN NEW ZEALAND FOR TENDERISING SQUID.

SERVES THREE TO FOUR

INGREDIENTS

about 450g/1lb squid
about 45ml/3 tbsp olive oil
15g/½oz/1 tbsp butter
1 onion, finely chopped
2 garlic cloves, crushed
1 fresh red chilli, seeded and finely
sliced
275g/10oz/1½ cups risotto rice
175ml/6fl oz/¾ cup dry white wine
1 litre/1¾ pints/4 cups simmering
fish stock
30ml/2 tbsp chopped fresh coriander
salt and freshly ground black pepper
For the marinade
2 ripe kiwi fruit, chopped and mashed
1 fresh red chilli, seeded and finely
sliced
30ml/2 tbsp fresh lime juice

1 If not already cleaned, prepare the squid by cutting off the tentacles at the base and pulling to remove the quill. Discard the quill and intestines, if necessary, and pull away the thin outer skin. Rinse the body and cut into thin strips: cut the tentacles into short pieces, discarding the beak and eyes.

2 Mash the kiwi fruit for the marinade in a bowl, then stir in the chilli and lime juice. Add the squid, stirring to coat all the strips in the mixture. Season with salt and freshly ground black pepper, cover with clear film and set aside in the fridge for 4 hours or overnight.

3 Drain the squid. Heat 15ml/1 tbsp of the olive oil in a frying pan and cook the strips, in batches if necessary, for about 30–60 seconds over a high heat. It is important that the squid cooks very quickly. Transfer the cooked squid to a plate and set aside. Don't worry if some of the marinade clings to the squid, but if too much juice accumulates in the pan, pour this into a jug and add more olive oil when cooking the next batch, so that the squid fries rather than simmers. Reserve the accumulated juices in a jug.

4 Heat the remaining oil with the butter in a large saucepan and gently fry the onion and garlic for 5–6 minutes until soft. Add the sliced chilli to the saucepan and fry for 1 minute more.

5 Add the rice. Cook for a few minutes, stirring, until the rice is coated with oil and is slightly translucent, then stir in the wine until it has been absorbed.

6 Gradually add the hot stock and the reserved cooking liquid from the squid, a ladleful at a time, stirring the rice constantly and waiting until each quantity of stock has been absorbed before adding the next.

7 When the rice is about three-quarters cooked, stir in the squid and continue cooking the risotto until all the stock has been absorbed and the rice is tender, but retains a bit of "bite". Stir in the chopped coriander, cover with the lid or a dish towel, and leave to rest for a few minutes before serving.

COOK'S TIP
Although fish stock underlines the flavour of the squid, a light chicken or vegetable stock would also work well in this recipe.

MUSSEL RISOTTO

FRESH ROOT GINGER AND CORIANDER ADD A DISTINCTIVE FLAVOUR TO THIS DISH, WHILE THE GREEN CHILLIES GIVE IT A LITTLE HEAT. THE CHILLIES COULD BE OMITTED FOR A MILDER DISH.

SERVES THREE TO FOUR

INGREDIENTS

900g/2lb fresh mussels
about 250ml/8fl oz/1 cup dry white
    wine
30ml/2 tbsp olive oil
1 onion, chopped
2 garlic cloves, crushed
1–2 fresh green chillies, seeded and
    finely sliced
2.5cm/1in piece of fresh root ginger,
    grated
275g/10oz/1½ cups risotto rice
900ml/1½ pints/3¾ cups simmering
    fish stock
30ml/2 tbsp chopped fresh coriander
30ml/2 tbsp double cream
salt and freshly ground black pepper

3 Add the rice and cook over a medium heat for 2 minutes, stirring, until the rice is coated in oil and becomes translucent.

4 Stir in the reserved cooking liquid from the mussels. When this has been absorbed, add the remaining wine and cook stirring, until this has been absorbed. Now add the hot fish stock, a little at a time, making sure each addition has been absorbed before adding the next.

5 When the rice is about three-quarters cooked, stir in the mussels. Add the coriander and season with salt and pepper. Continue adding stock to the risotto until it is creamy and the rice is tender but slightly firm in the centre.

6 Remove the risotto from the heat, stir in the cream, cover and leave to rest for a few minutes. Spoon into a warmed serving dish, decorate with the reserved mussels in their shells, and serve immediately.

1 Scrub the mussels, discarding any that do not close when sharply tapped. Place in a large saucepan. Add 120ml/4fl oz/½ cup of the wine and bring to the boil. Cover the pan and cook the mussels for 4–5 minutes until they have opened, shaking the pan occasionally. Drain, reserving the liquid and discarding any mussels that have not opened. Remove most of the mussels from their shells, reserving a few in their shells for decoration. Strain the mussel liquid.

2 Heat the oil and fry the onion and garlic for 3–4 minutes until beginning to soften. Add the chillies. Continue to cook over a low heat for 1–2 minutes, stirring frequently, then stir in the ginger and fry gently for 1 minute more.

SEAFOOD RISOTTO

YOU CAN USE ANY SHELLFISH OR SEAFOOD FOR THIS RISOTTO, AS LONG AS THE TOTAL WEIGHT IS SIMILAR TO THAT USED HERE. THE RISOTTO WOULD ALSO MAKE A VERY GOOD STARTER FOR EIGHT.

SERVES FOUR TO SIX

INGREDIENTS

450g/1lb fresh mussels
about 250ml/8fl oz/1 cup dry white
  wine
225g/8oz sea bass fillet, skinned and
  cut into pieces
seasoned flour
60ml/4 tbsp olive oil
8 scallops with corals separated,
  white parts halved or sliced, if large
225g/8oz squid, cleaned and cut
  into rings
12 large raw prawns or langoustines,
  heads removed
2 shallots, finely chopped
1 garlic clove, crushed
400g/14oz/2 cups risotto rice,
  preferably Carnaroli
3 tomatoes, peeled, seeded and
  chopped
1.5 litres/2½ pints/6¼ cups
  simmering fish stock
30ml/2 tbsp chopped fresh parsley
30ml/2 tbsp double cream
salt and freshly ground black pepper

1 Scrub the mussels, discarding any that do not close when sharply tapped. Place them in a large saucepan and add 90ml/6 tbsp of the wine. Bring to the boil, cover the pan and cook for 3–4 minutes until all the mussels have opened, shaking the pan occasionally. Drain, reserving the liquid and discarding any mussels that have not opened. Set aside a few mussels in their shells for garnishing; remove the others from their shells. Strain the cooking liquid.

2 Dust the pieces of sea bass in seasoned flour. Heat 30ml/2 tbsp of the olive oil in a frying pan and fry the fish for 3–4 minutes until cooked. Transfer to a plate. Add a little more oil to the pan and fry the white parts of the scallops for 1–2 minutes on both sides until tender. Transfer to a plate.

3 Fry the squid for 3–4 minutes in the same pan, adding a little more oil if necessary, then set aside. Lastly, add the prawns or langoustines and fry for a further 3–4 minutes until pink, turning frequently. Towards the end of cooking, add a splash of wine – about 30ml/ 2 tbsp – and continue cooking so that the prawns become tender, but do not burn. Remove the prawns from the pan. As soon as they are cool enough to handle, remove the shells and legs, leaving the tails intact.

4 In a large saucepan, heat the remaining olive oil and fry the shallots and garlic for 3–4 minutes over a gentle heat until the shallots are soft but not brown. Add the rice and cook for a few minutes, stirring, until the rice is coated with oil and the grains are slightly translucent. Stir in the tomatoes, with the reserved liquid from the mussels.

5 When all the free liquid has been absorbed, add the remaining wine, stirring constantly. When it has also been absorbed, gradually add the hot stock, one ladleful at a time, continuing to stir the rice constantly and waiting until each quantity of stock has been absorbed before adding the next.

6 When the risotto is three-quarters cooked, carefully stir in all the seafood, except the mussels reserved for the garnish. Continue to cook until all the stock has been absorbed and the rice is tender but still has a bit of "bite".

7 Stir in the parsley and cream and adjust the seasoning. Cover the pan and leave the risotto to stand for 2–3 minutes. Serve in individual bowls, garnished with the reserved mussels in their shells.

CHAMPAGNE RISOTTO

THIS MAY SEEM RATHER EXTRAVAGANT, BUT IT MAKES A REALLY BEAUTIFULLY FLAVOURED RISOTTO, PERFECT FOR THAT SPECIAL ANNIVERSARY DINNER.

SERVES THREE TO FOUR

INGREDIENTS
25g/1oz/2 tbsp butter
2 shallots, finely chopped
275g/10oz/1½ cups risotto rice,
  preferably Carnaroli
½ bottle or 300ml/½ pint/1¼ cups
  champagne
750ml/1¼ pints/3 cups simmering
  light vegetable or chicken stock
150ml/¼ pint/⅔ cup double cream
40g/1½oz/½ cup freshly grated
  Parmesan cheese
10ml/2 tsp very finely chopped fresh
  chervil
salt and freshly ground black pepper
black truffle shavings, to garnish
  (optional)

1 Melt the butter in a pan and fry the shallots for 2–3 minutes until softened. Add the rice and cook, stirring all the time, until the grains are evenly coated in butter and are beginning to look translucent around the edges.

2 Pour in about two-thirds of the champagne and cook over a high heat so that the liquid bubbles fiercely. Cook, stirring, until all the liquid has been absorbed before beginning to add the hot stock.

3 Add the stock, a ladleful at a time, making sure that each addition has been completely absorbed before adding the next. The risotto should gradually become creamy and velvety and all the stock should be absorbed.

4 When the rice is tender but retains a bit of "bite", stir in the remaining champagne and the double cream and Parmesan. Adjust the seasoning. Remove from the heat, cover and leave to stand for a few minutes. Stir in the chervil. If you want to gild the lily, garnish with a few truffle shavings.

ROASTED PEPPER RISOTTO

THIS MAKES AN EXCELLENT VEGETARIAN SUPPER DISH, OR A STARTER FOR SIX.

SERVES THREE TO FOUR

INGREDIENTS

1 red pepper
1 yellow pepper
15ml/1 tbsp olive oil
25g/1oz/2 tbsp butter
1 onion, chopped
2 garlic cloves, crushed
275g/10oz/1½ cups risotto rice
1 litre/1¾ pints/4 cups simmering
 vegetable stock
50g/2oz/⅔ cup freshly grated
 Parmesan cheese
salt and freshly ground black pepper
freshly grated Parmesan cheese, to
 serve (optional)

1 Preheat the grill to high. Cut the peppers in half, remove the seeds and pith and arrange, cut side down, on a baking sheet. Place under the grill for 5–6 minutes until the skin is charred. Put the peppers in a plastic bag, tie the ends and leave for 4–5 minutes.

2 Peel the peppers when they are cool enough to handle and the steam has loosened the skin. Cut into thin strips,

3 Heat the oil and butter in a pan and fry the onion and garlic for 4–5 minutes over a low heat until the onion begins to soften. Add the peppers and cook the mixture for 3–4 minutes more, stirring occasionally.

4 Stir in the rice. Cook over a medium heat for 3–4 minutes, stirring all the time, until the rice is evenly coated in oil and the outer part of each grain has become translucent.

5 Add a ladleful of stock. Cook, stirring, until all the liquid has been absorbed. Continue to add the stock, a ladleful at a time, making sure each quantity has been absorbed before adding the next.

6 When the rice is tender but retains a bit of "bite", stir in the Parmesan, and add seasoning to taste. Cover and leave to stand for 3–4 minutes, then serve, with extra Parmesan, if using.

Two Cheese Risotto

This undeniably rich and creamy risotto is just the thing to serve on cold winter evenings when everyone needs warming up.

SERVES THREE TO FOUR

INGREDIENTS

7.5ml/1½ tsp olive oil
50g/2oz/4 tbsp butter
1 onion, finely chopped
1 garlic clove, crushed
275g/10oz/1½ cups risotto rice,
  preferably Vialone Nano
175ml/6fl oz/¾ cup dry white wine
1 litre/1¾ pints/4 cups simmering
  vegetable or chicken stock
75g/3oz/¾ cup fontina cheese, cubed
50g/2oz/⅔ cup freshly grated
  Parmesan cheese, plus extra, to
  serve
salt and freshly ground black pepper

1 Heat the olive oil with half the butter in a pan and gently fry the onion and garlic for 5–6 minutes until soft. Add the rice and cook, stirring all the time, until the grains are coated in fat and have become slightly translucent around the edges.

2 Stir in the wine. Cook, stirring, until the liquid has been absorbed, then add a ladleful of hot stock. Stir until the stock has been absorbed, then add the remaining stock in the same way, waiting for each quantity of stock to be absorbed before adding more.

3 When the rice is half cooked, stir in the fontina cheese, and continue cooking and adding stock. Keep stirring the rice all the time.

4 When the risotto is creamy and the grains are tender but still have a bit of "bite", stir in the remaining butter and the Parmesan. Season, then remove the pan from the heat, cover and leave to rest for 3–4 minutes before serving.

Quick Risotto

This is rather a cheat's risotto as it defies all the rules that insist the stock is added gradually. Instead, the rice is cooked quickly in a conventional way, and the other ingredients are simply thrown in at the last minute. It tastes good for all that.

SERVES THREE TO FOUR

INGREDIENTS

275g/10oz/1½ cups risotto rice
1 litre/1¾ pints/4 cups simmering
  chicken stock
115g/4oz/1 cup mozzarella cheese,
  cut into small cubes
2 egg yolks
30ml/2 tbsp freshly grated Parmesan
  cheese
75g/3oz cooked ham, cut into small
  cubes
30ml/2 tbsp chopped fresh parsley
salt and freshly ground black pepper
fresh parsley sprigs, to garnish
freshly grated Parmesan cheese, to
  serve

1 Put the rice in a pan. Pour in the stock, bring to the boil and then cover and simmer for about 18–20 minutes until the rice is tender.

2 Remove the pan from the heat and quickly stir in the mozzarella, egg yolks, Parmesan, ham and parsley. Season well with salt and pepper.

3 Cover the pan and stand for 2–3 minutes to allow the cheese to melt, then stir again. Pile into warmed serving bowls and serve immediately, with extra Parmesan cheese.

PESTO RISOTTO

IF YOU BUY THE PESTO — AND THERE ARE SOME GOOD VARIETIES AVAILABLE NOWADAYS — THIS IS JUST ABOUT AS EASY AS A RISOTTO GETS.

SERVES THREE TO FOUR

INGREDIENTS
30ml/2 tbsp olive oil
2 shallots, finely chopped
1 garlic clove, crushed
275g/10oz/1½ cups risotto rice
175ml/6fl oz/¾ cup dry white wine
1 litre/1¾ pints/4 cups simmering
  vegetable stock
45ml/3 tbsp pesto
25g/1oz/⅓ cup freshly grated
  Parmesan cheese, plus extra, to
  serve (optional)
salt and freshly ground black pepper

1 Heat the olive oil in a pan and fry the shallots and garlic for 4–5 minutes until the shallots are soft but not browned.

2 Add the rice and cook over a medium heat, stirring all the time, until the grains of rice are coated in oil and the outer part of the grain is translucent and the inner part opaque.

3 Pour in the wine. Cook, stirring, until all of it has been absorbed, then start adding the hot stock, a ladleful at a time, stirring constantly and waiting until each addition of stock has been absorbed before adding the next.

4 After about 20 minutes, when all the stock has been absorbed and the rice is creamy and tender, stir in the pesto and Parmesan. Taste and adjust seasoning and then cover and rest for 3–4 minutes. Spoon into a bowl and serve, with extra Parmesan, if you like.

PUMPKIN AND APPLE RISOTTO

PUMPKIN AND OTHER WINTER SQUASH ARE VERY POPULAR IN ITALY AND APPEAR IN MANY CLASSIC RECIPES. IF PUMPKINS ARE OUT OF SEASON, USE BUTTERNUT OR ONION SQUASH — THE FLAVOURS WILL BE SLIGHTLY DIFFERENT, BUT THEY BOTH WORK WELL.

SERVES THREE TO FOUR

INGREDIENTS
225g/8oz butternut squash or
  pumpkin flesh
1 cooking apple
120ml/4fl oz/½ cup water
25g/1oz/2 tbsp butter
25ml/1½ tbsp olive oil
1 onion, finely chopped
1 garlic clove, crushed
275g/10oz/1½ cups risotto rice, such
  as Vialone Nano
175ml/6fl oz/¾ cup fruity white wine
900ml–1 litre/1½–1¾ pints/3¾–4
  cups simmering vegetable stock
75g/3oz/1 cup freshly grated
  Parmesan cheese
salt and freshly ground black pepper

1 Cut the squash into small pieces. Peel, core and roughly chop the apple. Place in a pan and pour in the water. Bring to the boil, then simmer for about 15–20 minutes until the squash is very tender. Drain, return the squash mixture to the pan and add half the butter. Mash the mixture roughly with a fork to break up any large pieces, but leave the mixture chunky.

2 Heat the oil and remaining butter in a pan and fry the onion and garlic until the onion is soft. Tip in the rice. Cook, stirring constantly, over a medium heat for 2 minutes until it is coated in oil and the grains are slightly translucent.

3 Add the wine and stir into the rice. When all the liquid has been absorbed, begin to add the stock a ladleful at a time, making sure each addition has been absorbed before adding the next. This should take about 20 minutes.

4 When roughly two ladlefuls of stock are left, add the squash and apple mixture together with another addition of stock. Continue to cook, stirring well and adding the rest of the stock, until the risotto is very creamy. Stir in the Parmesan cheese, adjust the seasoning and serve immediately.

ROSEMARY RISOTTO <u>WITH</u> BORLOTTI BEANS

THIS IS A CLASSIC RISOTTO WITH A SUBTLE AND COMPLEX TASTE, FROM THE HEADY FLAVOURS OF ROSEMARY TO THE SAVOURY BEANS AND THE FRUITY-SWEET FLAVOURS OF MASCARPONE AND PARMESAN.

SERVES THREE TO FOUR

INGREDIENTS
   400g/14oz can borlotti beans
   30ml/2 tbsp olive oil
   1 onion, chopped
   2 garlic cloves, crushed
   275g/10oz/1½ cups risotto rice
   175ml/6fl oz/¾ cup dry white wine
   900ml–1 litre/1½–1¾ pints/
      3¾–4 cups simmering vegetable or
      chicken stock
   60ml/4 tbsp mascarpone cheese
   65g/2½oz/scant 1 cup freshly grated
      Parmesan cheese, plus extra, to
      serve (optional)
   5ml/1 tsp chopped fresh rosemary
   salt and freshly ground black pepper

1 Drain the beans, rinse under cold water and drain again. Purée about two-thirds of the beans fairly coarsely in a food processor or blender. Set the remaining beans aside.

2 Heat the olive oil in a large pan and gently fry the onion and garlic for 6–8 minutes until very soft. Add the rice and cook over a medium heat for a few minutes, stirring constantly, until the grains are thoroughly coated in oil and are slightly translucent.

VARIATION
Fresh thyme or marjoram could be used for this risotto instead of rosemary, if preferred. One of the great virtues of risotto is that it lends itself well to variations. Experiment with different herbs to make your own speciality dish.

3 Pour in the wine. Cook over a medium heat for 2–3 minutes, stirring all the time, until the wine has been absorbed. Add the stock gradually, a ladleful at a time, waiting for each quantity to be absorbed before adding more, and continuing to stir.

4 When the rice is three-quarters cooked, stir in the bean purée. Continue to cook the risotto, adding the remaining stock, until it is creamy and the rice is tender but still has a bit of "bite". Add the reserved beans, with the mascarpone, Parmesan and rosemary, then season to taste. Stir thoroughly, then cover and leave to stand for about 5 minutes so that the risotto absorbs the flavours fully and the rice completes cooking. Serve with extra Parmesan, if you like.

JERUSALEM ARTICHOKE RISOTTO

THIS IS A SIMPLE AND WARMING RISOTTO, WHICH BENEFITS FROM THE DELICIOUS AND DISTINCTIVE FLAVOUR OF JERUSALEM ARTICHOKES.

SERVES THREE TO FOUR

INGREDIENTS

400g/14oz Jerusalem artichokes
40g/1½oz/3 tbsp butter
15ml/1 tbsp olive oil
1 onion, finely chopped
1 garlic clove, crushed
275g/10oz/1½ cups risotto rice
120ml/4fl oz/½ cup fruity white wine
1 litre/1¾ pints/4 cups simmering
    vegetable stock
10ml/2 tsp chopped fresh thyme
40g/1½oz/½ cup freshly grated
    Parmesan cheese, plus extra, to
    serve
salt and freshly ground black pepper
fresh thyme sprigs, to garnish

1 Peel the artichokes, cut them into pieces and immediately add them to a pan of lightly salted water. Simmer them until tender, then drain and mash with 15g/½oz/1 tbsp of the butter. Add a little more salt, if needed.

2 Heat the oil and the remaining butter in a pan and fry the onion and garlic for 5–6 minutes until soft. Add the rice and cook over a medium heat for about 2 minutes until the grains are translucent around the edges.

3 Pour in the wine, stir until it has been absorbed, then start adding the simmering stock, a ladleful at a time, making sure each quantity has been absorbed before adding more.

4 When you have just one last ladleful of stock to add, stir in the mashed artichokes and the chopped thyme. Season with salt and pepper. Continue cooking until the risotto is creamy and the artichokes are hot. Stir in the Parmesan. Remove from the heat, cover the pan and leave the risotto to stand for a few minutes. Spoon into a serving dish, garnish with thyme, and serve with Parmesan cheese.

DUCK RISOTTO

THIS MAKES AN EXCELLENT STARTER FOR SIX OR COULD BE SERVED FOR HALF THAT NUMBER AS A LUNCH OR SUPPER DISH. ADD A GREEN SALAD, OR SERVE WITH MANGETOUTS AND SAUTÉED RED PEPPER SLICES.

SERVES THREE TO FOUR

INGREDIENTS

2 duck breasts
30ml/2 tbsp brandy
30ml/2 tbsp orange juice
15ml/1 tbsp olive oil (optional)
1 onion, finely chopped
1 garlic clove, crushed
275g/10oz/1½ cups risotto rice
1–1.2 litres/1¾–2 pints/4–5 cups
  simmering duck, turkey or chicken
  stock
5ml/1 tsp chopped fresh thyme
5ml/1 tsp chopped fresh mint
10ml/2 tsp grated orange rind
40g/1½oz/½ cup freshly grated
  Parmesan cheese
salt and freshly ground black pepper
strips of thinly pared orange rind, to
  garnish

1 Score the fatty side of the duck breasts and rub them with salt. Put them, fat side down, in a heavy frying pan and dry-fry over a medium heat for 6–8 minutes to render the fat. Transfer the breasts to a plate and then pull away and discard the fat. Cut the flesh into strips about 2cm/¾in wide.

2 Pour all but 15ml/1 tbsp of the rendered duck fat from the pan into a cup or jug, then reheat the fat in the pan. Fry the duck slices for 2–3 minutes over a medium high heat until evenly brown but not overcooked. Add the brandy, heat to simmering point and then ignite, either by tilting the pan or using a taper. When the flames have died down, add the orange juice and season with salt and pepper. Remove from the heat and set aside.

3 In a saucepan, heat either 15ml/ 1 tbsp of the remaining duck fat or use olive oil. Fry the onion and garlic over a gentle heat until the onion is soft but not browned. Add the rice and cook, stirring all the time, until the grains are coated in oil and have become slightly translucent around the edges.

4 Add the stock, a ladleful at a time, waiting for each quantity of stock to be absorbed completely before adding the next. Just before adding the final ladleful of stock, stir in the duck, with the thyme and mint. Continue cooking until the risotto is creamy and the rice is tender but still has a bit of "bite".

5 Add the orange rind and Parmesan. Taste and adjust the seasoning, then remove from the heat, cover the pan and leave to stand for a few minutes. Serve on individual plates, garnished with the pared orange rind.

CHICKEN LIVER RISOTTO

*THE COMBINATION OF CHICKEN LIVERS, BACON, PARSLEY AND THYME GIVES THIS RISOTTO A
WONDERFULLY RICH FLAVOUR. SERVE IT AS A STARTER FOR FOUR OR A LUNCH FOR TWO OR THREE.*

SERVES TWO TO FOUR

INGREDIENTS

175g/6oz chicken livers
about 15ml/1 tbsp olive oil
about 25g/1oz/2 tbsp butter
about 40g/1½oz speck or 3 rindless
  streaky bacon rashers, finely
  chopped
2 shallots, finely chopped
1 garlic clove, crushed
1 celery stick, finely sliced
275g/10oz/1½ cups risotto rice
175ml/6fl oz/¾ cup dry white wine
900ml–1 litre/1½–1¾ pints/3¾–4
  cups simmering chicken stock
5ml/1 tsp chopped fresh thyme
15ml/1 tbsp chopped fresh parsley
salt and freshly ground black pepper
parsley and thyme sprigs to garnish

1 Clean the chicken livers carefully, removing any fat or membrane. Rinse well, pat dry with kitchen paper and cut into small, even pieces.

2 Heat the oil and butter in a frying pan and fry the speck or bacon for 2–3 minutes. Add the shallots, garlic and celery and continue frying for 3–4 minutes over a low heat until the vegetables are slightly softened. Increase the heat and add the chicken livers, stir-frying for a few minutes until they are brown all over.

3 Add the rice. Cook, stirring, for a few minutes, then pour over the wine. Allow to boil so that the alcohol is driven off. Stir frequently, taking care not to break up the chicken livers. When all the wine has been absorbed, add the hot stock, a ladleful at a time, stirring constantly.

4 About halfway through cooking, add the thyme and season with salt and pepper. Continue to add the stock as before, making sure that each quantity has been absorbed before adding more.

5 When the risotto is creamy and the rice is tender but still has a bit of "bite", stir in the parsley. Taste and adjust the seasoning. Remove the pan from the heat, cover and leave to rest for a few minutes before serving, garnished with parsley and thyme.

LEEK AND HAM RISOTTO

ANOTHER SIMPLE RISOTTO THAT MAKES AN EASY SUPPER, YET IS SPECIAL ENOUGH FOR A DINNER PARTY.

SERVES THREE TO FOUR

INGREDIENTS

7.5ml/1½ tsp olive oil
40g/1½oz/3 tbsp butter
2 leeks, cut in slices
175g/6oz prosciutto, torn into pieces
75g/3oz/generous 1 cup button
    mushrooms, sliced
275g/10oz/1½ cups risotto rice
1 litre/1¾ pints/4 cups simmering
    chicken stock
45ml/3 tbsp chopped fresh flat leaf
    parsley
40g/1½oz/½ cup freshly grated
    Parmesan cheese
salt and freshly ground black pepper

1 Heat the oil and butter in a pan and fry the leeks until soft. Set aside a few strips of prosciutto for the garnish and add the rest to the pan. Fry for 1 minute, then add the mushrooms and stir-fry for 2–3 minutes until lightly browned.

2 Add the rice. Cook, stirring, for 1–2 minutes until the grains are evenly coated in oil and have become translucent around the edges. Add a ladleful of hot stock. Stir until this has been absorbed completely, then add the next ladleful. Continue in this way until all the stock has been absorbed.

3 When the risotto is creamy and the rice is tender but still has a bit of "bite", stir in the parsley and Parmesan. Adjust the seasoning, remove from the heat and cover. Allow to rest for a few minutes. Spoon into a bowl, garnish with the reserved prosciutto and serve.

RABBIT AND LEMON GRASS RISOTTO

THE LEMON GRASS ADDS A PLEASANT TANG TO THIS RISOTTO. IF RABBIT ISN'T AVAILABLE, USE CHICKEN OR TURKEY INSTEAD.

SERVES THREE TO FOUR

INGREDIENTS

225g/8oz rabbit meat, cut into strips
seasoned flour
50g/2oz/¼ cup butter
15ml/1 tbsp olive oil
45ml/3 tbsp dry sherry
1 onion, finely chopped
1 garlic clove, crushed
1 lemon grass stalk, peeled and very
    finely sliced
275g/10oz/1½ cups risotto rice,
    preferably Carnaroli
1 litre/1¾ pints/4 cups simmering
    chicken stock
10ml/2 tsp chopped fresh thyme
45ml/3 tbsp double cream
25g/1oz/⅓ cup freshly grated
    Parmesan cheese
salt and freshly ground black pepper

1 Coat the rabbit strips in the seasoned flour. Heat half the butter and olive oil in a frying pan and fry the rabbit quickly until evenly brown. Add the sherry, and allow to boil briefly to burn off the alcohol. Season with salt and pepper and set aside.

2 Heat the remaining olive oil and butter in a large saucepan. Fry the onion and garlic over a low heat for 4–5 minutes until the onion is soft. Add the sliced lemon grass and cook for a few more minutes.

3 Add the rice and stir to coat in the oil. Add a ladleful of stock and cook, stirring, until the liquid has been absorbed. Continue adding the stock gradually, stirring constantly. When the rice is almost cooked, stir in three-quarters of the rabbit strips, with the pan juices. Add the thyme and seasoning.

4 Continue cooking until the rice is tender but still has a "bite". Stir in the cream and Parmesan, remove from the heat and cover. Leave to rest before serving, garnished with rabbit strips.

APPLE AND LEMON RISOTTO WITH POACHED PLUMS

ALTHOUGH IT'S ENTIRELY POSSIBLE TO COOK THIS BY THE CONVENTIONAL RISOTTO METHOD –
BY ADDING THE LIQUID SLOWLY – IT MAKES MORE SENSE TO COOK THE RICE WITH THE MILK,
IN THE SAME WAY AS FOR A RICE PUDDING.

SERVES FOUR

INGREDIENTS
  1 cooking apple
  15g/½oz/1 tbsp butter
  175g/6oz/scant 1 cup risotto rice
  600ml/1 pint/2½ cups creamy milk
  about 50g/2oz/¼ cup caster sugar
  1.5ml/¼ tsp ground cinnamon
  30ml/2 tbsp lemon juice
  45ml/3 tbsp double cream
  grated rind of 1 lemon, to decorate
For the poached plums
  50g/2oz/¼ cup light brown
    muscovado sugar
  200ml/7fl oz/scant 1 cup apple juice
  3 star anise
  cinnamon stick
  6 plums, halved and sliced

1 Peel and core the apple. Cut it into large chunks. Put these in a large, non-stick pan and add the butter. Heat gently until the butter melts.

2 Add the rice and milk and stir well. Bring to the boil over a medium heat, then simmer very gently for 20–25 minutes, stirring occasionally.

COOK'S TIP

If the apple is very sharp (acidic) the milk may curdle. There is no need to worry about this – it won't affect the look or taste of the sauce.

3 To make the poached plums, dissolve the sugar in 150ml/¼ pints/⅔ cup apple juice in a pan. Add the spices and bring to the boil. Boil for 2 minutes. Add the plums, and simmer for 2 minutes. Set aside until ready to serve.

4 Stir the sugar, cinnamon and lemon juice into the risotto. Cook for 2 minutes, stirring all the time, then stir in the cream. Taste and add more sugar if necessary. Decorate with the lemon rind and serve with the poached plums.

CHOCOLATE RISOTTO

*IF YOU'VE NEVER TASTED A SWEET RISOTTO, THERE'S A TREAT IN STORE. CHOCOLATE RISOTTO IS
DELECTABLE, AND CHILDREN OF ALL AGES LOVE IT.*

SERVES FOUR TO SIX

INGREDIENTS

175g/6oz/scant 1 cup risotto rice
600ml/1 pint/2½ cups creamy milk
75g/3oz plain chocolate, broken into
  pieces
25g/1oz/2 tbsp butter
about 50g/2oz/¼ cup caster sugar
pinch of ground cinnamon
60ml/4 tbsp double cream
fresh raspberries and chocolate
  caraque, to decorate
chocolate sauce, to serve

3 Remove the pan from the heat and
stir in the ground cinnamon and double
cream. Cover the pan and leave to
stand for a few minutes.

4 Spoon the risotto into individual
dishes or dessert plates, and decorate
with fresh raspberries and chocolate
caraque. Serve with chocolate sauce.

1 Put the rice in a non-stick pan. Pour
in the milk and bring to the boil over a
low to medium heat. Reduce the heat
to the lowest setting and simmer very
gently for about 20 minutes, stirring
occasionally, until the rice is very soft.

2 Stir in the chocolate, butter and
sugar. Cook, stirring all the time over
a very gentle heat for 1–2 minutes,
until the chocolate has melted.

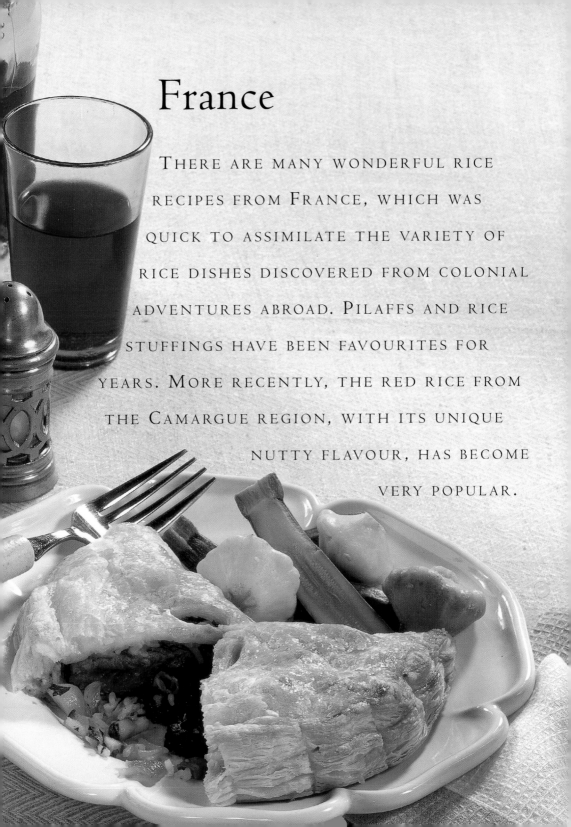

France

THERE ARE MANY WONDERFUL RICE
RECIPES FROM FRANCE, WHICH WAS
QUICK TO ASSIMILATE THE VARIETY OF
RICE DISHES DISCOVERED FROM COLONIAL
ADVENTURES ABROAD. PILAFFS AND RICE
STUFFINGS HAVE BEEN FAVOURITES FOR
YEARS. MORE RECENTLY, THE RED RICE FROM
THE CAMARGUE REGION, WITH ITS UNIQUE
NUTTY FLAVOUR, HAS BECOME
VERY POPULAR.

PROVENÇAL FISH SOUP

THE RICE MAKES THIS A SUBSTANTIAL MAIN MEAL SOUP. BASMATI OR THAI RICE HAS THE BEST FLAVOUR, BUT ANY LONG GRAIN RICE COULD BE USED. IF USING A QUICK-COOK RICE, COOK THE VEGETABLES FOR LONGER BEFORE ADDING THE RICE.

SERVES FOUR TO SIX

INGREDIENTS

450g/1lb fresh mussels
about 250ml/8fl oz/1 cup white wine
675–900g/1½–2lb mixed white fish
  fillets such as monkfish, plaice,
  cod or haddock
6 large scallops
30ml/2 tbsp olive oil
3 leeks, chopped
1 garlic clove, crushed
1 red pepper, seeded and cut into
  2.5cm/1in pieces
1 yellow pepper, seeded and cut into
  2.5cm/1in pieces
175g/6oz fennel, cut into 4cm/1½in
  pieces
400g/14oz can chopped tomatoes
about 1.2 litres/2 pints/5 cups
  well-flavoured fish stock
generous pinch of saffron threads,
  soaked in 15ml/1 tbsp hot water
175g/6oz/scant 1 cup basmati rice,
  soaked
8 large raw prawns, peeled and
  deveined
salt and freshly ground black pepper
30–45ml/2–3 tbsp fresh dill, to
  garnish
crusty bread, to serve (optional)

1 Clean the mussels, discarding any that do not close when tapped with a knife. Place them in a heavy-based pan. Add 90ml/6 tbsp of the wine, cover, bring to the boil over a high heat and cook for about 3 minutes or until all the mussels have opened. Strain, reserving the liquid. Set aside half the mussels in their shells for the garnish; shell the rest and put them in a bowl. Discard any mussels that have not opened.

2 Cut the fish into 2.5cm/1in cubes. Detach the corals from the scallops and slice the white flesh into three or four pieces. Add the scallops to the fish and the corals to the mussels.

3 Heat the olive oil in a saucepan and fry the leeks and garlic for 3–4 minutes until softened. Add the peppers and fennel and fry for 2 minutes more.

4 Add the tomatoes, stock, saffron water, reserved mussel liquid and the remaining wine. Season well and cook for 5 minutes. Drain the rice, stir it into the mixture, cover and simmer for 10 minutes until it is just tender.

5 Carefully stir in the white fish and cook over a low heat for 5 minutes. Add the prawns, cook for 2 minutes then add the scallop corals and mussels and cook for 2–3 minutes more, until all the fish is tender. If the soup seems dry, add a little extra white wine or stock, or a little of both. Spoon into warmed soup dishes, top with the mussels in their shells and sprinkle with the dill. Serve with fresh crusty bread, if liked.

COOK'S TIP
To make your own fish stock, place about 450g/1lb white fish trimmings – bones, heads, but not gills – in a large pan. Add a chopped onion, carrot, bay leaf, parsley sprig, 6 peppercorns and a 5cm/2in piece of pared lemon rind. Pour in 1.2 litres/2 pints/5 cups water, bring to the boil, then simmer gently for 25–30 minutes. Strain through muslin.

SALMON AND RICE GRATIN

THIS ALL-IN-ONE SUPPER DISH IS IDEAL FOR INFORMAL ENTERTAINING AS IT CAN BE MADE AHEAD OF TIME AND REHEATED FOR ABOUT HALF AN HOUR BEFORE BEING SERVED WITH A TOSSED SALAD.

SERVES SIX

INGREDIENTS

675g/1½lb fresh salmon fillet, skinned
1 bay leaf
a few parsley stalks
1 litre/1¾ pints/4 cups water
400g/14oz/2 cups basmati rice, soaked and drained
30–45ml/2–3 tbsp chopped fresh parsley, plus extra to garnish
175g/6oz/1½ cups Cheddar cheese, grated
3 hard-boiled eggs, chopped
salt and freshly ground black pepper
For the sauce
1 litre/1¾ pints/4 cups milk
40g/1½oz/⅓ cup plain flour
40g/1½oz/3 tbsp butter
5ml/1 tsp mild curry paste or French mustard

1 Put the salmon in a wide, shallow pan. Add the bay leaf and parsley stalks, with salt and pepper. Pour in the water and bring to simmering point. Poach the fish for about 12 minutes until just tender.

2 Lift the fish out of the pan using a slotted spoon, then strain the liquid into a saucepan. Leave the fish to cool, then remove any visible bones and flake the flesh gently with a fork.

3 Drain the rice and add it to the saucepan containing the fish-poaching liquid. Bring to the boil, then lower the heat, cover and simmer for 10 minutes without lifting the lid.

4 Remove the pan from the heat and, without lifting the lid, allow the rice to stand undisturbed for 5 minutes.

5 Meanwhile, make the sauce. Mix the milk, flour and butter in a saucepan. Bring to the boil over a low heat, whisking constantly until the sauce is smooth and thick. Stir in the curry paste or mustard, with salt and pepper to taste. Simmer for 2 minutes.

6 Preheat the grill. Remove the sauce from the heat and stir in the chopped parsley and rice, with half the cheese. Using a large metal spoon, fold in the flaked fish and eggs. Spoon into a shallow gratin dish and sprinkle with the rest of the cheese. Heat under the grill until the topping is golden brown and bubbling. Serve in individual dishes, garnished with chopped parsley.

VARIATIONS
Prawns could be substituted for the salmon, and other hard cheeses, such as Lancashire or Red Leicester, could be used instead of the Cheddar.

RED RICE SALAD NIÇOISE

RED RICE, WITH ITS SWEET NUTTINESS, GOES WELL IN THIS CLASSIC SALAD. THE TUNA OR SWORDFISH COULD BE BARBECUED OR PAN-FRIED BUT TAKE CARE THAT IT DOES NOT OVERCOOK.

SERVES SIX

INGREDIENTS
about 675g/1½lb fresh tuna or
    swordfish, sliced into 2cm/¾in thick
    steaks
350g/12oz/1¾ cups Camargue red
    rice
fish or vegetable stock or water
450g/1lb French beans
450g/1lb broad beans, shelled
1 cos lettuce
450g/1lb cherry tomatoes, halved
    unless very tiny
30ml/2 tbsp coarsely chopped fresh
    coriander
3 hard-boiled eggs
175g/6oz/1½ cups stoned black
    olives
olive oil, for brushing
For the marinade
1 red onion, roughly chopped
2 garlic cloves
½ bunch fresh parsley
½ bunch fresh coriander
10ml/2 tsp paprika
45ml/3 tbsp olive oil
45ml/3 tbsp water
30ml/2 tbsp white wine vinegar
15ml/1 tbsp fresh lime or lemon
    juice
salt and freshly ground black pepper
For the dressing
30ml/2 tbsp fresh lime or lemon
    juice
5ml/1 tsp Dijon mustard
½ garlic clove, crushed (optional)
60ml/4 tbsp olive oil
60ml/4 tbsp sunflower oil

COOK'S TIP
A good salad Niçoise is a feast for the
eyes as well as the palate. Arrange the
ingredients with care, either on a large
serving dish or individual salad plates.

1 Make the marinade by mixing all
the ingredients in a food processor
and processing them for 30–40
seconds until the vegetables and
herbs are finely chopped.

2 Prick the tuna or swordfish steaks
all over with a fork, lay them side by
side in a shallow dish and pour over
the marinade, turning the fish to coat
each piece. Cover with clear film and
leave in a cool place for 2–4 hours.

3 Cook the rice in stock or water,
following the instructions on the packet,
then drain, tip into a bowl and set aside.

4 Make the dressing. Mix the citrus
juice, mustard and garlic (if using) in
a bowl. Whisk in the oils, then add salt
and freshly ground black pepper to
taste. Stir 60ml/4 tbsp of the dressing
into the rice, then spoon the rice into
the centre of a large serving dish.

5 Cook the French beans and broad
beans in boiling salted water until
tender. Drain, refresh under cold water
and drain again. Remove the outer shell
from the broad beans and add them to
the rice.

6 Discard the outer leaves from the
lettuce and tear the inner leaves into
pieces. Add to the salad with the
tomatoes and coriander. Shell the
hard-boiled eggs and cut them into
sixths. Preheat the grill.

7 Arrange the tuna or swordfish steaks
on a grill pan. Brush with the marinade
and a little extra olive oil. Grill for 3–4
minutes on each side, until the fish is
tender and flakes easily when tested
with the tip of a sharp knife. Brush with
marinade and more olive oil when
turning the fish over.

8 Allow the fish to cool a little, then
break the steaks into large pieces. Toss
into the salad with the olives and the
remaining dressing. Decorate with the
eggs and serve.

BEEF IN PASTRY WITH WILD MUSHROOMS AND RICE

A TASTY LAYER OF RICE AND JUICY WILD MUSHROOMS TOPS EACH FILLET STEAK BEFORE IT IS WRAPPED IN PUFF PASTRY. THIS COOKS TO CRISP AND FLAKY PERFECTION, THE PERFECT FOIL FOR THE FILLING.

SERVES FOUR

INGREDIENTS
  20g/¾oz/¼ cup dried wild
    mushrooms, soaked for 10 minutes
    in warm water to cover
  115g/4oz/1½–1¾ cups morel
    mushrooms
  about 45ml/3 tbsp olive oil
  4 shallots, finely chopped
  1 garlic clove, crushed
  20g/¾oz/1½ tbsp butter
  175g/6oz/1½ cups cooked white long
    grain rice
  10ml/2 tsp chopped fresh marjoram
  15ml/1 tbsp finely chopped fresh
    parsley
  275g/10oz puff pastry, thawed if
    frozen
  4 fillet steaks, each about 90g/3½oz
    and 2.5cm/1in thick
  10ml/2 tsp Dijon mustard
  1 egg, beaten with 15ml/1 tbsp water
  salt and freshly ground black pepper
  roast potatoes and patty pan squash,
    to serve (optional)

1 Preheat the oven to 220°C/425°F/ Gas 7. Drain the dried mushrooms, reserving the liquid, and chop finely. Trim the morels and chop them.

2 Heat 15ml/1 tbsp of the olive oil in a frying pan and fry the shallots and garlic for 2–3 minutes until soft, stirring occasionally. Add the butter to the pan. When it begins to foam, add the mushrooms and cook for 3–4 minutes more, stirring occasionally.

3 Scrape the mixture into the bowl of rice and stir in the marjoram and parsley. Season to taste.

4 Cut the pastry into four and roll out each piece into an 18cm/7in circle. Trim the top and bottom edges.

5 Heat the remaining olive oil in the pan and fry the steaks for about 30 seconds on each side until browned. Spread a little mustard over each steak, then place on one side of a piece of pastry. Spoon a quarter of the mushroom and rice mixture on top of each steak.

6 Fold the pastry over to make a pasty, sealing the join with a little of the egg wash. Repeat to make four pasties, then place them on an oiled baking sheet. Slit the top of each pasty, decorate with the pastry trimmings, and glaze with more egg wash. Bake in the oven for about 15 minutes, until the pastry is golden.

CHICKEN PILAFF

THE FRENCH MARMITE POT IS IDEAL FOR THIS RECIPE. THE TALL SIDES SLANT INWARDS, REDUCING EVAPORATION AND ENSURING THAT THE RICE COOKS SLOWLY WITHOUT BECOMING DRY.

SERVES THREE TO FOUR

INGREDIENTS
    15–20 dried chanterelle mushrooms
    15–30ml/1–2 tbsp olive oil
    15g/½oz/1 tbsp butter
    4 thin rashers rindless smoked
        streaky bacon, chopped
    3 skinless, boneless chicken breasts,
        cut into thin slices
    4 spring onions, sliced
    225g/8oz/generous 1 cup basmati
        rice, soaked
    450ml/¾ pint/scant 2 cups hot
        chicken stock
    salt and freshly ground black pepper

1 Preheat the oven to 180°C/350°F/ Gas 4. Soak the mushrooms for 10 minutes in warm water. Drain, reserving the liquid. Slice the mushrooms, discarding the stalks.

2 Heat the olive oil and butter in a frying pan. Fry the bacon for 2–3 minutes. Add the chicken and stir-fry until the pieces are golden brown all over. Transfer the chicken and bacon mixture to a bowl using a slotted spoon.

3 Briefly fry the mushrooms and spring onions in the fat remaining in the pan, then add them to the chicken pieces. Drain the rice and add it to the pan, with a little olive oil if necessary. Stir-fry for 2–3 minutes. Spoon the rice into an earthenware marmite pot or casserole.

4 Pour the hot chicken stock and reserved mushroom liquid over the rice in the marmite pot or casserole. Stir in the reserved chicken and mushroom mixture and season.

5 Cover with a double piece of foil and secure with a lid. Cook in the oven for 30–35 minutes until the rice is tender.

RED RICE AND ROASTED RED PEPPER SALAD

PEPPERS, SUN-DRIED TOMATOES AND GARLIC GIVE A DISTINCTLY MEDITERRANEAN FLAVOUR TO THIS SALAD DISH. IT MAKES AN EXCELLENT ACCOMPANIMENT TO SPICY SAUSAGES OR FISH.

SERVES FOUR

INGREDIENTS

225g/8oz/generous 1 cup Camargue
  red rice
vegetable or chicken stock or water
  (see method)
45ml/3 tbsp olive oil
3 red peppers, seeded and sliced into
  strips
4–5 sun-dried tomatoes
4–5 whole garlic cloves, unpeeled
1 onion, chopped
30ml/2 tbsp chopped fresh parsley,
  plus extra to garnish
15ml/1 tbsp chopped fresh coriander
10ml/2 tsp balsamic vinegar
salt and freshly ground black pepper

1 Cook the rice in stock or water, following instructions on the packet. Heat the oil in a frying pan and add the peppers. Cook over a medium heat for 4 minutes, shaking occasionally.

2 Lower the heat, add the sun-dried tomatoes, whole garlic cloves and onion, cover the pan and cook for 8–10 minutes more, stirring occasionally. Remove the lid and cook for 3 minutes more.

3 Off the heat, stir in the parsley, coriander and vinegar, and season. Spread the rice out on a serving dish and spoon the pepper mixture on top. Peel the whole garlic cloves, cut the flesh into slices and scatter these over the salad. Serve at room temperature, garnished with more fresh parsley.

CREAMY FISH PILAU

THIS DISH IS INSPIRED BY A FUSION OF CUISINES – THE METHOD COMES FROM INDIA AND USES THAT COUNTRY'S FAVOURITE RICE, BASMATI, BUT THE DELICIOUS WINE AND CREAM SAUCE IS VERY MUCH FRENCH IN FLAVOUR.

SERVES FOUR TO SIX

INGREDIENTS

450g/1lb fresh mussels, scrubbed
350ml/12fl oz/1½ cups white wine
fresh parsley sprig
about 675g/1½lb salmon
225g/8oz scallops
about 15ml/1 tbsp olive oil
40g/1½oz/3 tbsp butter
2 shallots, finely chopped
225g/8oz/3 cups button mushrooms,
  halved if large
275g/10oz/1½ cups basmati rice,
  soaked
300ml/½ pint/1¼ cups fish stock
150ml/¼ pint/⅔ cup double cream
15ml/1 tbsp chopped fresh parsley
225g/8oz large cooked prawns,
  peeled and deveined
salt and freshly ground black pepper
fresh flat leaf parsley sprigs, to
  garnish

1 Preheat the oven to 160°C/325°F/ Gas 3. Place the mussels in a pan with 90ml/6 tbsp of the wine and parsley, cover and cook for 4–5 minutes until they have opened. Drain, reserving the cooking liquid. Remove the mussels from their shells, discarding any that have not opened.

2 Cut the fish into bite-size pieces. Detach the corals from the scallops and cut the white scallop flesh into thick pieces.

3 Heat half the olive oil and butter and fry the shallots and mushrooms for 3–4 minutes. Transfer to a large bowl. Heat the remaining oil in the frying pan and fry the rice for 2–3 minutes, stirring until it is coated in oil. Spoon the rice into a deep casserole.

4 Pour the stock, remaining wine and reserved mussel liquid into the frying pan, and bring to the boil. Off the heat, stir in the cream and parsley; season lightly. Pour over the rice and then add the salmon and the scallop flesh, together with the mushroom mixture. Stir carefully to mix.

5 Cover the casserole tightly. Bake for 30–35 minutes, then add the corals, replace the cover and cook for 4 minutes more. Add the mussels and prawns, cover and cook for 3–4 minutes until the seafood is heated through and the rice is tender. Serve garnished with the parsley sprigs.

COURGETTE ROULADE

THIS MAKES A REALLY IMPRESSIVE BUFFET SUPPER OR DINNER PARTY DISH, OR CAN BE WRAPPED AND SERVED CHILLED AS THE PIÈCE DE RÉSISTANCE AT A PICNIC.

5 Bake for 10–15 minutes until the roulade is firm and lightly golden on top. Carefully turn it out on to a sheet of greaseproof or non-stick baking paper sprinkled with 30ml/2 tbsp grated Parmesan. Peel away the lining paper. Roll the roulade up, using the paper as a guide, and leave it to cool.

6 To make the filling, mix the goat's cheese, fromage frais, rice and herbs in a bowl. Season with salt and pepper. Heat the olive oil and butter in a small pan and fry the mushrooms until soft.

SERVES SIX

INGREDIENTS
40g/1½oz/3 tbsp butter
50g/2oz/½ cup plain flour
300ml/½ pint/1¼ cups milk
4 eggs, separated
3 courgettes, grated
25g/1oz/⅓ cup freshly grated
  Parmesan cheese
salt and freshly ground black pepper
herb and green leaf salad, to serve
For the filling
75g/3oz/⅔ cup soft goat's cheese
60ml/4 tbsp fromage frais
225g/8oz/2 cups cooked rice, such
  as Thai fragrant rice or Japanese
  short grain
15ml/1 tbsp chopped mixed fresh
  herbs
15ml/1 tbsp olive oil
15g/½oz/1 tbsp butter
75g/3oz/generous 1 cup button
  mushrooms, very finely chopped

1 Preheat the oven to 200°C/400°F/
Gas 6. Line a 33 x 23cm/13 x 9in Swiss
roll tin with non-stick baking paper.

2 Melt the butter in a saucepan, stir
in the flour and cook for 1–2 minutes,
stirring all the time. Gradually add the
milk, stirring until the mixture forms a
smooth sauce. Remove from the heat
and cool for a few minutes.

3 Stir the egg yolks into the sauce,
one at a time, and then add the grated
courgettes and the Parmesan, and
check the seasoning.

4 Whisk the egg whites until stiff, fold
them into the courgette mixture and
scrape into the prepared tin. Spread
evenly, smoothing the surface with a
palette knife.

7 Unwrap the roulade, spread with the
rice filling and lay the mushrooms along
the centre. Roll up again. The roulade
can be served warm or chilled. To heat,
place on a baking sheet, cover with foil
and heat for 15–20 minutes in a
moderately hot oven. To eat cold, wrap
in clear film and chill in the fridge.
Serve with a herb and green leaf salad.

PROVENÇAL RICE

ONE OF THE GLORIOUS THINGS ABOUT FOOD FROM THE SOUTH OF FRANCE IS ITS COLOUR, AND THIS DISH IS NO EXCEPTION. TO SERVE AS A MAIN COURSE, ALLOW 50G/2OZ/¼ CUP RICE PER PERSON.

SERVES FOUR

INGREDIENTS

2 onions
90ml/6 tbsp olive oil
175g/6oz/scant 1 cup brown long
  grain rice
10ml/2 tsp mustard seeds
475ml/16fl oz/2 cups vegetable stock
1 large or 2 small red peppers,
  seeded and cut into chunks
1 small aubergine, cut into cubes
2–3 courgettes, sliced
about 12 cherry tomatoes
5–6 fresh basil leaves, torn into
  pieces
2 garlic cloves, finely chopped
60ml/4 tbsp white wine
60ml/4 tbsp passata or tomato
  juice
2 hard-boiled eggs, cut into wedges
8 stuffed green olives, sliced
15ml/1 tbsp capers
3 drained sun-dried tomatoes in oil,
  sliced (optional)
butter
sea salt and freshly ground black
  pepper

1 Preheat the oven to 200°C/400°F/ Gas 6. Finely chop one onion. Heat 30ml/2 tbsp of the oil in a saucepan and fry the chopped onion over a gentle heat for 5–6 minutes until softened.

2 Add the rice and mustard seeds. Cook, stirring, for 2 minutes, then add the stock and a little salt. Bring to the boil, then lower the heat, cover and simmer for 35 minutes until the rice is tender.

3 Meanwhile, cut the remaining onion into wedges. Put these in a roasting tin with the peppers, aubergine, courgettes and cherry tomatoes. Scatter over the torn basil leaves and chopped garlic. Pour over the remaining olive oil and sprinkle with sea salt and black pepper. Roast for 15–20 minutes until the vegetables begin to char, stirring halfway through cooking. Reduce the oven temperature to 180°C/350°F/Gas 4.

4 Spoon the rice into an earthenware casserole. Put the roasted vegetables on top, together with any vegetable juices from the roasting tin, then pour over the wine and passata.

5 Arrange the egg wedges on top of the vegetables, with the sliced olives, capers and sun-dried tomatoes, if using. Dot with butter, cover and cook for 15–20 minutes until heated through.

VEGETABLE TARTE TATIN

THIS UPSIDE-DOWN TART COMBINES MEDITERRANEAN VEGETABLES WITH A MEDLEY OF RICE, GARLIC, ONIONS AND OLIVES.

SERVES FOUR AS A STARTER

INGREDIENTS

30ml/2 tbsp sunflower oil
about 25ml/1½ tbsp olive oil
1 aubergine, sliced lengthways
1 large red pepper, seeded and cut into long strips
5 tomatoes
2 red shallots, finely chopped
1–2 garlic cloves, crushed
150ml/¼ pint/⅔ cup white wine
10ml/2 tsp chopped fresh basil
225g/8oz/2 cups cooked white or brown long grain rice
40g/1½oz/⅓ cup stoned black olives, chopped
350g/12oz puff pastry, thawed if frozen
freshly ground black pepper

VARIATION
Courgettes and mushrooms could be used as well, or instead of, the aubergines and peppers, or use strips of lightly browned chicken breast and serve for two as a main meal.

1 Preheat the oven to 190°C/375°F/Gas 5. Heat the sunflower oil with 15ml/1 tbsp of the olive oil in a frying pan and fry the aubergine slices for 4–5 minutes on each side until golden brown. Lift out and drain on kitchen paper.

2 Add the pepper strips to the oil remaining in the pan, turning them to coat. Cover the pan with a lid or foil and sweat the peppers over a moderately high heat for 5–6 minutes, stirring occasionally, until the pepper strips are soft and flecked with brown.

3 Slice two of the tomatoes and set them aside. Plunge the remaining tomatoes briefly into boiling water, then peel them, cut them into quarters and remove the core and seeds. Chop them roughly.

4 Heat the remaining oil in the frying pan and fry the shallots and garlic for 3–4 minutes until softened. Add the chopped tomatoes and cook for a few minutes until softened. Stir in the wine and basil, with black pepper to taste. Bring to the boil, then remove from the heat and stir in the cooked rice and black olives.

5 Arrange the tomato slices, aubergine slices and peppers in a single layer over the bottom of a heavy, 30cm/12in, shallow ovenproof dish. Spread the rice mixture on top.

6 Roll out the pastry to a circle slightly larger than the diameter of the dish and place on top of the rice, tucking the overlap down inside the dish.

7 Bake for 25–30 minutes, until the pastry is golden and risen. Cool slightly, then invert the tart on to a large, warmed serving plate. Serve in slices, with a leafy green salad or simply dressed lamb's lettuce.

COOK'S TIP
This tart would make a lovely lunch or supper dish for two people. Serve it hot with buttered new potatoes and a green vegetable, such as mangetouts or French beans.

SOUFFLÉED RICE PUDDING

USING SKIMMED MILK TO MAKE THIS PUDDING IS A HEALTHY OPTION, BUT YOU COULD USE WHOLE MILK IF YOU PREFER A CREAMIER TASTE.

SERVES FOUR

INGREDIENTS

65g/2½oz/⅓ cup short grain pudding rice
45ml/3 tbsp clear honey
750ml/1¼ pints/3 cups skimmed milk
1 vanilla pod or 2.5ml/½ tsp vanilla essence
butter, for greasing
2 egg whites
5ml/1 tsp freshly grated nutmeg
wafer biscuits, to serve (optional)

1 Place the rice, honey and milk in a heavy or non-stick saucepan, and bring the milk to just below boiling point, watching it closely to prevent it from boiling over. Add the vanilla pod, if using.

2 Reduce the heat to the lowest setting and cover the pan. Leave to cook for about 1–1¼ hours, stirring occasionally to prevent sticking, until most of the liquid has been absorbed.

3 Remove the vanilla pod or, if using vanilla essence, add this to the rice mixture now. Preheat the oven to 220°C/425°F/Gas 7. Grease a 1 litre/1¾ pint/4 cup baking dish with butter.

4 Place the egg whites in a large grease-free bowl and whisk them until they hold soft peaks. Using either a large metal spoon or a spatula, carefully fold the egg whites evenly into the rice and milk mixture. Tip into the baking dish.

5 Sprinkle with grated nutmeg and bake in the oven for about 15–20 minutes, until the rice pudding has risen well and the surface is golden brown. Serve the pudding hot, with wafer biscuits, if you like.

COOK'S TIP
This pudding is delicious topped with a stewed, dried fruit salad.

PEAR, ALMOND AND GROUND RICE FLAN

GROUND RICE GIVES A DISTINCTIVE, SLIGHTLY GRAINY TEXTURE TO PUDDINGS THAT GOES PARTICULARLY WELL WITH AUTUMN FRUIT. PEARS AND ALMONDS ARE A DIVINE COMBINATION.

2 Cream the butter and caster sugar until light and fluffy, then beat in the eggs and almond essence. Fold in the flour and ground rice.

3 Carefully spoon the almond-flavoured egg and ground rice mixture over the quartered pears and level the surface with a palette knife.

SERVES SIX

INGREDIENTS
    4 ripe pears
    30ml/2 tbsp soft light brown sugar
    115g/4oz/½ cup unsalted butter
    115g/4oz/generous ½ cup caster
      sugar
    2 eggs
    a few drops of almond essence
    75g/3oz/⅔ cup self-raising flour
    50g/2oz/⅓ cup ground rice
    25g/1oz/¼ cup flaked almonds
    custard or crème fraîche, to serve
      (optional)

1 Preheat the oven to 180°C/350°F/ Gas 4. Grease a shallow 25cm/10in flan dish. Peel and quarter the pears and arrange them in the flan dish. Sprinkle with the brown sugar.

4 Sprinkle the top with the flaked almonds, then bake the flan for 30–35 minutes until the topping is golden. Serve with custard or crème fraîche.

Cajun, Creole and South America

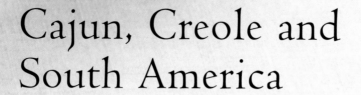

RICE IS GROWN IN LOUISIANA IN THE
SOUTH OF THE UNITED STATES, AND
ACROSS THE BORDER IN CENTRAL AND
SOUTH AMERICA. THE DISHES FROM
THESE REGIONS MAKE USE OF A WEALTH
OF INGREDIENTS, AND MANY ARE NOW
WORLD CLASSICS – CAJUN JAMBALAYAS AND
GUMBOS, TORTILLAS FROM MEXICO
AND CASSEROLES FROM BRAZIL.

LOUISIANA RICE

AUBERGINE AND PORK COMBINE WITH HERBS AND SPICES TO MAKE A HIGHLY FLAVOURSOME DISH.

SERVES FOUR

INGREDIENTS
60ml/4 tbsp vegetable oil
1 onion, chopped
1 small aubergine, diced
225g/8oz minced pork
1 green pepper, seeded and
  chopped
2 celery sticks, chopped
1 garlic clove, crushed
5ml/1 tsp cayenne pepper
5ml/1 tsp paprika
5ml/1 tsp freshly ground black
  pepper
2.5ml/½ tsp salt
5ml/1 tsp dried thyme
2.5ml/½ tsp dried oregano
475ml/16fl oz/2 cups chicken stock
225g/8oz chicken livers, chopped
150g/5oz/¾ cup white long grain rice
1 bay leaf
45ml/3 tbsp chopped fresh parsley

1 Heat the oil in a frying pan. When it is piping hot, add the onion and aubergine and stir-fry for about 5 minutes.

2 Add the pork and cook for 6–8 minutes until browned, using a wooden spoon to break up any lumps.

3 Stir in the green pepper, celery and garlic, with all the spices and herbs. Cover and cook over a high heat for 9–10 minutes, stirring frequently from the bottom of the pan to scrape up and distribute the crispy brown bits.

4 Pour in the chicken stock and stir to remove any sediment from the bottom of the pan. Cover and cook for 6 minutes over a moderate heat. Stir in the chicken livers and cook for 2 minutes more.

5 Stir in the rice and add the bay leaf. Lower the heat, cover and simmer for 6–7 minutes. Turn off the heat and leave to stand, still covered, for 10–15 minutes more until the rice is tender. Remove the bay leaf and stir in the chopped parsley. Serve the rice hot.

DIRTY RICE

CONTRARY TO POPULAR BELIEF, THIS DISH DOESN'T GET ITS NAME FROM ITS APPEARANCE, BUT FROM ITS ASSOCIATION WITH NEW ORLEANS, THE HOME OF JAZZ, WHICH HAS OFTEN BEEN REFERRED TO AS "DIRTY MUSIC".

SERVES FOUR

INGREDIENTS

60ml/4 tbsp vegetable oil
25g/1oz/¼ cup plain flour
50g/2oz/4 tbsp butter
1 large onion, chopped
2 garlic cloves, crushed
200g/7oz minced pork
225g/8oz chicken livers, trimmed
  and finely chopped
dash of Tabasco sauce
1 green pepper, seeded and sliced
2 celery sticks, sliced
300ml/½ pint/1¼ cups chicken stock
225g/8oz/generous 1 cup cooked
  white long grain rice
4 spring onions, chopped
45ml/3 tbsp chopped fresh parsley
salt and freshly ground black pepper
celery leaves, to garnish

1 Heat half the oil in a heavy-based saucepan. Stir in the flour and cook over a low heat, stirring constantly, until the roux is smooth and the colour is a rich chestnut-brown. Immediately remove the pan from the heat and place it on a cold surface such as the draining board of a sink.

2 Heat the remaining oil with the butter in a frying pan and stir-fry the onion for 5 minutes.

3 Add the garlic and pork. Cook for 5 minutes, breaking up the pork and stirring until it is evenly browned, then stir in the chicken livers and fry for 2–3 minutes until they have changed colour all over. Season with salt, pepper and Tabasco sauce. Stir in the green pepper and celery.

4 Stir the roux into the stir-fried mixture, then gradually add in the stock. When the mixture begins to bubble, cover and cook for 30 minutes, stirring occasionally. Stir in the rice, spring onions and parsley. Toss over the heat until the rice has heated through. Serve garnished with celery leaves.

LOUISIANA SEAFOOD GUMBO

GUMBO IS A SOUP, BUT IS SERVED OVER RICE AS A MAIN COURSE. IN LOUISIANA, OYSTERS ARE CHEAP AND PROLIFIC, AND WOULD BE USED HERE INSTEAD OF MUSSELS.

SERVES SIX

INGREDIENTS
450g/1lb fresh mussels
450g/1lb raw prawns, in the shell
1 cooked crab, about 1kg/2¼lb
small bunch of parsley, leaves
  chopped and stalks reserved
150ml/¼ pint/⅔ cup vegetable oil
115g/4oz/1 cup plain flour
1 green pepper, seeded and chopped
1 large onion, chopped
2 celery sticks, sliced
3 garlic cloves, finely chopped
75g/3oz smoked spiced sausage,
  skinned and sliced
275g/10oz/1½ cups white long grain
  rice
6 spring onions, shredded
cayenne pepper, to taste
Tabasco sauce, to taste
salt

1 Wash the mussels in several changes of cold water, pulling away the black "beards". Discard any mussels that are broken or do not close when you tap them firmly.

2 Bring 250ml/8fl oz/1 cup water to the boil in a deep saucepan. Add the mussels, cover the pan tightly and cook over a high heat, shaking frequently, for 3 minutes. As the mussels open, lift them out with tongs into a sieve set over a bowl. Discard any that fail to open. Shell the mussels, discarding the shells. Return the liquid from the bowl to the pan and make the quantity up to 2 litres/3½ pints/8 cups with water.

3 Peel the prawns and set them aside, reserving a few for the garnish. Put the shells and heads into the saucepan.

4 Remove all the meat from the crab, separating the brown and white meat. Add all the pieces of shell to the saucepan with 5ml/2 tsp salt.

5 Bring the shellfish stock to the boil, skimming it regularly. When there is no more froth on the surface, add the parsley stalks and simmer for 15 minutes. Cool the stock, then strain it into a measuring jug and make up to 2 litres/3½ pints/8 cups with water.

6 Heat the oil in a heavy-based pan and stir in the flour. Stir constantly over a medium heat with a wooden spoon or whisk until the roux reaches a golden-brown colour. Immediately add the pepper, onion, celery and garlic. Continue cooking for about 3 minutes until the onion is soft. Stir in the sausage. Reheat the stock.

7 Stir the brown crab meat into the roux, then ladle in the hot stock a little at a time, stirring constantly until it has all been smoothly incorporated. Bring to a low boil, partially cover the pan, then simmer the gumbo for 30 minutes.

8 Meanwhile, cook the rice in plenty of lightly salted boiling water until the grains are tender.

9 Add the prawns, mussels, white crab meat and spring onions to the gumbo. Return to the boil and season with salt if necessary, cayenne and a dash or two of Tabasco sauce. Simmer for a further minute, then add the chopped parsley leaves. Serve immediately, ladling the soup over the hot rice in soup plates.

COOK'S TIP
It is vital to stir constantly to darken the roux without burning. Should black specks occur at any stage of cooking, discard the roux and start again. Have the onion, green pepper and celery ready to add to the roux the minute it reaches the correct golden-brown stage, as this arrests its darkening.

CHICKEN AND PRAWN JAMBALAYA

THE MIXTURE OF CHICKEN, SEAFOOD AND RICE SUGGESTS A CLOSE RELATIONSHIP TO THE SPANISH
PAELLA, BUT THE NAME IS MORE LIKELY TO HAVE DERIVED FROM JAMBON (THE FRENCH FOR HAM),
À LA YA (CREOLE FOR RICE). JAMBALAYAS ARE A COLOURFUL MIXTURE OF HIGHLY FLAVOURED
INGREDIENTS, AND ARE ALWAYS MADE IN LARGE QUANTITIES FOR FEASTS AND CELEBRATION MEALS.

SERVES TEN

INGREDIENTS

2 chickens, each about 1.5kg/3–3½lb
450g/1lb piece raw smoked gammon
50g/2oz/4 tbsp lard or bacon fat
50g/2oz/½ cup plain flour
3 medium onions, finely sliced
2 green peppers, seeded and sliced
675g/1½lb tomatoes, peeled and
  chopped
2–3 garlic cloves, crushed
10ml/2 tsp chopped fresh thyme or
  5ml/1 tsp dried thyme
24 raw Mediterranean prawns, peeled
  and deveined
500g/1¼lb/3 cups white long grain rice
1.2 litres/2 pints/5 cups water
2–3 dashes Tabasco sauce
45ml/3 tbsp chopped fresh flat leaf
  parsley, plus tiny fresh parsley
  sprigs, to garnish
salt and freshly ground black pepper

4 Add the diced gammon, onions, green peppers, tomatoes, garlic and thyme. Cook, stirring regularly, for 10 minutes, then add the prawns and mix lightly.

5 Stir the rice into the pan and pour in the water. Season with salt, pepper and Tabasco sauce. Bring to the boil, then cook gently until the rice is tender and all the liquid has been absorbed. Add a little extra boiling water if the rice looks like drying out before it is cooked.

6 Mix the parsley into the finished dish, garnish with tiny sprigs of flat leaf parsley and serve immediately.

1 Cut each chicken into 10 pieces and season with salt and pepper. Dice the gammon, discarding the rind and fat.

2 Melt the lard or bacon fat in a large, heavy-based frying pan. Add the chicken pieces in batches, brown them all over, then lift them out with a slotted spoon and set them aside.

3 Reduce the heat. Sprinkle the flour into the fat in the pan and stir until the roux turns golden brown. Return the chicken pieces to the pan.

BRAZILIAN PORK AND RICE CASSEROLE

*WE TEND TO ASSOCIATE BRAZIL WITH BEEF, BUT THERE ARE ALSO SOME EXCELLENT PORK RECIPES,
INCLUDING THIS HEARTY DISH OF MARINATED PORK, VEGETABLES AND RICE.*

SERVES FOUR TO SIX

INGREDIENTS

500g/1¼lb lean pork, such as fillet,
   cut into strips
60ml/4 tbsp corn oil
1 onion, chopped
1 garlic clove, crushed
1 green pepper, cut into pieces
about 300ml/½ pint/1¼ cups chicken
   stock
225g/8oz/generous 1 cup white long
   grain rice
150ml/¼ pint/⅔ cup double cream
40g/1½oz/½ cup freshly grated
   Parmesan cheese
salt and freshly ground black pepper
For the marinade
120ml/4fl oz/½ cup dry white wine
30ml/2 tbsp lemon juice
1 onion, chopped
4 juniper berries, lightly crushed
3 cloves
1 fresh red chilli, seeded and finely
   sliced

1 Mix all the marinade ingredients,
add the pork and set aside to marinate
for 3–4 hours, turning occasionally.
Transfer the pork to a plate and pat dry.
Strain the marinade and set aside.

2 Heat the oil in a heavy-based
saucepan and fry the pork for a few
minutes until evenly brown. Transfer
to a plate using a slotted spoon.

3 Add the chopped onion and the
garlic to the saucepan and fry for
3–4 minutes. Stir in the pepper, cook
for 3–4 minutes more, then return the
pork to the pan. Pour in the reserved
marinade and the stock. Bring to the
boil and season with salt and fresh
black pepper, then lower the heat,
cover and simmer gently for 10 minutes
until the meat is nearly tender.

4 Preheat the oven to 160°C/325°F/
Gas 3. Cook the rice in plenty of lightly
salted boiling water for 8 minutes or
until three-quarters cooked. Drain well.
Spread half the rice over the bottom of
a buttered, oval baking dish. Using a
slotted spoon, make a neat layer of
meat and vegetables on top, then
spread over the remaining rice.

5 Stir the cream and 30ml/2 tbsp of
the Parmesan into the liquid in which
the pork was cooked. Tip into a jug.
Carefully pour the cream mixture over
the rice and sprinkle with the remaining
Parmesan cheese. Cover with foil and
bake for 20 minutes, then remove the
foil and cook for 5 minutes more, until
the top is lightly brown.

CHICKEN FAJITAS

FAJITAS ARE WARMED SOFT TORTILLAS, FILLED AND FOLDED LIKE AN ENVELOPE. THEY ARE
TRADITIONAL MEXICAN FAST FOOD, DELICIOUS AND EASY TO PREPARE, AND A FAVOURITE FOR SUPPER.

SERVES FOUR

INGREDIENTS
    115g/4oz/generous ½ cup white long
        grain rice
    15g/1oz/3 tbsp wild rice
    15ml/1 tbsp olive oil
    15ml/1 tbsp sunflower oil
    1 onion, cut into thin wedges
    4 skinless, boneless chicken breasts,
        cut into thin strips
    1 red pepper, seeded and finely
        sliced
    5ml/1 tsp ground cumin
    generous pinch of cayenne pepper
    2.5ml/½ tsp ground turmeric
    175ml/6fl oz/¾ cup passata
    120–175ml/4–6fl oz/½–¾ cup
        chicken stock
    12 small or 8 large wheat tortillas,
        warmed
    soured cream, to serve
For the salsa
    1 shallot, roughly chopped
    1 small garlic clove
    ½–1 fresh green chilli, seeded and
        roughly chopped
    small bunch of fresh parsley
    5 tomatoes, peeled, seeded and
        chopped
    10ml/2 tsp olive oil
    15ml/1 tbsp lemon juice
    30ml/2 tbsp tomato juice
    salt and freshly ground black pepper
For the guacamole
    1 large ripe avocado
    2 spring onions, chopped
    15–30ml/1–2 tbsp fresh lime or
        lemon juice
    generous pinch of cayenne pepper
    15ml/1 tbsp chopped fresh coriander

COOK'S TIP
To warm the tortillas, either wrap them
in foil and place them in a warm oven
for 5 minutes, or wrap 4 or 5 at a time
in microwave film and microwave for
20 seconds on 100% Full Power.

1 Cook the long grain and wild rice
separately, following the instructions
on the packets. Drain and set aside.

2 Make the salsa. Finely chop the
shallot, garlic, chilli and parsley in a
blender or food processor. Spoon into
a bowl. Stir in the chopped tomatoes,
olive oil, lemon juice and tomato juice.
Season to taste with salt and pepper.
Cover with clear film and chill.

3 Make the guacamole. Scoop the
avocado flesh into a bowl. Mash it
lightly with the spring onions, citrus
juice, cayenne, fresh coriander and
seasoning, so that small pieces still
remain. Cover the surface closely with
clear film and chill.

4 Heat the olive and sunflower oils in
a frying pan and fry the onion wedges
for 4–5 minutes until softened. Add
the chicken strips and red pepper
slices and fry until evenly browned.

5 Stir in the cumin, cayenne and
turmeric. Fry, stirring, for about
1 minute, then stir in the passata and
chicken stock. Bring to the boil, then
lower the heat and simmer gently for
5–6 minutes until the chicken is
cooked through. Season to taste.

6 Stir both types of rice into the
chicken and cook for 1–2 minutes
until the rice is warmed through.

7 Spoon a little of the chicken and
rice mixture on to each warmed tortilla.
Top with salsa, guacamole and soured
cream and roll up. Alternatively, let
everyone assemble their own fajita
at the table.

VARIATION
Fajitas are very popular family fare, so
don't be surprised if there are demands
for this dish time and time again. To ring
the changes, use brown long grain and
red Camargue rice instead of the white
rice and wild rice, and try using pork fillet
or beef steak in place of the chicken.

MEXICAN SPICY BEEF TORTILLA

THIS DISH IS NOT UNLIKE A LASAGNE, EXCEPT THAT THE SPICY MEAT IS MIXED WITH RICE AND IS LAYERED BETWEEN MEXICAN TORTILLAS, WITH A HOT SALSA SAUCE FOR AN EXTRA KICK.

SERVES FOUR

INGREDIENTS

1 onion, chopped
2 garlic cloves, crushed
1 fresh red chilli, seeded and sliced
350g/12oz rump steak, cut into
  small cubes
15ml/1 tbsp oil
225g/8oz/2 cups cooked long grain
  rice
beef stock, to moisten
3 large wheat tortillas
For the salsa picante
2 x 400g/14oz cans chopped tomatoes
2 garlic cloves, halved
1 onion, quartered
1–2 fresh red chillies, seeded and
  roughly chopped
5ml/1 tsp ground cumin
2.5–5ml/½–1 tsp cayenne pepper
5ml/1 tsp fresh oregano or 2.5ml/½
  tsp dried oregano
tomato juice or water, if required
For the cheese sauce
50g/2oz/4 tbsp butter
50g/2oz/½ cup plain flour
600ml/1 pint/2½ cups milk
115g/4oz/1 cup grated Cheddar cheese
salt and freshly ground black pepper

1 Preheat the oven to 180°C/350°F/ Gas 4. Make the salsa picante. Place the tomatoes, garlic, onion and chillies in a blender or food processor and process until smooth. Pour into a small saucepan, add the spices and oregano and season with salt. Gradually bring to the boil, stirring occasionally. Boil for 1–2 minutes, then lower the heat, cover and simmer for 15 minutes. The sauce should be thick, but of a pouring consistency. If it is too thick, dilute it with a little tomato juice or water.

2 Make the cheese sauce. Melt the butter in a pan and stir in the flour. Cook for 1 minute. Add the milk, stirring all the time until the sauce boils and thickens. Stir in all but 30ml/2 tbsp of the cheese and season to taste. Cover the pan closely and set aside.

3 Mix the onion, garlic and chilli in a large bowl. Add the steak cubes and mix well. Heat the oil in a frying pan and stir-fry the meat mixture for about 10 minutes, until the meat cubes have browned and the onion is soft. Stir in the rice and enough beef stock to moisten. Season to taste with salt and freshly ground black pepper.

4 Pour about a quarter of the cheese sauce into the bottom of a round ovenproof dish. Add a tortilla and then spread over half the salsa followed by half the meat mixture.

5 Repeat these layers, then add half the remaining cheese sauce and the final tortilla. Pour over the remaining cheese sauce and sprinkle the reserved cheese on top. Bake in the oven for 15–20 minutes until golden on top.

COOK'S TIP

You can use any type of beef for this dish. If braising or stewing steak are used, they should be very finely chopped or even minced and the bake should be cooked for an extra 10–15 minutes.

TOMATO RICE

PROOF POSITIVE THAT YOU DON'T NEED ELABORATE INGREDIENTS OR COMPLICATED COOKING METHODS TO MAKE A DELICIOUS DISH.

SERVES FOUR

INGREDIENTS
    30ml/2 tbsp sunflower oil
    2.5ml/½ tsp onion seeds
    1 onion, sliced
    2 tomatoes, chopped
    1 orange or yellow pepper, seeded
        and sliced
    5ml/1 tsp crushed fresh root ginger
    1 garlic clove, crushed
    5ml/1 tsp chilli powder
    1 potato, diced
    7.5ml/1½ tsp salt
    400g/14oz/2 cups basmati rice,
        soaked
    750ml/1¼ pints/3 cups water
    30–45ml/2–3 tbsp chopped fresh
        coriander

1 Heat the oil and fry the onion seeds for about 30 seconds. Add the sliced onion and fry for about 5 minutes.

2 Stir in the tomatoes, pepper, ginger, garlic, chilli powder, potato and salt. Stir-fry over a medium heat for about 5 minutes more.

3 Drain the rice and add to the pan, then stir for about 1 minute until the grains are well coated.

4 Pour in the water and bring the rice to the boil, then lower the heat, cover the pan and cook the rice for 12–15 minutes. Remove from the heat, without lifting the lid, and leave the rice to stand for 5 minutes. Stir in the chopped coriander and serve.

PERUVIAN DUCK WITH RICE

THIS IS A VERY RICH DISH, BRIGHTLY COLOURED WITH SPANISH TOMATOES AND FRESH HERBS.

SERVES FOUR TO SIX

INGREDIENTS

4 boned duck breasts
1 Spanish onion, chopped
2 garlic cloves, crushed
10ml/2 tsp grated fresh root ginger
4 tomatoes (peeled, if liked),
   chopped
225g/8oz Kabocha or onion squash,
   cut into 1cm/½in cubes
275g/10oz/1½ cups long grain rice
750ml/1¼ pints/3 cups chicken
   stock
15ml/1 tbsp finely chopped fresh
   coriander
15ml/1 tbsp finely chopped fresh
   mint
salt and freshly ground black
   pepper

2 Pour all but 15ml/1 tbsp of the fat into a jar or cup, then fry the breasts, meat side down, in the fat remaining in the pan for 3–4 minutes until brown all over. Transfer to a board, slice thickly and set aside in a shallow dish. Deglaze the pan with a little water and pour this liquid over the duck.

4 Add the squash, stir-fry for a few minutes, then cover and allow to steam for about 4 minutes.

5 Stir in the rice and cook, stirring, until the rice is coated in the tomato and onion mixture. Pour in the stock, return the slices of duck to the pan and season with salt and pepper.

1 Heat a heavy-based frying pan or flameproof casserole. Using a sharp knife, score the fatty side of the duck breasts in a criss-cross pattern, rub the fat with a little salt, then dry-fry the duck, skin side down, for 6–8 minutes to render some of the fat.

3 Fry the onion and garlic in the same pan for 4–5 minutes until the onion is fairly soft, adding a little extra duck fat if necessary. Stir in the ginger, cook for 1–2 minutes more, then add the tomatoes and cook, stirring, for another 2 minutes.

6 Bring to the boil, then lower the heat, cover and simmer gently for 30–35 minutes until the rice is tender. Stir in the coriander and mint and serve.

COOK'S TIP
While rice was originally imported to South America, squash was very much an indigenous vegetable. Pumpkin could also be used for this recipe. Kabocha squash has a thick skin and lots of seeds, which need to be removed before the flesh is cubed.

VARIATION
In Peru, these kinds of all-in-one dishes are based around whatever meat is available in the shops, or, in the case of vegetables, what is growing in the garden. Chicken or rabbit can be used instead of duck, and courgettes and carrots would work well when squash is out of season.

PERUVIAN SALAD

THIS REALLY IS A SPECTACULAR-LOOKING SALAD. IT COULD BE SERVED AS A SIDE DISH OR WOULD MAKE A DELICIOUS LIGHT LUNCH. IN PERU, WHITE RICE WOULD BE USED, BUT BROWN RICE ADDS AN INTERESTING TEXTURE AND FLAVOUR.

SERVES FOUR

INGREDIENTS

225g/8oz/2 cups cooked long grain
   brown or white rice
15ml/1 tbsp chopped fresh parsley
1 red pepper
1 small onion, sliced
olive oil, for sprinkling
115g/4oz green beans, halved
50g/2oz/½ cup baby sweetcorn
4 quails' eggs, hard-boiled
25–50g/1–2oz Spanish ham, cut into
   thin slices (optional)
1 small avocado
lemon juice, for sprinkling
75g/3oz mixed salad
15ml/1 tbsp capers
about 10 stuffed olives, halved
For the dressing
1 garlic clove, crushed
60ml/4 tbsp olive oil
45ml/3 tbsp sunflower oil
30ml/2 tbsp lemon juice
45ml/3 tbsp natural yogurt
2.5ml/½ tsp mustard
2.5ml/½ tsp granulated sugar
salt and freshly ground black pepper

1 Make the dressing by placing all the ingredients in a bowl and whisking with a fork until smooth. Alternatively, shake the ingredients together in a jam jar.

2 Put the cooked rice into a large, glass salad bowl and spoon in half the dressing. Add the chopped parsley, stir well and set aside.

3 Cut the pepper in half, remove the seeds and pith, then place the halves, cut side down, in a small roasting tin. Add the onion rings. Sprinkle the onion with a little olive oil, place the tin under a hot grill and grill for 5–6 minutes until the pepper blackens and blisters and the onion turns golden. You may need to stir the onion once or twice so that it grills evenly.

4 Stir the onion in with the rice. Put the pepper in a plastic bag and knot the bag. When the steam has loosened the skin on the pepper halves and they are cool enough to handle, peel them and cut the flesh into thin strips.

COOK'S TIP
This dish looks particularly attractive if served in a deep, glass salad bowl. Guests can then see the various layers, starting with the white rice, then the green salad leaves, topped by the bright colours of peppers, corn, eggs and olives.

5 Cook the green beans in boiling water for 2 minutes, then add the sweetcorn and cook for 1–2 minutes more, until tender. Drain both vegetables, refresh them under cold water, then drain again. Place in a large mixing bowl and add the red pepper strips, quails' eggs and ham, if using.

6 Peel the avocado, remove the stone, and cut the flesh into slices or chunks. Sprinkle with the lemon juice. Put the salad in a separate mixing bowl, add the avocado and mix lightly. Arrange the salad on top of the rice.

7 Stir about 45ml/3 tbsp of the remaining dressing into the green bean and pepper mixture. Pile this on top of the salad.

8 Scatter the capers and stuffed olives on top and serve the salad with the remaining dressing.

CALAS

THESE SWEET RICE FRITTERS ARE A CREOLE SPECIALITY, SOLD BY "CALAS" WOMEN ON THE STREETS OF THE FRENCH QUARTER OF NEW ORLEANS TO RESIDENTS AND OFFICE WORKERS, FOR WHOM THEY MAKE A POPULAR AND TASTY BREAKFAST.

MAKES OVER 40

INGREDIENTS

115g/4oz/generous ½ cup short grain
   pudding rice
900ml/1½ pints/3¾ cups mixed milk
   and water
30ml/2 tbsp caster sugar
50g/2oz/½ cup plain flour
7.5ml/1½ tsp baking powder
5ml/1 tsp grated lemon rind
2.5ml/½ tsp ground cinnamon
1.5ml/¼ tsp ground ginger
generous pinch of grated nutmeg
2 eggs
sunflower oil, for deep frying
salt
icing sugar, for dusting
cherry or strawberry jam and thick
   cream, to serve

1 Put the rice in a saucepan and pour in the milk and water. Add a pinch of salt and bring to the boil. Stir, then cover and simmer over a very gentle heat for 15–20 minutes until the rice is tender.

2 Switch off the heat under the pan, then add the sugar. Stir well, cover and leave until completely cool, by which time the rice should have absorbed all the liquid and become very soft.

3 Put the rice in a food processor or blender and add the flour, baking powder, lemon rind, spices and eggs. Process for about 20–30 seconds so that the mixture is like a thick batter.

4 Heat the oil in a wok or deep-fryer to 160°C/325°F. Scoop up a generous teaspoon of the rice batter and, using a second spoon, push this off carefully into the hot oil. Add four or five more and fry for 3–4 minutes, turning them occasionally, until the calas are a deep golden brown. Drain on kitchen paper and keep warm while cooking successive batches.

5 Dust the calas generously with icing sugar and serve warm with fruit jam and thick cream.

FRUITY RICE PUDDING CUSTARD

THERE ARE MANY DELICIOUS VARIATIONS ON RICE PUDDING IN LATIN AMERICA, THANKS TO SPANISH, PORTUGUESE AND FRENCH SETTLERS WHO ADAPTED FAVOURITE RECIPES FROM THEIR NATIVE COUNTRIES AND ADDED LOCAL INGREDIENTS LIKE RUM, THAT THEY HAD ACQUIRED A LIKING FOR.

SERVES FOUR TO SIX

INGREDIENTS
  60ml/4 tbsp rum or brandy
  75g/3oz/½ cup sultanas
  75g/3oz/scant ½ cup short grain
    pudding rice
  600ml/1 pint/2½ cups creamy milk
  1 strip pared lemon rind
  ½ cinnamon stick
  115g/4oz/scant ½ cup caster sugar
  150ml/¼ pint/⅔ cup single cream
  2 eggs, plus 1 egg yolk
  almond biscuits, to serve (optional)

1 Warm the rum or brandy in a small pan, then pour it over the sultanas. Soak for 3–4 hours or overnight.

2 Cook the rice in boiling water for 10 minutes until slightly softened. Drain well and return to the saucepan.

3 Stir 300ml/½ pint/1¼ cups of milk into the rice in the pan. Add the strip of lemon rind and the cinnamon stick, bring to the boil, then lower the heat and simmer for about 5 minutes. Remove the pan from the heat and stir in half of the sugar. Cover tightly with a damp dish towel held firmly in place with the saucepan lid. Leave the rice to cool for 1–2 hours.

4 Preheat the oven to 180°C/350°F/ Gas 4. Butter a medium-size baking dish and scatter the sultanas (with any remaining rum or brandy) over the bottom. Stir the rice, which should by now be thick and creamy, most of the liquid having been absorbed, and discard the cinnamon stick and lemon rind. Spoon the rice over the sultanas in the baking dish.

5 Heat the remaining milk with the cream until just boiling. Meanwhile, mix the eggs and egg yolk in a jug. Whisk in the remaining sugar, then the hot milk. Pour the mixture over the rice.

6 Stand the dish in a roasting tin, pour in hot water to come halfway up the sides of the dish and bake for 1–1¼ hours until the top is firm. Serve hot, with almond biscuits, if you like.

COOK'S TIP
This makes a light, creamy rice pudding. If you like your pudding to be denser, cook it for longer.

Africa and the Caribbean

RICE HAS BEEN AN IMPORTANT CROP IN
AFRICA FOR CENTURIES, AND SOME OF
THE OLDEST RICE DISHES, ALTHOUGH NOT
NECESSARILY THE BEST KNOWN, COME FROM
HERE. TRADITIONAL RECIPES AND, PROBABLY,
THE RICE SEEDS, WERE BROUGHT FROM AFRICA
TO THE CARIBBEAN, AND A NEW CUISINE
EVOLVED — AN UNFORGETTABLE BLEND OF
TRADITION AND EXOTIC PRODUCE.

JOLOFF CHICKEN AND RICE

IN WEST AFRICA, WHERE IT ORIGINATED, THIS DISH IS USUALLY MADE IN LARGE QUANTITIES, USING
JOINTED WHOLE CHICKENS. THIS VERSION IS SOMEWHAT MORE SOPHISTICATED, BUT STILL HAS THE
TRADITIONAL FLAVOUR.

SERVES FOUR

INGREDIENTS

2 garlic cloves, crushed
5ml/1 tsp dried thyme
4 skinless, boneless chicken breasts
30ml/2 tbsp palm or vegetable oil
400g/14oz can chopped tomatoes
15ml/1 tbsp tomato purée
1 onion, chopped
450ml/¾ pint/scant 2 cups chicken
   stock
30ml/2 tbsp dried shrimps or
   crayfish, ground
1 fresh green chilli, seeded and
   finely chopped
350g/12oz//1¾ cups white long grain
   rice
750ml/18fl oz/2½ cups water
chopped fresh thyme, to garnish

1 Mix the garlic and thyme in a bowl.
Rub the mixture into the chicken
breasts. Heat the oil in a frying pan.

2 Add the chicken breasts to the pan
to brown in the oil, then remove to a
plate. Add the chopped tomatoes,
tomato purée and onion to the pan.
Cook over a moderately high heat for
about 15 minutes until the tomatoes
are well reduced, stirring occasionally
at first and then more frequently as the
tomatoes thicken.

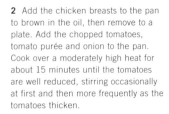

3 Lower the heat a little, return the
chicken pieces to the pan and stir well
to coat with the sauce. Cook for 10
minutes, stirring, then add the stock,
the dried shrimps or crayfish and the
chilli. Bring to the boil, then simmer
for 5 minutes or until the chicken is
cooked, stirring occasionally.

4 Meanwhile, put the rice in a separate
saucepan. Pour in 750ml/18 fl oz/
2½ cups of water, and top up with the
sauce from the chicken. Bring to the
boil, then lower the heat and cover the
pan. Cook over a low heat for 12–15
minutes until the liquid has been
absorbed and the rice is tender.

5 Pack the rice in four individual
moulds and set aside. Lift out the
chicken breasts from the sauce and
put them on a board. If the sauce is
runny, cook it over a high heat to
reduce it a little. Unmould a rice
timbale on each of four serving plates.
Spoon the sauce around, then quickly
slice the chicken breasts and fan them
on the sauce. Garnish with fresh thyme
sprigs and serve immediately.

TANZANIAN VEGETABLE RICE

SERVE THIS TASTY DISH WITH BAKED CHICKEN OR FISH. ADD THE VEGETABLES NEAR THE END OF COOKING SO THAT THEY REMAIN CRISP.

SERVES FOUR

INGREDIENTS

    350g/12oz/1¾ cups basmati rice
    45ml/3 tbsp vegetable oil
    1 onion, chopped
    2 garlic cloves, crushed
    750ml/1¼ pints/3 cups vegetable
      stock or water
    115g/4oz/⅔ cup fresh or drained
      canned sweetcorn kernels
    ½ red or green pepper, seeded and
      chopped
    1 large carrot, grated
    fresh chervil sprigs, to garnish

1 Rinse the rice in a sieve under cold water, then leave to drain thoroughly for about 15 minutes.

2 Heat the oil in a large saucepan and fry the onion for a few minutes over a medium heat until it starts to soften.

3 Add the rice and fry for about 10 minutes, stirring constantly to prevent the rice sticking to the pan. Then stir in the crushed garlic.

4 Pour in the stock or water and stir well. Bring to the boil, then lower the heat, cover and simmer for 10 minutes.

5 Scatter the sweetcorn kernels over the rice, then spread the chopped pepper on top. Sprinkle over the grated carrot. Cover the saucepan tightly. Steam over a low heat until the rice is tender, then mix together with a fork, pile on to a platter and garnish with chervil. Serve immediately.

MOROCCAN PAELLA

PAELLA IS PERENNIALLY POPULAR. THIS VERSION HAS CROSSED THE SEA FROM SPAIN TO MOROCCO, AND ACQUIRED SOME SPICY TOUCHES. UNLIKE SPANISH PAELLA, IT IS MADE WITH LONG GRAIN RICE.

SERVES SIX

INGREDIENTS
    2 large skinless, boneless chicken
        breasts
    about 150g/5oz prepared squid, cut
        into rings
    275g/10oz cod or haddock fillets,
        skinned and cut into bite-size
        chunks
    8–10 raw king prawns, peeled and
        deveined
    8 scallops, trimmed and halved
    350g/12oz fresh mussels
    250g/9oz/1¼ cups white long grain
        rice
    30ml/2 tbsp sunflower oil
    1 bunch spring onions, cut into strips
    2 small courgettes, cut into strips
    1 red pepper, cored, seeded and cut
        into strips
    400ml/14fl oz/1⅔ cups chicken stock
    250ml/8fl oz/1 cup passata
    salt and freshly ground black pepper
    fresh coriander sprigs and lemon
        wedges, to garnish
For the marinade
    2 fresh red chillies, seeded and
        roughly chopped
    generous handful of fresh coriander
    10–15ml/2–3 tsp ground cumin
    15ml/1 tbsp paprika
    2 garlic cloves
    45ml/3 tbsp olive oil
    60ml/4 tbsp sunflower oil
    juice of 1 lemon

1 Make the marinade. Place all the ingredients in a food processor with 5ml/1 tsp salt and process until thoroughly blended. Cut the chicken into bite-size pieces. Place in a bowl.

2 Place the fish and shellfish (apart from the mussels) in a separate glass bowl. Divide the marinade between the fish and chicken and stir well. Cover with clear film and leave to marinate for at least 2 hours.

3 Scrub the mussels, discarding any that do not close when tapped sharply, and keep in a bowl in the fridge until ready to use. Place the rice in a bowl, cover with boiling water and set aside for about 30 minutes. Drain the chicken and fish, and reserve both lots of the marinade. Heat the oil in a wok, balti pan or paella pan and fry the chicken pieces for a few minutes until lightly browned.

4 Add the spring onions to the pan, fry for 1 minute and then add the courgettes and red pepper and fry for 3–4 minutes more until slightly softened. Transfer the chicken and then the vegetables to separate plates.

5 Scrape all the marinade into the pan and cook for 1 minute. Drain the rice, add to the pan and cook for 1 minute. Add the chicken stock, passata and reserved chicken, season with salt and pepper and stir well. Bring the mixture to the boil, then cover the pan with a large lid or foil and simmer very gently for 10–15 minutes until the rice is almost tender.

6 Add the reserved vegetables to the pan and place all the fish and mussels on top. Cover again with a lid or foil and cook over a moderate heat for 10–12 minutes until the fish is cooked and the mussels have opened. Discard any mussels that remain closed. Serve garnished with fresh coriander and lemon wedges.

SAVOURY GROUND RICE

SAVOURY GROUND RICE IS OFTEN SERVED AS AN ACCOMPANIMENT TO SOUPS AND STEWS IN WEST AFRICA.

SERVES FOUR

INGREDIENTS

300ml/½ pint/1¼ cups water
300ml/½ pint/1¼ cups milk
2.5ml/½ tsp salt
15ml/1 tbsp chopped fresh parsley
25g/1oz/2 tbsp butter or margarine
275g/10oz/1⅔ cups ground rice

COOK'S TIP
Ground rice is a creamy white colour, with a slightly grainy texture. Although often used in sweet dishes, it is a tasty grain to serve with savoury dishes too. The addition of milk gives a creamier flavour, but a double quantity of water can be used instead, if preferred.

3 Cover the pan and cook over a low heat for about 15 minutes, beating the mixture every 2 minutes to prevent the formation of lumps.

4 To test if the rice is cooked, rub a pinch of the mixture between your fingers: if it feels smooth and fairly dry, it is ready. Serve hot.

1 Place the water in a saucepan. Pour in the milk, bring to the boil and add the salt and parsley.

2 Add the butter or margarine and the ground rice, stirring with a wooden spoon to prevent the rice from becoming lumpy.

MOROCCAN SPICY MEATBALLS WITH RED RICE

CAMARGUE RED RICE IS NATIVE TO FRANCE, BUT IS RAPIDLY GROWING IN POPULARITY THROUGHOUT THE MEDITERRANEAN. IN THIS MOROCCAN DISH, THE NUTTY FLAVOUR OF THE RICE IS A PERFECT MATCH FOR THE SPICY MEATBALLS.

SERVES FOUR TO SIX

INGREDIENTS

225g/8oz/generous 1 cup Camargue
  red rice
675g/1½lb lamb leg steaks
2 onions
3–4 fresh parsley sprigs
3 fresh coriander sprigs, plus
  30ml/2 tbsp chopped fresh coriander
1–2 fresh mint sprigs
2.5ml/½ tsp ground cumin
2.5ml/½ tsp ground cinnamon
2.5ml/½ tsp ground ginger
5ml/1 tsp paprika
30ml/2 tbsp sunflower oil
1 garlic clove, crushed
300ml/½ pint/1¼ cups tomato juice
450ml/¾ pint/scant 2 cups chicken
  or vegetable stock
salt and freshly ground black pepper
Moroccan flat bread and yogurt
  dressing, to serve (optional)

1 Cook the rice in plenty of lightly salted water or stock for 30 minutes or according to the instructions on the packet. Drain.

2 Meanwhile, prepare the meatballs. Chop the lamb roughly, then place it in a food processor and process until finely chopped. Scrape the meat into a large bowl.

3 Cut 1 onion into quarters and add it to the processor with the parsley, coriander and mint sprigs; process until finely chopped. Return the lamb to the processor, add the spices and seasoning and process again until smooth. Scrape the mixture into a bowl and chill for about 1 hour.

4 Shape the mixture into about 30 small balls. Heat half the oil in a frying pan, add the meatballs, in batches if necessary, and brown them evenly. Transfer to a plate. Chop the remaining onion finely.

5 Drain off the excess fat, leaving around 30ml/2 tbsp in the pan, and fry the chopped onion with the garlic for a few minutes until softened. Stir in the rice. Cook, stirring for 1–2 minutes, then stir in the tomato juice, stock and chopped fresh coriander. Season to taste with salt and pepper.

6 Arrange the meatballs over the rice, cover with a lid or foil and simmer very gently for 15 minutes. Serve solo, or with Moroccan flat bread and a yogurt dressing, if you like.

COOK'S TIP
A yogurt dressing is delicious with these meatballs. Simply stir 10ml/2 tsp finely chopped fresh mint into 90ml/6 tbsp natural yogurt.

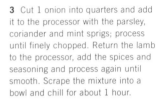

AFRICAN LAMB AND VEGETABLE PILAU

SPICY LAMB IS SERVED IN THIS DISH WITH BASMATI RICE AND A COLOURFUL SELECTION OF DIFFERENT
VEGETABLES AND CASHEW NUTS. LAMB AND RICE ARE A POPULAR COMBINATION IN AFRICAN COOKING.

SERVES FOUR

INGREDIENTS
    450g/1lb boned shoulder of lamb,
        cubed
    2.5ml/½ tsp dried thyme
    2.5ml/½ tsp paprika
    5ml/1 tsp garam masala
    1 garlic clove, crushed
    25ml/1½ tbsp vegetable oil
    900ml/1½ pints/3¾ cups lamb stock
    savoy cabbage or crisp lettuce
        leaves, to serve
For the rice
    25g/1oz/2 tbsp butter
    1 onion, chopped
    1 medium potato, diced
    1 carrot, sliced
    ½ red pepper, seeded and chopped
    1 fresh green chilli, seeded and
        chopped
    115g/4oz/1 cup sliced green cabbage
    60ml/4 tbsp natural yogurt
    2.5ml/½ tsp ground cumin
    5 green cardamom pods
    2 garlic cloves, crushed
    225g/8oz/generous 1 cup basmati
        rice, soaked
    about 50g/2oz/½ cup cashew nuts
    salt and freshly ground black pepper

1 Put the lamb cubes in a large bowl and add the thyme, paprika, garam masala and garlic, with plenty of salt and pepper. Stir, cover, and leave in a cool place for 2–3 hours.

2 Heat the oil in a saucepan and fry the lamb, in batches if necessary, over a medium heat for 5–6 minutes, until browned. Stir in the stock, cover the pan and cook for 35–40 minutes. Using a slotted spoon, transfer the lamb to a bowl. Pour the liquid into a measuring jug, topping it up with water if necessary to make 600ml/1 pint/2½ cups.

COOK'S TIP
If the stock looks a bit fatty after cooking the lamb cubes, blot the surface with kitchen paper to remove the excess grease before pouring the stock into the measuring jug.

3 Melt the butter in a separate pan and fry the onion, potato and carrot for 5 minutes. Add the red pepper and chilli and fry for 3 minutes more, then stir in the cabbage, yogurt, spices, garlic and the reserved lamb stock. Stir well, cover, then simmer gently for 5–10 minutes, until the cabbage has wilted.

4 Drain the rice and stir into the stew with the lamb. Cover and simmer over a low heat for 20 minutes or until the rice is cooked. Sprinkle in the cashew nuts and season to taste with salt and pepper. Serve hot, cupped in cabbage or lettuce leaves.

NORTH AFRICAN FISH WITH PUMPKIN RICE

THIS IS A DISH OF CONTRASTS — THE SLIGHTLY SWEET FLAVOUR OF PUMPKIN, THE MILDLY SPICY FISH, AND THE CORIANDER AND GINGER MIXTURE THAT IS STIRRED IN AT THE END — ALL BOUND TOGETHER WITH WELL-FLAVOURED RICE.

SERVES FOUR

INGREDIENTS

450g/1lb sea bass or other firm fish fillets
30ml/2 tbsp plain flour
5ml/1 tsp ground coriander
1.5–2.5ml/¼–½ tsp ground turmeric
1 wedge of pumpkin, about 500g/1¼lb
30–45ml/2–3 tbsp olive oil
6 spring onions, sliced diagonally
1 garlic clove, finely chopped
275g/10oz/1½ cups basmati rice, soaked
550ml/18fl oz/2½ cups fish stock
salt and freshly ground black pepper
lime or lemon wedges and fresh coriander sprigs, to serve

For the coriander and ginger flavouring mixture
45ml/3 tbsp finely chopped fresh coriander
10ml/2 tsp finely chopped fresh root ginger
½–1 fresh chilli, seeded and very finely chopped
45ml/3 tbsp lime or lemon juice

1 Remove and discard any skin or stray bones from the fish, and cut into 2cm/¾in chunks. Mix the flour, ground coriander, turmeric and a little salt and pepper in a plastic bag, add the fish and shake for a few seconds so that the fish is evenly coated in the spice mixture. Set aside. Make the coriander and ginger flavouring mixture by mixing all the ingredients in a small bowl.

2 Cut away the skin and scoop out the seeds from the pumpkin. Cut the flesh into 2cm/¾in chunks.

3 Heat 15ml/1 tbsp oil in a flameproof casserole and stir-fry the spring onions and garlic for a few minutes until slightly softened. Add the pumpkin and cook over a fairly low heat, stirring frequently, for 4–5 minutes or until the flesh begins to soften.

4 Drain the rice, add it to the mixture and toss over a brisk heat for 2–3 minutes. Stir in the stock, with a little salt. Bring to simmering point, then lower the heat, cover and cook for 12–15 minutes until both the rice and the pumpkin are tender.

5 About 4 minutes before the rice is ready, heat the remaining oil in a frying pan and fry the spiced fish over a moderately high heat for about 3 minutes until the outside is lightly browned and crisp and the flesh is cooked through but still moist.

6 Stir the coriander and ginger flavouring mixture into the rice and transfer to a warmed serving dish. Lay the fish pieces on top. Serve immediately, garnished with coriander, and offer lemon or lime wedges for squeezing over the fish.

COOK'S TIP
This dish can also be cooked – and served – in a wok, if preferred.

CHICKEN AND VEGETABLE TAGINE

MOROCCAN TAGINES ARE USUALLY SERVED WITH COUSCOUS, BUT RICE MAKES AN EQUALLY DELICIOUS ACCOMPANIMENT. HERE, COUSCOUS IS STIRRED INTO THE RICE TO CREATE AN UNUSUAL AND TASTY DISH, ALTHOUGH YOU COULD USE RICE BY ITSELF.

SERVES FOUR

INGREDIENTS

30ml/2 tbsp groundnut oil
4 skinless, boneless chicken breasts,
  cut into large pieces
1 large onion, chopped
2 garlic cloves, crushed
1 small parsnip, cut into 2.5cm/1in
  pieces
1 small turnip, cut into 2cm/¾in
  pieces
3 carrots, cut into 4cm/1½in pieces
4 tomatoes, chopped
1 cinnamon stick
4 cloves
5ml/1 tsp ground ginger
1 bay leaf
1.5–2.5ml/¼–½ tsp cayenne pepper
350ml/12fl oz/1½ cups chicken stock
400g/14oz can chick-peas, drained
  and skinned
1 red pepper, seeded and sliced
150g/5oz green beans, halved
1 piece of preserved lemon peel,
  thinly sliced
20–30 stoned brown or green olives
salt
For the rice and couscous
750ml/1¼ pints/3 cups chicken stock
225g/8oz/generous 1 cup long grain
  rice
115g/4oz/⅔ cup couscous
45ml/3 tbsp chopped fresh coriander

1 Heat half of the oil in a large, flameproof casserole and fry the chicken pieces for a few minutes until evenly browned. Transfer to a plate. Heat the remaining oil and fry the onion, garlic, parsnip, turnip and carrots together over a medium heat for 4–5 minutes until the vegetables are lightly flecked with brown, stirring frequently. Lower the heat, cover and sweat the vegetables for 5 minutes more, stirring occasionally.

2 Add the tomatoes, cook for a few minutes, then add the cinnamon stick, cloves, ginger, bay leaf and cayenne. Cook for 1–2 minutes.

3 Pour in the chicken stock, add the chick-peas and browned chicken pieces, and season with salt. Cover and simmer for 25 minutes.

4 Meanwhile, cook the rice and couscous mixture. Bring the chicken stock to the boil. Add the rice and simmer for about 5 minutes until almost tender. Remove the pan from the heat, stir in the couscous, cover tightly and leave for about 5 minutes.

5 When the vegetables in the tagine are almost tender, stir in the pepper slices and green beans and simmer for 10 minutes. Add the preserved lemon and olives, stir well and cook for 5 minutes more, or until the vegetables are perfectly tender.

6 Stir the chopped coriander into the rice and couscous mixture and pile it on to a plate. Serve the chicken tagine in the traditional dish, if you have one, or in a casserole.

RICE AND PEAS

THIS IS A POPULAR DISH ON THE ISLANDS OF THE EASTERN CARIBBEAN. THE BEANS MUST BE SOAKED OVERNIGHT, SO ALLOW PLENTY OF TIME FOR THIS RECIPE.

SERVES FOUR TO SIX

INGREDIENTS
175g/6oz/¾ cup red kidney beans
2 fresh thyme sprigs
50g/2oz piece of creamed coconut
2 bay leaves
1 onion, finely chopped
2 garlic cloves, crushed
2.5ml/½ tsp ground allspice
115g/4oz/¾ cup chopped red pepper
600ml/1 pint/2½ cups water
450g/1lb/2⅓ cups white long grain rice
salt and freshly ground black pepper

1 Place the red kidney beans in a large bowl. Cover with water and leave to soak overnight.

2 Drain the beans, place in a large pan and pour in enough water to cover them by 2.5cm/1in. Bring to the boil. Boil over a high heat for 10 minutes, then lower the heat and simmer for 1½ hours or until the beans are tender.

3 Add the thyme, creamed coconut, bay leaves, onion, garlic, allspice and red pepper. Season well and stir in the measured water.

4 Bring to the boil and add the rice. Stir well, lower the heat and cover the pan. Simmer for 25–30 minutes, until all the liquid has been absorbed. Serve as an accompaniment to fish, meat or vegetarian dishes.

COOK'S TIP
To save time, use a 400g/14oz can of red kidney beans. Add them along with the rice.

CARIBBEAN PEANUT CHICKEN

PEANUT BUTTER IS USED A LOT IN MANY CARIBBEAN DISHES. IT ADDS A RICHNESS, AS WELL AS A DELICIOUS DEPTH OF FLAVOUR ALL OF ITS OWN.

SERVES FOUR

INGREDIENTS

4 skinless, boneless chicken breasts, cut into thin strips
225g/8oz/generous 1 cup white long grain rice
30ml/2 tbsp groundnut oil
15g/$\frac{1}{2}$oz/1 tbsp butter, plus extra for greasing
1 onion, finely chopped
2 tomatoes, peeled, seeded and chopped
1 fresh green chilli, seeded and sliced
60ml/4 tbsp smooth peanut butter
450ml/$\frac{3}{4}$ pint/scant 2 cups chicken stock
lemon juice, to taste
salt and freshly ground black pepper
lime wedges and sprigs of fresh flat leaf parsley, to garnish
For the marinade
15ml/1 tbsp sunflower oil
1–2 garlic cloves, crushed
5ml/1 tsp chopped fresh thyme
25ml/1$\frac{1}{2}$ tbsp medium curry powder
juice of half a lemon

1 Mix all the marinade ingredients in a large bowl and stir in the chicken. Cover loosely with clear film and set aside in a cool place for 2–3 hours.

2 Meanwhile, cook the rice in plenty of lightly salted boiling water until tender. Drain well and turn into a generously buttered casserole.

3 Preheat the oven to 180°C/350°F/Gas 4. Heat 15ml/1 tbsp of the oil and butter in a flameproof casserole and fry the chicken pieces for 4–5 minutes until evenly brown. Add more oil if necessary.

4 Transfer the chicken to a plate. Add the onion to the casserole and fry for 5–6 minutes until lightly browned, adding more oil if necessary. Stir in the chopped tomatoes and chilli. Cook over a gentle heat for 3–4 minutes, stirring occasionally. Remove from the heat.

5 Mix the peanut butter with the chicken stock. Stir into the tomato and onion mixture, then add the chicken. Stir in the lemon juice, season to taste, then spoon the mixture over the rice in the casserole.

6 Cover the casserole. Cook in the oven for 15–20 minutes or until piping hot. Use a large spoon to toss the rice with the chicken mixture. Serve at once, garnished with the lime wedges and parsley sprigs.

COOK'S TIP
If the casserole is not large enough to allow you to toss the rice with the chicken mixture before serving, invert a large, deep plate over the casserole, turn both over and toss the mixture on the plate.

SPICY PEANUT BALLS

*TASTY RICE BALLS, ROLLED IN CHOPPED PEANUTS AND DEEP-FRIED, MAKE A DELICIOUS SNACK.
SERVE THEM AS THEY ARE, OR WITH A CHILLI SAUCE FOR DIPPING.*

MAKES SIXTEEN

INGREDIENTS

1 garlic clove, crushed
1cm/½in piece of fresh root ginger,
  peeled and finely chopped
1.5ml/¼ tsp ground turmeric
5ml/1 tsp granulated sugar
2.5ml/½ tsp salt
5ml/1 tsp chilli sauce
10ml/2 tsp fish sauce or soy sauce
30ml/2 tbsp chopped fresh coriander
225g/8oz/2 cups cooked white long
  grain rice
115g/4oz peanuts, chopped
vegetable oil, for deep-frying
lime wedges and chilli dipping
  sauce, to serve (optional)

1 Process the garlic, ginger and turmeric in a food processor until the mixture forms a paste. Add the granulated sugar, salt, chilli sauce and fish sauce or soy sauce, with the chopped coriander and lime juice. Process briefly to mix.

2 Add three-quarters of the cooked rice to the paste in the food processor, and process until smooth and sticky. Scrape into a mixing bowl and stir in the remainder of the rice. Wet your hands and shape the mixture into thumb-size balls.

3 Roll the balls in chopped peanuts, making sure they are evenly coated.

4 Heat the oil in a deep-fryer or wok. Deep-fry the peanut balls until crisp. Drain on kitchen paper and then pile on to a platter. Serve hot with lime wedges and a chilli dipping sauce, if you like.

CARIBBEAN CHICKEN WITH PIGEON PEA RICE

GOLDEN, SPICY CARAMELIZED CHICKEN TOPS A RICHLY FLAVOURED VEGETABLE RICE IN THIS HEARTY AND DELICIOUS SUPPER DISH. PIGEON PEAS ARE A COMMON INGREDIENT IN CARIBBEAN COOKING.

SERVES FOUR

INGREDIENTS
    5ml/1 tsp allspice
    2.5ml/½ tsp ground cinnamon
    5ml/1 tsp dried thyme
    pinch of ground cloves
    1.5ml/¼ tsp freshly grated nutmeg
    4 skinless, boneless chicken breasts
    45ml/3 tbsp groundnut or sunflower
        oil
    15g/½oz/1 tbsp butter
    1 onion, chopped
    2 garlic cloves, crushed
    1 carrot, diced
    1 celery stick, chopped
    3 spring onions, chopped
    1 fresh red chilli, seeded and thinly
        sliced
    400g/14oz can pigeon peas
    225g/8oz/generous 1 cup long grain
        rice
    120ml/4fl oz/½ cup coconut milk
    550ml/18fl oz/2½ cups chicken
        stock
    30ml/2 tbsp demerara sugar
    salt and cayenne pepper

1 Mix together the allspice, cinnamon, thyme, cloves and nutmeg. Rub the mixture all over the pieces of chicken. Set aside for 30 minutes.

2 Heat 15ml/1 tbsp of the oil with the butter in a saucepan. Fry the onion and garlic over a medium heat until soft and beginning to brown. Add the carrot, celery, spring onions and chilli. Sauté for a few minutes, then stir in the pigeon peas, rice, coconut milk and chicken stock. Season with salt and cayenne pepper. Bring to simmering point, cover and cook over a low heat for about 25 minutes.

COOK'S TIP
Pigeon peas are sometimes called gungo beans, especially when sold in ethnic markets. If they are not available, use borlotti beans instead.

3 About 10 minutes before the rice mixture is cooked, heat the remaining oil in a heavy-based frying pan, add the sugar and cook, without stirring, until it begins to caramelize.

4 Carefully add the chicken to the pan. Cook for 8–10 minutes until the chicken has a browned, glazed appearance and is cooked through. Transfer the chicken to a board and slice it thickly. Serve the pigeon pea rice in individual bowls, with the chicken on top.

JAMAICAN FISH CURRY

ALTHOUGH THE RICE IS SIMPLY BOILED FOR THIS RECIPE, IT IS AN INTEGRAL PART OF THIS DISH AND IS AN EXCELLENT EXAMPLE OF HOW THE PLAINEST RICE TAKES ON THE FLAVOUR OF THE SAUCE WITH WHICH IT IS SERVED.

SERVES FOUR

INGREDIENTS

2 halibut steaks, total weight about
   500–675g/1¼–1½lb
30ml/2 tbsp groundnut oil
2 cardamom pods
1 cinnamon stick
6 allspice berries
4 cloves
1 large onion, chopped
3 garlic cloves, crushed
10–15ml/2–3 tsp grated fresh root
   ginger
10ml/2 tsp ground cumin
5ml/1 tsp ground coriander
2.5ml/½ tsp cayenne pepper or to
   taste
4 tomatoes, peeled, seeded and
   chopped
1 sweet potato, about 225g/8oz,
   cut into 2cm/¾in cubes
475ml/16fl oz/2 cups fish stock or
   water
115g/4oz piece of creamed coconut
1 bay leaf
225g/8oz/generous 1 cup white long
   grain rice
salt

COOK'S TIP
Sweet potato discolours very quickly.
If preparing ingredients in advance, put
the potato into a bowl of cold water with
30–45ml/2–3 tbsp lemon juice until
ready to use.
   This recipe uses some of the most
common spices to appear in dishes from
Africa and the Caribbean, where the
influence of India is clearly visible.
The taste is for pungent flavours rather
than fiery heat. Allspice is widely
used throughout the Caribbean, while
cardamom and cayenne pepper are
essential ingredients in curries.

1 Rub the halibut steaks well with salt and set aside.

2 Heat the oil in a flameproof casserole and stir-fry the cardamom pods, cinnamon stick, allspice berries and cloves for about 3 minutes to release the aroma.

3 Add the onion, garlic and ginger. Continue cooking for 4–5 minutes over a gentle heat until the onion is fairly soft, stirring frequently, then add the cumin, coriander and cayenne pepper and cook briefly, stirring all the time.

4 Stir in the tomatoes, sweet potato, fish stock or water, creamed coconut and bay leaf. Season well with salt. Bring to the boil, then lower the heat, cover and simmer for 15–18 minutes until the sweet potato is tender.

5 Cook the rice according to your preferred method. Meanwhile, add the fish steaks to the pan of sauce and spoon the sauce over to cover them completely. Put a lid on the pan and simmer for about 10 minutes until the fish is just tender and flakes easily.

6 Spoon the rice into a warmed serving dish, spoon over the curry sauce and arrange the halibut steaks on top. Garnish with chopped coriander, if you like, and serve immediately.

ORANGE RICE PUDDING

IN MOROCCO, AS IN SPAIN, GREECE AND ITALY, THICK, CREAMY RICE PUDDINGS ARE VERY POPULAR, ESPECIALLY WHEN SWEETENED WITH HONEY AND FLAVOURED WITH ORANGE.

SERVES FOUR

INGREDIENTS

50g/2oz/generous ¼ cup short grain
   pudding rice
600ml/1 pint/2½ cups milk
finely grated rind of ½ small orange
30–45ml/2–3 tbsp clear honey
150ml/¼ pint/⅔ cup double cream
15ml/1 tbsp chopped pistachios,
   toasted (optional)
grated orange rind, to garnish

1 Mix the rice with the milk and orange rind in a saucepan. Pour in the honey and stir well.

2 Bring to the boil, then lower the heat, cover and simmer very gently for about 1¼ hours, stirring frequently.

VARIATION
Instead of adding double cream, stir in Greek yogurt. Serve immediately (without reheating), topped with toasted pine nuts and fresh orange segments.

3 Remove the lid and continue cooking and stirring for 15–20 minutes, until the rice is creamy.

4 Pour in the cream, stirring constantly, then simmer for 5–8 minutes more. Spoon the rice pudding into warmed individual bowls. Sprinkle with the pistachios and orange rind and serve.

CARIBBEAN SPICED RICE PUDDING

CARIBBEAN RECIPES CAN BE EXTREMELY SWEET, AND YOU MAY FIND YOU CAN REDUCE THE SUGAR QUANTITY IN THIS PUDDING BECAUSE OF THE NATURAL SWEETNESS OF THE FRUIT.

SERVES FOUR TO SIX

INGREDIENTS
    25g/1oz/2 tbsp butter
    1 cinnamon stick
    115g/4oz/½ cup soft brown sugar
    115g/4oz/⅔ cup ground rice
    1.2 litres/2 pints/5 cups milk
    2.5ml/½ tsp allspice
    50g/2oz/⅓ cup sultanas
    75g/3oz chopped mandarin oranges
    75g/3oz chopped pineapple

1 Melt the butter in a non-stick pan and then add the cinnamon stick and sugar. Heat over a medium heat until the sugar begins to caramelize: remove from the heat as soon as this happens.

2 Carefully stir in the rice and three-quarters of the milk. Bring to the boil, stirring all the time, without letting the milk burn. Reduce the heat and simmer for 10 minutes until the rice is cooked, stirring constantly.

3 Add the remaining milk, the allspice and the sultanas. Leave to simmer for 5 minutes, stirring occasionally.

4 When the rice is thick and creamy, allow to cool slightly, then stir in the mandarin and pineapple pieces. As an alternative, the fruit can be served separately, with warm or cold rice.

Britain

RICE IS A RELATIVE NEWCOMER
TO BRITAIN. FOR A SURPRISINGLY
LONG TIME, THE ONLY WAY TO USE
RICE WAS TO CREAM IT WITH MILK
AND SUGAR IN A RICE PUDDING, BUT
THE LAST TWENTY YEARS HAVE
SEEN RICE EARN ITS RIGHTFUL PLACE
AT THE DINNER TABLE. OF TODAY'S RICE
DISHES, SOME HAVE BEEN ADAPTED FROM ORIENTAL
CUISINES; OTHERS ARE ENTIRELY HOME-GROWN.

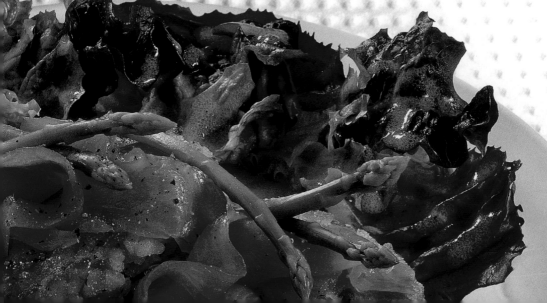

PUMPKIN, RICE AND CHICKEN SOUP

THIS IS A WARM, COMFORTING SOUP WHICH, DESPITE THE SPICE AND BASMATI RICE, IS QUINTESSENTIALLY ENGLISH. FOR AN EVEN MORE SUBSTANTIAL MEAL, ADD A LITTLE MORE RICE AND MAKE SURE YOU USE ALL THE CHICKEN FROM THE STOCK.

SERVES FOUR

INGREDIENTS
  1 wedge of pumpkin, about 450g/1lb
  15ml/1 tbsp sunflower oil
  25g/1oz/2 tbsp butter
  6 green cardamom pods
  2 leeks, chopped
  115g/4oz/generous ½ cup basmati
    rice, soaked
  350ml/12fl oz/1½ cups milk
  salt and freshly ground black pepper
  generous strips of pared orange rind,
    to garnish
For the chicken stock
  2 chicken quarters
  1 onion, quartered
  2 carrots, chopped
  1 celery stalk, chopped
  6–8 peppercorns
  900ml/1½ pints/3¾ cups water

1 First make the chicken stock. Place the chicken quarters, onion, carrots, celery and peppercorns in a large saucepan. Pour in the water and slowly bring to the boil. Skim the surface if necessary, then lower the heat, cover and simmer gently for 1 hour.

2 Strain the chicken stock into a clean, large bowl, discarding the vegetables. Skin and bone one or both chicken pieces and cut the flesh into strips. (If not using both chicken pieces for the soup, reserve the other piece for another recipe.)

3 Skin the pumpkin and remove all the seeds and pith, so that you have about 350g/12oz flesh. Cut the flesh into 2.5cm/1in cubes.

4 Heat the oil and butter in a saucepan and fry the cardamom pods for 2–3 minutes until slightly swollen. Add the leeks and pumpkin. Cook, stirring, for 3–4 minutes over a medium heat, then lower the heat, cover and sweat for 5 minutes more or until the pumpkin is quite soft, stirring once or twice.

5 Measure out 600ml/1 pint/2½ cups of the stock and add to the pumpkin mixture. Bring to the boil, then lower the heat, cover and simmer gently for 10–15 minutes, until the pumpkin is soft.

6 Pour the remaining stock into a measuring jug and make up with water to 300ml/½ pint/1¼ cups. Drain the rice and put it into a saucepan. Pour in the stock, bring to the boil, then simmer for about 10 minutes until the rice is tender. Add seasoning to taste.

7 Remove the cardamom pods, then process the soup in a blender or food processor until smooth. Pour back into a clean saucepan and stir in the milk, chicken and rice (with any stock that has not been absorbed). Heat until simmering. Garnish with the strips of pared orange rind and freshly ground black pepper, and serve with granary or wholemeal bread.

RICE CAKES WITH SMOKED SALMON

THESE ELEGANT RICE CAKES ARE MADE USING A RISOTTO BASE. YOU COULD SKIP THIS STAGE AND USE LEFTOVER SEAFOOD OR MUSHROOM RISOTTO. ALTERNATIVELY, USE LEFTOVER LONG GRAIN RICE AND ADD EXTRA FLAVOUR WITH SPRING ONIONS.

SERVES FOUR

INGREDIENTS

30ml/2 tbsp olive oil
1 medium onion, chopped
225g/8oz/generous 1 cup risotto rice
about 90ml/6 tbsp white wine
about 750ml/1¼ pints/3 cups fish or
    chicken stock
15g/½oz/2 tbsp dried porcini
    mushrooms, soaked for 10 minutes
    in warm water to cover
15ml/1 tbsp chopped fresh parsley
15ml/1 tbsp snipped fresh chives
5ml/1 tsp chopped fresh dill
1 egg, lightly beaten
about 45ml/3 tbsp ground rice, plus
    extra for dusting
oil, for frying
60ml/4 tbsp soured cream
175g/6oz smoked salmon
salt and freshly ground black pepper
radicchio and oakleaf salad, tossed
    in French dressing, to serve

1 Heat the olive oil in a pan and fry the onion for 3–4 minutes until soft. Add the rice and cook, stirring, until the grains are thoroughly coated in oil. Pour in the wine and stock, a little at a time, stirring constantly over a gentle heat until each quantity of liquid has been absorbed before adding more.

2 Drain the mushrooms and chop them into small pieces. When the rice is tender, and all the liquid has been absorbed, stir in the mushrooms, parsley, chives, dill and seasoning. Remove from the heat and set aside for a few minutes to cool.

COOK'S TIP
For a sophisticated occasion, garnish the rice cakes with roasted baby asparagus spears, lemon slices and dill.

3 Add the beaten egg, then stir in enough ground rice to bind the mixture – it should be soft but manageable. Dust your hands with ground rice and shape the mixture into four patties, about 13cm/5in in diameter and about 2cm/¾in thick.

4 Heat the oil in a shallow pan and fry the rice cakes, in batches if necessary, for 4–5 minutes until evenly browned on both sides. Drain on kitchen paper and cool slightly. Place each rice cake on a plate and top with 15ml/1 tbsp soured cream. Twist two or three thin slices of smoked salmon on top, and serve with a dressed salad garnish.

SALMON IN PUFF PASTRY

THIS IS AN ELEGANT PARTY DISH, MADE WITH RICE, EGGS AND SALMON AND ENCLOSED IN PUFF PASTRY.

SERVES SIX

INGREDIENTS

450g/1lb puff pastry, thawed if
    frozen
1 egg, beaten
3 hard-boiled eggs
90ml/6 tbsp single cream
200g/7oz/1¾ cups cooked long grain
    rice
30ml/2 tbsp finely chopped fresh
    parsley
10ml/2 tsp chopped fresh tarragon
675g/1½lb fresh salmon fillets
40g/1½oz/3 tbsp butter
juice of ½ lemon
salt and freshly ground black pepper

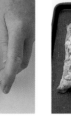

2 In a bowl, mash the hard-boiled eggs with the cream, then stir in the cooked rice. Add the parsley and tarragon and season well. Spoon this mixture on to the prepared pastry.

5 Roll out the remaining pastry and cut out a semi-circle piece to cover the head portion and a tail shape to cover the tail. Brush both pieces of pastry with a little beaten egg and place on top of the fish, pressing down firmly to secure. Score a criss-cross pattern on the tail.

1 Preheat the oven to 190°C/375°F/Gas 5. Roll out two-thirds of the pastry into a large oval, measuring about 35cm/14in in length. Cut into a curved fish shape and place on a lightly greased baking sheet. Use the trimmings to make narrow strips. Brush one side of each strip with a little beaten egg and secure in place around the rim of the pastry to make a raised edge. Prick the base all over with a fork, then bake for 8–10 minutes until the sides are well risen and the pastry is lightly golden. Leave to cool.

3 Cut the salmon into 2cm/¾in chunks. Melt the butter until it starts to sizzle, then add the salmon. Turn the pieces over in the butter so that they begin to colour but do not cook through.

6 Cut the remaining pastry into small circles and, starting from the tail end, arrange the circles in overlapping lines to represent scales. Add an extra one for an eye. Brush the whole fish shape with the remaining beaten egg.

7 Bake for 10 minutes, then reduce the temperature to 160°C/325°F/Gas 3 and cook for a further 15–20 minutes until the pastry is evenly golden. Slide the fish on to a serving plate and serve.

COOK'S TIP

If the pastry seems to be browning too quickly, cover it with foil during cooking and remove from the oven for the last 5 minutes. It is important that the "fish" cooks for the recommended time, so that the salmon is sufficiently cooked through.

4 Remove from the heat and arrange the salmon pieces on top of the rice, piled in the centre. Stir the lemon juice into the butter in the pan, then spoon the mixture over the salmon pieces.

VARIATION

If time is short you may prefer to use this simplified version of the recipe. Roll out the pastry into a rectangle, then make pastry edges to contain the filling. Part bake the "fish", top with plain, rolled out pastry and return it to the oven.

KEDGEREE

A POPULAR VICTORIAN BREAKFAST DISH, KEDGEREE HAS ITS ORIGINS IN KITCHIRI, AN INDIAN RICE AND LENTIL DISH. KEDGEREE CAN BE FLAVOURED WITH CURRY POWDER, BUT THIS RECIPE IS MILD.

SERVES FOUR

INGREDIENTS

500g/1¼lb smoked haddock
115g/4oz/generous ½ cup basmati
  rice
30ml/2 tbsp lemon juice
150ml/¼ pint/⅔ cup single cream or
  soured cream
pinch of freshly grated nutmeg
pinch of cayenne pepper
2 hard-boiled eggs, peeled and cut
  into wedges
50g/2oz/4 tbsp butter, diced
30ml/2 tbsp chopped fresh parsley
salt and freshly ground black pepper

COOK'S TIP
Taste the kedgeree before you add salt,
as the smoked haddock may already be
quite salty.

1 Put the haddock in a shallow pan,
pour in just enough water to cover and
heat to simmering point. Poach the fish
for about 10 minutes, until the flesh
flakes easily when tested with the tip
of a sharp knife. Lift the fish out of the
cooking liquid, then remove any skin
and bones and flake the flesh. Reserve
the cooking liquid,

2 Pour the cooking liquid into a
measuring jug and make up the volume
with water to 250ml/8fl oz/1 cup.

3 Pour the measured liquid into a pan
and bring it to the boil. Add the rice,
stir, then lower the heat, cover and
simmer for about 10 minutes, until the
rice is tender and the liquid has been
absorbed. Meanwhile, preheat the oven
to 180°C/350°F/Gas 4 and butter a
baking dish.

4 When the rice is cooked, remove
it from the heat and stir in the lemon
juice, cream, flaked haddock, grated
nutmeg and cayenne pepper. Add the
egg wedges to the rice mixture and stir
in gently.

5 Tip the rice mixture into the prepared
baking dish. Level the surface and dot
with butter. Cover the dish loosely with
foil and bake for about 25 minutes.

6 Stir the chopped parsley into the
baked kedgeree and add seasoning to
taste. Serve immediately.

CHICKEN AND MANGO SALAD WITH ORANGE RICE

CONTEMPORARY BRITISH COOKING DRAWS ITS INSPIRATION FROM ALL OVER THE WORLD.

SERVES FOUR

INGREDIENTS
  15ml/1 tbsp sunflower oil
  1 onion, chopped
  1 garlic clove, crushed
  30ml/2 tbsp red curry paste
  10ml/2 tsp apricot jam
  30ml/2 tbsp chicken stock
  about 450g/1lb cooked chicken, cut
    into small pieces
  150ml/¼ pint/⅔ cup natural yogurt
  60–75ml/4–5 tbsp mayonnaise
  1 large mango, cut into 1cm/½in dice
  fresh flat leaf parsley sprigs, to
    garnish
  poppadums, to serve
For the orange rice
  175g/6oz/scant 1 cup white long
    grain rice
  225g/8oz carrots, grated (about 1⅓
    cups)
  1 large orange, cut into segments
  40g/1½oz/⅓ cup roasted flaked
    almonds
For the dressing
  45ml/3 tbsp olive oil
  60ml/4 tbsp sunflower oil
  45ml/3 tbsp lemon juice
  1 garlic clove, crushed
  15ml/1 tbsp chopped mixed fresh
    herbs (tarragon, parsley, chives)
  salt and freshly ground black pepper

1 Heat the oil in a frying pan and fry the onion and garlic for 3–4 minutes until soft.

2 Stir in the curry paste, cook for about 1 minute, then lower the heat and stir in the apricot jam and stock. Mix well, add the chopped chicken and stir until the chicken is thoroughly coated in the paste. Spoon the mixture into a large bowl and leave to cool.

3 Meanwhile, boil the rice in plenty of lightly salted water until just tender. Drain, rinse under cold water and drain again. When cool, stir into the grated carrots and add the orange segments and flaked almonds.

4 Make the dressing by whisking all the ingredients together in a bowl.

5 When the chicken mixture is cool, stir in the yogurt and mayonnaise, then add the mango, stirring it in carefully so as not to break the flesh. Chill for about 30 minutes.

6 When ready to serve, pour the dressing into the rice salad and mix well. Spoon on to a platter and mound the cold curried chicken on top. Garnish with flat leaf parsley and serve with poppadums.

COOK'S TIP
A simple way of dicing a mango is to take two thick slices from either side of the large flat stone without peeling the fruit. Make criss-cross cuts in the flesh on each slice and then turn inside out. The cubes of flesh will stand proud of the skin and can be easily cut off.

LOIN OF PORK WITH CASHEW AND ORANGE STUFFING

THE ORANGES AND CASHEW NUTS ADD CONTRASTING FLAVOURS AND TEXTURES TO THIS STUFFING, AND COMBINE WELL WITH THE BROWN RICE. DON'T WORRY IF THE STUFFING DOESN'T BIND – THE BEST THING ABOUT BROWN RICE IS THAT IT RETAINS ITS OWN TEXTURE.

SERVES SIX

INGREDIENTS
   1.5kg/3–3½lb boned loin of pork
   15ml/1 tbsp plain flour
   300ml/½ pint/1¼ cups dry white
      wine
   salt and freshly ground black pepper
   fresh rosemary sprig and orange
      slices, to garnish
For the stuffing
   25g/1oz/2 tbsp butter
   1 small onion, finely chopped
   75g/3oz/scant ½ cup brown basmati
      rice, soaked and drained
   350ml/12fl oz/scant 1½ cups chicken
      stock
   50g/2oz/½ cup cashew nuts
   1 orange
   50g/2oz/⅓ cup sultanas

1 First cook the rice for the stuffing. Melt the butter in a frying pan and fry the chopped onion for 2–3 minutes until softened but not browned. Add the rice and cook for 1 minute, then pour in the chicken stock and bring to the boil. Stir, then lower the heat, cover and simmer for 35 minutes until the rice is tender and the liquid has been absorbed. Preheat the oven to 220°C/425°F/Gas 7.

2 While the rice is cooking, open out the loin of pork and cut two lengthways slits through the meat, making sure not to cut right through. Turn the meat over. Remove any excess fat, but leave a good layer; this will keep the meat moist during cooking.

3 Spread out the cashew nuts for the stuffing in a roasting tin and roast for 2–4 minutes until golden. Allow to cool, then chop roughly in a food processor or blender. Leave the oven on.

4 Grate 5ml/1 tsp of the orange rind into a bowl, then peel the orange. Working over a bowl to catch the juice, cut the orange into segments. Chop them roughly.

5 Add the chopped orange segments to the cooked rice with the orange rind, roast cashew nuts and sultanas. Season well, then stir in 15–30ml/1–2 tbsp of the reserved orange juice. Don't worry if the rice doesn't bind – it should have a fairly loose consistency.

6 Spread a generous layer of stuffing along the centre of the pork. If you have any stuffing left over, put it in a heatproof bowl and set aside.

7 Roll up the loin and tie securely with kitchen string. Rub a little salt and pepper into the surface of the meat and place it in a roasting tin. Roast for 15 minutes then lower the oven temperature to 180°C/350°F/Gas 4. Roast for 2–2¼ hours more or until the meat juices run clear and without any sign of pinkness. Heat any extra stuffing in the covered bowl alongside the meat for the final 15 minutes.

8 Transfer the meat to a warmed serving plate and keep warm. Stir the flour into the meat juices remaining in the roasting tin, cook for 1 minute, then stir in the white wine. Bring to the boil, stirring until thickened, then strain into a gravy boat.

9 Remove the string from the meat before carving. Stud the pork with the rosemary and garnish with the orange slices. Serve with the gravy and any extra stuffing.

COOK'S TIP
Pork is usually roasted until well done, though cooking times depend on your oven and the size of the joint. As a rule, allow 35–40 minutes at 180°C/350°F/Gas 4 per 450g/1lb for stuffed pork, plus an extra 15–20 minutes. If you like crackling, make sure the skin is completely dry. Just before cooking score it in a diamond pattern and rub generously with salt.

STRAWBERRY SHORTCAKE

GROUND RICE IS WIDELY USED FOR BAKING. IT ADDS A LIGHT, FINE TEXTURE TO THIS SHORTBREAD.

SERVES EIGHT

INGREDIENTS
350g/12oz/3 cups strawberries
300ml/½ pint/1¼ cups double cream
30ml/2 tbsp caster sugar
15ml/1 tbsp icing sugar (optional)
For the shortbread
115g/4oz/1 cup plain flour
50g/2oz/⅓ cup ground rice
75g/3oz/6 tbsp caster sugar
115g/4oz/½ cup unsalted butter
1 egg yolk
about 15ml/1 tbsp milk

1 Preheat the oven to 180°C/350°F/Gas 4. Make the shortbread. Sift the flour and ground rice into a bowl. Stir in the sugar, then rub in the butter. Stir in the egg yolk and milk, and mix to a dough.

2 Knead the dough lightly, break in half and roll each piece into a 20cm/8in round. Place on a greased baking sheet or in two fluted flan tins. Mark one of the rounds in to eight wedges.

3 Bake the shortbreads for 15–20 minutes until golden. Allow to cool a little on the baking sheet or in the tins. Cut the marked shortbread into wedges, then transfer the whole round and wedges to a wire rack and leave to cool.

4 Reserve the best-looking strawberry for the central decoration, and hull and slice the remainder. Set aside about eight of the strawberry slices to use as decoration. Whip the cream until it is fairly thick and stir in the caster sugar.

5 Spoon about one-third of the cream into a piping bag. Spread the remaining cream mixture over the whole shortbread base, and top with the sliced strawberries.

6 Top with the shortbread wedges, standing them at an angle and piping cream between them. Decorate with the reserved strawberry slices. Slice the whole strawberry almost, but not quite through and fan the slices. Place it in the centre of the shortcake, dust with icing sugar, if you like, and serve.

COOK'S TIP
Ground rice makes a good substitute for wheat flour, and is especially popular with people who cannot tolerate gluten.

TRADITIONAL ENGLISH RICE PUDDING

DON'T BE PUT OFF BY MEMORIES OF SCHOOL-DAYS RICE PUDDING. A PROPER RICE PUDDING IS SMOOTH AND CREAMY WITH JUST A HINT OF FRAGRANT SPICES. SERVE IT WITH A SPOONFUL OF THICK CHERRY JAM, IF LIKED.

SERVES FOUR

INGREDIENTS
600ml/1 pint/2½ cups creamy milk
1 vanilla pod
50g/2oz/generous ¼ cup short grain pudding rice
45ml/3 tbsp caster sugar
25g/1oz/2 tbsp butter
freshly grated nutmeg

1 Pour the milk into a pan and add the vanilla pod. Bring to simmering point, then remove from the heat, cover and leave to infuse for 1 hour. Preheat the oven to 150°C/300°F/Gas 2.

2 Put the rice and sugar in an ovenproof dish. Strain the milk over the rice, discarding the vanilla pod. Stir to mix, then dot the surface with the butter.

3 Bake, uncovered, for 2 hours. After about 40 minutes, stir the surface skin into the pudding, and repeat this after a further 40 minutes. At this point, sprinkle the surface of the pudding with grated nutmeg. Allow the pudding to finish cooking without stirring.

COOK'S TIP
If possible, always use a non-stick saucepan when heating milk, otherwise it is likely to stick to the bottom of the pan and burn.

North America

NORTH AMERICA IS ONE OF THE WORLD'S
LARGEST RICE PRODUCING COUNTRIES. IT
IS NO SURPRISE TO FIND HERE A LARGE
NUMBER OF HOME-GROWN RICE RECIPES,
AS WELL AS A DIVERSE COLLECTION OF
"IMPORTS" INTRODUCED AND ADAPTED
OVER GENERATIONS BY THE CULTURALLY
RICH MIGRANT COMMUNITIES, AMONGST
THEM ITALIANS, JAPANESE AND CHINESE.

SEAFOOD CHOWDER

CHOWDER TAKES ITS NAME FROM THE FRENCH WORD FOR CAULDRON – CHAUDIÈRE – THE TYPE OF POT ONCE TRADITIONALLY USED FOR SOUPS AND STEWS. LIKE MOST CHOWDERS, THIS IS A SUBSTANTIAL DISH, WHICH COULD EASILY BE SERVED WITH CRUSTY BREAD FOR A LUNCH OR SUPPER.

SERVES FOUR TO SIX

INGREDIENTS
- 200g/7oz/generous 1 cup drained, canned sweetcorn kernels
- 600ml/1 pint/2½ cups milk
- 15g/½oz/1 tbsp butter
- 1 small leek, sliced
- 1 small garlic clove, crushed
- 2 rindless smoked streaky bacon rashers, finely chopped
- 1 small green pepper, seeded and diced
- 1 celery stalk, chopped
- 115g/4oz/generous ½ cup white long grain rice
- 5ml/1 tsp plain flour
- about 450ml/¾ pint/scant 2 cups hot chicken or vegetable stock
- 4 large scallops, preferably with corals
- 115g/4oz white fish fillet, such as monkfish or plaice
- 15ml/1 tbsp finely chopped fresh parsley
- good pinch of cayenne pepper
- 30–45ml/2–3 tbsp single cream (optional)
- salt and freshly ground black pepper

1 Place half the sweetcorn kernels in a food processor or blender. Add a little of the milk and process until thick and creamy.

2 Melt the butter in a large saucepan and gently fry the leek, garlic and bacon for 4–5 minutes until the leek has softened but not browned. Add the green pepper and celery and sweat over a very gentle heat for 3–4 minutes more, stirring frequently.

3 Stir in the rice and cook for a few minutes until the grains begin to swell. Sprinkle over the flour. Cook, stirring, for about 1 minute, then gradually stir in the remaining milk and the stock.

4 Bring the mixture to the boil over a medium heat, then lower the heat and stir in the creamed corn mixture, with the whole corn kernels. Season well.

5 Cover the pan and simmer the chowder very gently for 20 minutes or until the rice is tender, stirring occasionally, and adding a little more chicken stock or water if the mixture thickens too quickly or the rice begins to stick to the bottom of the pan.

6 Pull the corals away from the scallops and slice the white flesh into 5mm/¼in pieces. Cut the fish fillet into bite-size chunks.

7 Stir the scallops and fish into the chowder, cook for 4 minutes, then stir in the corals, parsley and cayenne. Cook for a few minutes to heat through, then stir in the cream, if liked. Adjust the seasoning and serve.

THAI-STYLE SEAFOOD PASTIES

THAI-STYLE FOOD IS HUGELY POPULAR IN MANY PARTS OF AMERICA, ESPECIALLY ALONG THE WEST COAST, WHERE RICE IS ONE OF THE MOST IMPORTANT CROPS.

MAKES EIGHTEEN

INGREDIENTS
  500g/1¼lb puff pastry, thawed if
    frozen
  1 egg, beaten with 30ml/2 tbsp water
  fresh coriander leaves and lime
    twists, to garnish
For the filling
  275g/10oz skinned white fish fillets,
    such as cod or haddock
  plain flour seasoned with salt and
    freshly ground black pepper
  8–10 large raw prawns
  15ml/1 tbsp sunflower oil
  about 75g/3oz/6 tbsp butter
  6 spring onions, finely sliced
  1 garlic clove, crushed
  225g/8oz/2 cups cooked Thai
    fragrant rice
  4cm/1½in piece of fresh root ginger,
    grated
  10ml/2 tsp finely chopped fresh
    coriander
  5ml/1 tsp finely grated lime rind

1 Preheat the oven to 190°C/375°F/ Gas 5. Make the filling. Cut the fish into 2cm/¾in cubes and dust with the flour. Peel and devein the prawns and cut each one into four pieces.

2 Heat half of the oil and 15g/½oz/ 1 tbsp of the butter in a frying pan. Add the spring onions and fry them over a gentle heat for 2 minutes. Add the garlic and fry for about 5 minutes more, until the onions are very soft. Transfer to a large bowl.

3 Heat the remaining oil and a further 25g/1oz/2 tbsp of the butter in a clean pan. Fry the fish pieces briefly. As soon as they begin to turn opaque, use a slotted spoon to transfer them to the bowl with the spring onions. Cook the prawns in the fat remaining in the pan. When they begin to change colour, lift them out and add them to the bowl.

4 Add the cooked rice to the bowl, with the ginger, coriander and lime rind. Mix, taking care not to break up the fish.

5 Dust the work surface with a little flour. Roll out the pastry and cut into 10cm/4in rounds. Place spoonfuls of filling just off centre on the pastry rounds. Dot with a little butter. Dampen the edges of the pastry with a little of the egg wash, fold one side of the pastry over the filling and press the edges together firmly.

6 Place these on a lightly greased baking sheet. Decorate the pasties with the pastry trimmings, if you like. Brush them with egg wash and bake for 12–15 minutes or until golden.

7 Transfer to a plate and garnish with fresh coriander leaves and lime twists.

COOK'S TIP
If you prefer, you could make 6 larger pasties to serve as a main course.

CALIFORNIAN CITRUS FRIED RICE

AS WITH ALL FRIED RICE DISHES, THE IMPORTANT THING HERE IS TO MAKE SURE THE RICE IS COLD.
ADD IT AFTER COOKING ALL THE OTHER INGREDIENTS, AND STIR TO HEAT IT THROUGH COMPLETELY.

SERVES FOUR TO SIX

INGREDIENTS

4 eggs
10ml/2 tsp Japanese rice vinegar
30ml/2 tbsp light soy sauce
about 45ml/3 tbsp groundnut oil
50g/2oz/½ cup cashew nuts
2 garlic cloves, crushed
6 spring onions, diagonally sliced
2 small carrots, cut into julienne
   strips
225g/8oz asparagus, each spear cut
   diagonally into 4 pieces
175g/6oz/2¼ cups button
   mushrooms, halved
30ml/2 tbsp rice wine
30ml/2 tbsp water
450g/1lb/4 cups cooked white long
   grain rice
about 10ml/2 tsp sesame oil
1 pink grapefruit or orange,
   segmented
thin strips of orange rind, to garnish
For the hot dressing
5ml/1 tsp grated orange rind
30ml/2 tbsp Japanese rice wine
45ml/3 tbsp oyster sauce
30ml/2 tbsp freshly squeezed pink
   grapefruit or orange juice
5ml/1 tsp medium or hot chilli sauce

3 Heat the remaining oil and add the garlic and spring onions. Cook over a medium heat for 1–2 minutes until the onions begin to soften, then add the carrots and stir-fry for 4 minutes.

4 Add the asparagus and cook for 2–3 minutes, then stir in the mushrooms and stir-fry for a further 1 minute. Stir in the rice wine, the remaining soy sauce and the water. Simmer for a few minutes until the vegetables are just tender but still firm.

5 Mix the ingredients for the dressing, then add to the wok and bring to the boil. Add the rice, scrambled eggs and cashew nuts. Toss over a low heat for 3–4 minutes, until the rice is heated through. Just before serving, stir in the sesame oil and the grapefruit or orange segments. Garnish with strips of orange rind and serve at once.

1 Beat the eggs with the vinegar and 10ml/2 tsp of the soy sauce. Heat 15ml/1 tbsp of the oil in a wok and cook the eggs until lightly scrambled. Transfer to a plate and set aside.

2 Add the cashew nuts to the wok and stir-fry for 1–2 minutes. Set aside.

WALDORF RICE SALAD

WALDORF SALAD TAKES ITS NAME FROM THE WALDORF HOTEL IN NEW YORK, WHERE IT WAS FIRST MADE. THE RICE MAKES THIS SALAD SLIGHTLY MORE SUBSTANTIAL THAN USUAL. IT CAN BE SERVED AS AN ACCOMPANIMENT, OR AS A MAIN MEAL FOR TWO.

SERVES TWO TO FOUR

INGREDIENTS
115g/4oz/generous ½ cup white long
  grain rice
1 red apple
1 green apple
60ml/4 tbsp lemon juice
3 celery stalks
2–3 slices thick cooked ham
90ml/6 tbsp good quality
  mayonnaise, preferably home-made
60ml/4 tbsp soured cream
generous pinch of saffron, dissolved
  in 15ml/1 tbsp hot water
10ml/2 tsp chopped fresh basil
15ml/1 tbsp chopped fresh parsley
several cos or iceberg lettuce leaves
50g/2oz/½ cup walnuts, roughly
  chopped
salt and freshly ground black pepper

1 Cook the rice in plenty of boiling salted water until tender. Drain and set aside in a bowl to cool.

2 Cut the apples into quarters, remove the cores and finely slice one red and one green apple quarter. Place the slices in a bowl with half the lemon juice and reserve for the garnish. Peel the remaining apple quarters and cut into julienne strips. Place in a separate bowl and toss with another 15ml/1 tbsp of the lemon juice.

3 Cut the celery into thin strips. Roll up each slice of ham, slice finely and add to the apple sticks, with the celery.

4 Mix together the mayonnaise, soured cream and saffron water, then stir in salt and pepper to taste.

5 Stir the mayonnaise mixture and herbs into the rice. Add the apple and celery, with the remaining lemon juice.

6 Arrange the lettuce leaves around the outside of a salad bowl and pile the rice and apple mixture into the centre. Scatter with the chopped walnuts and garnish with fans of apple slices.

SMOKED SALMON AND RICE SALAD PARCELS

FETA, CUCUMBER AND TOMATOES GIVE A GREEK FLAVOUR TO THE SALAD IN THESE PARCELS, A COMBINATION WHICH GOES WELL WITH THE RICE, ESPECIALLY IF A LITTLE WILD RICE IS ADDED.

SERVES FOUR

INGREDIENTS
175g/6oz/scant 1 cup mixed wild
  rice and basmati rice
8 slices smoked salmon, total weight
  about 350g/12oz
10cm/4in piece of cucumber, finely
  diced
about 225g/8oz feta cheese, cubed
8 cherry tomatoes, quartered
30ml/2 tbsp mayonnaise
10ml/2 tsp fresh lime juice
15ml/1 tbsp chopped fresh chervil
salt and freshly ground black pepper
lime slices and fresh chervil, to
  garnish

1 Cook the rice according to the instructions on the packet. Drain, tip into a bowl and allow to cool.

2 Line four ramekins with clear film, then line each ramekin with two slices of smoked salmon. Reserve any extra pieces of smoked salmon for the tops of the parcels.

3 Add the cucumber, feta and tomatoes to the rice, and stir in the mayonnaise, lime juice and chervil. Mix together well. Season with salt and pepper to taste.

4 Spoon the rice mixture into the salmon-lined ramekins. (Any leftover mixture can be used to make a rice salad.) Place any extra pieces of smoked salmon on top, then fold over the overlapping pieces of salmon so that the rice mixture is completely encased.

5 Chill the parcels in the fridge for 30–60 minutes, then invert each parcel on to a plate, using the clear film to ease them out of the ramekins. Carefully peel off the clear film, then garnish each parcel with slices of lime and a sprig of fresh chervil and serve.

STUFFED PANCAKES WITH TURKEY AND CRANBERRIES

THIS IS A WONDERFUL WAY OF USING LEFTOVER ROAST TURKEY. CRANBERRIES ADD THEIR OWN BITTER-SWEET FLAVOUR, WHILE THE WILD RICE CONTRIBUTES A NUTTY FLAVOUR AND TEXTURE.

MAKES SIX TO EIGHT

INGREDIENTS

    50g/2oz/generous ¼ cup wild rice
    stock or water
    15g/½oz/1 tbsp butter
    2.5ml/½ tsp sunflower oil
    1 small onion, finely chopped
    50g/2oz/½ cup small chestnut
      mushrooms, quartered
    75g/3oz/¾ cup cranberries, fresh or
      frozen
    25ml/1½ tbsp granulated sugar
    60–75ml/4–5 tbsp water
    about 275g/10oz cooked turkey
      breast, cut into 2cm/¾in cubes
    150ml/¼ pint/⅔ cup soured cream
    30ml/2 tbsp freshly grated Parmesan
    salt and freshly ground black pepper
For the pancakes
    175g/6oz/1½ cups plain flour
    1 egg
    350ml/12fl oz/1½ cups milk,
      preferably semi-skimmed
    oil, for frying

1 Cook the wild rice in simmering stock or water for 40–50 minutes or according to the instructions on the packet. Drain. Preheat the oven to 190°C/375°F/Gas 5.

2 Meanwhile, make the pancakes. Sift the flour and a pinch of salt into a bowl. Beat in the egg and milk to make a smooth batter. Heat a little oil in a frying pan, pour in about 30ml/2 tbsp of the batter and tilt to cover the bottom of the pan. Cook until the underside is a pale brown colour, then flip the pancake over and cook the other side briefly. Carefully slide it out of the pan and cook 5–7 more pancakes in the same way.

3 Heat the butter and sunflower oil in a separate frying pan and fry the chopped onion for 3–4 minutes until soft. Add the chestnut mushrooms and fry for 2–3 minutes, until they are a pale golden colour.

4 Put the cranberries in a small saucepan and add the sugar and measured water. Bring to simmering point and then cover and simmer over a very low heat until the cranberries burst. This will take about 10 minutes if the cranberries are fresh, and about 2–3 minutes if frozen.

5 Transfer the cooked cranberries to a bowl with a slotted spoon, and pour in 45ml/3 tbsp of the cooking liquid. Add the rice, turkey, onion and mushroom mixture and 60ml/4 tbsp of the soured cream. Season with a little salt and pepper and stir to mix, taking care not to break up the cranberries.

6 Fold the pancakes in four and spoon the stuffing into one of the pockets. Arrange in a lightly greased baking dish. Mix the remaining soured cream with the grated Parmesan and spoon over the top of the pancakes. Bake for 10 minutes to heat through, then serve.

FISH PIE WITH SWEET POTATO TOPPING

THIS TASTY DISH IS FULL OF CONTRASTING FLAVOURS — THE SWEET, SLIGHTLY SPICY SWEET POTATO MAKING AN INTERESTING PARTNER FOR THE MILD-FLAVOURED FISH. WITH ITS BRIGHT TOPPING, IT LOOKS ATTRACTIVE, TOO, AND IS DELICIOUS SERVED WITH SUGAR SNAP PEAS.

SERVES FOUR

INGREDIENTS
175g/6oz/scant 1 cup basmati or
  Texmati rice, soaked
450ml/¾ pint/scant 2 cups
  well-flavoured stock
175g/6oz/1½ cups podded broad
  beans
675g/1½lb haddock or cod fillets,
  skinned
about 450ml/¾ pint/scant 2 cups
  milk
For the sauce
40g/1½oz/3 tbsp butter
30–45ml/2–3 tbsp plain flour
15ml/1 tbsp chopped fresh parsley
salt and freshly ground black pepper
For the topping
450g/1lb sweet potatoes, peeled and
  cut in large chunks
450g/1lb floury white potatoes, such
  as King Edwards, peeled and cut in
  large chunks
milk and butter, for mashing
10ml/2 tsp freshly chopped parsley
5ml/1 tsp freshly chopped dill
15ml/1 tbsp single cream (optional)

1 Preheat the oven to 190ºC/375ºF/
Gas 5. Drain the rice and put it in a
saucepan. Pour in the stock, with a little
salt and pepper, if needed, and bring to
the boil. Cover the pan, lower the heat
and simmer for about 10 minutes or
until all the liquid has been absorbed.

2 Cook the broad beans in a little
lightly salted water until tender. Drain
thoroughly. When cool enough to
handle, pop the bright green beans
out of their skins.

3 To make the potato topping, cook the
sweet and white potatoes separately in
boiling salted water until tender. Drain
them both, then mash them with a little
milk and butter. Spoon the mashed
potato into separate bowls. Beat parsley
and dill into the sweet potatoes, with
the single cream, if using.

4 Place the fish in a large frying pan
and pour in enough of the milk (about
350ml/12fl oz/1½ cups) to just cover.
Dot with 15g/½oz/1 tbsp of the butter
and season with salt and pepper. Heat
gently and simmer for 5–6 minutes until
the fish is just tender. Lift out the fish
and break it into large pieces. Pour the
cooking liquid into a measuring jug and
make up to 450ml/¾ pint/scant 2 cups
with the remaining milk.

5 Make a white sauce. Melt the butter
in a saucepan, stir in the flour and cook
for 1 minute. Gradually add the cooking
liquid and milk mixture, stirring, until a
fairly thin white sauce is formed. Stir in
the parsley, taste and season with a
little more salt and pepper, if necessary.

6 Spread out the cooked rice on the
bottom of a large oval gratin dish. Add
the broad beans and fish and pour over
the white sauce. Spoon the mashed
potatoes over the top, to make an
attractive pattern. Dot with a little extra
butter and bake for 15 minutes until
lightly browned.

COOK'S TIP
There are several types of sweet potato.
The lighter skinned variety, surprisingly,
has the redder flesh. If preferred, you
could top this pie entirely with sweet
potatoes, or you could mash the two
types together. Cook them separately,
however, as the sweet potato tends to
cook more quickly.

WILD RICE PILAFF

WILD RICE ISN'T A RICE AT ALL, BUT IS ACTUALLY A TYPE OF WILD GRASS. CALL IT WHAT YOU WILL, IT HAS A WONDERFUL NUTTY FLAVOUR AND COMBINES WELL WITH LONG GRAIN RICE IN THIS FRUITY MIXTURE. SERVE AS A SIDE DISH.

SERVES SIX

INGREDIENTS
200g/7oz/1 cup wild rice
40g/1½oz/3 tbsp butter
½ onion, finely chopped
200g/7oz/1 cup long grain rice
475ml/16fl oz/2 cups chicken stock
75g/3oz/¾ cup sliced or flaked
    almonds
115g/4oz/⅔ cup sultanas
30ml/2 tbsp chopped fresh parsley
salt and freshly ground black pepper

1 Bring a large saucepan of water to the boil. Add the wild rice and 5ml/ 1 tsp salt. Lower the heat, cover and simmer gently for 45–60 minutes, until the rice is tender. Drain well.

2 Meanwhile, melt 15g/½oz/1 tbsp of the butter in another saucepan. Add the onion and cook over a medium heat for about 5 minutes until it is just softened. Stir in the long grain rice and cook for 1 minute more.

3 Stir in the stock and bring to the boil. Cover and simmer gently for 30–40 minutes, until the rice is tender and the liquid has been absorbed.

COOK'S TIP
Like all rice dishes, this one must be made with well-flavoured stock. If you haven't time to make your own, use a carton or can of good quality stock.

4 Melt the remaining butter in a small pan. Add the almonds and cook until they are just golden. Set aside.

5 Put the rice mixture in a bowl and add the almonds, sultanas and half the parsley. Stir to mix. Taste and adjust the seasoning if necessary. Transfer to a warmed serving dish, sprinkle with the remaining parsley and serve.

WILD RICE WITH GRILLED VEGETABLES

THE MIXTURE OF WILD RICE — WHICH IS NOT REALLY RICE AT ALL BUT A GRASS — AND LONG GRAIN RICE IN THIS DISH WORKS VERY WELL, AND MAKES AN EXTREMELY TASTY VEGETARIAN MEAL.

SERVES FOUR

INGREDIENTS

225g/8oz/generous 1 cup mixed wild
   and long grain rice
1 large aubergine, thickly sliced
1 red, 1 yellow and 1 green pepper,
   seeded and cut into quarters
2 red onions, sliced
225g/8oz/generous 3 cups brown cap
   or shiitake mushrooms
2 small courgettes, cut in half
   lengthways
olive oil, for brushing
30ml/2 tbsp chopped fresh thyme,
   plus extra to garnish
For the dressing
90ml/6 tbsp extra virgin olive oil
30ml/2 tbsp balsamic vinegar
2 garlic cloves, crushed
salt and freshly ground black pepper

1 Put all the rice in a pan of cold salted water. Bring to the boil, then lower the heat, cover and cook gently for 30–40 minutes (or according to the instructions on the packet) until tender.

2 Make the dressing. Whisk the olive oil, vinegar, garlic and seasoning together in a bowl or shake in a screw-top jar until thoroughly blended. Set aside while you grill the vegetables.

3 Arrange all the vegetables on a grill rack. Brush with olive oil and grill for about 5 minutes.

4 Turn the vegetables over, brush them with more olive oil and grill for 5–8 minutes more, or until tender and charred in places.

5 Drain the rice, tip into a bowl and toss in half the dressing. Spoon on to individual plates and arrange the grilled vegetables on top. Pour over the remaining dressing, scatter over the chopped thyme and serve.

SOUTH-WESTERN RICE PUDDING

COCONUT IS THE SECRET INGREDIENT IN THIS UNUSUAL RICE PUDDING. DO NOT OVERCOOK THE RICE OR IT WILL BECOME STODGY. FRESH FRUITS, SUCH AS STRAWBERRIES, MAKE THE IDEAL PARTNER.

SERVES FOUR

INGREDIENTS

40g/1½oz/¼ cup raisins
about 475ml/16fl oz/2 cups water
200g/7oz/1 cup short grain pudding
   rice
1 cinnamon stick
30ml/2 tbsp granulated sugar
475ml/16fl oz/2 cups milk
250ml/8fl oz/1 cup canned
   sweetened coconut cream
2.5ml/½ tsp vanilla essence
15g/½oz/1 tbsp butter
25g/1oz/⅓ cup shredded coconut
ground cinnamon, for sprinkling

1 Put the raisins in a small bowl and pour over enough water to cover. Leave the raisins to soak.

2 Pour the measured water into a heavy or non-stick pan and bring it to the boil. Add the rice, cinnamon stick and sugar and stir. Return to the boil, then lower the heat, cover, and simmer gently for 15–20 minutes until the liquid has been absorbed.

3 Remove the cinnamon stick from the rice. Drain the raisins and add them to the rice with the milk, coconut cream and vanilla essence. Stir to mix. Replace the lid and cook the mixture for about 20 minutes more, until it is just thick. Do not overcook the rice. Preheat the grill.

4 Transfer the mixture to a serving dish that can safely be used under the grill. Dot with the butter and sprinkle coconut evenly over the surface. Grill about 13cm/5in from the heat until the top is just browned. Sprinkle with cinnamon. Serve the pudding warm or cold.

CARAMEL RICE PUDDING

THIS RICE PUDDING IS DELICIOUS SERVED WITH CRUNCHY FRESH FRUIT.

SERVES FOUR

INGREDIENTS

15g/½oz/1 tbsp butter
50g/2oz/¼ cup short grain pudding
   rice
75ml/5 tbsp demerara sugar
400g/14oz can evaporated milk
   made up to 600ml/1 pint/2½ cups
   with water
2 fresh baby pineapples
2 figs
1 crisp eating apple
10ml/2 tsp lemon juice
salt

1 Preheat the oven to 150°C/300°F/
Gas 2. Grease a soufflé dish lightly with
a little of the butter. Put the rice in a
sieve and wash it thoroughly under cold
water. Drain well and put into the
soufflé dish.

2 Add 30ml/2 tbsp of the sugar to the
dish, with a pinch of salt. Pour on the
diluted evaporated milk and stir gently.

3 Dot the surface of the rice with
butter. Bake for 2 hours, then leave to
cool for 30 minutes.

4 Meanwhile, quarter the pineapple
and the figs. Cut the apple into
segments and toss in the lemon juice.
Preheat the grill.

5 Sprinkle the remaining sugar evenly
over the rice. Grill for 5 minutes or until
the sugar has caramelized. Leave the
rice to stand for 5 minutes to allow the
caramel to harden, then serve with the
fresh fruit.

INDEX

ACKNOWLEDGEMENTS

Picture Credits

All pictures in the POTATO section taken by Steve Moss (potatoes and techniques) and Sam Stowell (recipes) and Walt Chrynwski (US potatoes) except for the following:
p12 (top and bottom), p13 (top), p14 E. T. Archive; p13 (bottom) Illustrated London News; p15 (bottom) The British Potato Council; p16 (middle and bottom) The International Potato Centre, Peru.

All pictures in the RICE section taken by Dave Jordan (rices and techniques) and Dave King (recipes) except for the following:
p262 Life File/Emma Lee; p263 (top) E. T. Archive/Free Library Philadelphia; (bottom) E. T. Archive/Domenica del Corriere; p264 (top) E. T. Archive/Freer Gallery of Art; p265 Life File/Emma Lee; p266 Life File/Emma Lee; p267 (top and bottom) Life File/Emma Lee.